Bull horns are so awesome. I wish I could grow horns. Guys the world over have wanted to have them since ancient times. You see them pop up all over the place. They make you look tough. Do they get in the way when you go to sleep, I wonder? It'd be hard to pull off headers in soccer. I can imagine sitting down at your desk and accidentally knocking over the lamp with your horns. You'd be like, "Mrooh*!!*" Hey, wait! Cows make that sound too*!!* *I bull-ieve it's time to start volume 70!!!*

—Eiichiro Oda, 2013

Eiichiro Oda began his manga career at the age of 17, when his one-shot cowboy manga **Wanted!** won second place in the coveted Tezuka manga awards. Oda went on to work as an assistant to some of the biggest manga artists in the industry, including Nobuhiro Watsuki, before winning the Hop Step Award for new artists. His pirate adventure **One Piece**, which debuted in **Weekly Shonen Jump** in 1997, quickly became one of the most popular manga in Japan.

ONE PIECE VOL. 70
NEW WORLD PART 10

SHONEN JUMP Manga Edition

STORY AND ART BY EIICHIRO ODA

Translation/Stephen Paul
Touch-up Art & Lettering/Vanessa Satone
Design/Fawn Lau
Editor/Alexis Kirsch

Printed in the U.S.A.

Published by VIZ Media, LLC
P.O. Box 77010
San Francisco, CA 94107

10 9 8 7 6 5 4 3 2 1
First printing, March 2014

www.viz.com

THE WORLD'S
MOST POPULAR MANGA

www.shonenjump.com

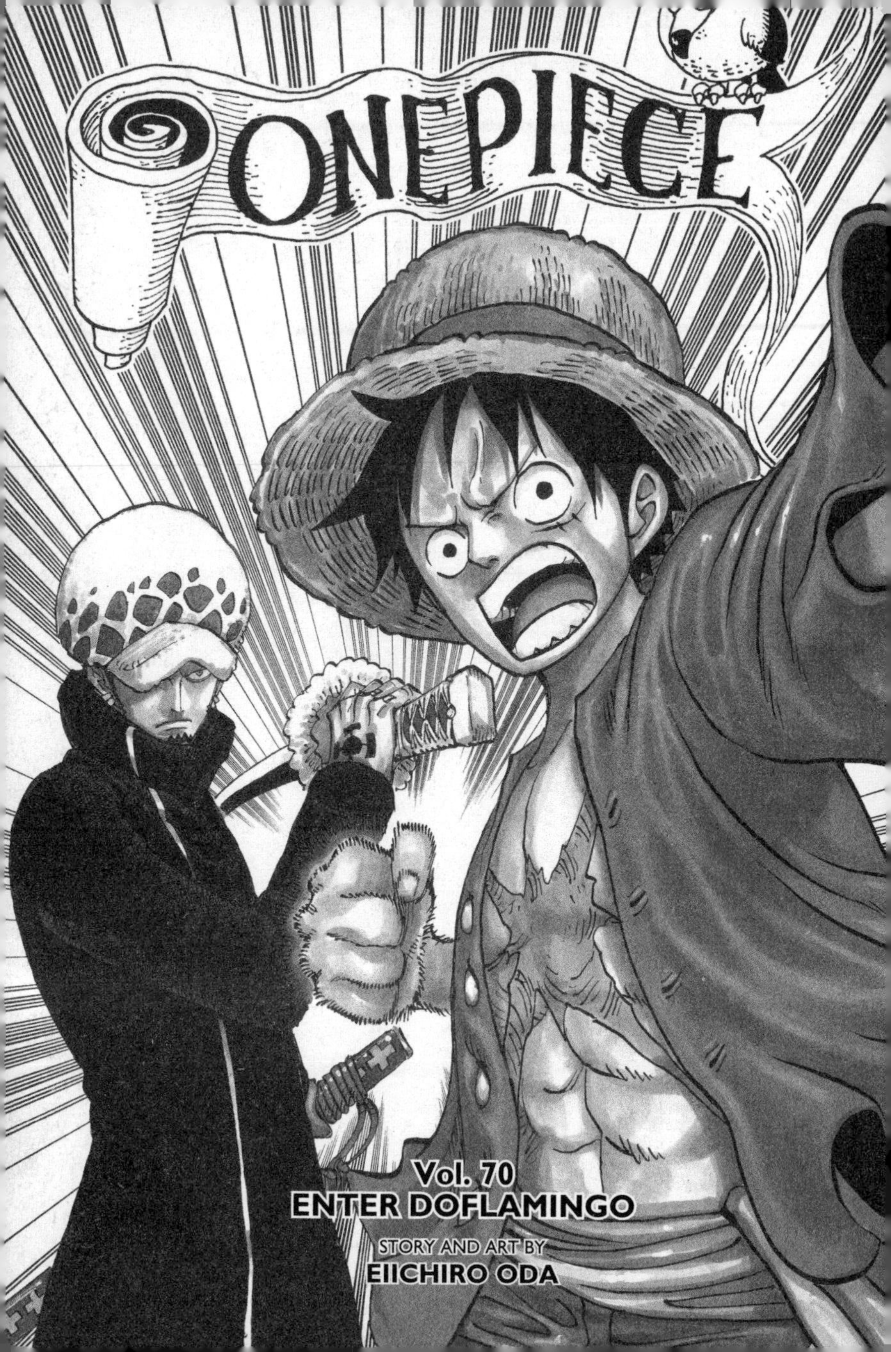

ONE PIECE

Vol. 70
ENTER DOFLAMINGO

STORY AND ART BY
EIICHIRO ODA

The Straw Hat Crew

Monkey D. Luffy

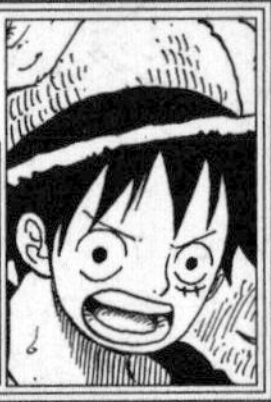

A young man who dreams of becoming the Pirate King. After training with Rayleigh, he and his crew head for the New World!

Captain, Bounty: 400 million berries

Roronoa Zolo

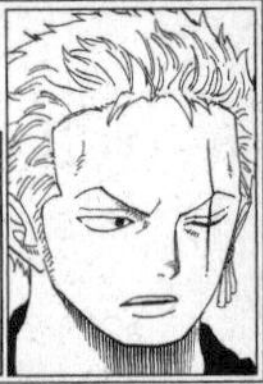

He swallowed his pride and asked to be trained by Mihawk on Gloom Island before reuniting with the rest of the crew.

Fighter, Bounty: 120 million berries

Tony Tony Chopper

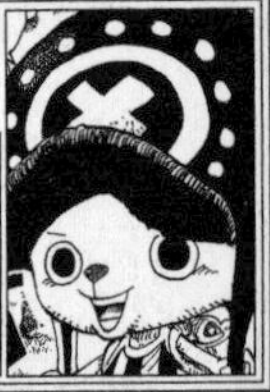

After researching powerful medicine in Birdie Kingdom, he reunites with the rest of the crew.

Ship's Doctor, Bounty: 50 berries

Nami

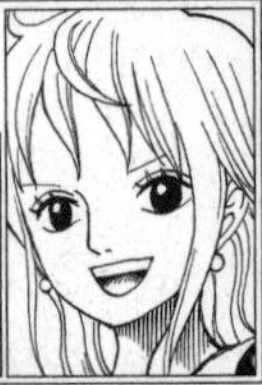

She studied the weather of the New World on the small Sky Island Weatheria, a place where weather is studied as a science.

Navigator, Bounty: 16 million berries

Nico Robin

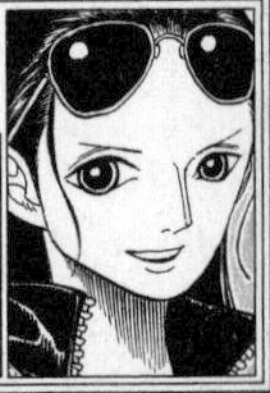

She spent her time in Baltigo with the leader of the Revolutionary Army: Luffy's father, Dragon.

Archeologist, Bounty: 80 million berries

Usopp

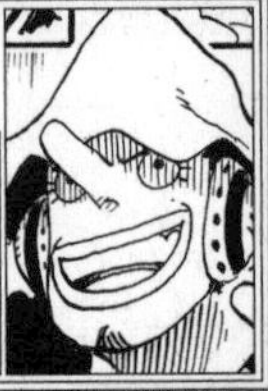

He trained under Heracles at the Bowin Islands to become the King of Snipers.

Sniper, Bounty: 30 million berries

Franky

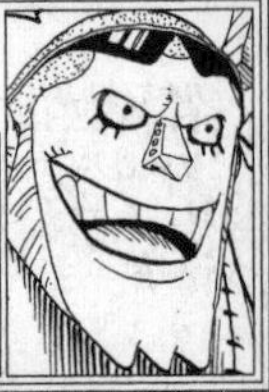

He modified himself in Future Land Baldimore and turned himself into Armored Franky before reuniting with the rest of the crew.

Shipwright, Bounty: 44 million berries

Sanji

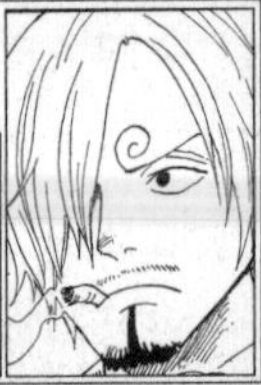

After fighting the New Kama Karate masters in the Kamabakka Kingdom, he returned to the crew.

Cook, Bounty: 77 million berries

Brook

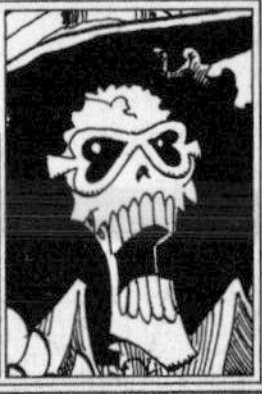

After being captured and used as a freak show by the Longarm Tribe, he became a famous rock star called "Soul King" Brook.

Musician, Bounty: 33 million berries

Luffy forms a new pirate alliance for the purpose of capturing Caesar and bringing down one of the mighty Four Emperors. Capturing Caesar would effectively cut off his employer Doflamingo's supply of "Smile," the artificial Devil Fruit being offered to the Emperor in question. Luffy and crew's journey into the new era begins by throwing a wrench into this heinous scheme...

The story of ONE PIECE 1»70

Shanks

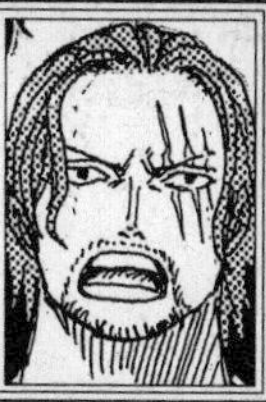

One of the Four Emperors. He continues to wait for Luffy in the second half of the Grand Line, called the New World.

Captain of the Red-Haired Pirates

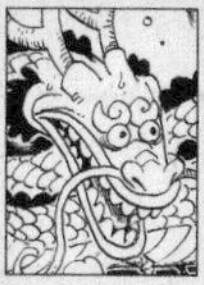

Momonosuke

Kin'emon's Son, Dragon

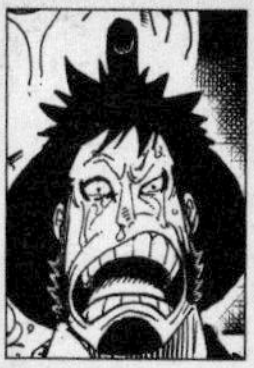

Foxfire Kin'emon

Samurai of Wano

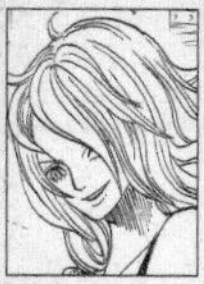

Monet

Harpy

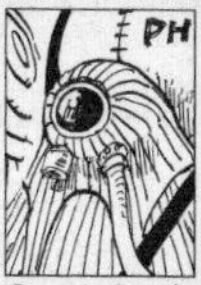
PH

Caesar's Guards

Caesar's followers

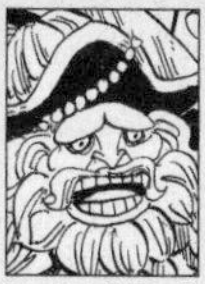

Brownbeard ("Boss")

Punk Hazard Patrol

Naval G-5:

5th Branch of the Naval Grand Line

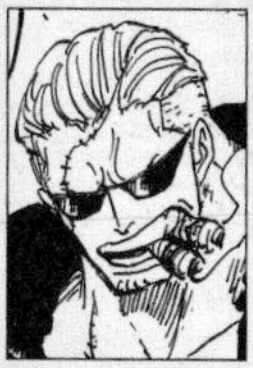

White Chase Smoker

G-5 Vice Admiral

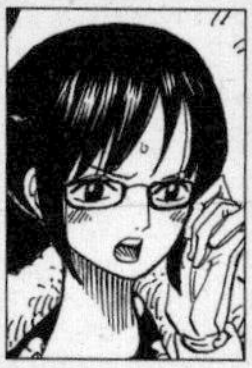

Tashigi

G-5 Captain

Punk Hazard

Master Caesar Clown

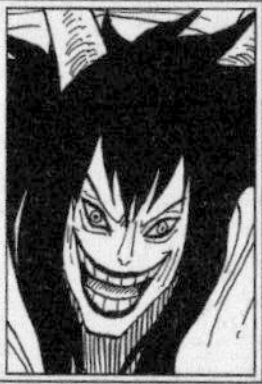

Dr. Vegapunk's former colleague. An authority on weapons of mass murder, now wanted by the government.

Former gov't scientist

Vice Admiral Vergo

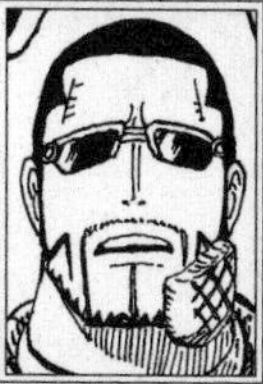

A Navy officer who secretly works for Doflamingo's organization. He helped orchestrate the child abductions.

G-5 Commander

Don Quixote Doflamingo (Joker)

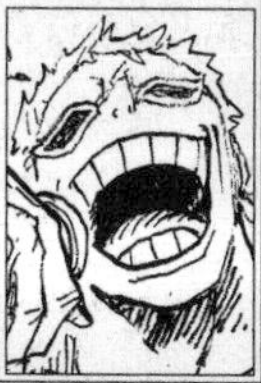

One of the Seven Warlords of the sea and a weapons broker. He works under the alias of "Joker."

Pirate, Warlord

Trafalgar Law

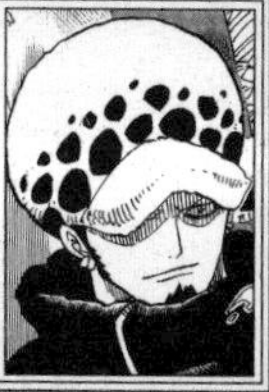

The Surgeon of Death, wielder of the Op-Op Fruit's powers. One of the Seven Warlords of the Sea.

Pirate, Warlord

Story

After two years of hard training, the Straw Hat Pirates are back together, first at the Sabaody Archipelago and then through Fish-Man Island to their next stage: the New World!!

The crew lands on Punk Hazard, where the mad scientist and wanted man Caesar Clown rules over the ruins of a government laboratory. With the arrival of the newly appointed Warlord of the Sea Trafalgar Law, the Straw Hats, and the pursuing Navy, the island bursts into chaos! At Law's suggestion,

Vol. 70
Enter Doflamingo

CONTENTS

Chapter 691: KING OF THE LAND OF THE DEAD

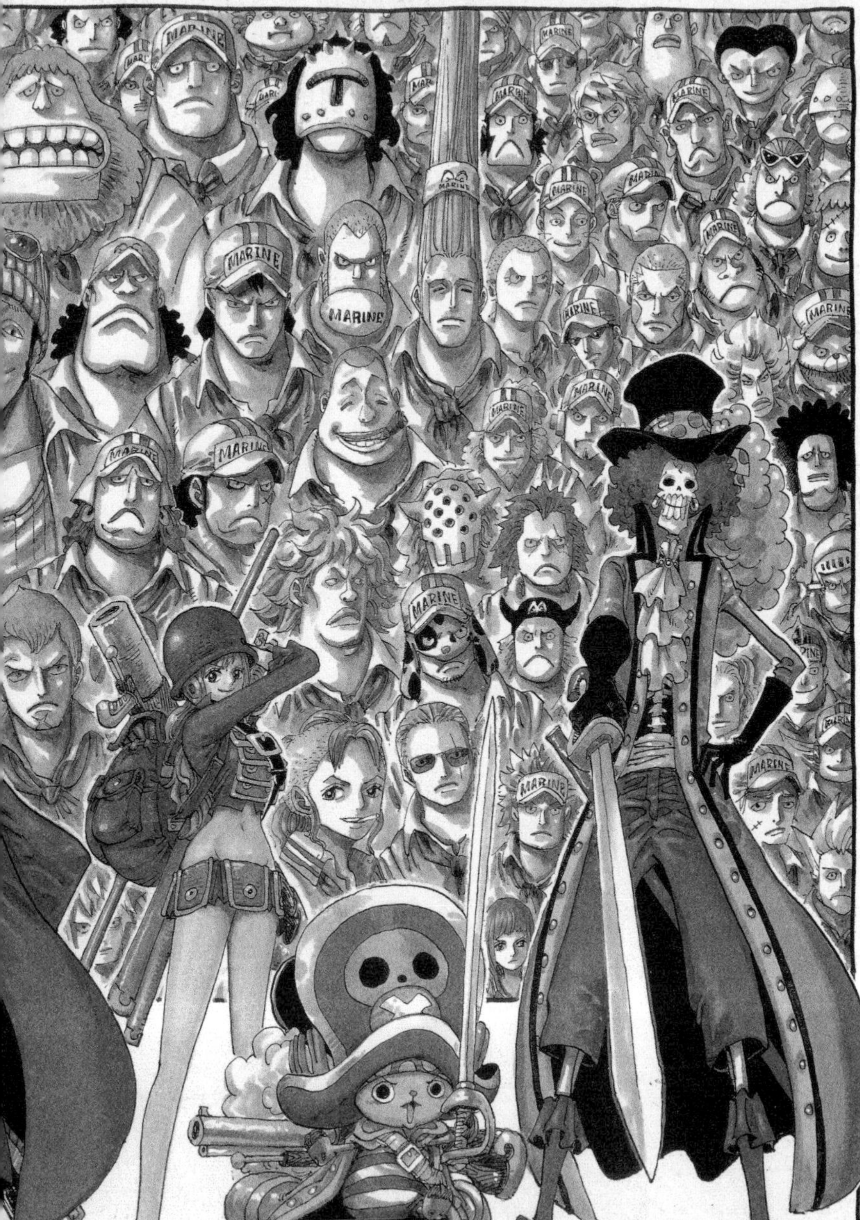

OF THE LAND OF THE DEAD

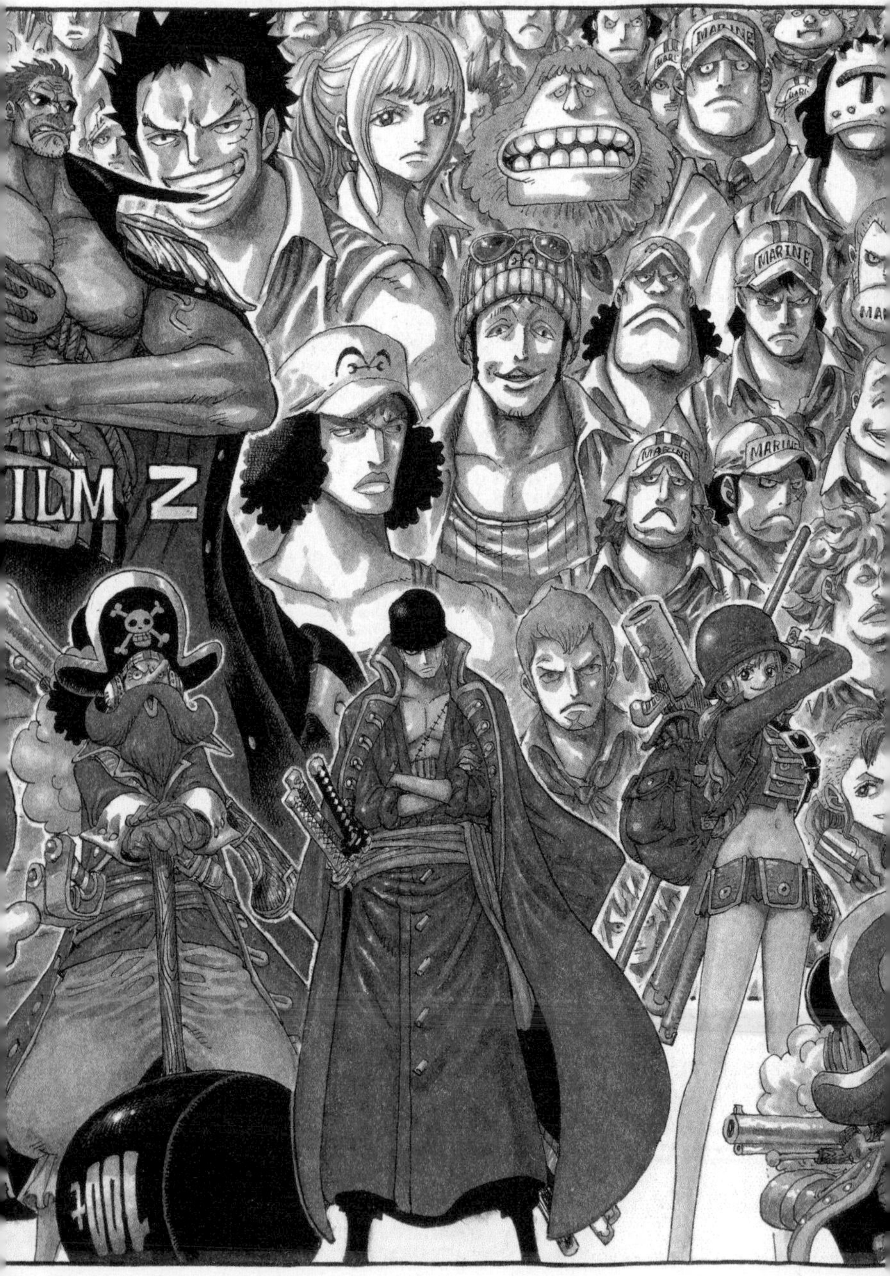
MARINE
ILM Z

Chapter 691: KING

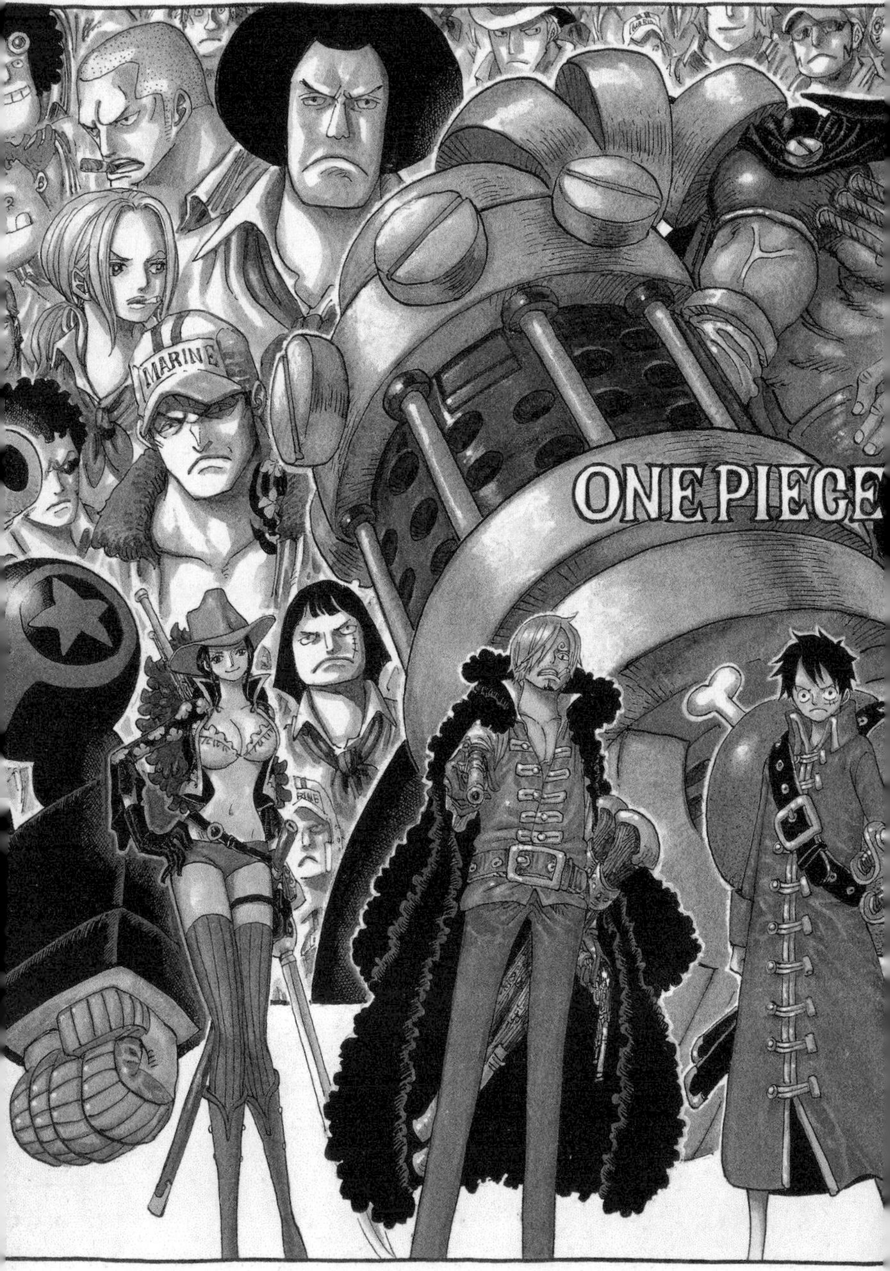
ONE PIECE
MARINE

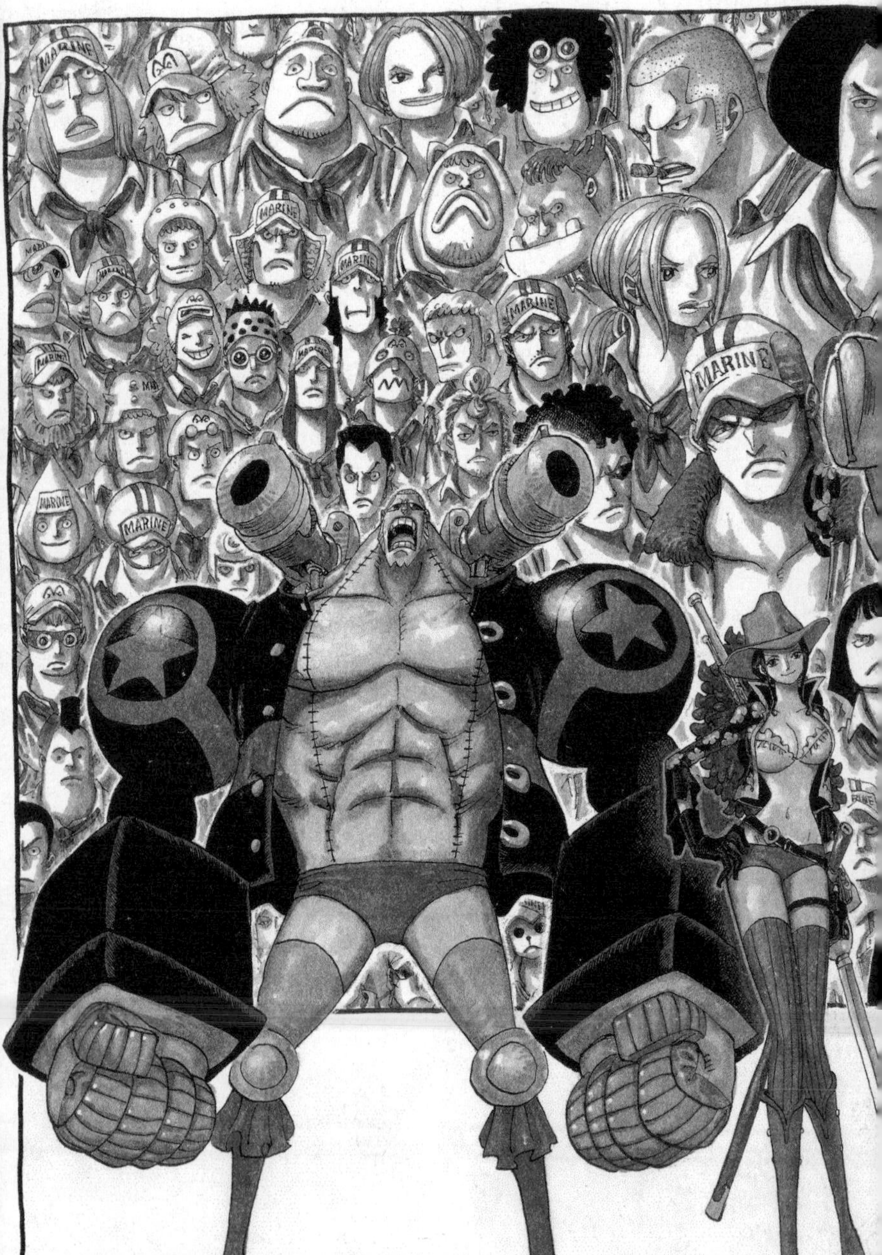
MARINE

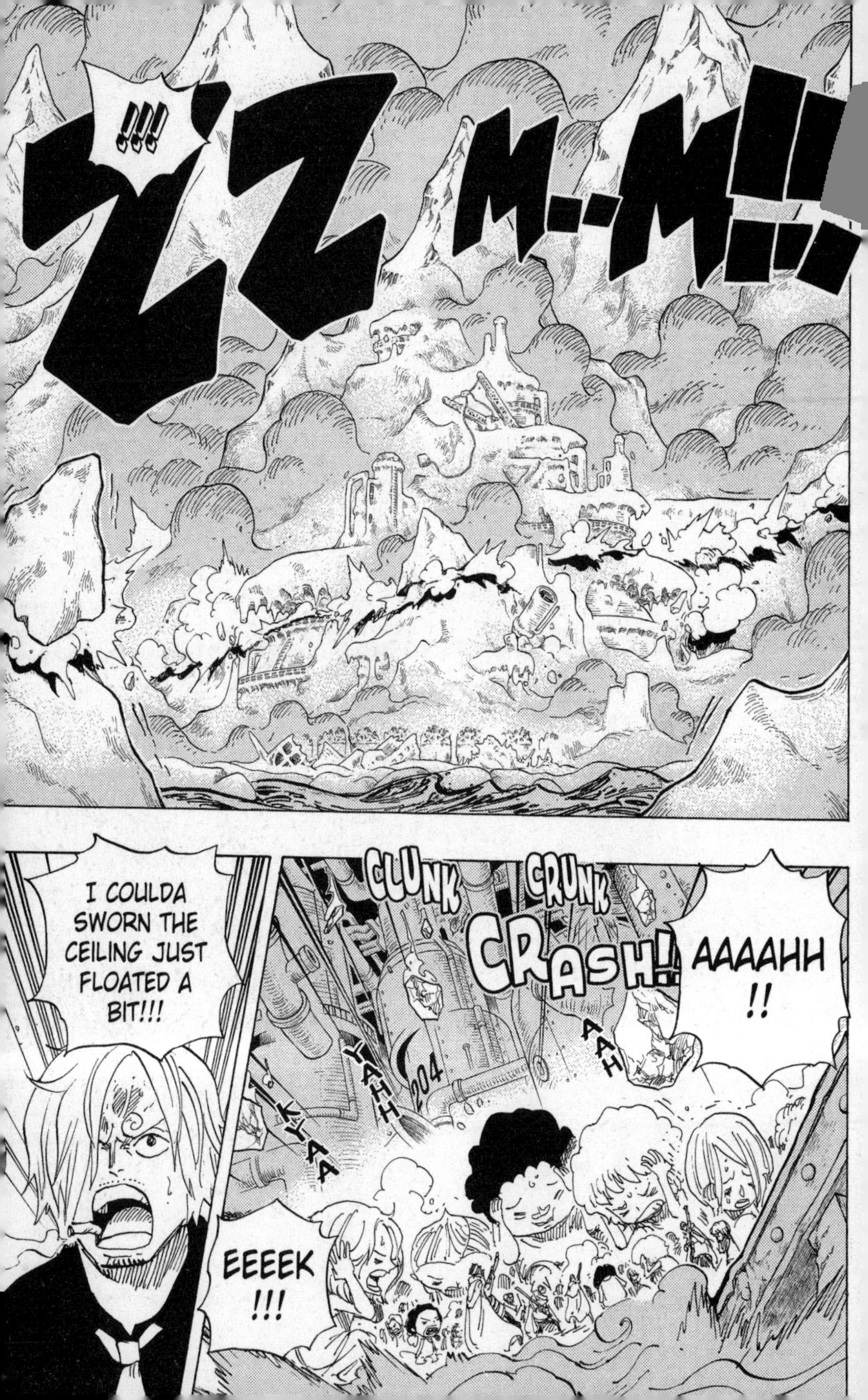
!!!
ZZM-M!!
AAAAHH !!
CLUNK
CRUNK
CRASH!!
AAH
YAHH
204
KYAA
EEEEK !!!
I COULDA SWORN THE CEILING JUST FLOATED A BIT!!!

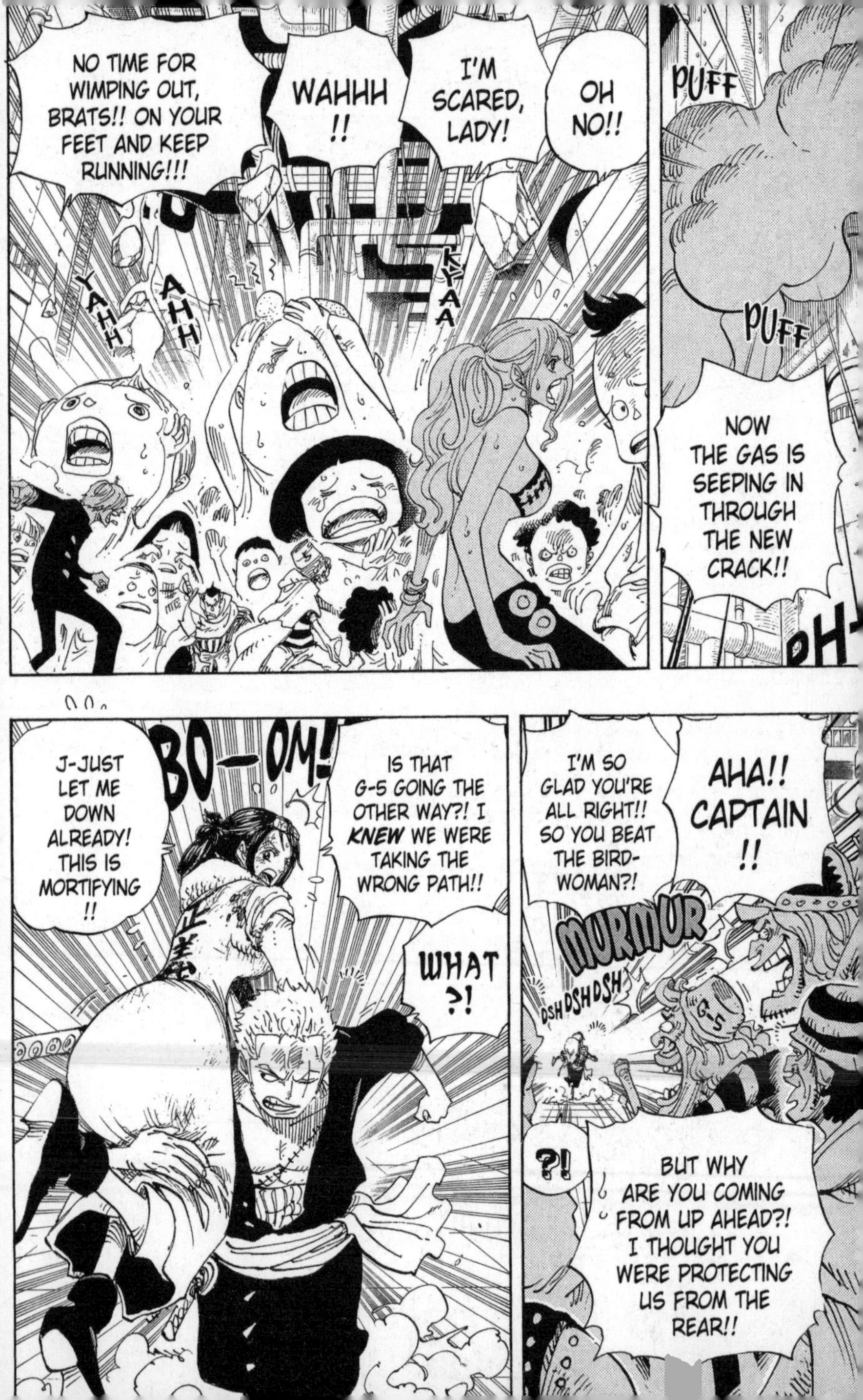
PUFF
PUFF
NOW THE GAS IS SEEPING IN THROUGH THE NEW CRACK!!
PH-
OH NO!!
I'M SCARED, LADY!
WAHHH!!
NO TIME FOR WIMPING OUT, BRATS!! ON YOUR FEET AND KEEP RUNNING!!!
KYAA
AHH
YAHH
AHA!! CAPTAIN!!
I'M SO GLAD YOU'RE ALL RIGHT!! SO YOU BEAT THE BIRD-WOMAN?!
MURMUR
DSH DSH DSH
?!
BUT WHY ARE YOU COMING FROM UP AHEAD?! I THOUGHT YOU WERE PROTECTING US FROM THE REAR!!
IS THAT G-5 GOING THE OTHER WAY?! I *KNEW* WE WERE TAKING THE WRONG PATH!!
BO-OM!
J-JUST LET ME DOWN ALREADY! THIS IS MORTIFYING!!
WHAT?!

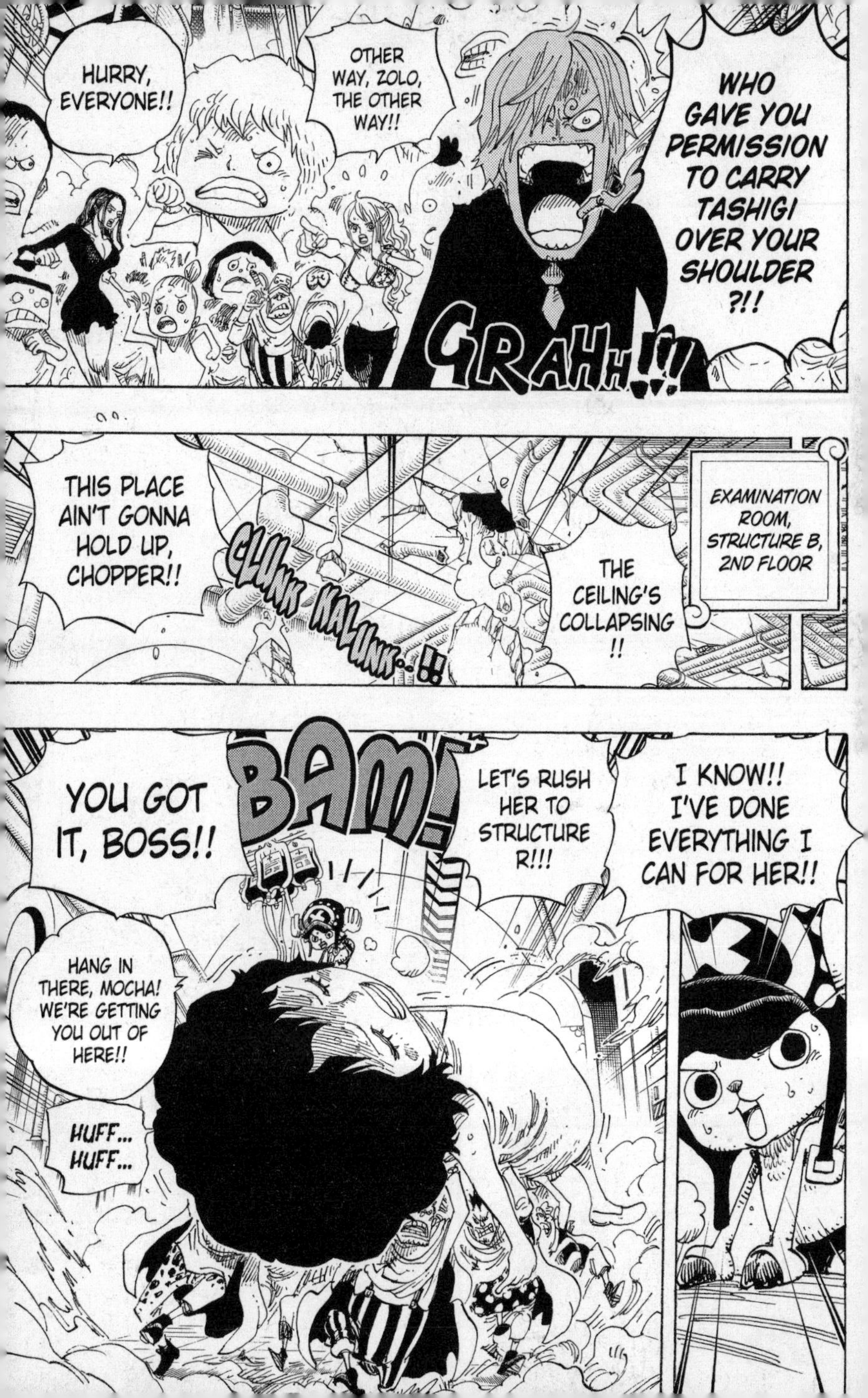
WHO GAVE YOU PERMISSION TO CARRY TASHIGI OVER YOUR SHOULDER ?!!
GRAHH!!!
OTHER WAY, ZOLO, THE OTHER WAY!!
HURRY, EVERYONE!!
EXAMINATION ROOM, STRUCTURE B, 2ND FLOOR
THE CEILING'S COLLAPSING !!
CLUNK KALUNK..!!
THIS PLACE AIN'T GONNA HOLD UP, CHOPPER!!
I KNOW!! I'VE DONE EVERYTHING I CAN FOR HER!!
LET'S RUSH HER TO STRUCTURE R!!!
BAM!
YOU GOT IT, BOSS!!
HANG IN THERE, MOCHA! WE'RE GETTING YOU OUT OF HERE!!
HUFF... HUFF...

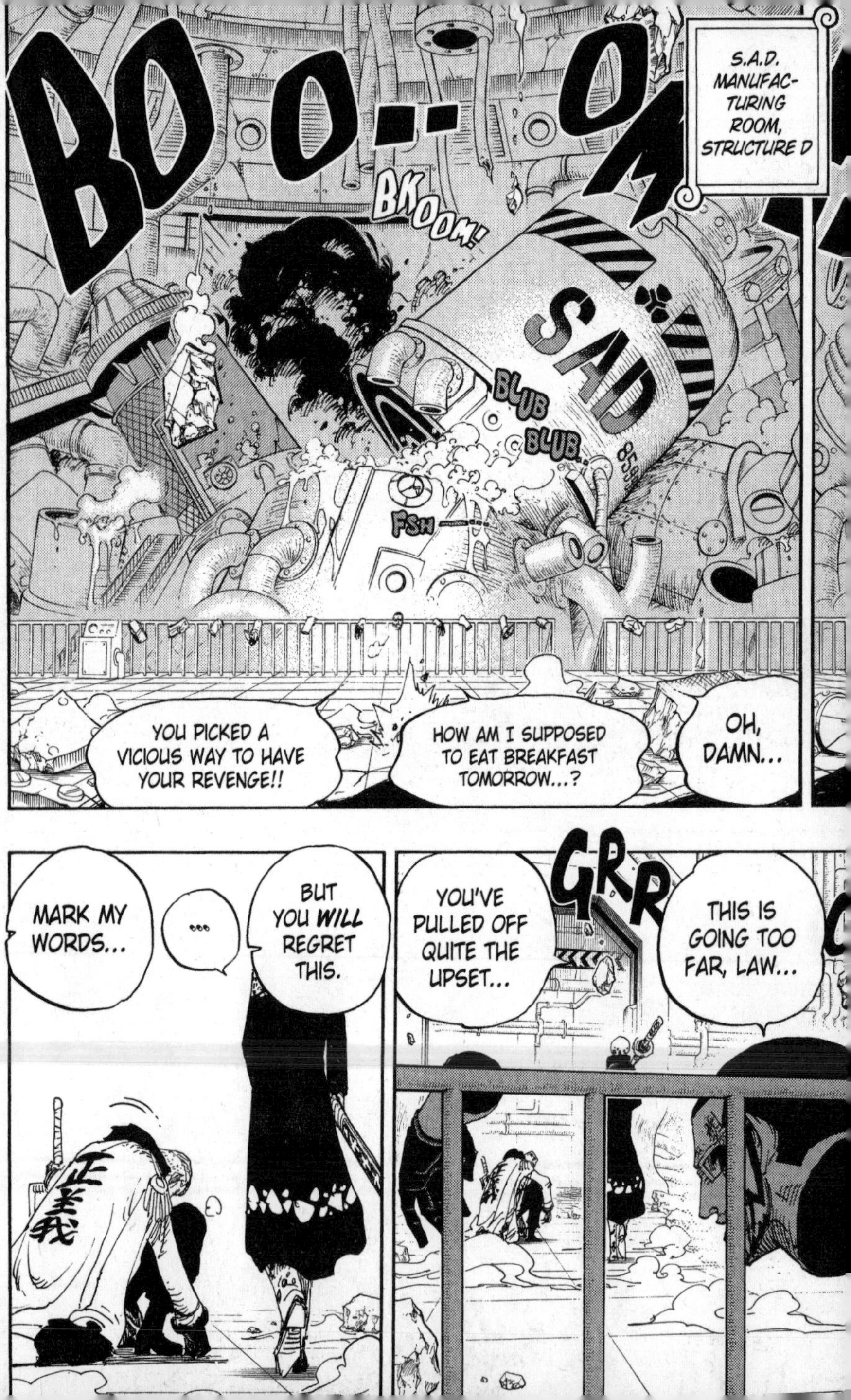
S.A.D. MANUFAC-TURING ROOM, STRUCTURE D
BOO..OM
BKOOM!
SAD
BLUB
BLUB..
FSH
OH, DAMN...
HOW AM I SUPPOSED TO EAT BREAKFAST TOMORROW...?
YOU PICKED A VICIOUS WAY TO HAVE YOUR REVENGE!!
GRR
THIS IS GOING TOO FAR, LAW...
YOU'VE PULLED OFF QUITE THE UPSET...
BUT YOU *WILL* REGRET THIS.
...
MARK MY WORDS...

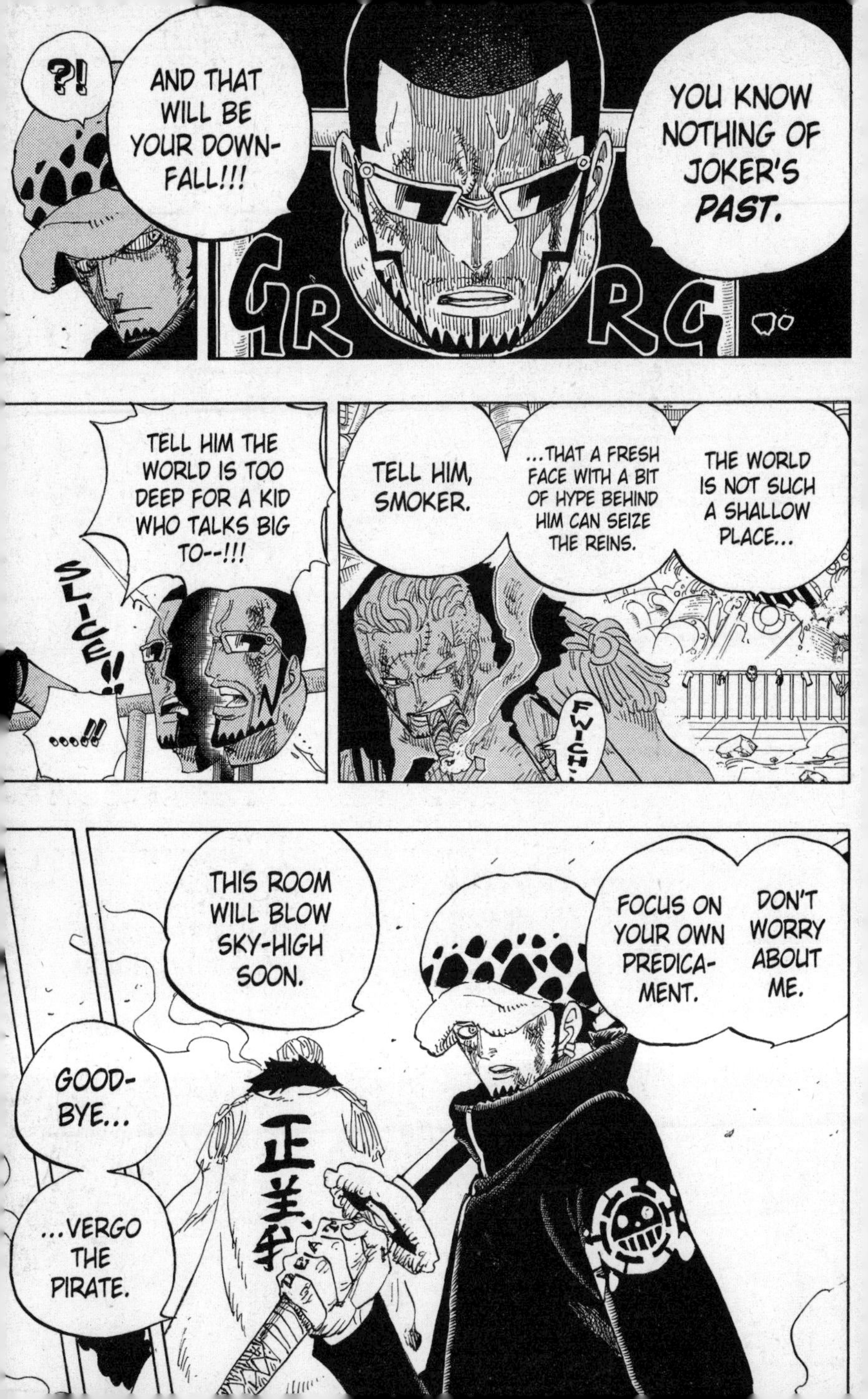
YOU KNOW NOTHING OF JOKER'S PAST.
AND THAT WILL BE YOUR DOWN-FALL!!!
?!
GR RG
THE WORLD IS NOT SUCH A SHALLOW PLACE...
...THAT A FRESH FACE WITH A BIT OF HYPE BEHIND HIM CAN SEIZE THE REINS.
TELL HIM, SMOKER.
FWICH
TELL HIM THE WORLD IS TOO DEEP FOR A KID WHO TALKS BIG TO--!!!
SLICE!!
....!!
DON'T WORRY ABOUT ME.
FOCUS ON YOUR OWN PREDICA-MENT.
THIS ROOM WILL BLOW SKY-HIGH SOON.
GOOD-BYE...
...VERGO THE PIRATE.

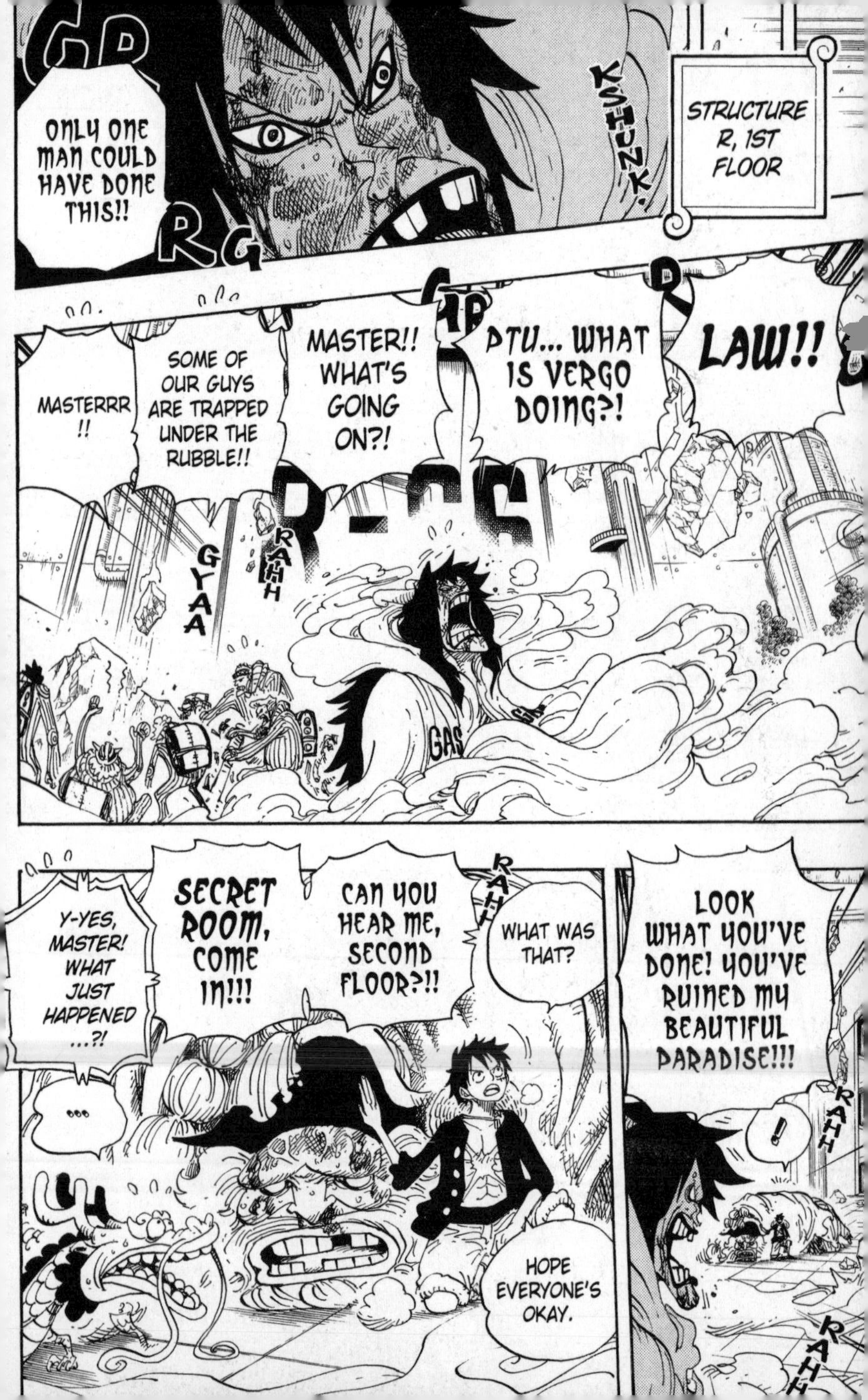
STRUCTURE R, 1ST FLOOR
KSHUNK.
GR
RG
ONLY ONE MAN COULD HAVE DONE THIS!!
GR
R
LAW!!
PTU... WHAT IS VERGO DOING?!
MASTER!! WHAT'S GOING ON?!
SOME OF OUR GUYS ARE TRAPPED UNDER THE RUBBLE!!
MASTERRR!!
RAHHH
GYAA
GAS
LOOK WHAT YOU'VE DONE! YOU'VE RUINED MY BEAUTIFUL PARADISE!!!
RAHH
!
RAHH
WHAT WAS THAT?
RAHH
CAN YOU HEAR ME, SECOND FLOOR?!!
SECRET ROOM, COME IN!!!
Y-YES, MASTER! WHAT JUST HAPPENED...?!
...
HOPE EVERYONE'S OKAY.

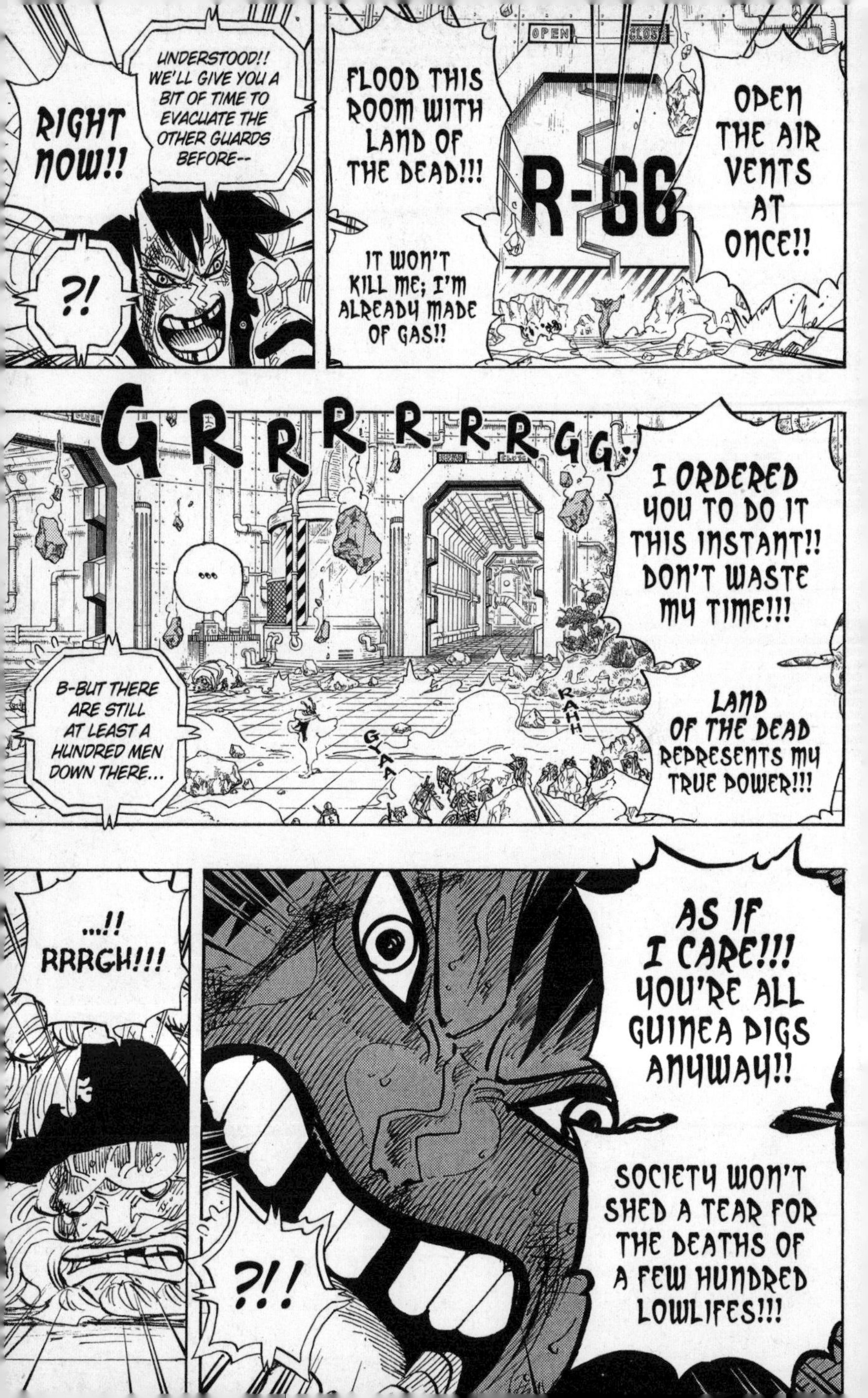
OPEN
R-66
OPEN THE AIR VENTS AT ONCE!!
FLOOD THIS ROOM WITH LAND OF THE DEAD!!!
IT WON'T KILL ME; I'M ALREADY MADE OF GAS!!
UNDERSTOOD!! WE'LL GIVE YOU A BIT OF TIME TO EVACUATE THE OTHER GUARDS BEFORE--
RIGHT NOW!!
?!
I ORDERED YOU TO DO IT THIS INSTANT!! DON'T WASTE MY TIME!!!
GRRRRRRGG
LAND OF THE DEAD REPRESENTS MY TRUE POWER!!!
...
RAHH
B-BUT THERE ARE STILL AT LEAST A HUNDRED MEN DOWN THERE...
GYAA
AS IF I CARE!!! YOU'RE ALL GUINEA PIGS ANYWAY!!
SOCIETY WON'T SHED A TEAR FOR THE DEATHS OF A FEW HUNDRED LOWLIFES!!!
?!!
...!! RRRGH!!!

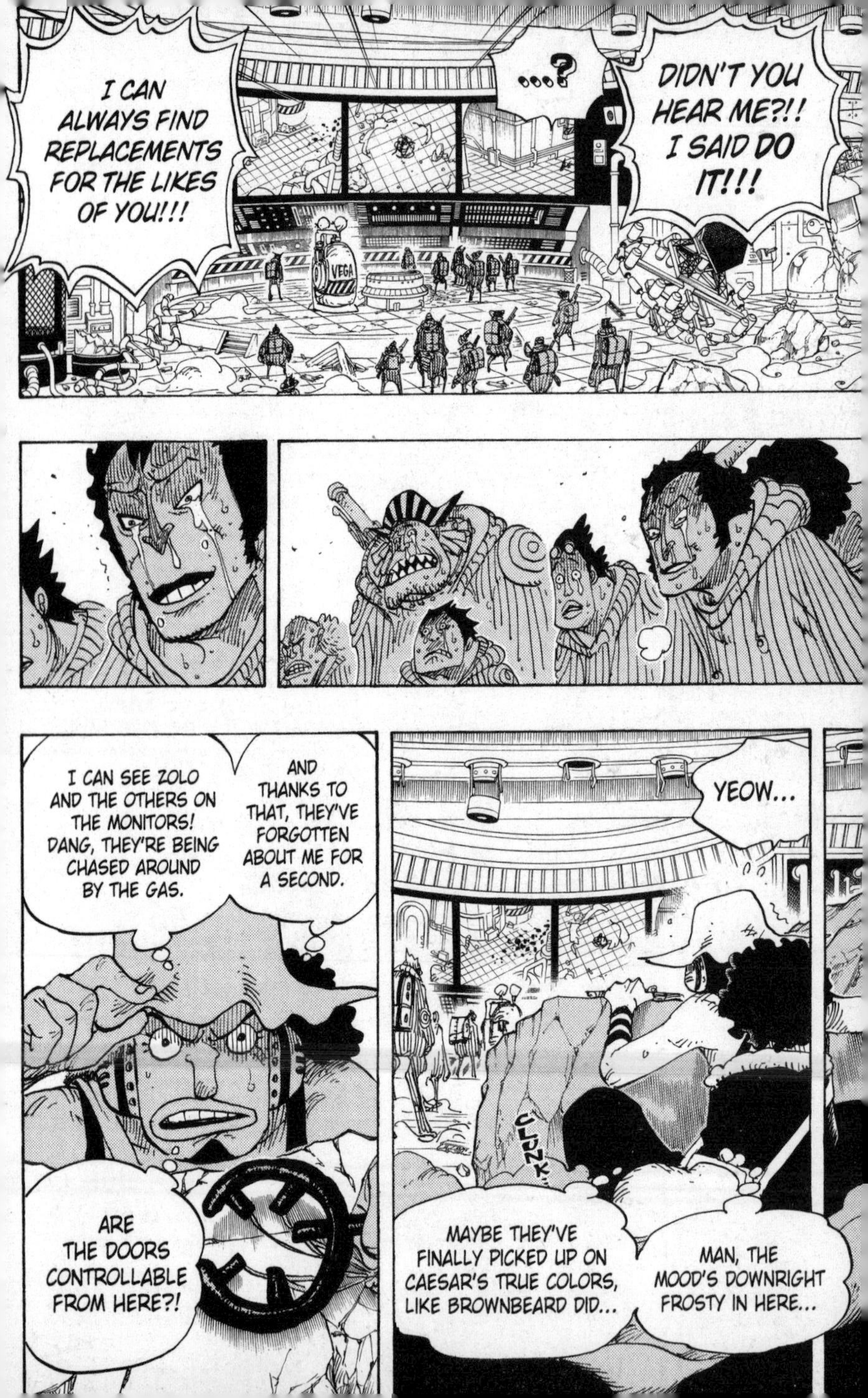
DIDN'T YOU HEAR ME?!! I SAID DO IT!!!
...?
I CAN ALWAYS FIND REPLACEMENTS FOR THE LIKES OF YOU!!!
YEOW...
CLUNK
MAN, THE MOOD'S DOWNRIGHT FROSTY IN HERE...
MAYBE THEY'VE FINALLY PICKED UP ON CAESAR'S TRUE COLORS, LIKE BROWNBEARD DID...
I CAN SEE ZOLO AND THE OTHERS ON THE MONITORS! DANG, THEY'RE BEING CHASED AROUND BY THE GAS.
AND THANKS TO THAT, THEY'VE FORGOTTEN ABOUT ME FOR A SECOND.
ARE THE DOORS CONTROLLABLE FROM HERE?!

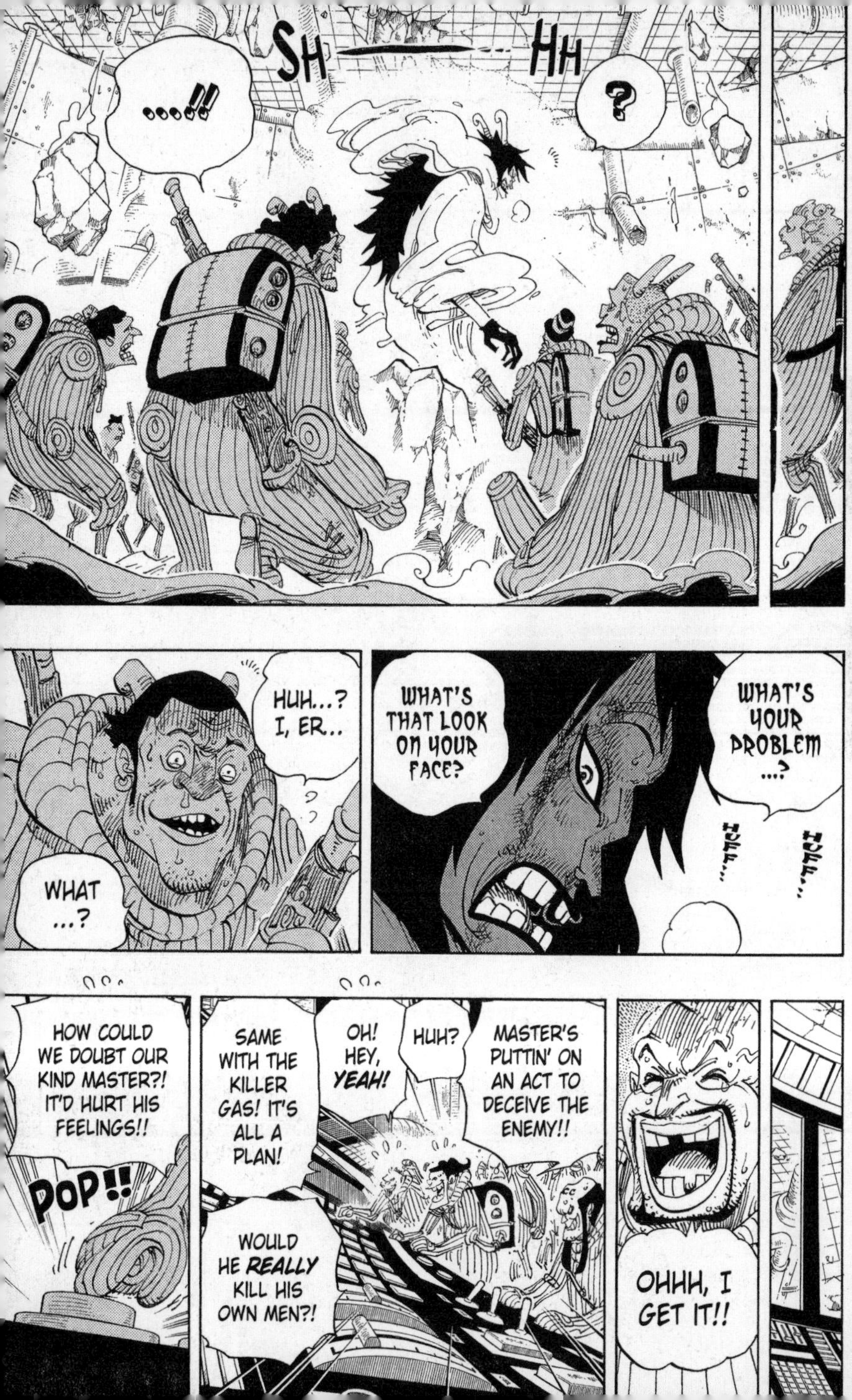
SH——HH
?
....!!
WHAT'S YOUR PROBLEM ...?
HUFF... HUFF...
WHAT'S THAT LOOK ON YOUR FACE?
HUH...? I, ER...
WHAT ...?
OHHH, I GET IT!!
MASTER'S PUTTIN' ON AN ACT TO DECEIVE THE ENEMY!!
HUH?
OH! HEY, *YEAH!*
SAME WITH THE KILLER GAS! IT'S ALL A PLAN!
WOULD HE *REALLY* KILL HIS OWN MEN?!
HOW COULD WE DOUBT OUR KIND MASTER?! IT'D HURT HIS FEELINGS!!
POP!!

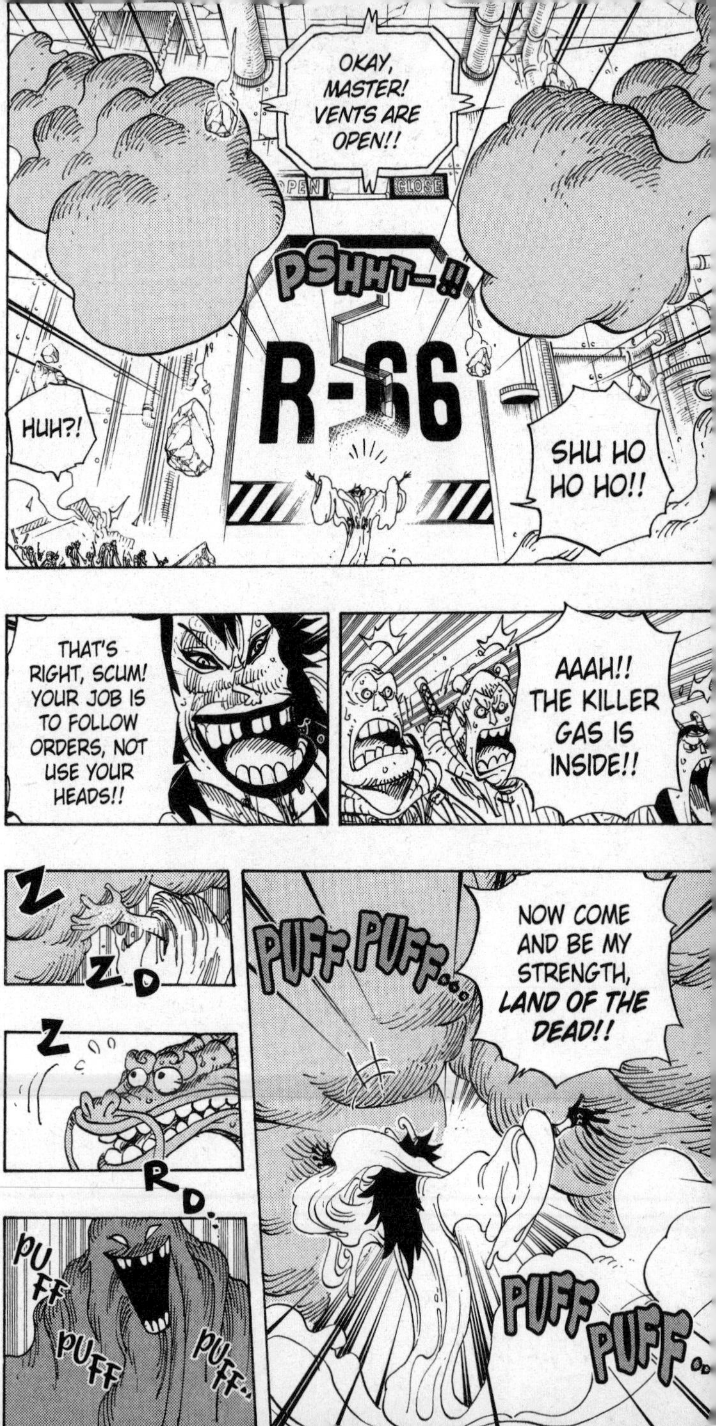
OKAY, MASTER! VENTS ARE OPEN!!
OPEN
CLOSE
PSHHT--!!
SHU HO HO HO!!
R-66
HUH?!
AAAH!! THE KILLER GAS IS INSIDE!!
THAT'S RIGHT, SCUM! YOUR JOB IS TO FOLLOW ORDERS, NOT USE YOUR HEADS!!
NOW COME AND BE MY STRENGTH, LAND OF THE DEAD!!
PUFF PUFF...
PUFF PUFF...
Z
ZD
Z
RD..
PUFF
PUFF
PUFF..
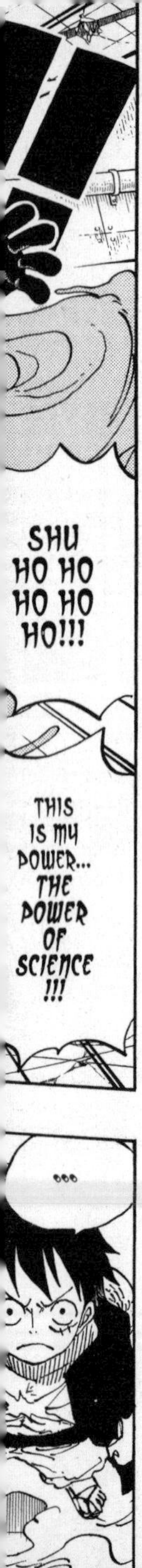
SHU HO HO HO HO HO!!!
THIS IS MY POWER... THE POWER OF SCIENCE!!!
...

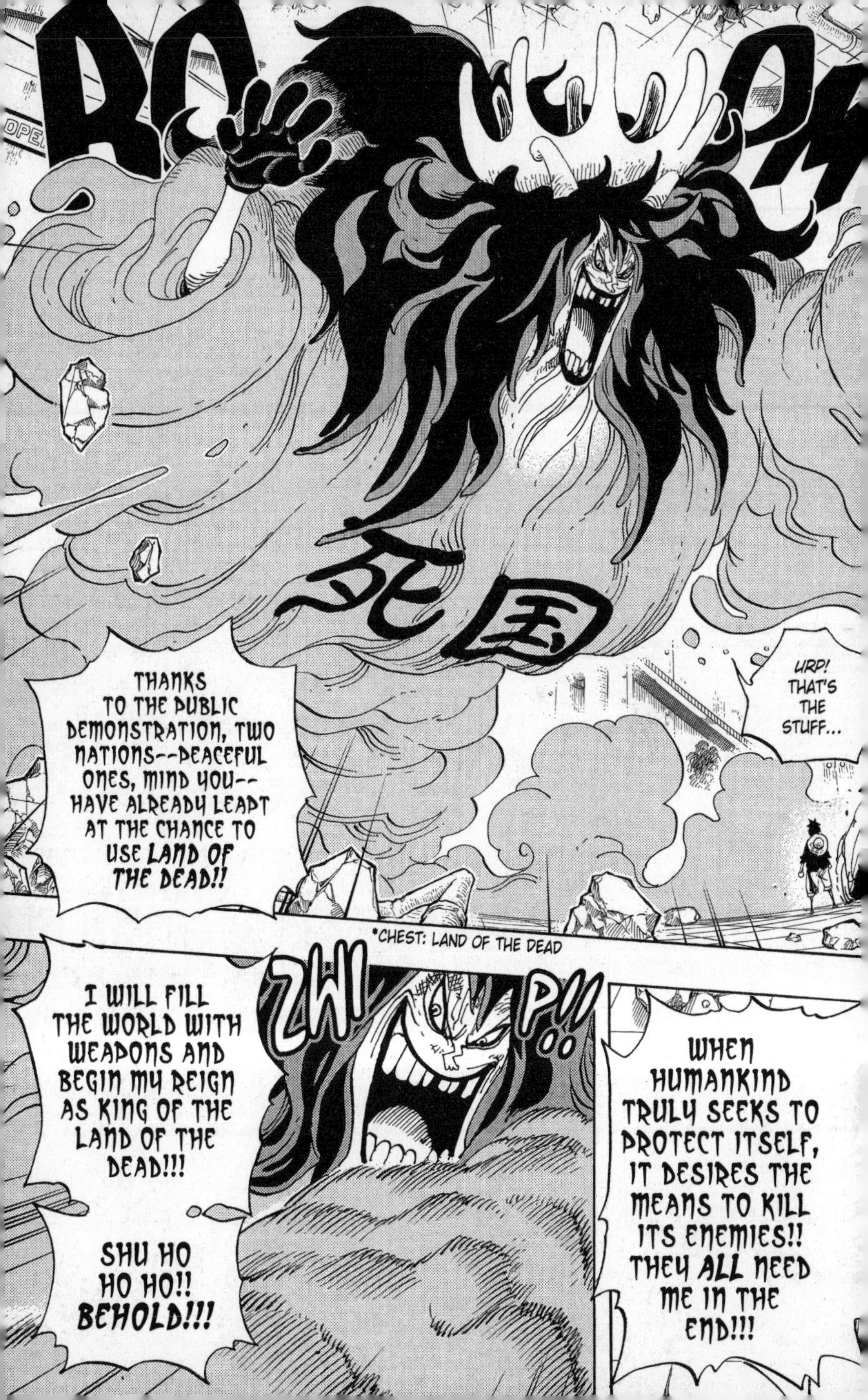
URP! THAT'S THE STUFF...
THANKS TO THE PUBLIC DEMONSTRATION, TWO NATIONS--PEACEFUL ONES, MIND YOU--HAVE ALREADY LEAPT AT THE CHANCE TO USE LAND OF THE DEAD!!
死国
*CHEST: LAND OF THE DEAD
WHEN HUMANKIND TRULY SEEKS TO PROTECT ITSELF, IT DESIRES THE MEANS TO KILL ITS ENEMIES!! THEY ALL NEED ME IN THE END!!!
ZWIP!!
I WILL FILL THE WORLD WITH WEAPONS AND BEGIN MY REIGN AS KING OF THE LAND OF THE DEAD!!!
SHU HO HO HO!! BEHOLD!!!

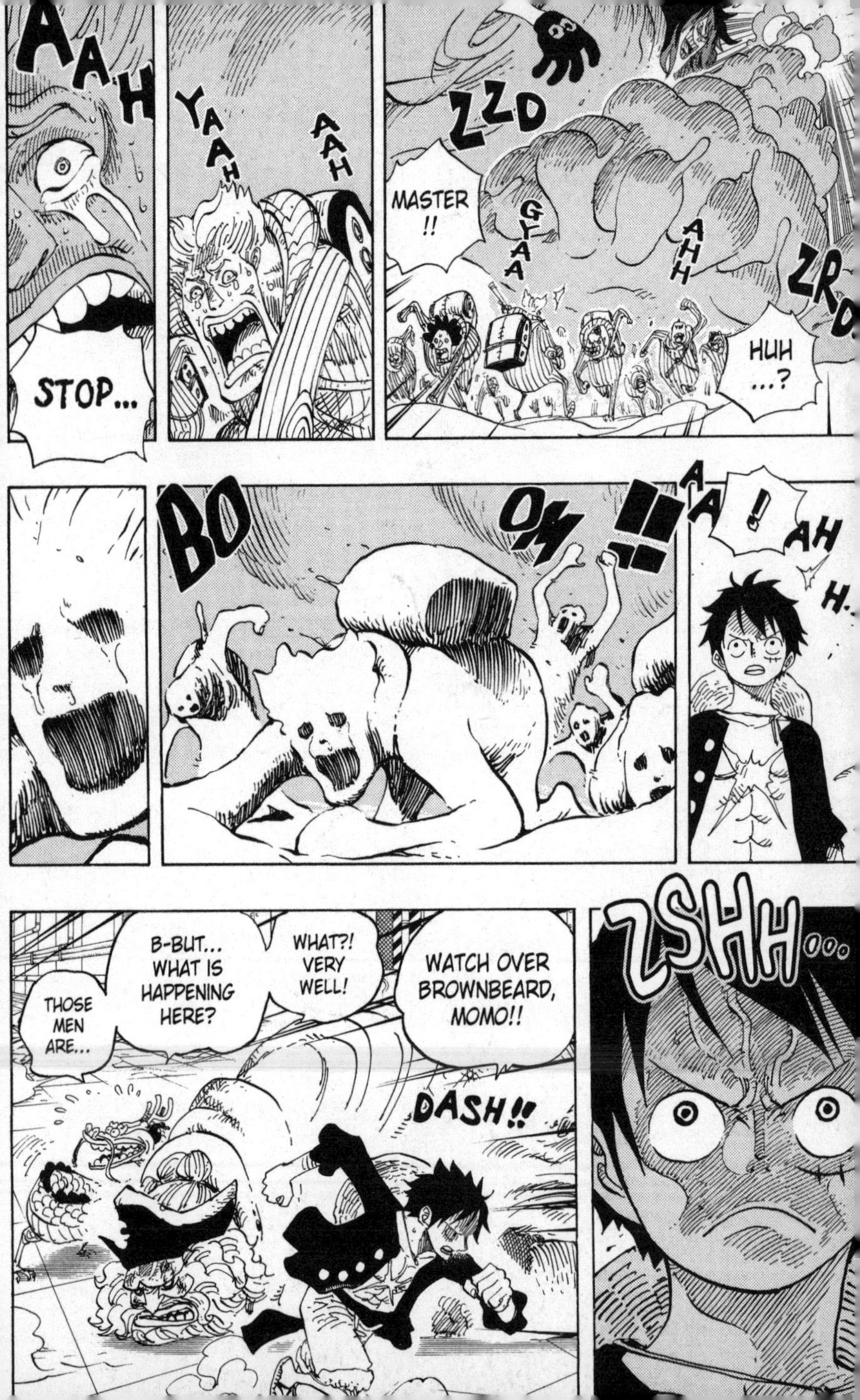
ZRD
HUH ...?
AHH
ZZD
MASTER !!
GYAA
YAAH
AAH
AAH
STOP...
AA ! AH
H..
BO OM!!
ZSHH...
WATCH OVER BROWNBEARD, MOMO!!
WHAT?! VERY WELL!
B-BUT... WHAT IS HAPPENING HERE?
THOSE MEN ARE...
DASH!!

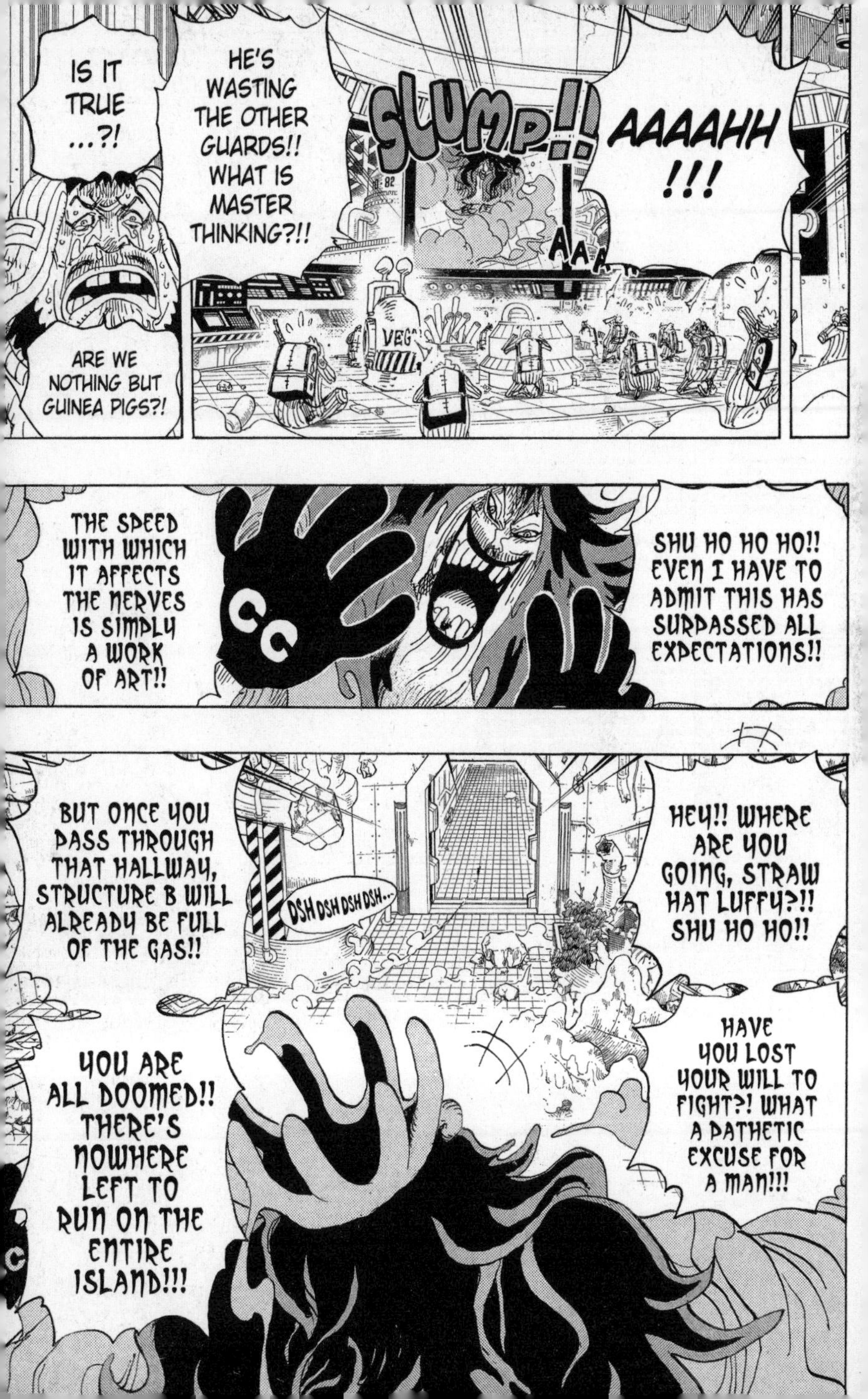
AAAAHH !!!
SLUMP!!
HE'S WASTING THE OTHER GUARDS!! WHAT IS MASTER THINKING?!!
IS IT TRUE ...?!
ARE WE NOTHING BUT GUINEA PIGS?!
SHU HO HO HO!! EVEN I HAVE TO ADMIT THIS HAS SURPASSED ALL EXPECTATIONS!!
THE SPEED WITH WHICH IT AFFECTS THE NERVES IS SIMPLY A WORK OF ART!!
HEY!! WHERE ARE YOU GOING, STRAW HAT LUFFY?!! SHU HO HO!!
BUT ONCE YOU PASS THROUGH THAT HALLWAY, STRUCTURE B WILL ALREADY BE FULL OF THE GAS!!
DSH DSH DSH DSH...
HAVE YOU LOST YOUR WILL TO FIGHT?! WHAT A PATHETIC EXCUSE FOR A MAN!!!
YOU ARE ALL DOOMED!! THERE'S NOWHERE LEFT TO RUN ON THE ENTIRE ISLAND!!!

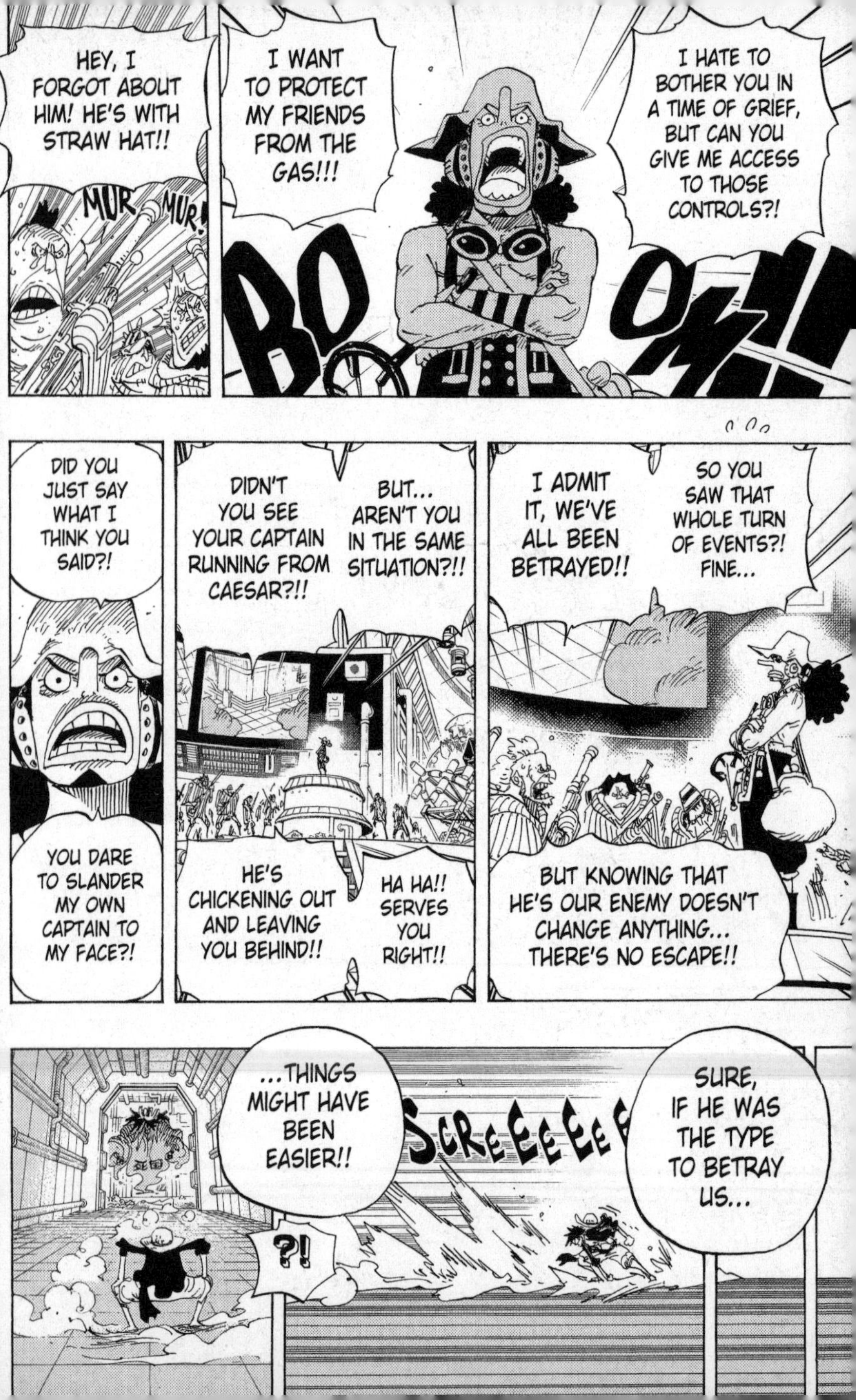
I HATE TO BOTHER YOU IN A TIME OF GRIEF, BUT CAN YOU GIVE ME ACCESS TO THOSE CONTROLS?!
I WANT TO PROTECT MY FRIENDS FROM THE GAS!!!
BO OM!!
HEY, I FORGOT ABOUT HIM! HE'S WITH STRAW HAT!!
MUR MUR
SO YOU SAW THAT WHOLE TURN OF EVENTS?! FINE...
I ADMIT IT, WE'VE ALL BEEN BETRAYED!!
BUT KNOWING THAT HE'S OUR ENEMY DOESN'T CHANGE ANYTHING... THERE'S NO ESCAPE!!
BUT... AREN'T YOU IN THE SAME SITUATION?!!
DIDN'T YOU SEE YOUR CAPTAIN RUNNING FROM CAESAR?!!
HA HA!! SERVES YOU RIGHT!!
HE'S CHICKENING OUT AND LEAVING YOU BEHIND!!
DID YOU JUST SAY WHAT I THINK YOU SAID?!
YOU DARE TO SLANDER MY OWN CAPTAIN TO MY FACE?!
SURE, IF HE WAS THE TYPE TO BETRAY US...
SCREEEEEE
...THINGS MIGHT HAVE BEEN EASIER!!
?!

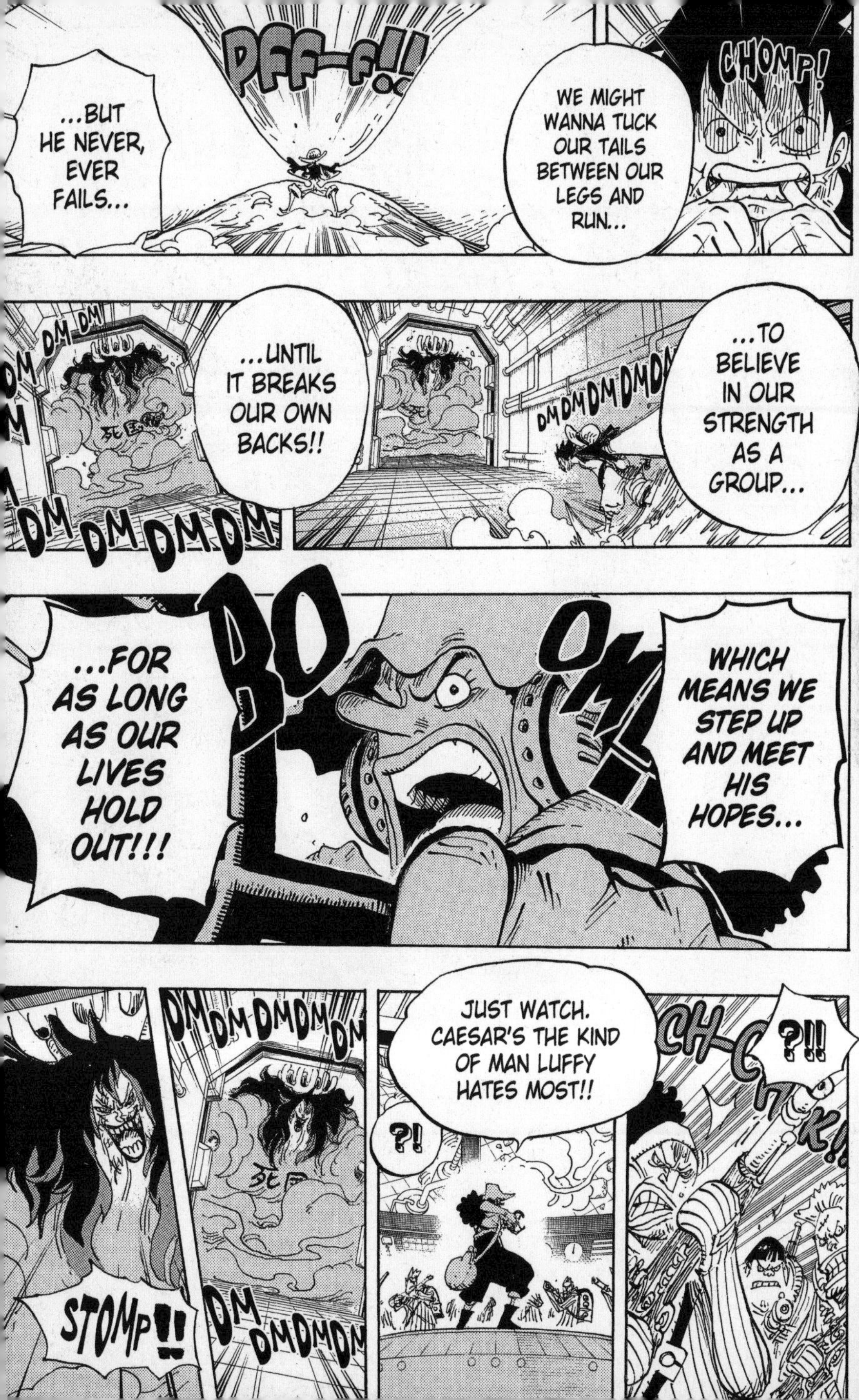
CHOMP!
WE MIGHT WANNA TUCK OUR TAILS BETWEEN OUR LEGS AND RUN...
PFF—F!!
...BUT HE NEVER, EVER FAILS...
...TO BELIEVE IN OUR STRENGTH AS A GROUP...
DM DM DM DMDM
...UNTIL IT BREAKS OUR OWN BACKS!!
DM DM
DM DM DMDM
WHICH MEANS WE STEP UP AND MEET HIS HOPES...
BOOM
...FOR AS LONG AS OUR LIVES HOLD OUT!!!
?!!
JUST WATCH. CAESAR'S THE KIND OF MAN LUFFY HATES MOST!!
?!
DM DM DMDM
DM DMDM
STOMP!!

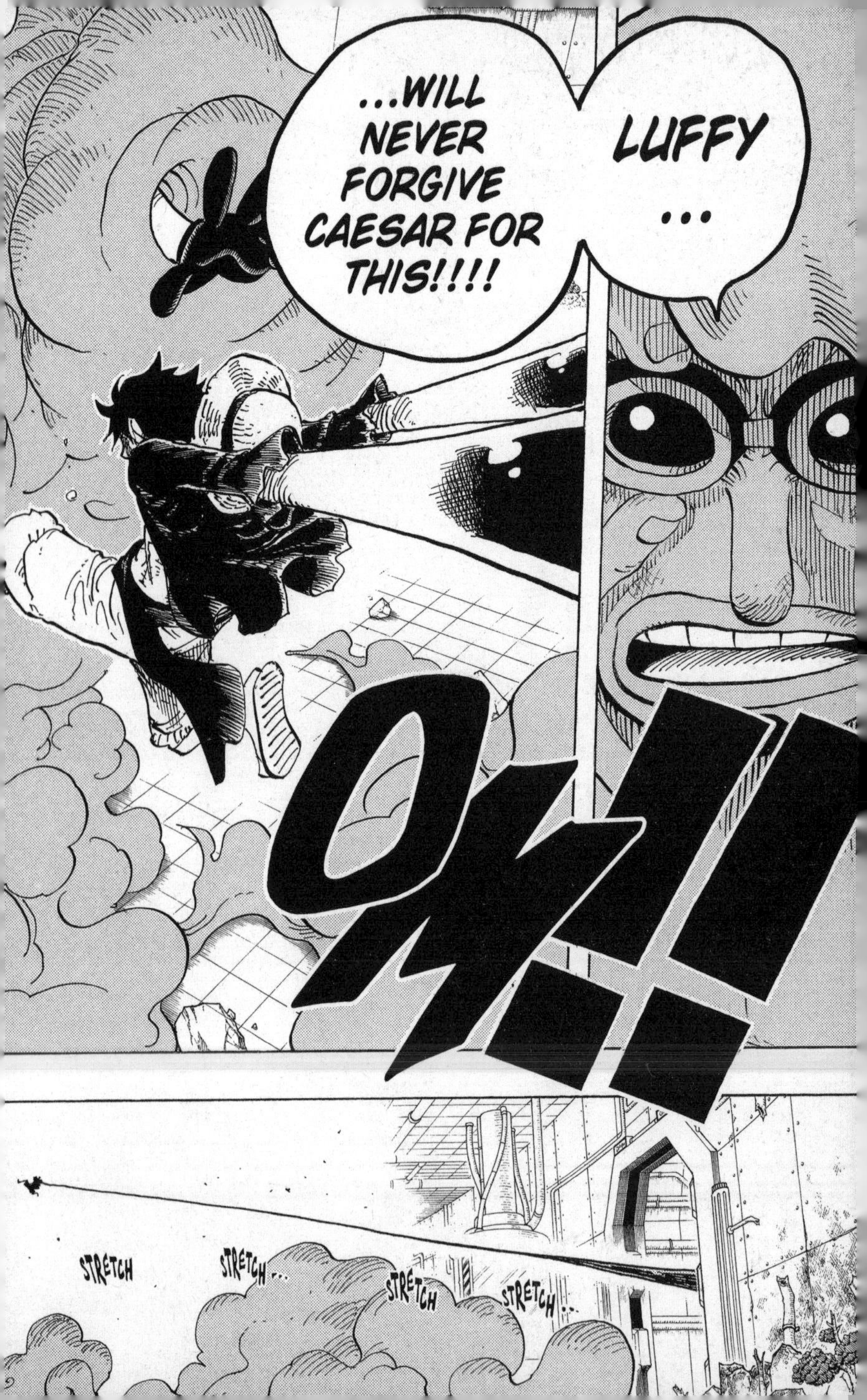
LUFFY ...
...WILL NEVER FORGIVE CAESAR FOR THIS!!!!
OH!!
STRETCH...
STRETCH
STRETCH...
STRETCH

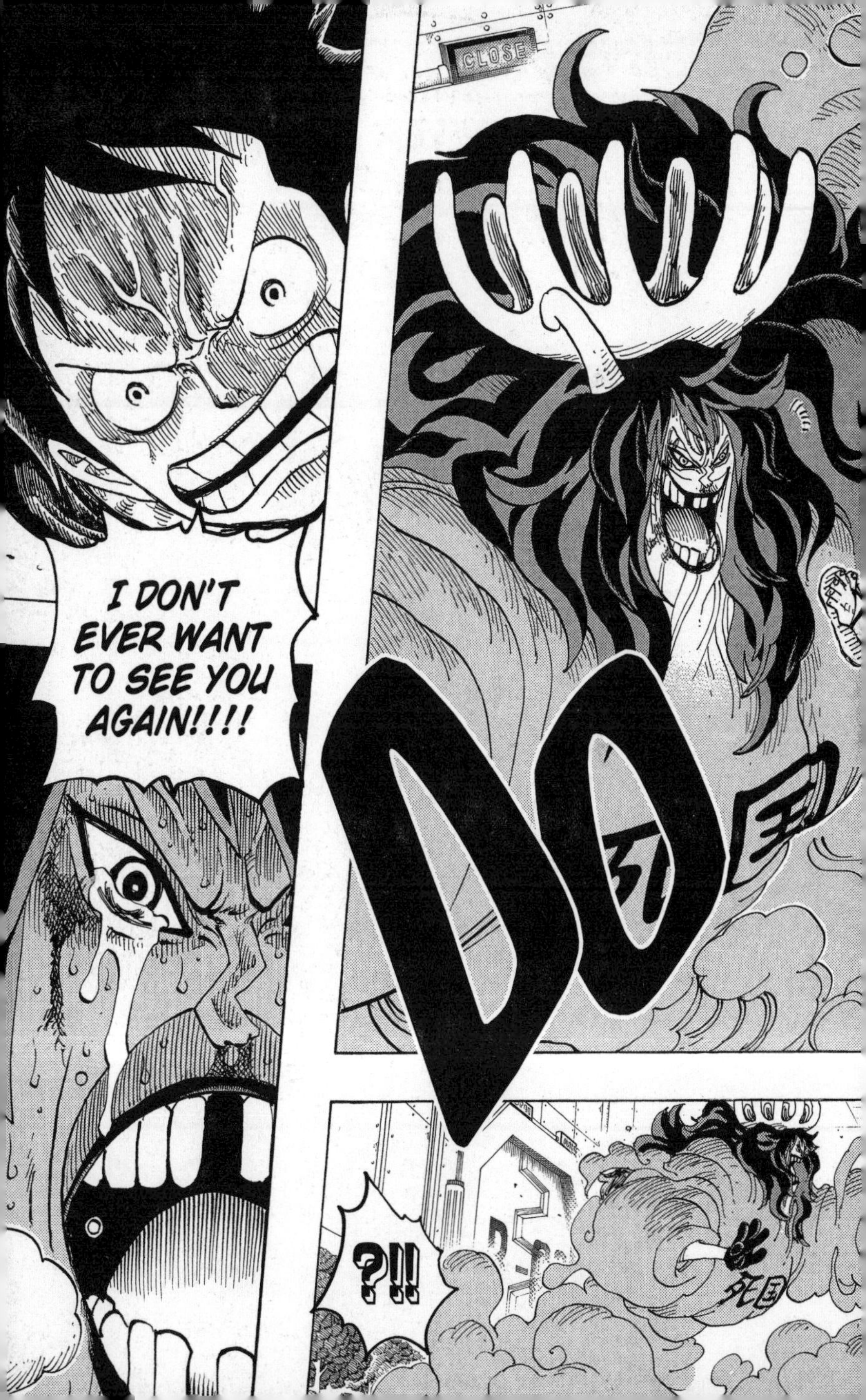
CLOSE
I DON'T EVER WANT TO SEE YOU AGAIN!!!!
DO
?!!

ASSASSINS FROM DRESSROSA

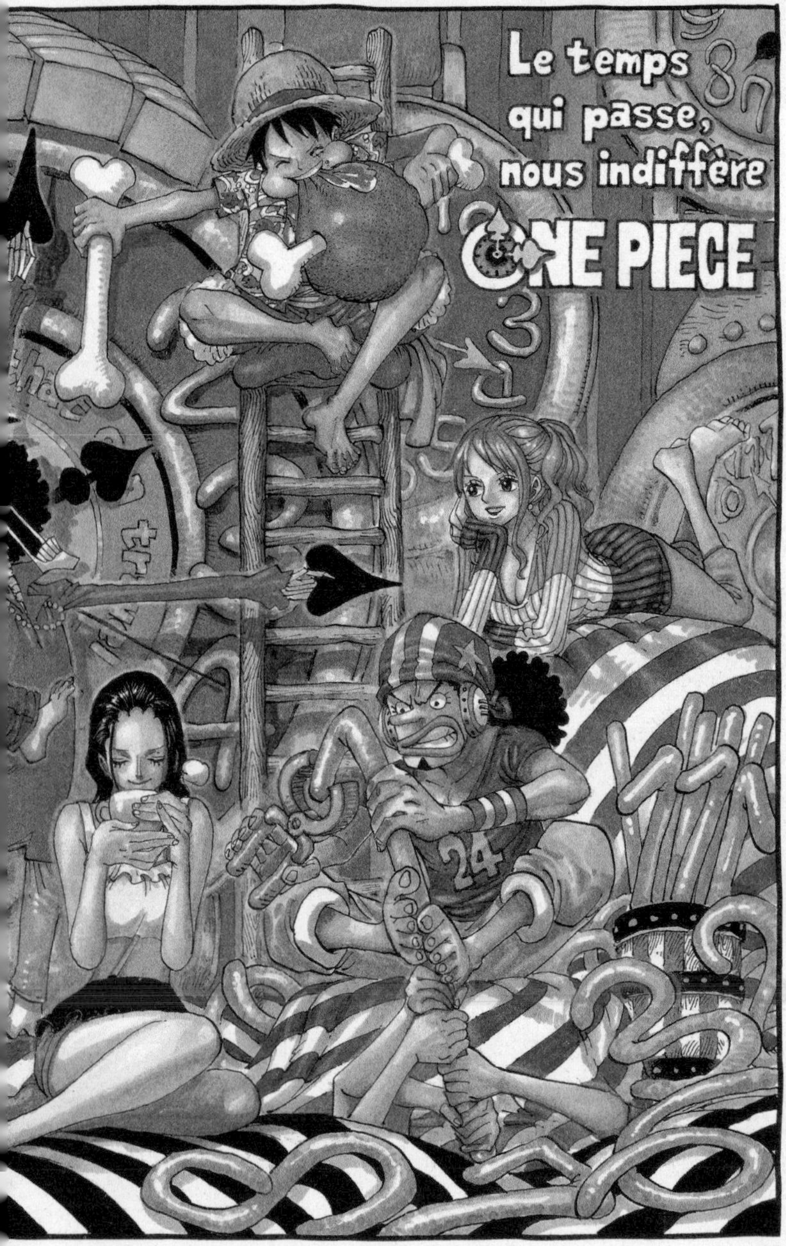
Le temps qui passe, nous indiffère
ONE PIECE
24

Chapter 692:

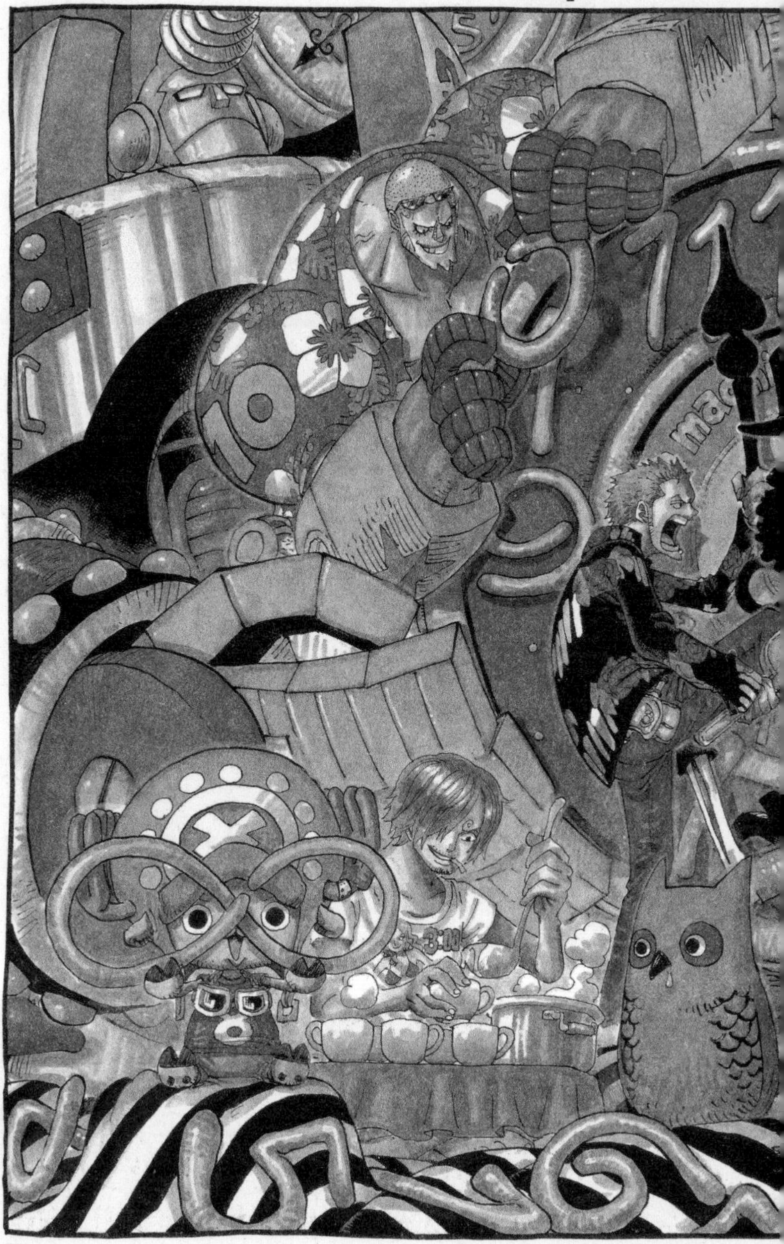

vol.70
ONE PIECE

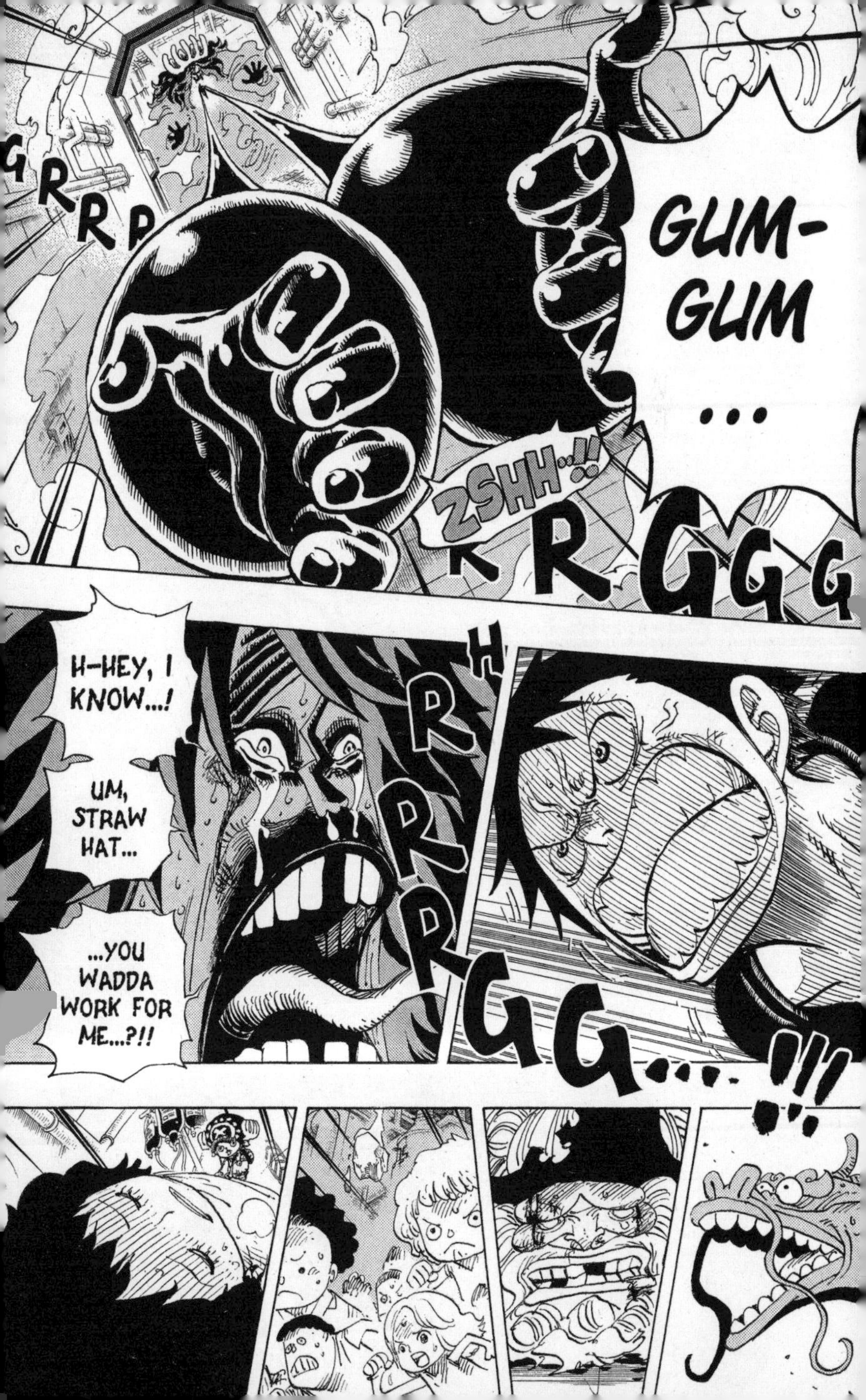

GUM-GUM
...
ZSHH..!!
KRGGGG
GRRP
HRRRGG...!!!
H-HEY, I KNOW...!
UM, STRAW HAT...
...YOU WADDA WORK FOR ME...?!!

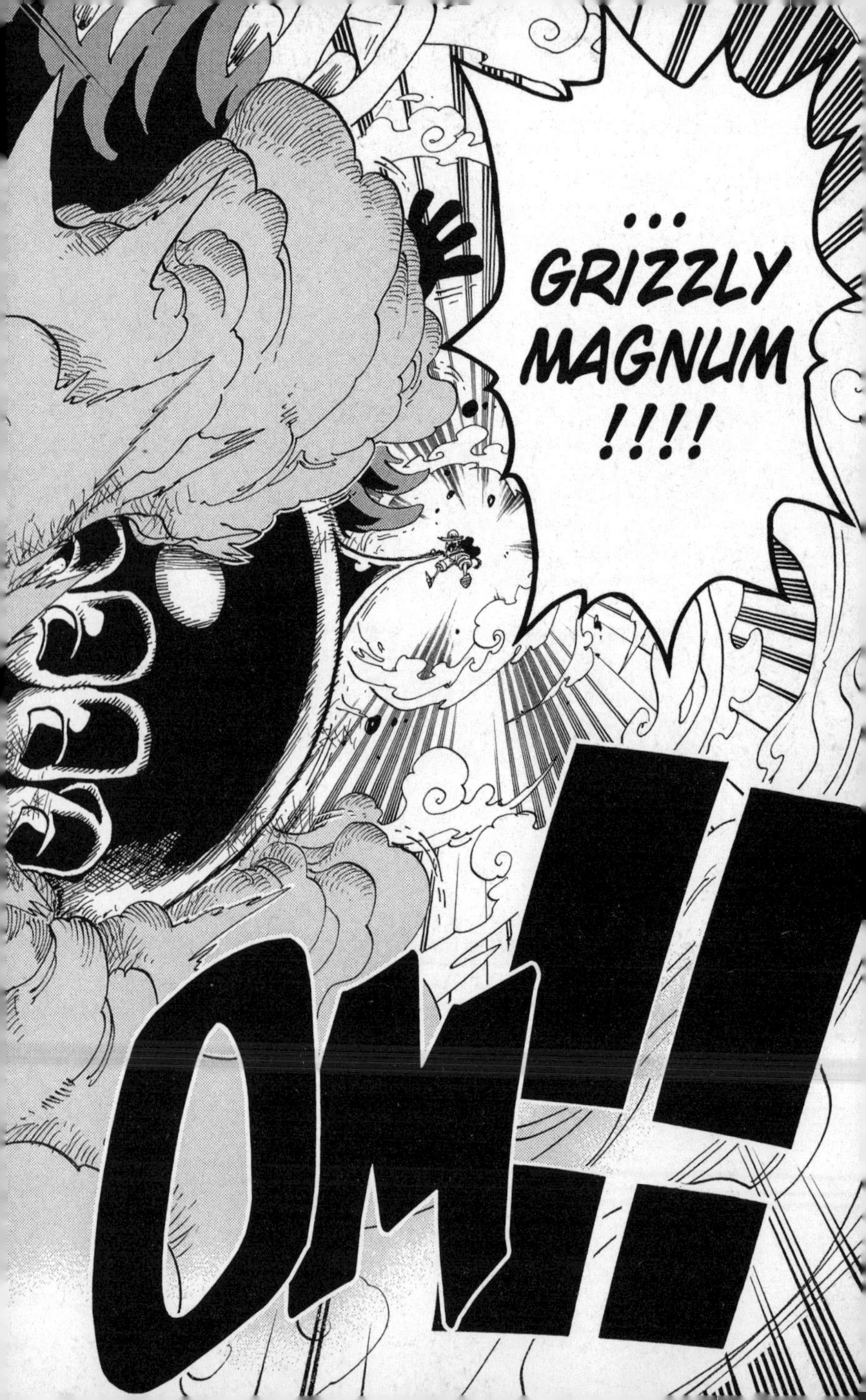
...GRIZZLY MAGNUM!!!!
OM!!

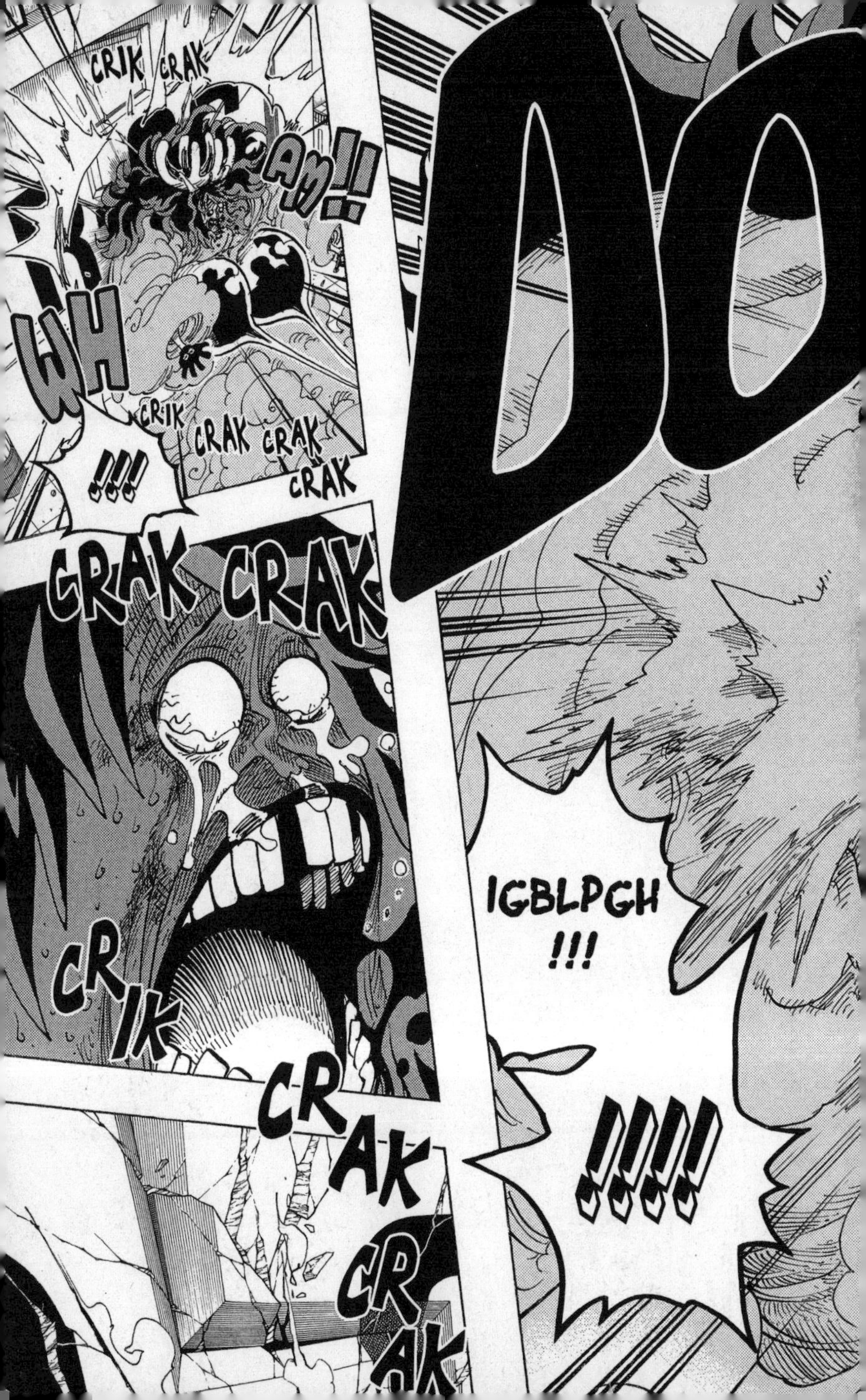
DO
IGBLPGH !!!
!!!!
CRIK CRAK
WHAM!!
CRIK CRAK CRAK CRAK
!!!
CRAK CRAK
CRIK
CRAK
CRAK

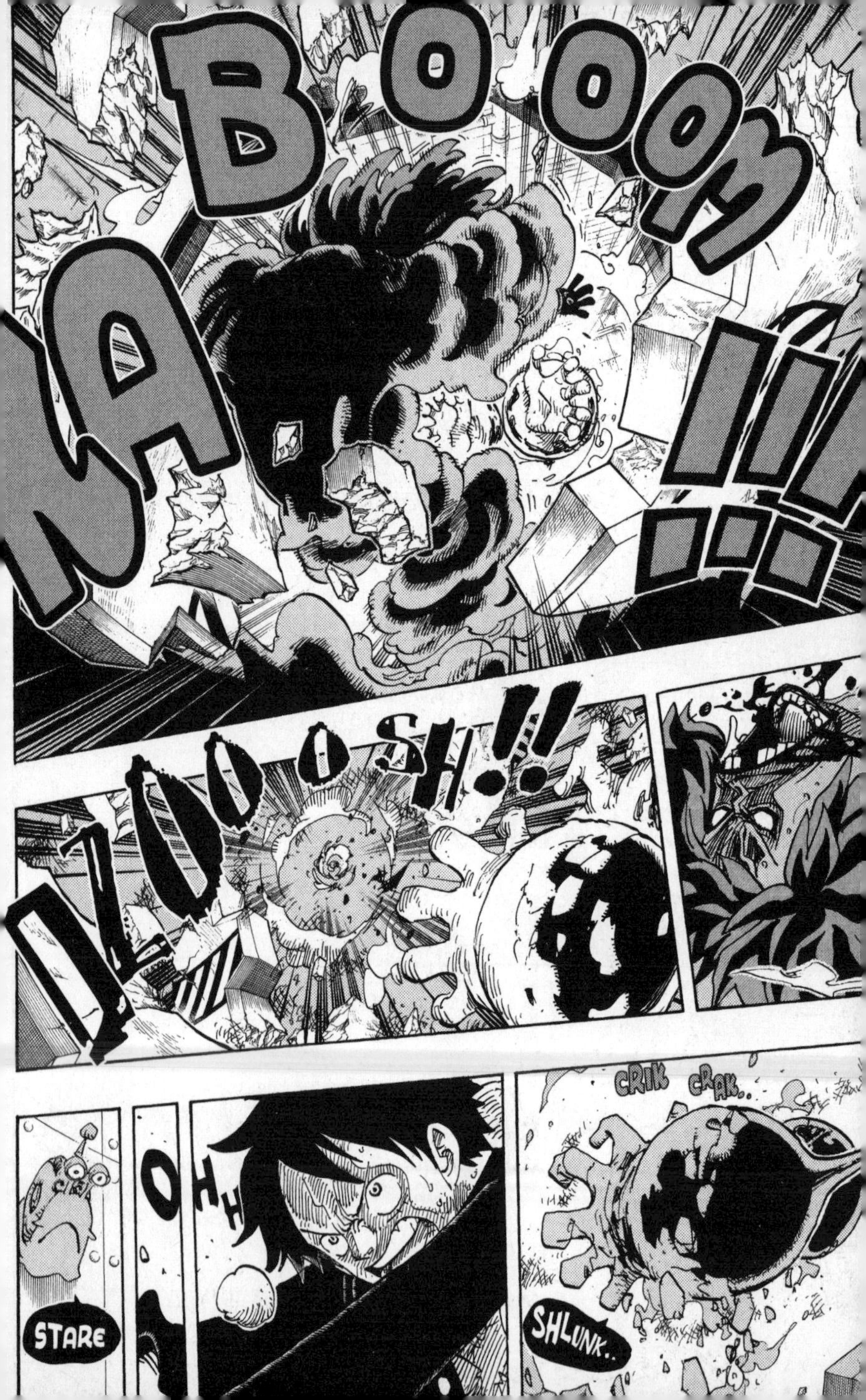

A BOOOM!!!
ZOOOSH!!
CRIK CRAK..
SHLUNK..
OHH
STARE

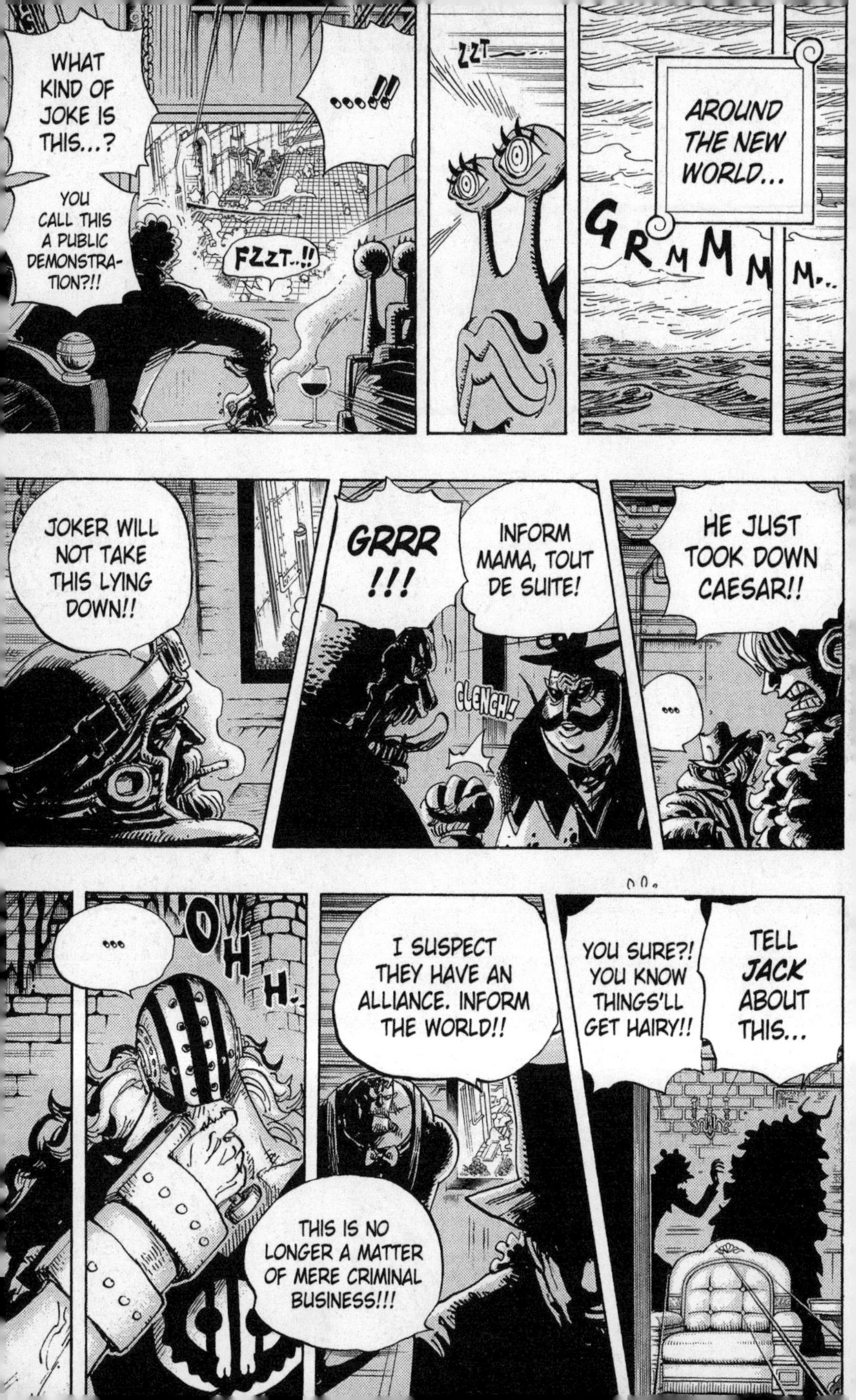
AROUND THE NEW WORLD...
GRMMMMM...
ZZT~
...!!
WHAT KIND OF JOKE IS THIS...?
YOU CALL THIS A PUBLIC DEMONSTRATION?!!
FZZT..!!
HE JUST TOOK DOWN CAESAR!!
...
INFORM MAMA, TOUT DE SUITE!
GRRR!!!
CLENCH!
JOKER WILL NOT TAKE THIS LYING DOWN!!
TELL JACK ABOUT THIS...
YOU SURE?! YOU KNOW THINGS'LL GET HAIRY!!
I SUSPECT THEY HAVE AN ALLIANCE. INFORM THE WORLD!!
THIS IS NO LONGER A MATTER OF MERE CRIMINAL BUSINESS!!!
OHH.
...

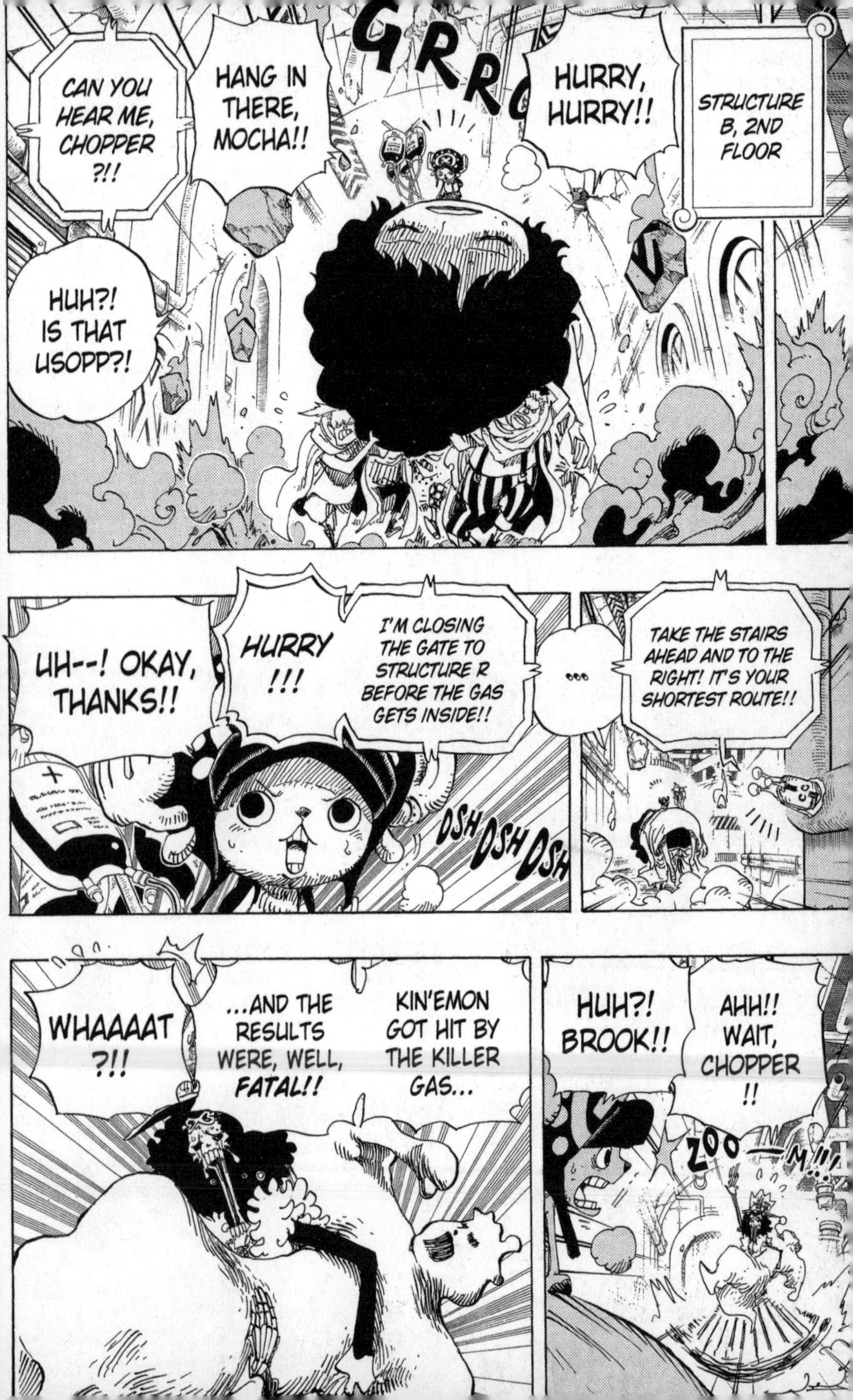
STRUCTURE B, 2ND FLOOR
GRRO
HURRY, HURRY!!
HANG IN THERE, MOCHA!!
CAN YOU HEAR ME, CHOPPER?!!
HUH?! IS THAT USOPP?!
TAKE THE STAIRS AHEAD AND TO THE RIGHT! IT'S YOUR SHORTEST ROUTE!!
...
I'M CLOSING THE GATE TO STRUCTURE R BEFORE THE GAS GETS INSIDE!!
HURRY!!!
UH--! OKAY, THANKS!!
DSH DSH DSH
AHH!! WAIT, CHOPPER!!
HUH?! BROOK!!
ZOOOM!!
KIN'EMON GOT HIT BY THE KILLER GAS...
...AND THE RESULTS WERE, WELL, FATAL!!
WHAAAAT?!!

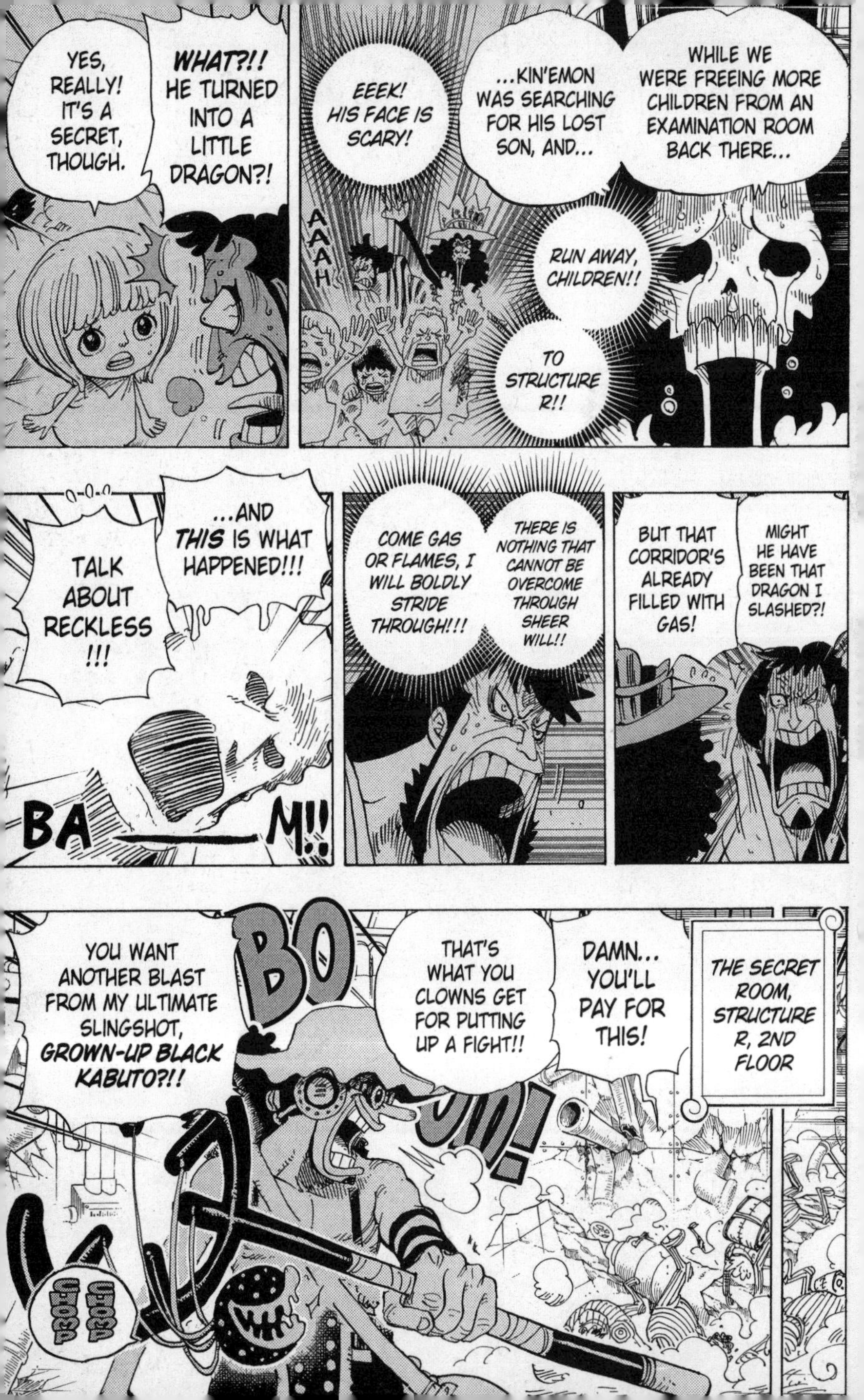
WHILE WE WERE FREEING MORE CHILDREN FROM AN EXAMINATION ROOM BACK THERE...
...KIN'EMON WAS SEARCHING FOR HIS LOST SON, AND...
EEEK! HIS FACE IS SCARY!
AAAH
RUN AWAY, CHILDREN!!
TO STRUCTURE R!!
WHAT?!! HE TURNED INTO A LITTLE DRAGON?!
YES, REALLY! IT'S A SECRET, THOUGH.
MIGHT HE HAVE BEEN THAT DRAGON I SLASHED?!
BUT THAT CORRIDOR'S ALREADY FILLED WITH GAS!
THERE IS NOTHING THAT CANNOT BE OVERCOME THROUGH SHEER WILL!!
COME GAS OR FLAMES, I WILL BOLDLY STRIDE THROUGH!!!
...AND THIS IS WHAT HAPPENED!!!
TALK ABOUT RECKLESS!!!
BA—M!!
THE SECRET ROOM, STRUCTURE R, 2ND FLOOR
DAMN... YOU'LL PAY FOR THIS!
THAT'S WHAT YOU CLOWNS GET FOR PUTTING UP A FIGHT!!
BO OM!
YOU WANT ANOTHER BLAST FROM MY ULTIMATE SLINGSHOT, GROWN-UP BLACK KABUTO?!!

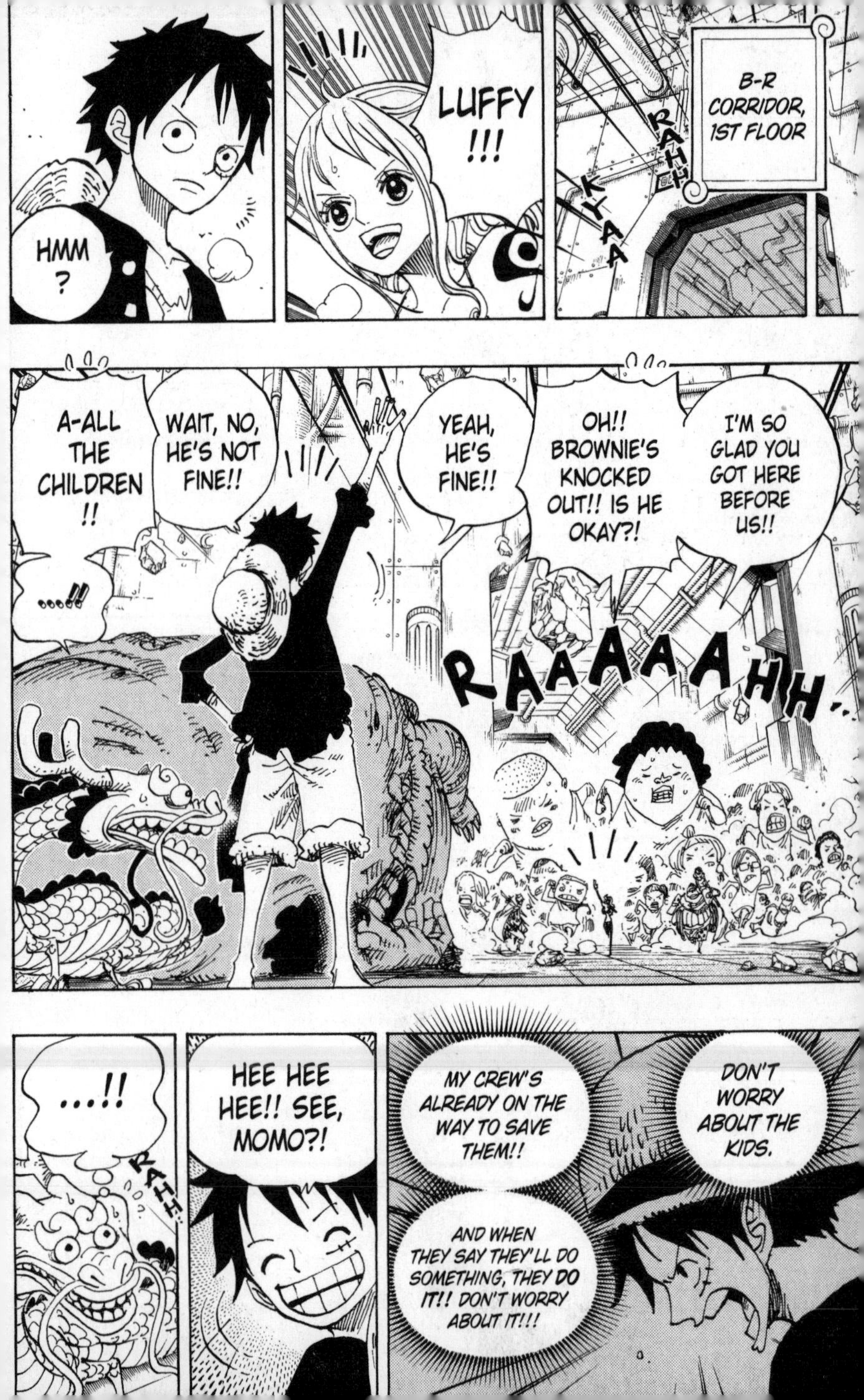
B-R CORRIDOR, 1ST FLOOR
RAHH
KYAA
LUFFY!!!
HMM?
I'M SO GLAD YOU GOT HERE BEFORE US!!
OH!! BROWNIE'S KNOCKED OUT!! IS HE OKAY?!
YEAH, HE'S FINE!!
WAIT, NO, HE'S NOT FINE!!
A-ALL THE CHILDREN!!
....!!
RAAAAAHH...
DON'T WORRY ABOUT THE KIDS.
MY CREW'S ALREADY ON THE WAY TO SAVE THEM!!
AND WHEN THEY SAY THEY'LL DO SOMETHING, THEY DO IT!! DON'T WORRY ABOUT IT!!!
HEE HEE HEE!! SEE, MOMO?!
...!!
RAHH

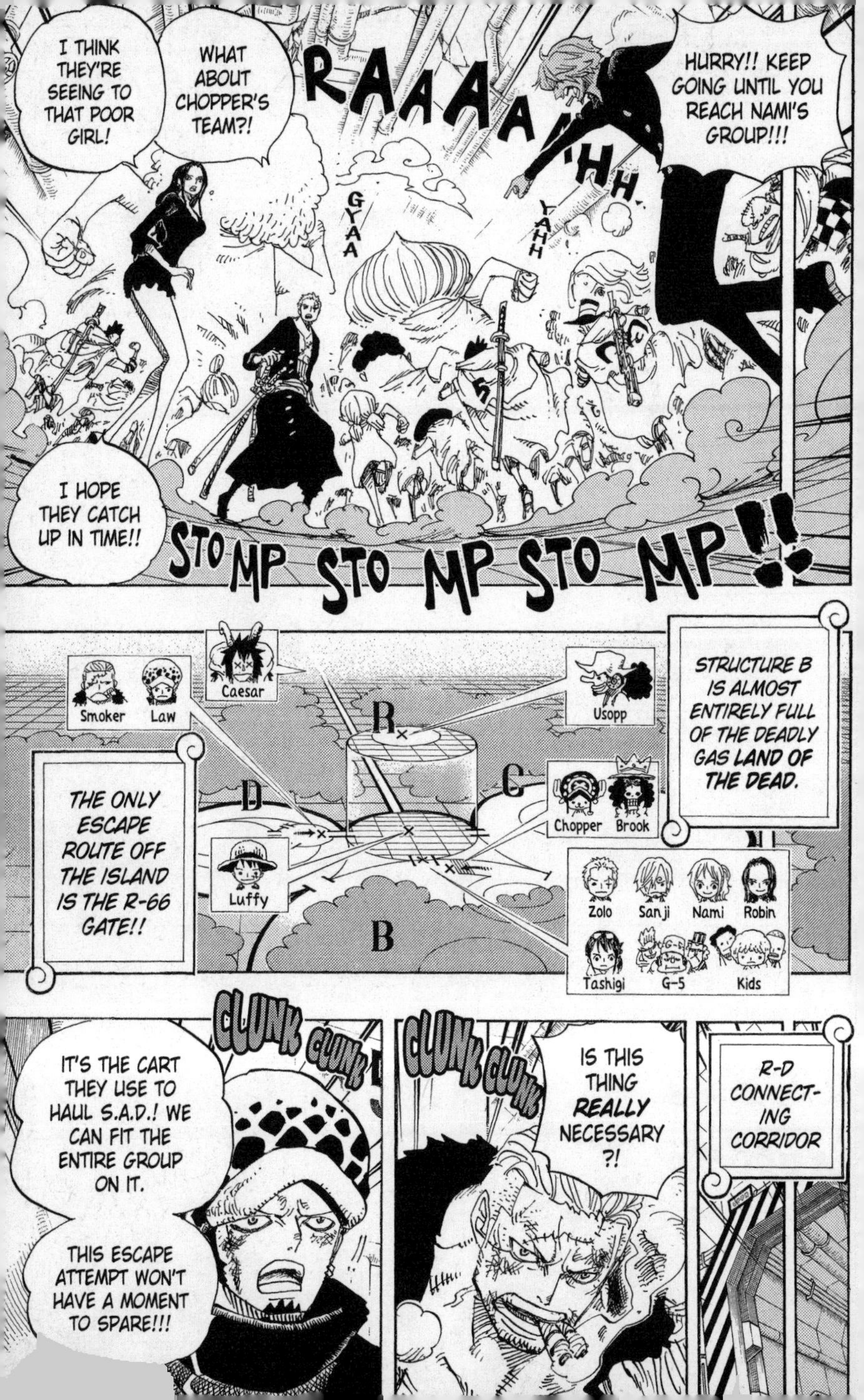
HURRY!! KEEP GOING UNTIL YOU REACH NAMI'S GROUP!!!
RAAAAAHH
WHAT ABOUT CHOPPER'S TEAM?!
I THINK THEY'RE SEEING TO THAT POOR GIRL!
YAHH
GYAA
I HOPE THEY CATCH UP IN TIME!!
STOMP STOMP STOMP!!
STRUCTURE B IS ALMOST ENTIRELY FULL OF THE DEADLY GAS LAND OF THE DEAD.
Usopp
R
Caesar
Smoker
Law
C
Chopper
Brook
D
Luffy
Zolo
Sanji
Nami
Robin
Tashigi
G-5
Kids
B
THE ONLY ESCAPE ROUTE OFF THE ISLAND IS THE R-66 GATE!!
R-D CONNECTING CORRIDOR
CLUNK CLUNK
IS THIS THING REALLY NECESSARY?!
CLUNK CLUNK
IT'S THE CART THEY USE TO HAUL S.A.D.! WE CAN FIT THE ENTIRE GROUP ON IT.
THIS ESCAPE ATTEMPT WON'T HAVE A MOMENT TO SPARE!!!

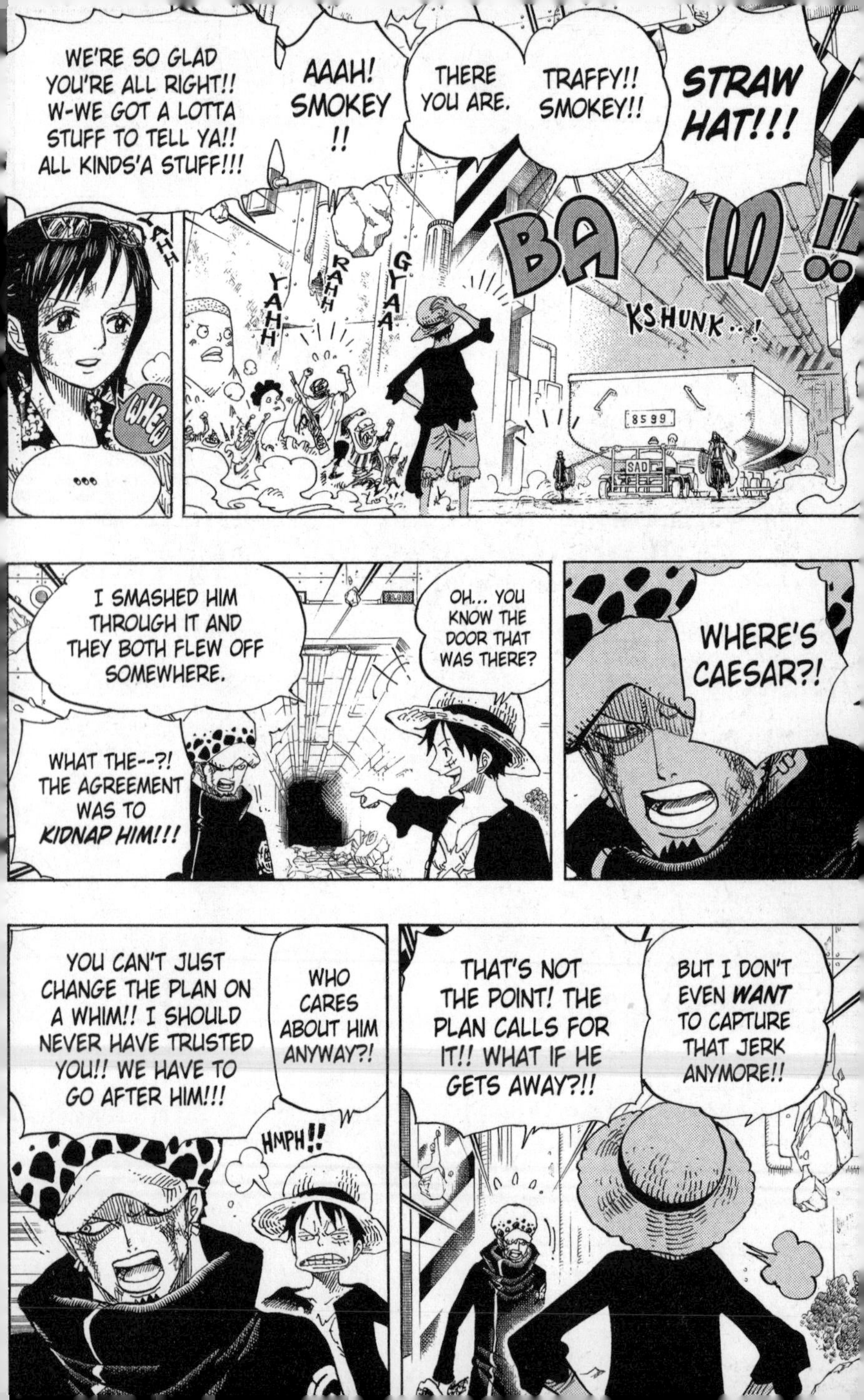
STRAW HAT!!!
TRAFFY!! SMOKEY!!
THERE YOU ARE.
BAM!!
KSHUNK..!
AAAH! SMOKEY!!
GYAA
RAHH
YAHH
WE'RE SO GLAD YOU'RE ALL RIGHT!! W-WE GOT A LOTTA STUFF TO TELL YA!! ALL KINDS'A STUFF!!!
YAHH
WHEW
...
WHERE'S CAESAR?!
OH... YOU KNOW THE DOOR THAT WAS THERE?
I SMASHED HIM THROUGH IT AND THEY BOTH FLEW OFF SOMEWHERE.
WHAT THE--?! THE AGREEMENT WAS TO *KIDNAP HIM!!!*
BUT I DON'T EVEN *WANT* TO CAPTURE THAT JERK ANYMORE!!
THAT'S NOT THE POINT! THE PLAN CALLS FOR IT!! WHAT IF HE GETS AWAY?!!
WHO CARES ABOUT HIM ANYWAY?!
HMPH!!
YOU CAN'T JUST CHANGE THE PLAN ON A WHIM!! I SHOULD NEVER HAVE TRUSTED YOU!! WE HAVE TO GO AFTER HIM!!!

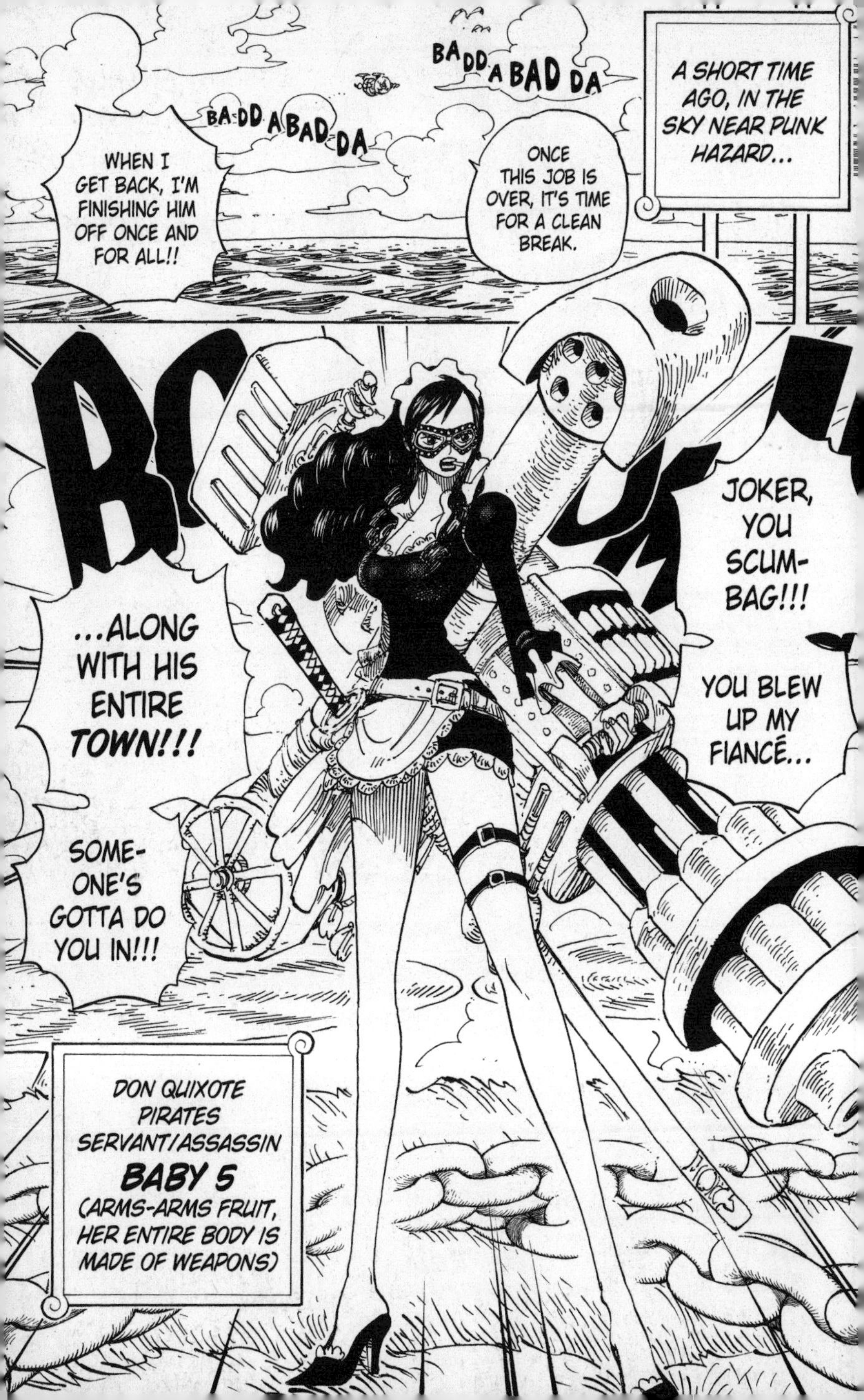
A SHORT TIME AGO, IN THE SKY NEAR PUNK HAZARD...
BADDA BAD DA
ONCE THIS JOB IS OVER, IT'S TIME FOR A CLEAN BREAK.
BADDA BAD DA
WHEN I GET BACK, I'M FINISHING HIM OFF ONCE AND FOR ALL!!
JOKER, YOU SCUM-BAG!!!
YOU BLEW UP MY FIANCÉ...
...ALONG WITH HIS ENTIRE TOWN!!!
SOME-ONE'S GOTTA DO YOU IN!!!
DON QUIXOTE PIRATES SERVANT/ASSASSIN
BABY 5
(ARMS-ARMS FRUIT, HER ENTIRE BODY IS MADE OF WEAPONS)

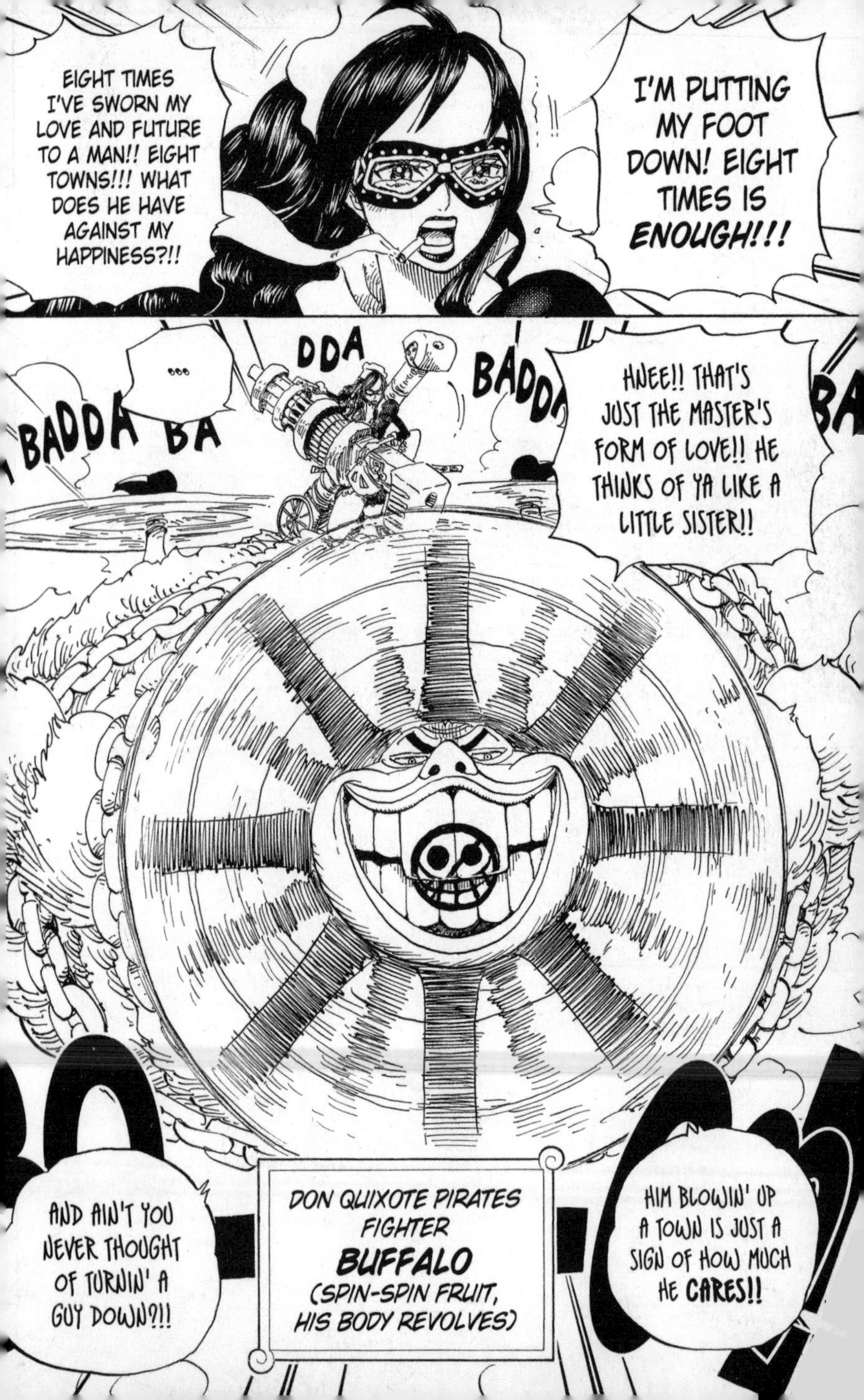
I'M PUTTING MY FOOT DOWN! EIGHT TIMES IS ENOUGH!!!
EIGHT TIMES I'VE SWORN MY LOVE AND FUTURE TO A MAN!! EIGHT TOWNS!!! WHAT DOES HE HAVE AGAINST MY HAPPINESS?!!
BA
HWEE!! THAT'S JUST THE MASTER'S FORM OF LOVE!! HE THINKS OF YA LIKE A LITTLE SISTER!!
BADD
DDA
...
BADDA BA
HIM BLOWIN' UP A TOWN IS JUST A SIGN OF HOW MUCH HE CARES!!
DON QUIXOTE PIRATES FIGHTER
BUFFALO
(SPIN-SPIN FRUIT, HIS BODY REVOLVES)
AND AIN'T YOU NEVER THOUGHT OF TURNIN' A GUY DOWN?!!

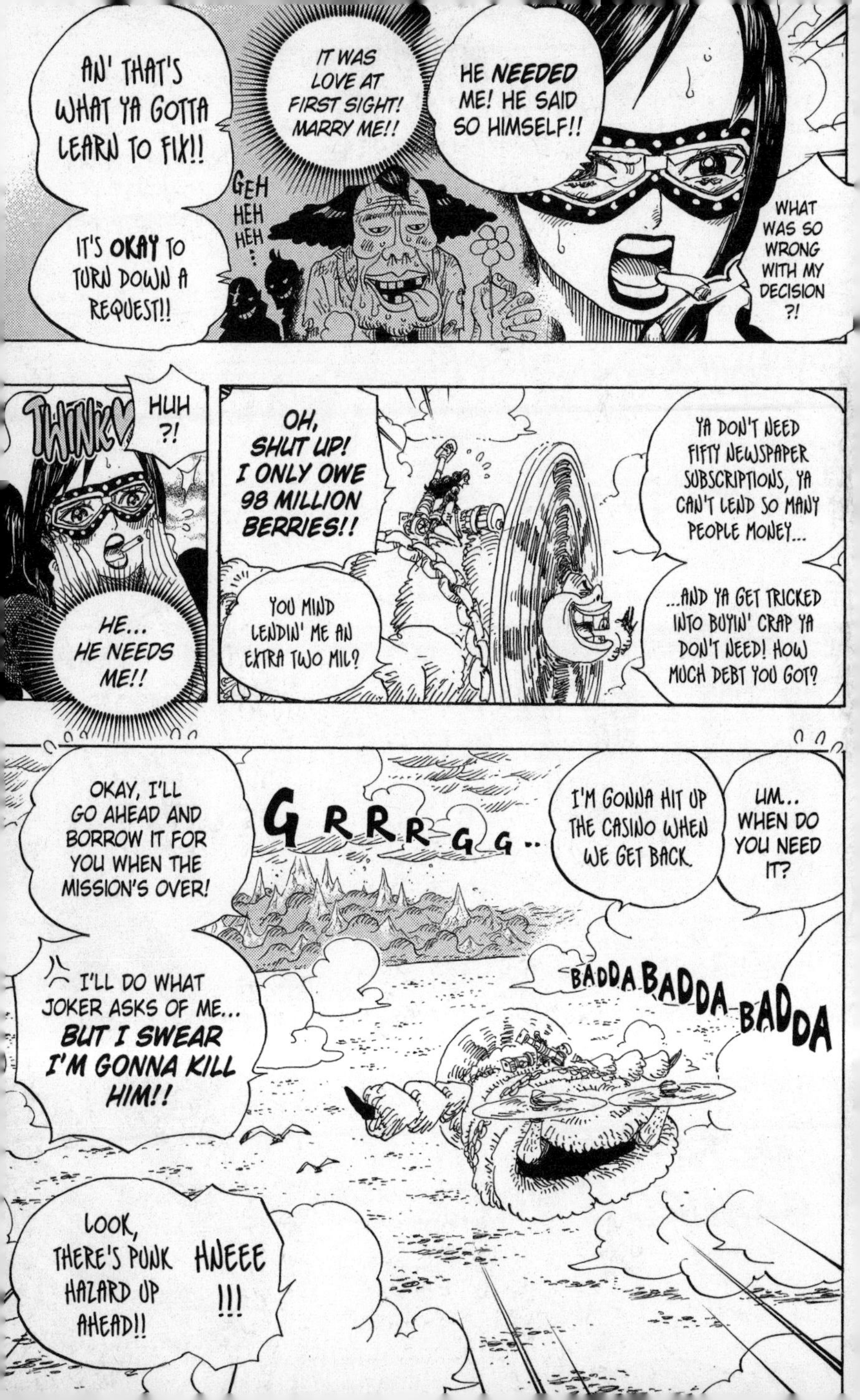
WHAT WAS SO WRONG WITH MY DECISION ?!
HE NEEDED ME! HE SAID SO HIMSELF!!
IT WAS LOVE AT FIRST SIGHT! MARRY ME!!
GEH HEH HEH...
AN' THAT'S WHAT YA GOTTA LEARN TO FIX!!
IT'S OKAY TO TURN DOWN A REQUEST!!
YA DON'T NEED FIFTY NEWSPAPER SUBSCRIPTIONS, YA CAN'T LEND SO MANY PEOPLE MONEY...
...AND YA GET TRICKED INTO BUYIN' CRAP YA DON'T NEED! HOW MUCH DEBT YOU GOT?
OH, SHUT UP! I ONLY OWE 98 MILLION BERRIES!!
YOU MIND LENDIN' ME AN EXTRA TWO MIL?
THINK♥
HUH ?!
HE... HE NEEDS ME!!
UM.. WHEN DO YOU NEED IT?
I'M GONNA HIT UP THE CASINO WHEN WE GET BACK.
GRRRRGG..
OKAY, I'LL GO AHEAD AND BORROW IT FOR YOU WHEN THE MISSION'S OVER!
BADDA BADDA BADDA
I'LL DO WHAT JOKER ASKS OF ME... BUT I SWEAR I'M GONNA KILL HIM!!
HNEEE !!!
LOOK, THERE'S PUNK HAZARD UP AHEAD!!

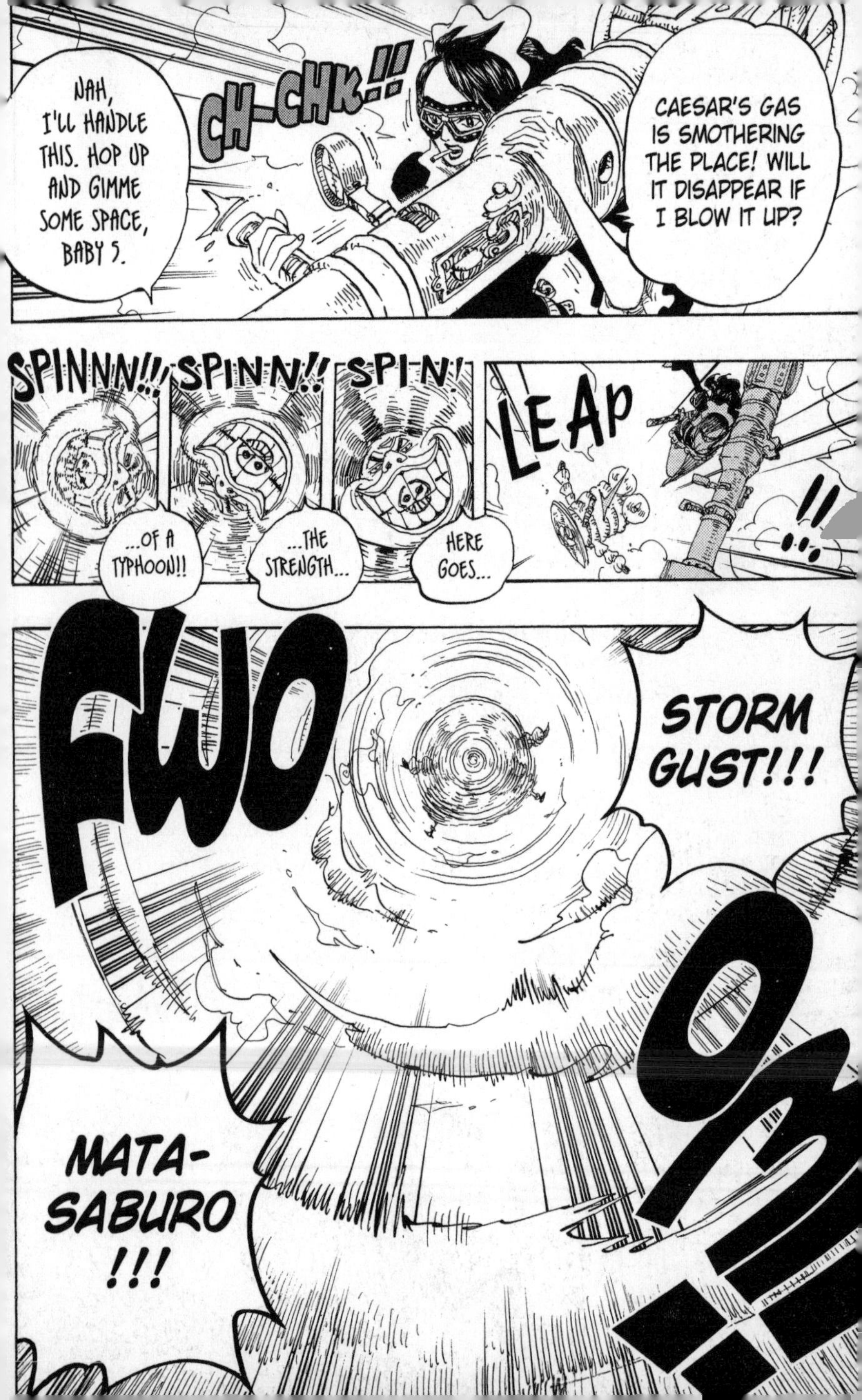
CAESAR'S GAS IS SMOTHERING THE PLACE! WILL IT DISAPPEAR IF I BLOW IT UP?
CH-CHK!!
NAH, I'LL HANDLE THIS. HOP UP AND GIMME SOME SPACE, BABY 5.
LEAP
!!
SPIN!
HERE GOES...
SPINN!!
...THE STRENGTH...
SPINNN!!
...OF A TYPHOON!!
STORM GUST!!!
FWO
OM!!
MATA-SABURO!!!

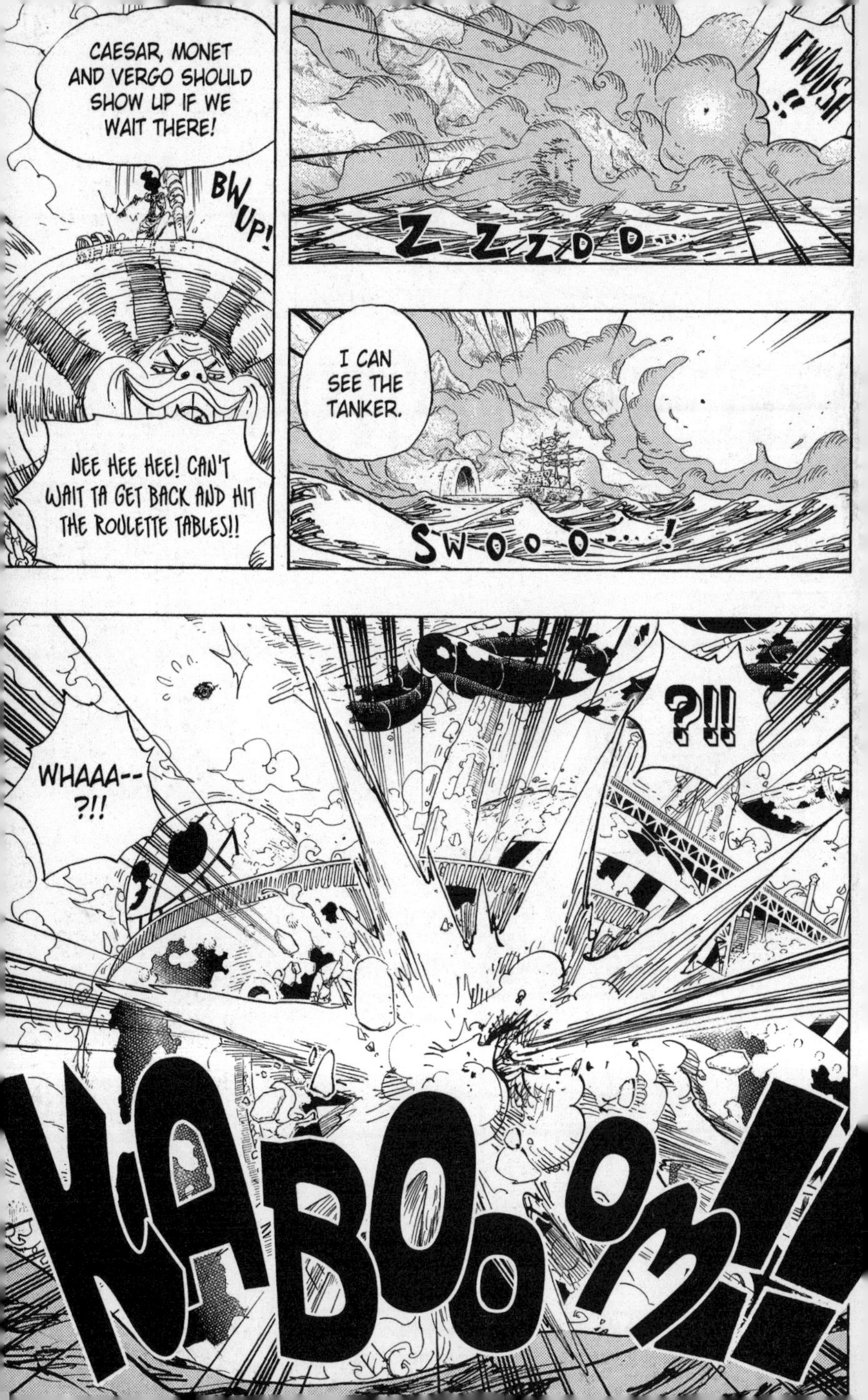
FWOOSH!!
ZZZZDD...
I CAN SEE THE TANKER.
SWOOO...!
CAESAR, MONET AND VERGO SHOULD SHOW UP IF WE WAIT THERE!
BWUP!
NEE HEE HEE! CAN'T WAIT TA GET BACK AND HIT THE ROULETTE TABLES!!
?!!
WHAAA--?!!
KABOOOM!!

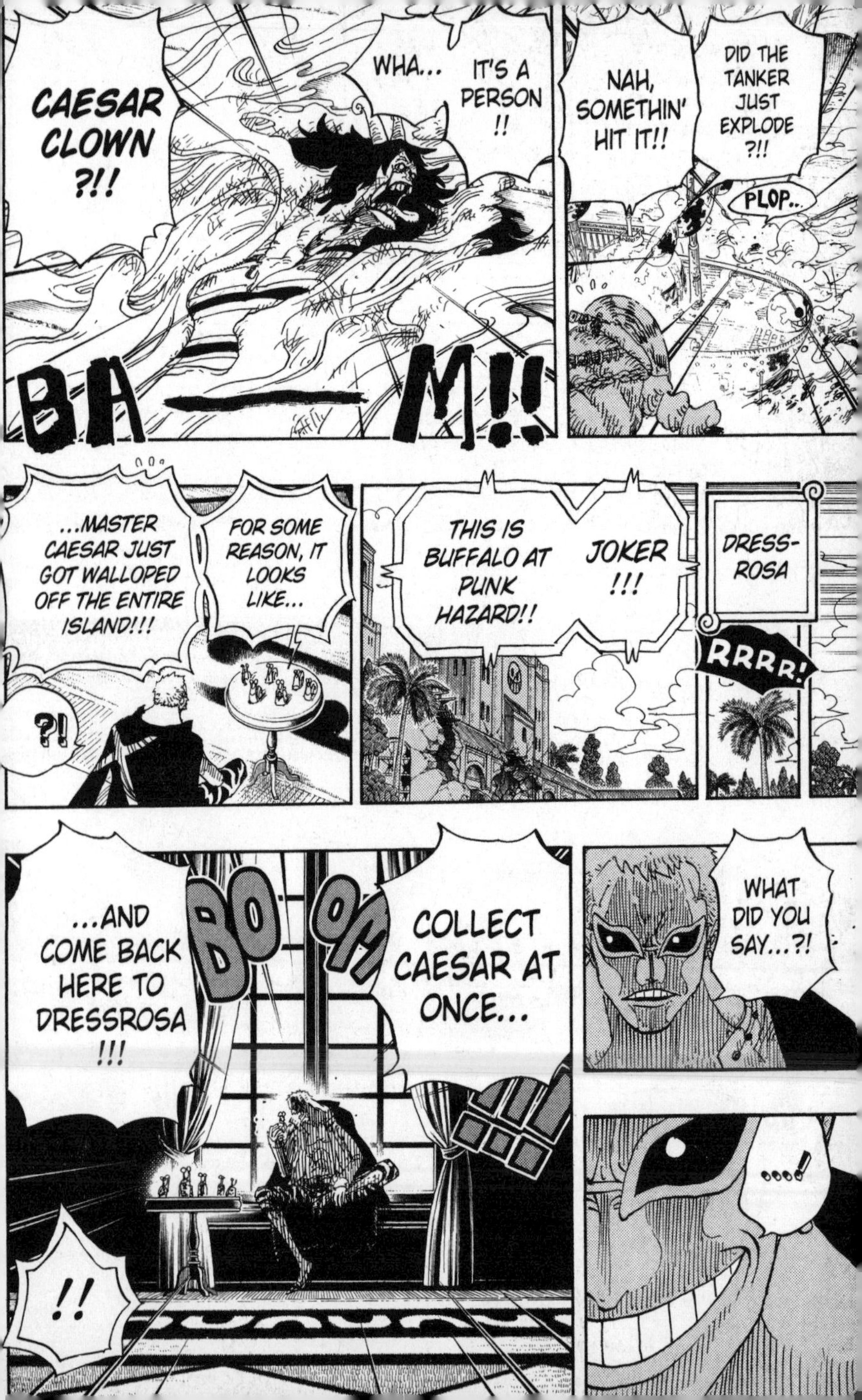
DID THE TANKER JUST EXPLODE ?!!
NAH, SOMETHIN' HIT IT!!
PLOP...
IT'S A PERSON !!
WHA...
CAESAR CLOWN ?!!
BA—M!!
DRESS-ROSA
RRRR!
JOKER !!!
THIS IS BUFFALO AT PUNK HAZARD!!
FOR SOME REASON, IT LOOKS LIKE...
...MASTER CAESAR JUST GOT WALLOPED OFF THE ENTIRE ISLAND!!!
?!
WHAT DID YOU SAY...?!
...!
COLLECT CAESAR AT ONCE...
BOOM
...AND COME BACK HERE TO DRESSROSA !!!
!!

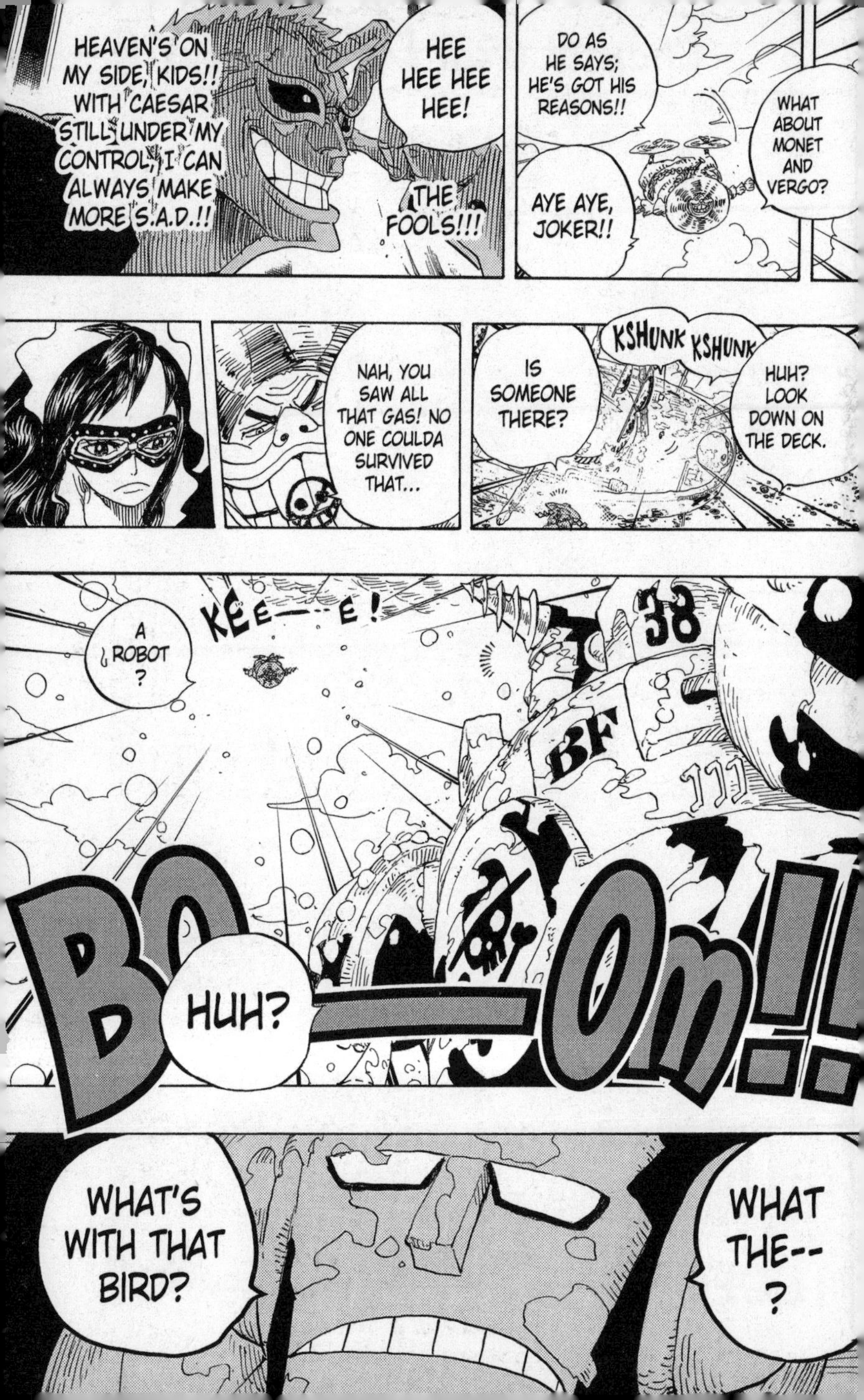
WHAT ABOUT MONET AND VERGO?
DO AS HE SAYS; HE'S GOT HIS REASONS!!
AYE AYE, JOKER!!
HEE HEE HEE HEE!
HEAVEN'S ON MY SIDE, KIDS!! WITH CAESAR STILL UNDER MY CONTROL, I CAN ALWAYS MAKE MORE S.A.D.!!
THE FOOLS!!!
HUH? LOOK DOWN ON THE DECK.
KSHUNK KSHUNK
IS SOMEONE THERE?
NAH, YOU SAW ALL THAT GAS! NO ONE COULDA SURVIVED THAT...
KEE---E!
A ¿ROBOT?
BO--OM!!
HUH?
WHAT THE-- ?
WHAT'S WITH THAT BIRD?

Chapter 693: DIE FOR ME

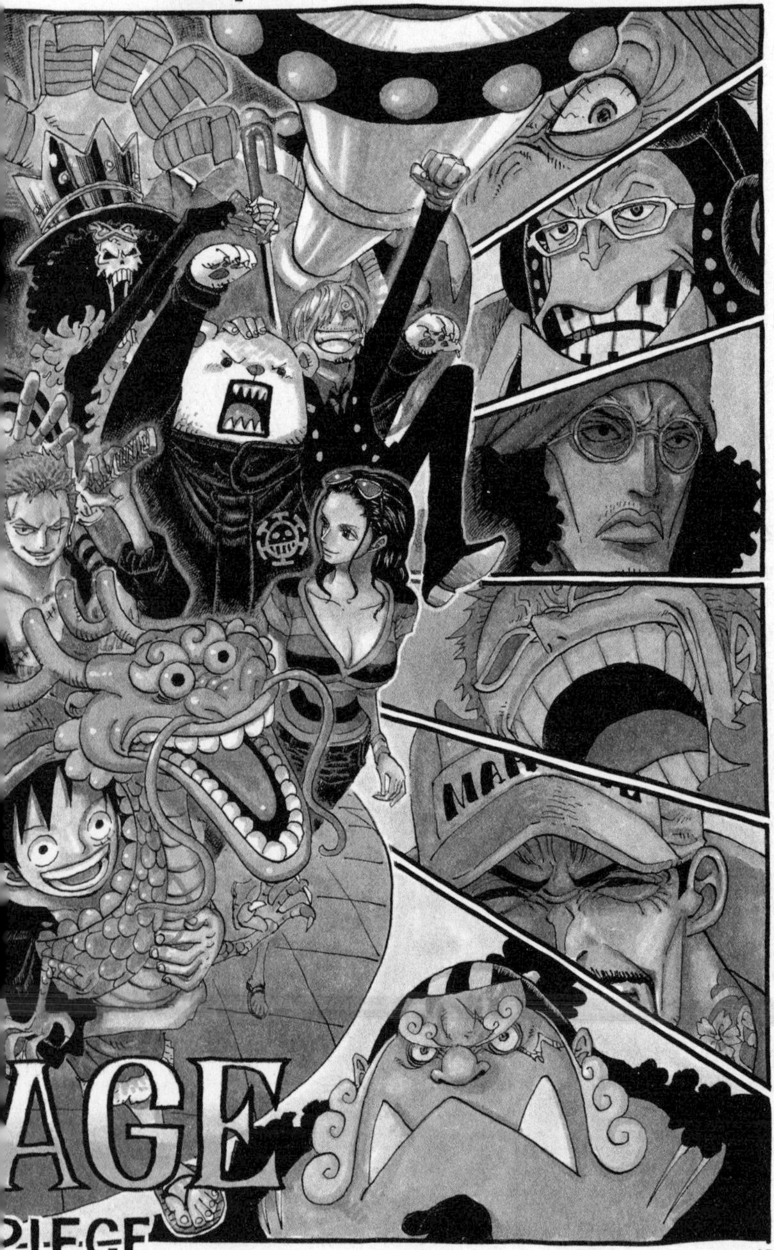

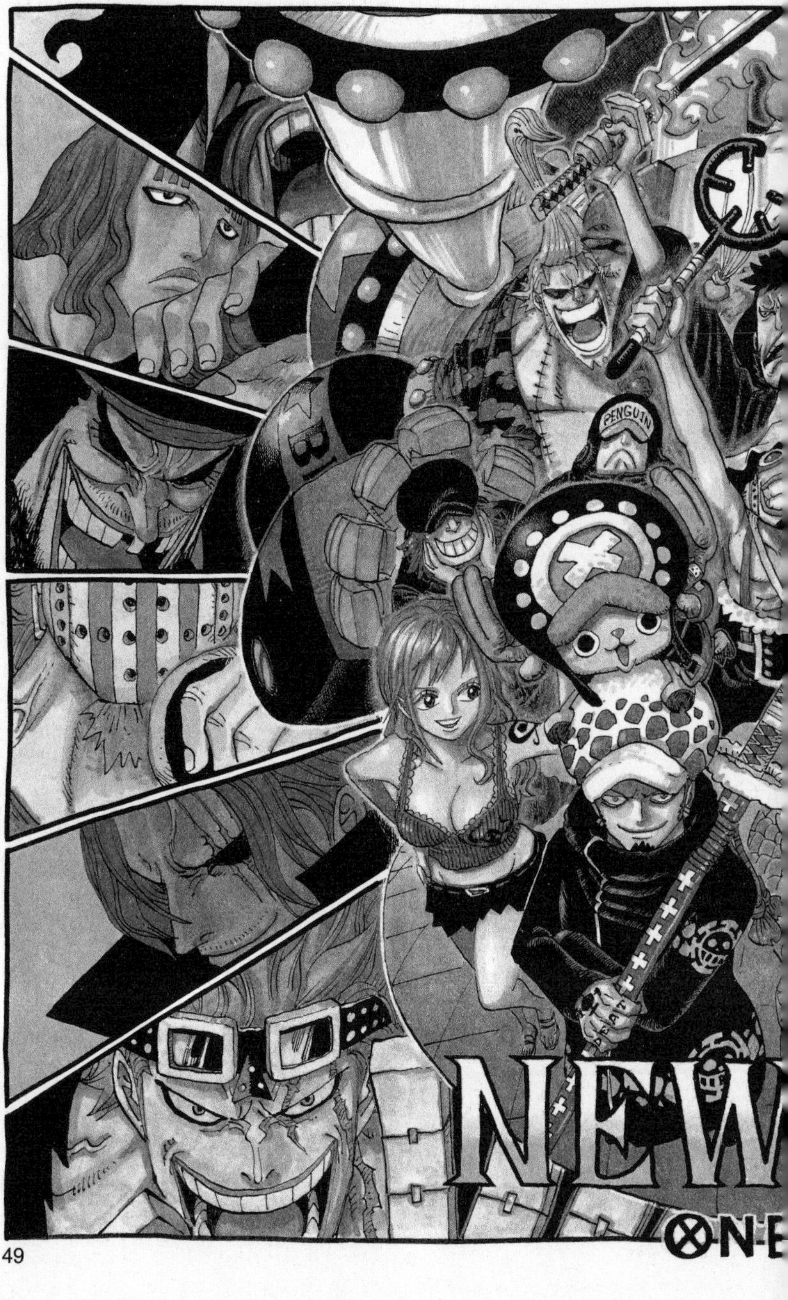
PENGUIN
NEW

vol. 70
ONE PIECE

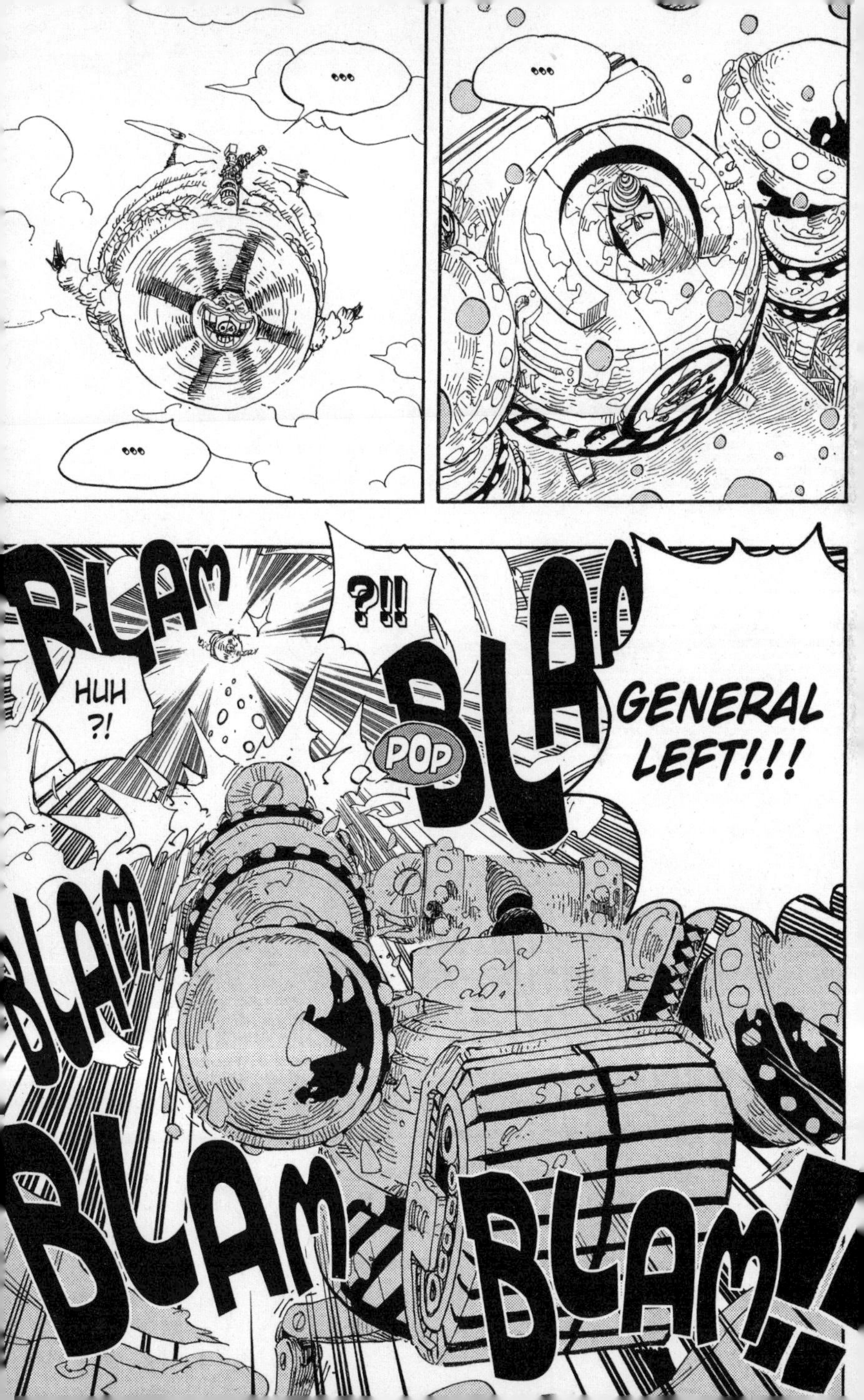
...
...
...
GENERAL LEFT!!!
?!!
BLAM
HUH ?!
POP
BLAM
BLAM
BLAM!!

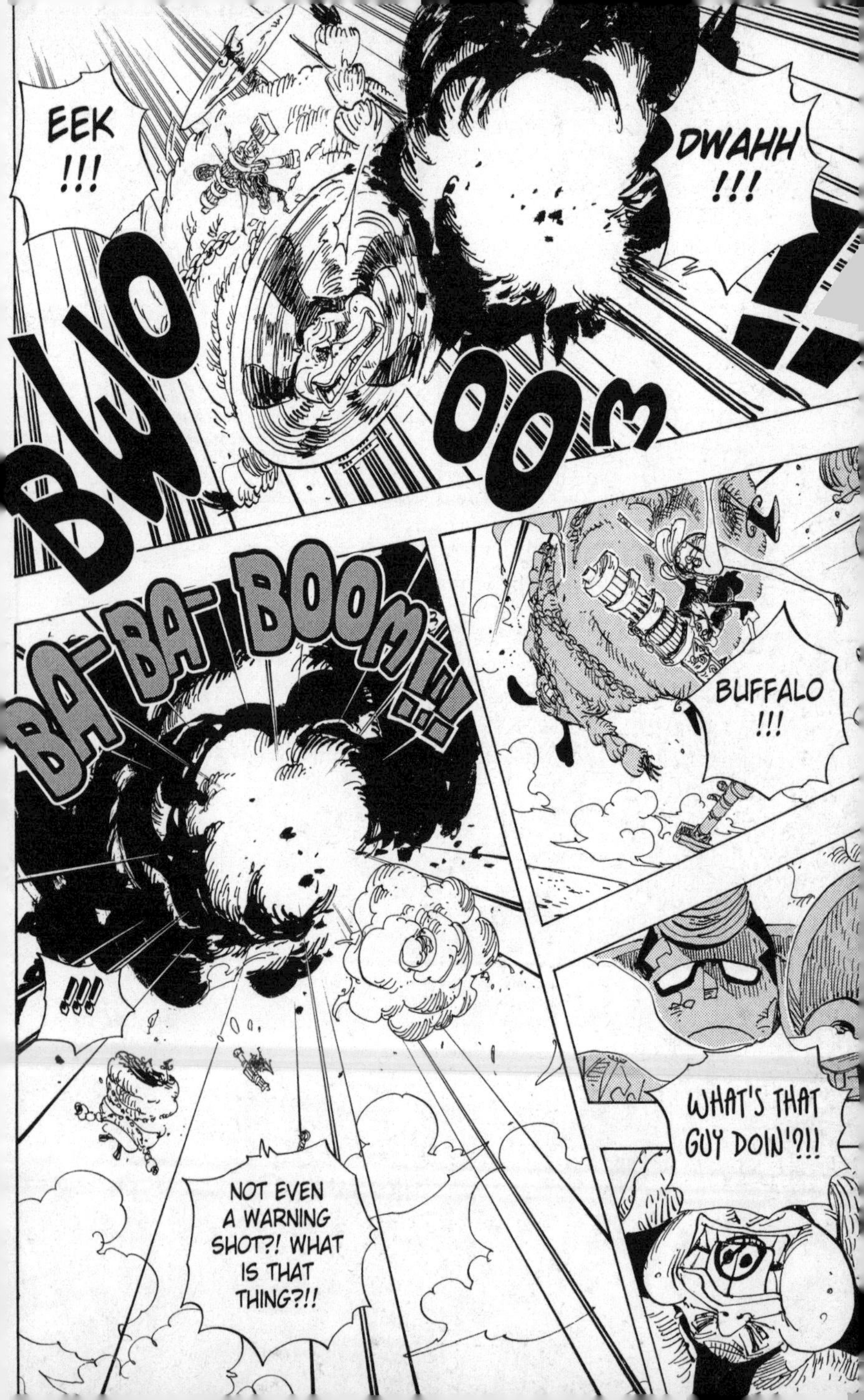
DWAHH !!!
EEK !!!
BWOOOM
BUFFALO !!!
BA-BA-BOOM!!!
!!!
WHAT'S THAT GUY DOIN'?!!
NOT EVEN A WARNING SHOT?! WHAT IS THAT THING?!!

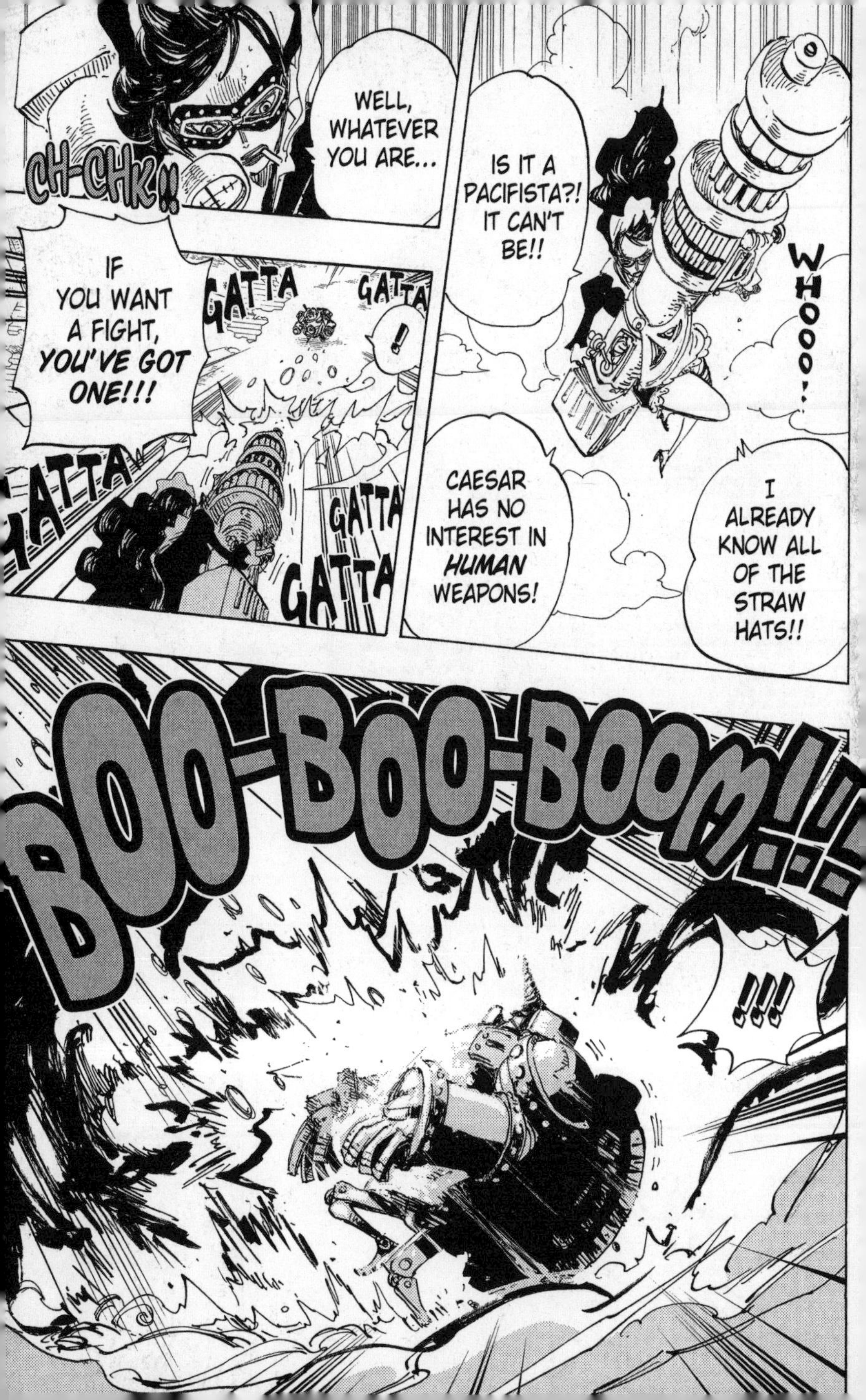
IS IT A PACIFISTA?! IT CAN'T BE!!
WHOOO!
I ALREADY KNOW ALL OF THE STRAW HATS!!
CAESAR HAS NO INTEREST IN *HUMAN* WEAPONS!
WELL, WHATEVER YOU ARE...
CH-CHK!!
IF YOU WANT A FIGHT, *YOU'VE GOT ONE!!!*
GATTA
GATTA
!
GATTA
GATTA
GATTA
BOO-BOO-BOOM!!!
!!!

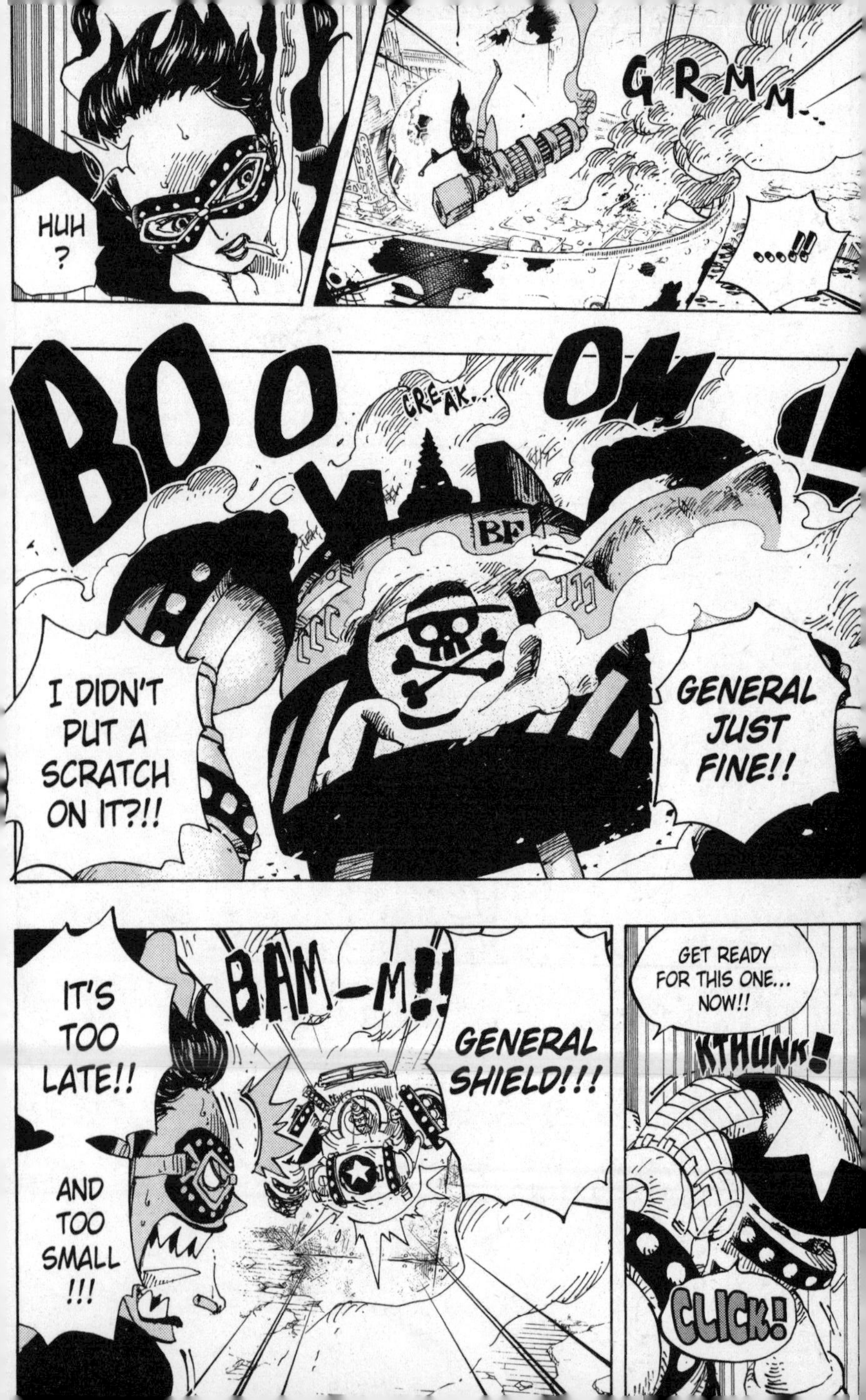
GRMM...
...!!
HUH?
BOOOM!!
CREAK...
GENERAL JUST FINE!!
I DIDN'T PUT A SCRATCH ON IT?!!
GET READY FOR THIS ONE... NOW!!
KTHUNK!
CLICK!
GENERAL SHIELD!!!
BAM-M!!
IT'S TOO LATE!!
AND TOO SMALL!!!

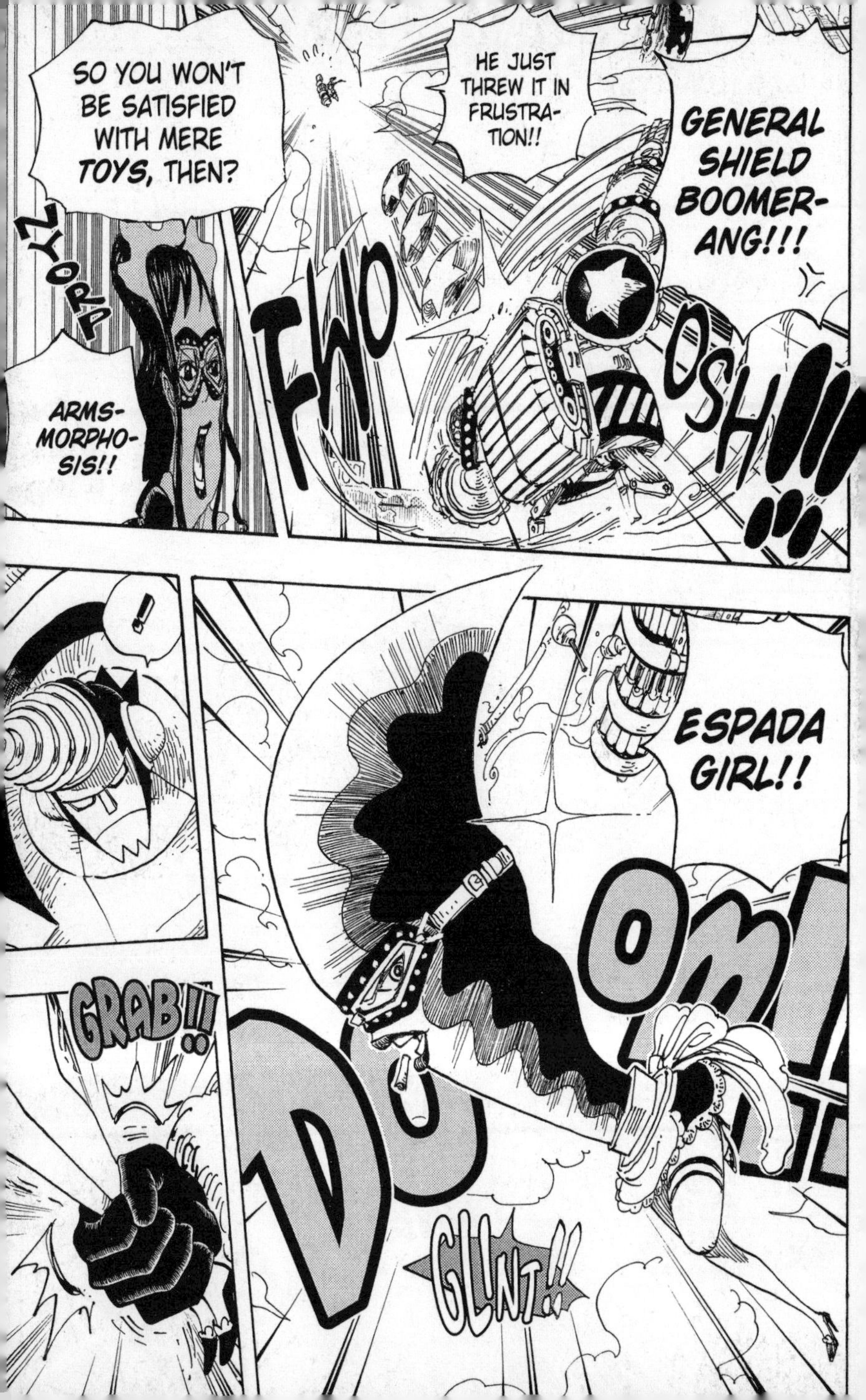
GENERAL SHIELD BOOMER-ANG!!!
HE JUST THREW IT IN FRUSTRA-TION!!
FWO
OSH!!!
SO YOU WON'T BE SATISFIED WITH MERE TOYS, THEN?
ZYORA
ARMS-MORPHO-SIS!!
ESPADA GIRL!!
DOOM!!
GLINT!!
!
GRAB!!

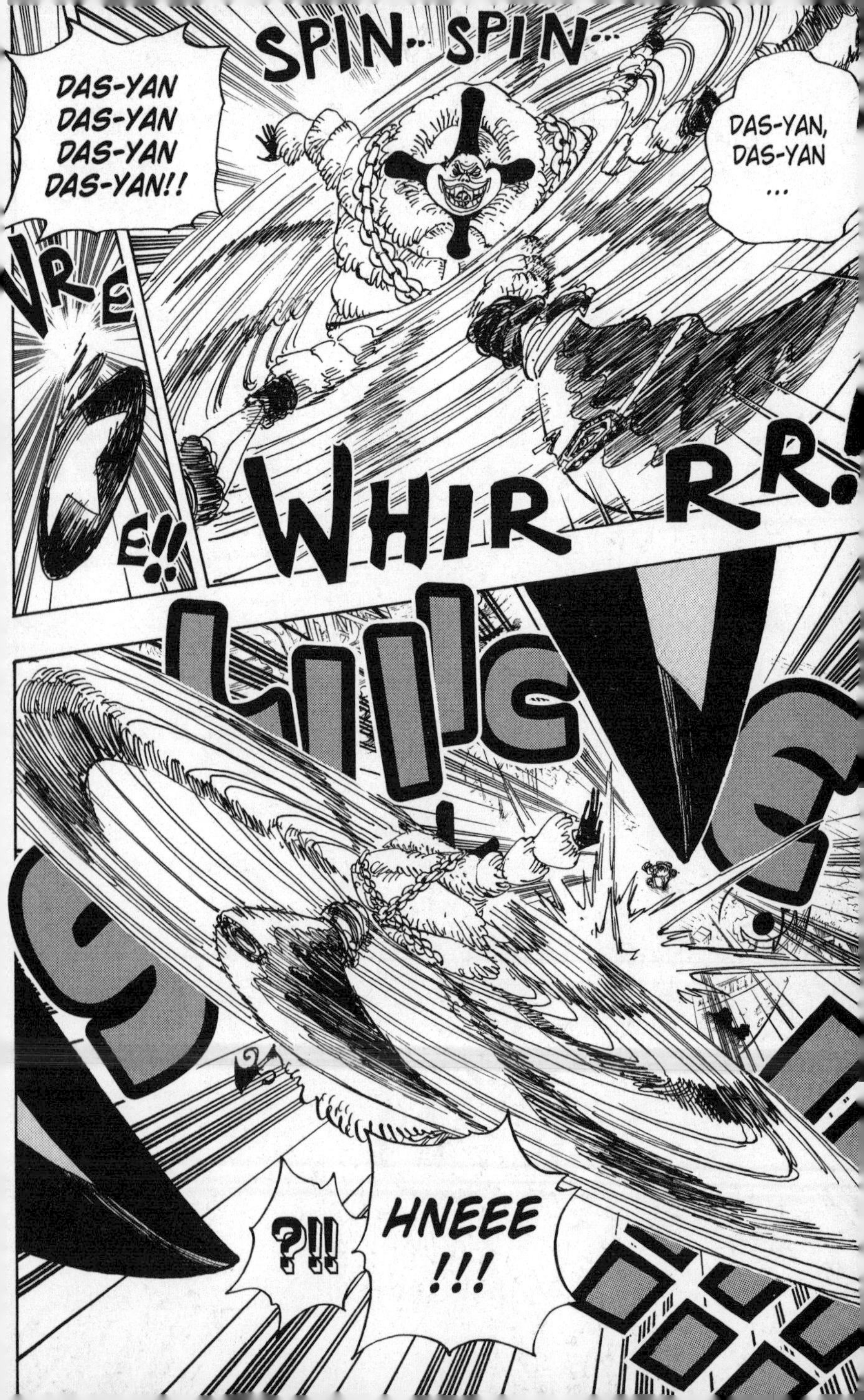
SPIN... SPIN...
DAS-YAN, DAS-YAN ...
DAS-YAN DAS-YAN DAS-YAN DAS-YAN!!
WHIRRR!
VRRE E!!
HNEEE !!!
?!!

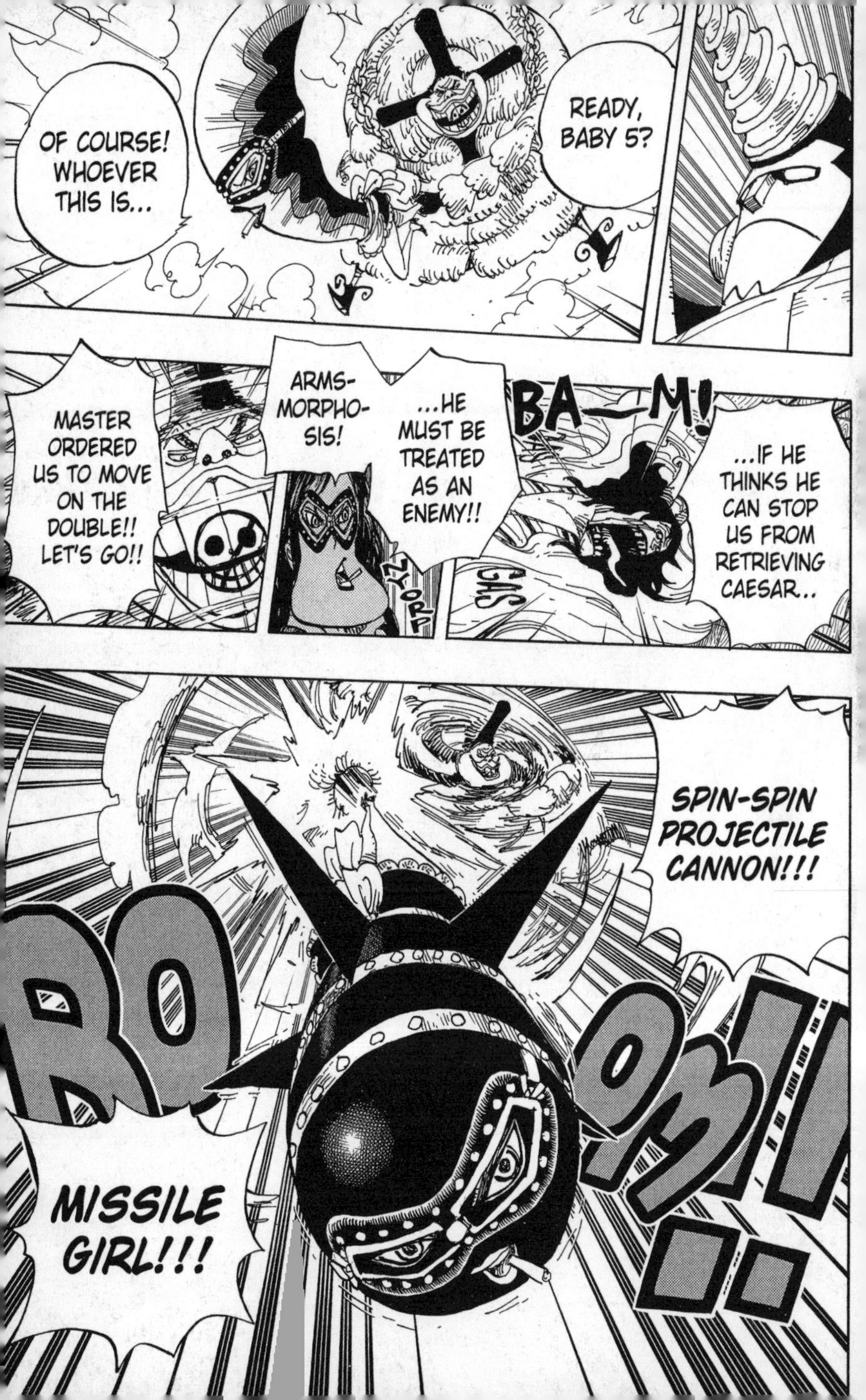
READY, BABY 5?
OF COURSE! WHOEVER THIS IS...
BA-M!
...IF HE THINKS HE CAN STOP US FROM RETRIEVING CAESAR...
...HE MUST BE TREATED AS AN ENEMY!!
ARMS-MORPHO-SIS!
NYORP
MASTER ORDERED US TO MOVE ON THE DOUBLE!! LET'S GO!!
SPIN-SPIN PROJECTILE CANNON!!!
MISSILE GIRL!!!
BOOM!!

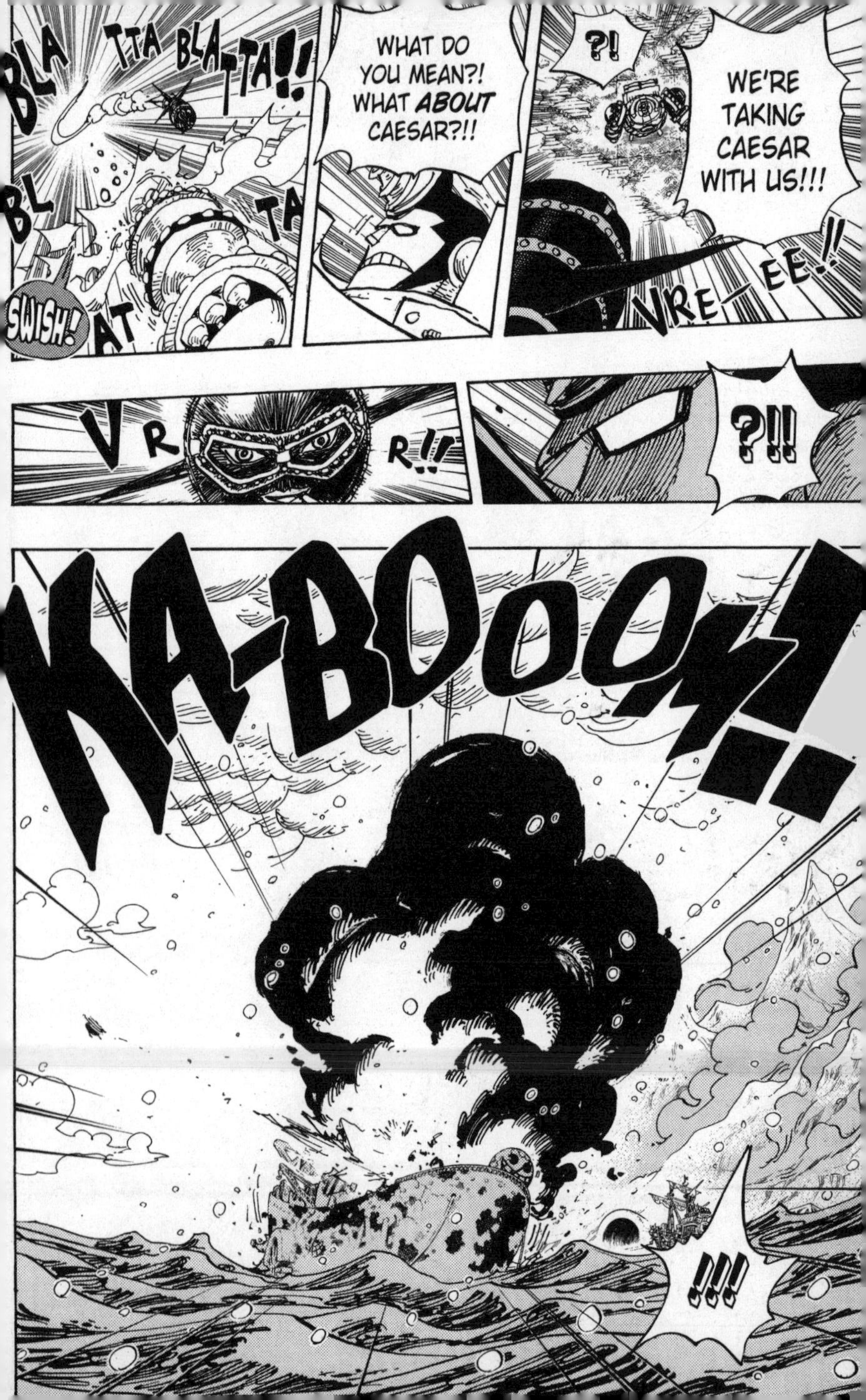
?!
WE'RE TAKING CAESAR WITH US!!!
VRE-EE!!
WHAT DO YOU MEAN?! WHAT *ABOUT* CAESAR?!!
BLA TTA BLATTA!!
BL TA AT
SWISH!
?!!
VR R!!
KA-BOOOM!!
!!!

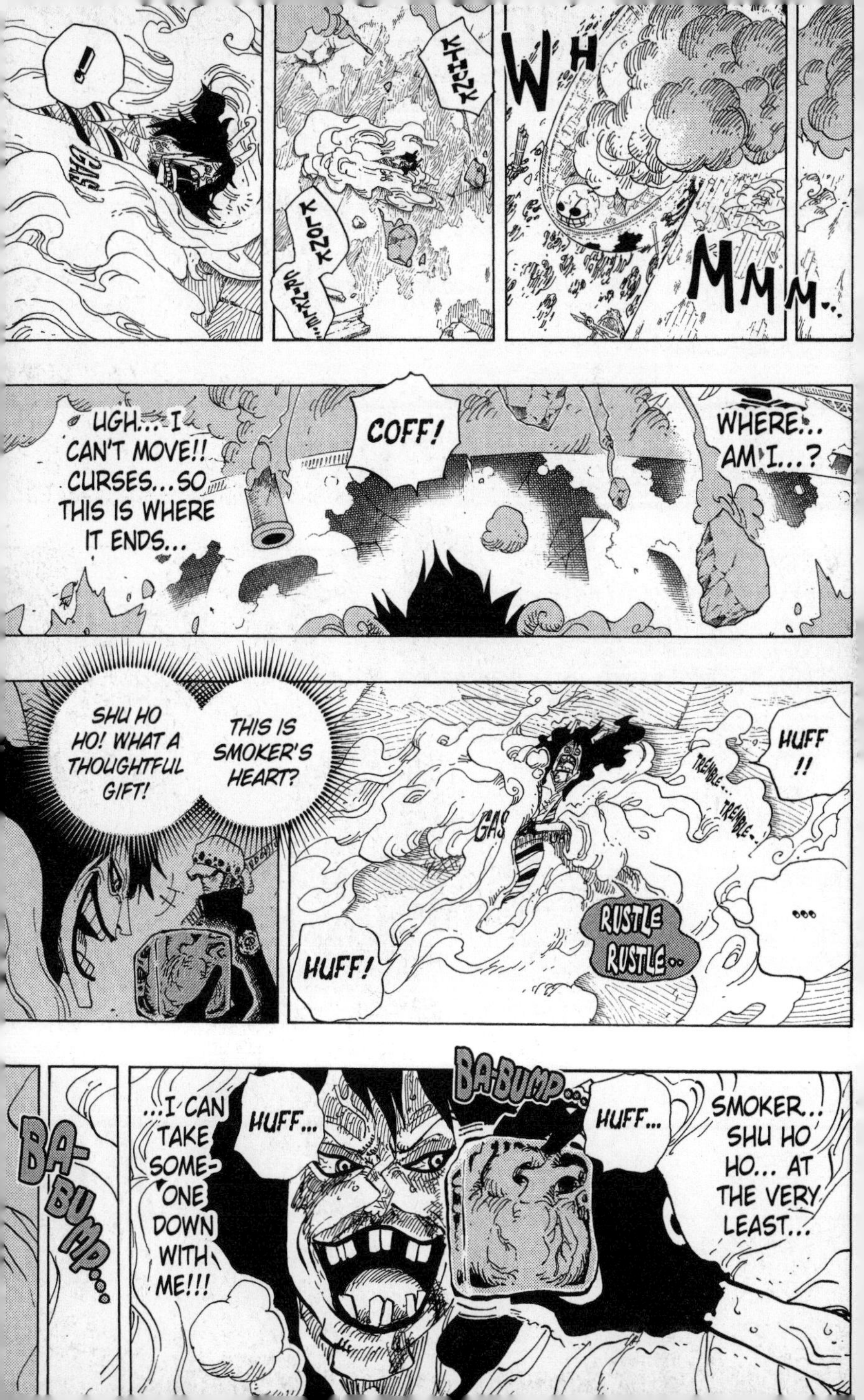
WH
MMM...
KTHUNK
KLONK
CRINKLE...
!
GAS
WHERE... AM I...?
COFF!
UGH... I CAN'T MOVE!! CURSES...SO THIS IS WHERE IT ENDS...
HUFF !!
TREMBLE... TREMBLE...
GAS
...
RUSTLE RUSTLE..
HUFF!
THIS IS SMOKER'S HEART?
SHU HO HO! WHAT A THOUGHTFUL GIFT!
SMOKER... SHU HO HO... AT THE VERY LEAST...
HUFF...
BA-BUMP...
HUFF...
...I CAN TAKE SOME-ONE DOWN WITH ME!!!
BA-BUMP...

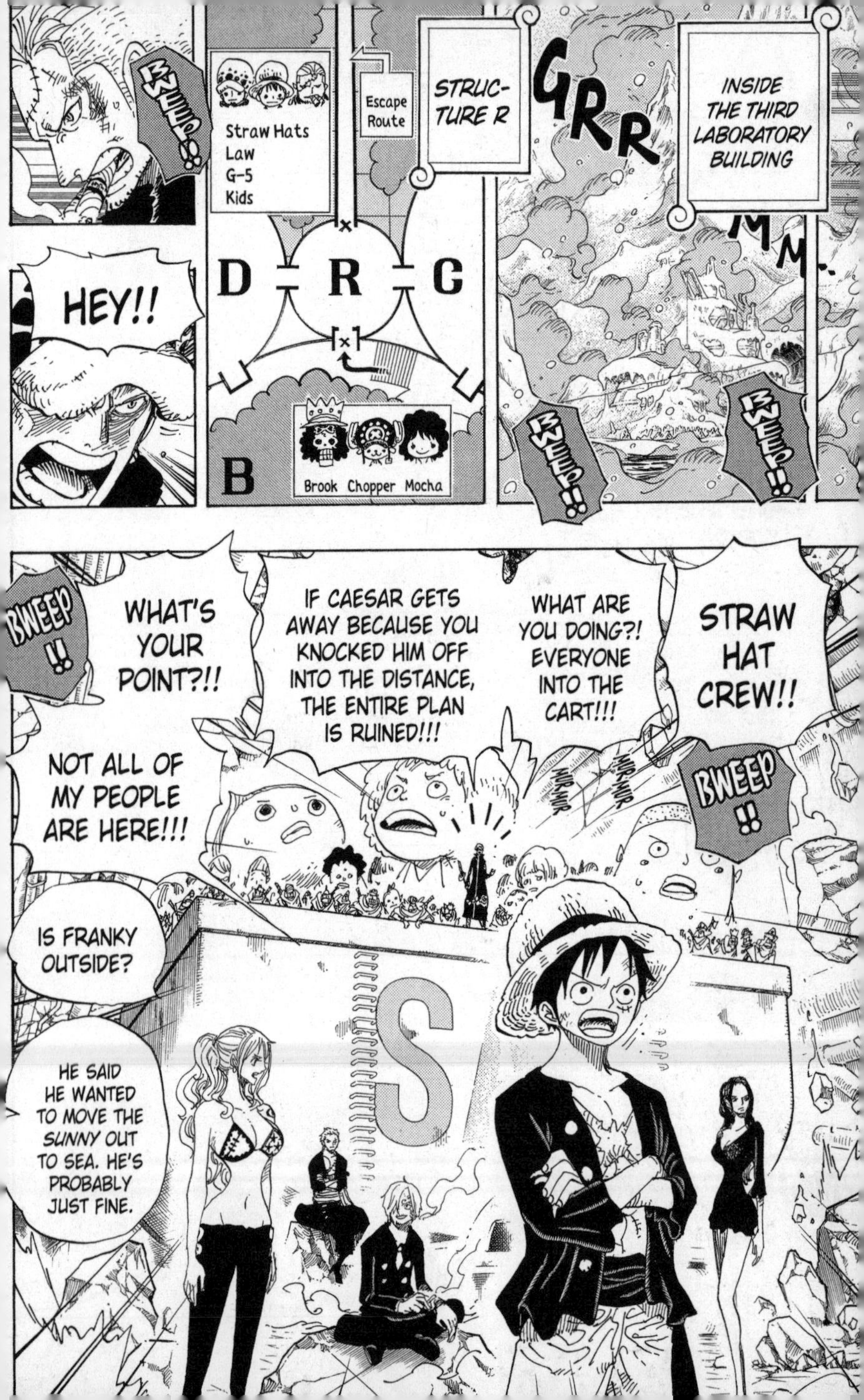
INSIDE THE THIRD LABORATORY BUILDING
GRR
MM...
BWEEP!!
BWEEP!!
STRUC-TURE R
Escape Route
Straw Hats
Law
G-5
Kids
D
R
C
B
Brook Chopper Mocha
BWEEP!!
HEY!!
STRAW HAT CREW!!
BWEEP!!
WHAT ARE YOU DOING?! EVERYONE INTO THE CART!!!
MUR MUR
MUR MUR
IF CAESAR GETS AWAY BECAUSE YOU KNOCKED HIM OFF INTO THE DISTANCE, THE ENTIRE PLAN IS RUINED!!!
WHAT'S YOUR POINT?!!
BWEEP!!
NOT ALL OF MY PEOPLE ARE HERE!!!
IS FRANKY OUTSIDE?
S
HE SAID HE WANTED TO MOVE THE SUNNY OUT TO SEA. HE'S PROBABLY JUST FINE.

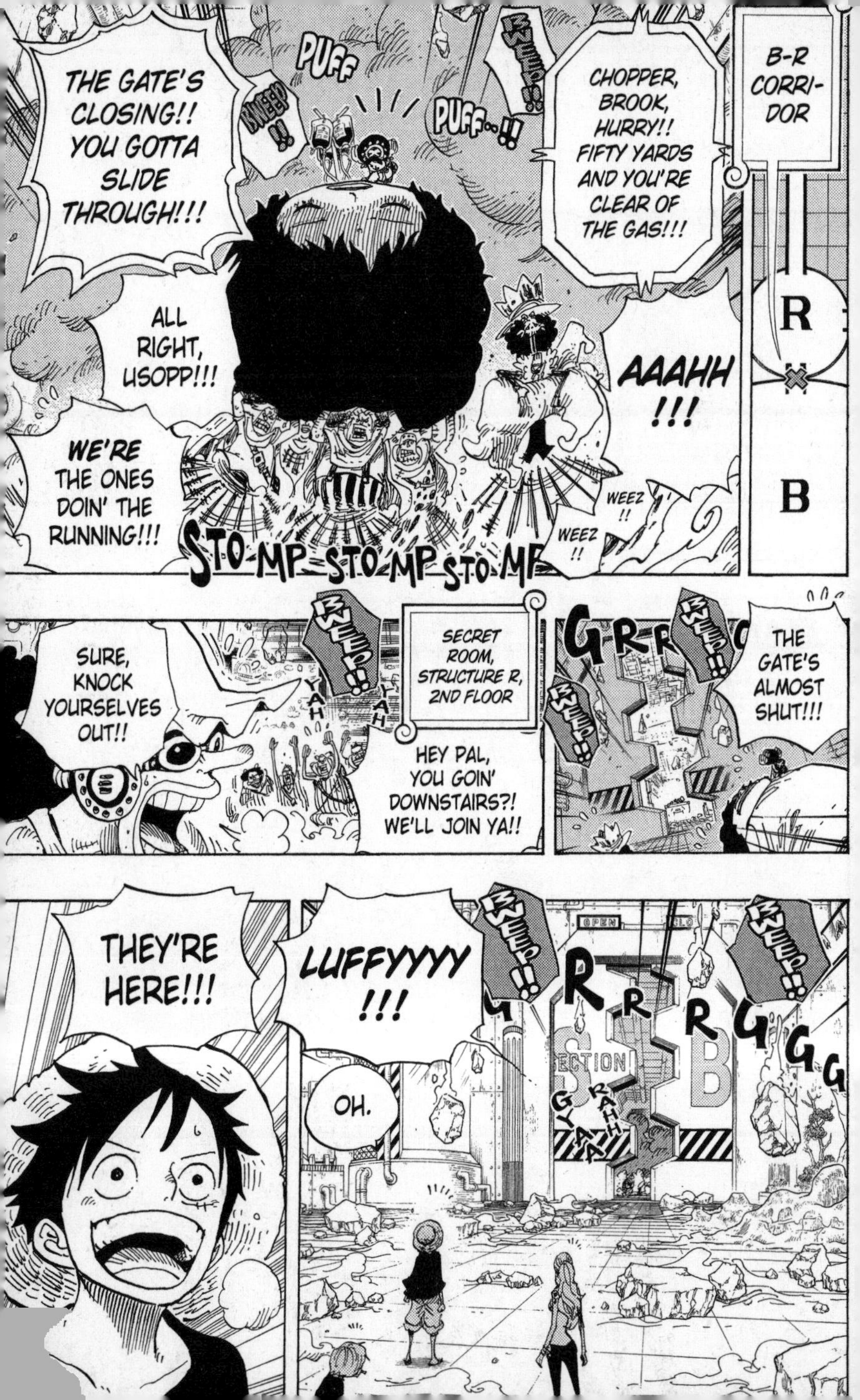
B-R CORRIDOR
R
B
CHOPPER, BROOK, HURRY!! FIFTY YARDS AND YOU'RE CLEAR OF THE GAS!!!
BWEEP!!
PUFF...!!
PUFF
BWEEP!!
THE GATE'S CLOSING!! YOU GOTTA SLIDE THROUGH!!!
AAAHH!!!
WEEZ!!
WEEZ!!
ALL RIGHT, USOPP!!!
WE'RE THE ONES DOIN' THE RUNNING!!!
STO-MP STO-MP STO-MP
THE GATE'S ALMOST SHUT!!!
BWEEP!!
GRRR
BWEEP!!
SECRET ROOM, STRUCTURE R, 2ND FLOOR
BWEEP!!
YAH
YAH
HEY PAL, YOU GOIN' DOWNSTAIRS?! WE'LL JOIN YA!!
SURE, KNOCK YOURSELVES OUT!!
BWEEP!!
RRRRGGG
BWEEP!!
SECTION
OPEN
RAHH
GYAA
LUFFYYYY!!!
OH.
THEY'RE HERE!!!

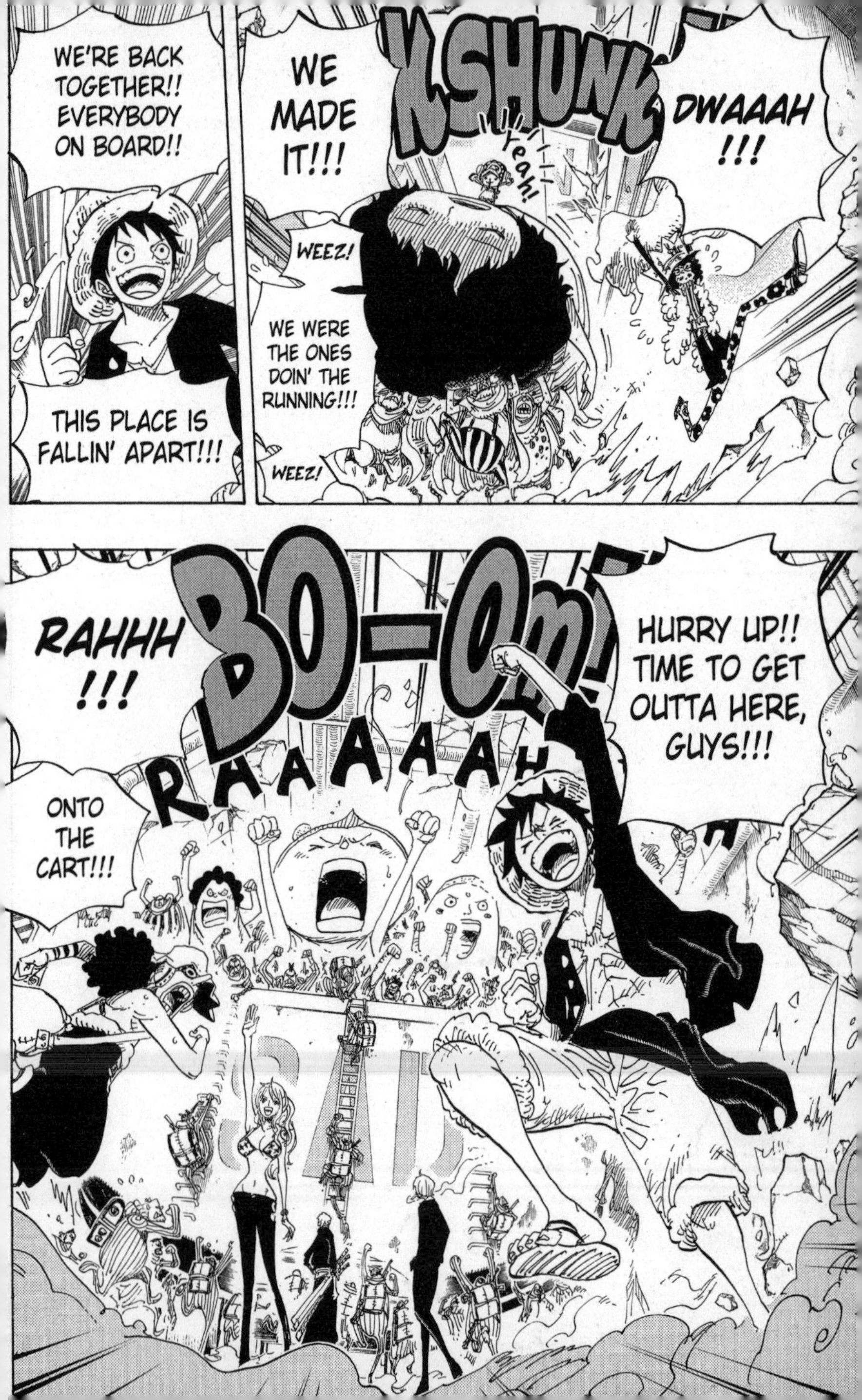
DWAAAH!!!
K-SHUNK
Yeah!
WE MADE IT!!!
WEEZ!
WE WERE THE ONES DOIN' THE RUNNING!!!
WEEZ!
WE'RE BACK TOGETHER!! EVERYBODY ON BOARD!!
THIS PLACE IS FALLIN' APART!!!
HURRY UP!! TIME TO GET OUTTA HERE, GUYS!!!
BO-OM!
RAHHH!!!
RAAAAAH
ONTO THE CART!!!

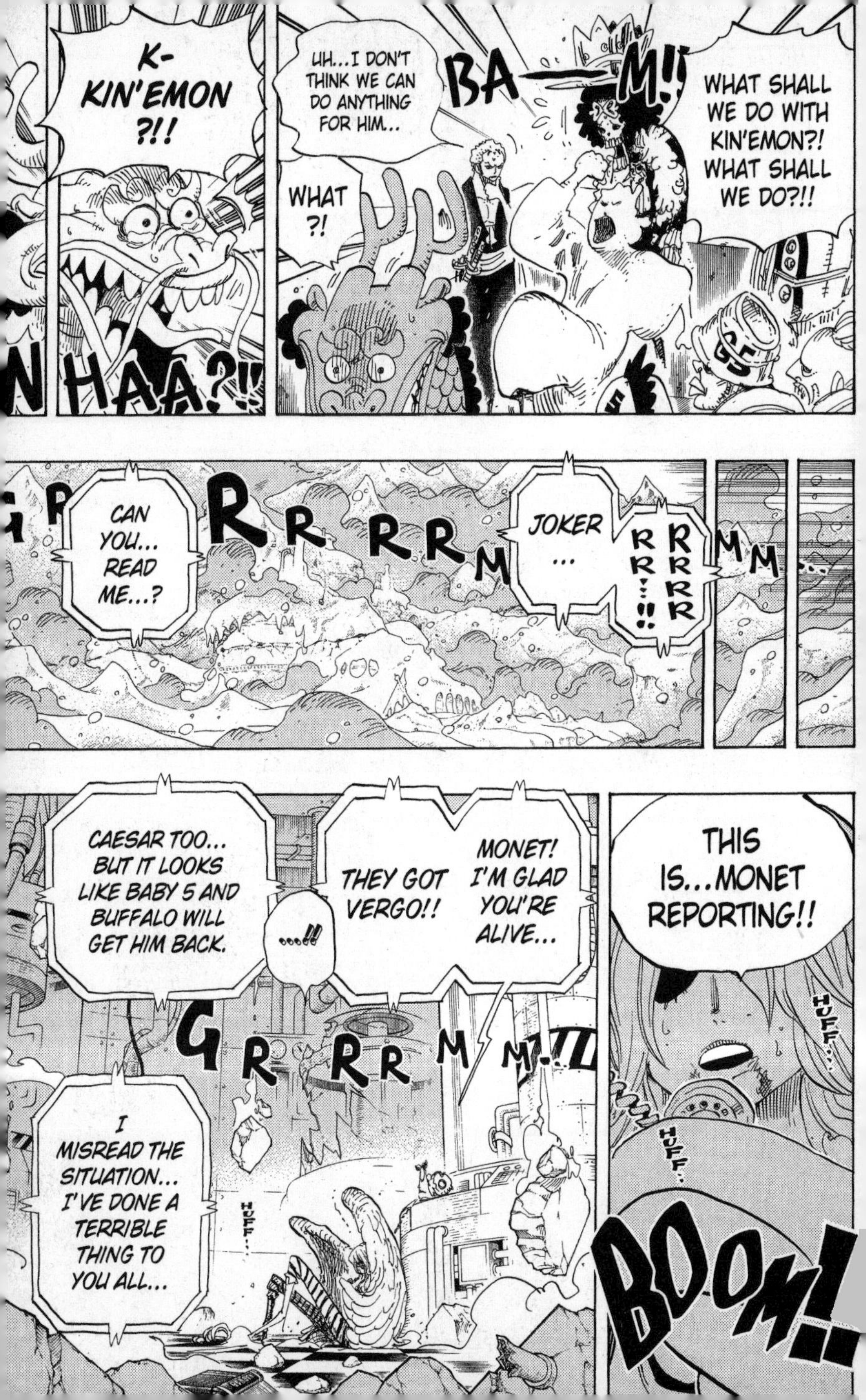

WHAT SHALL WE DO WITH KIN'EMON?! WHAT SHALL WE DO?!!
BA—M!!
UH...I DON'T THINK WE CAN DO ANYTHING FOR HIM...
WHAT ?!
K-KIN'EMON ?!!
NHAA?!!
JOKER ...
RRRRR RR...!!
RRRR
MM
CAN YOU... READ ME...?
GRRRRRM
THIS IS...MONET REPORTING!!
HUFF...
HUFF...
BOOM!!
MONET! I'M GLAD YOU'RE ALIVE...
THEY GOT VERGO!!
...!!
CAESAR TOO... BUT IT LOOKS LIKE BABY 5 AND BUFFALO WILL GET HIM BACK.
GRRRRMM!!
I MISREAD THE SITUATION... I'VE DONE A TERRIBLE THING TO YOU ALL...
HUFF...

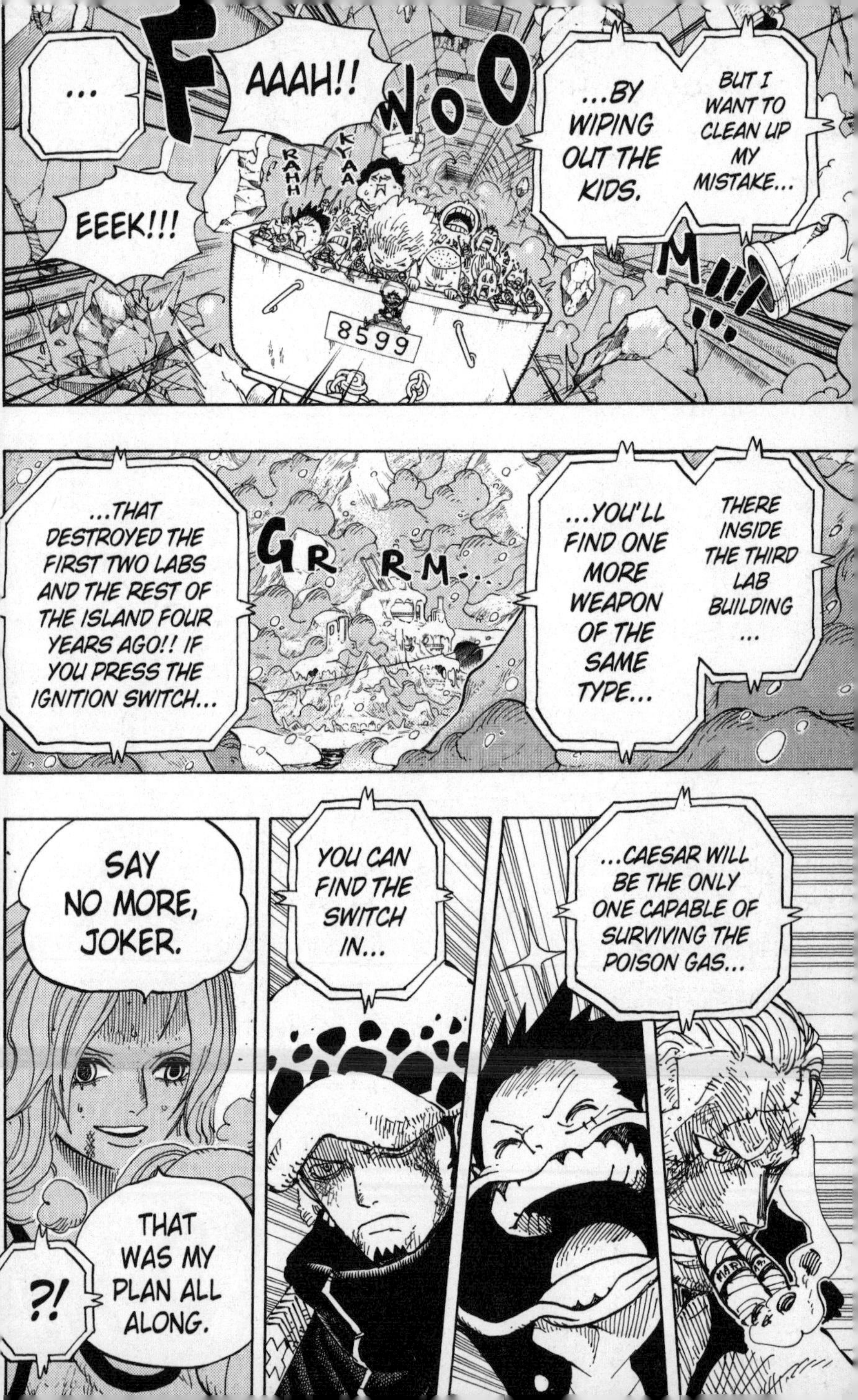
BUT I WANT TO CLEAN UP MY MISTAKE...
...BY WIPING OUT THE KIDS.
WOO
AAAH!!
F
...
KYAA
RAHH
EEEK!!!
M!!!
THERE INSIDE THE THIRD LAB BUILDING...
...YOU'LL FIND ONE MORE WEAPON OF THE SAME TYPE...
GRRM...
...THAT DESTROYED THE FIRST TWO LABS AND THE REST OF THE ISLAND FOUR YEARS AGO!! IF YOU PRESS THE IGNITION SWITCH...
...CAESAR WILL BE THE ONLY ONE CAPABLE OF SURVIVING THE POISON GAS...
YOU CAN FIND THE SWITCH IN...
SAY NO MORE, JOKER.
THAT WAS MY PLAN ALL ALONG.
?!

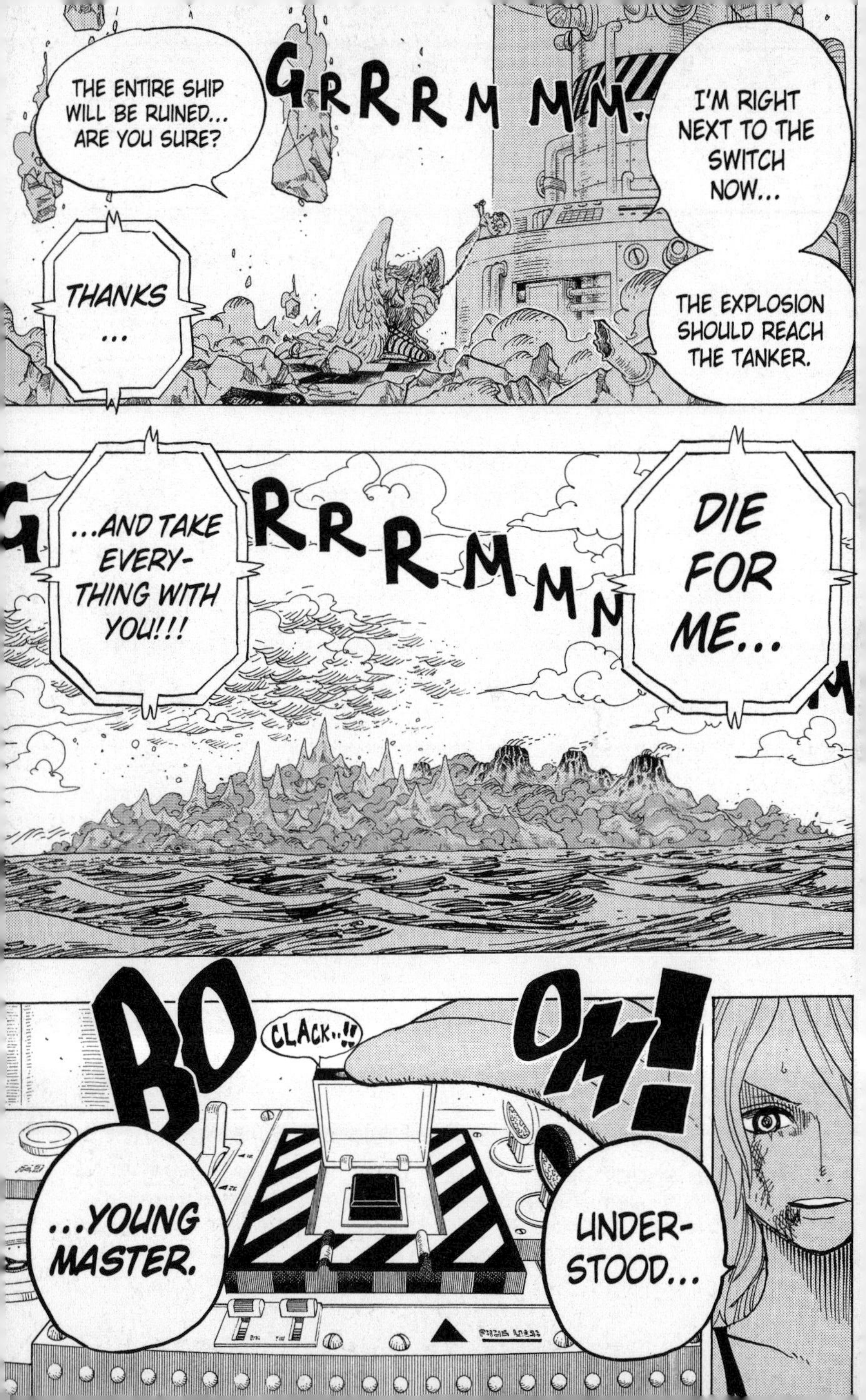
I'M RIGHT NEXT TO THE SWITCH NOW...
THE EXPLOSION SHOULD REACH THE TANKER.
GRRRM MMM
THE ENTIRE SHIP WILL BE RUINED... ARE YOU SURE?
THANKS...
DIE FOR ME...
GRRRRMMMM
...AND TAKE EVERY-THING WITH YOU!!!
UNDER-STOOD...
BOOM!
CLACK..!!
...YOUNG MASTER.

SBS Question Corner

(Hippo Iron, Saitama)

Q: Who's going to slip in the first **"Start the SBS!!"** this volume? I can't wait to find out…
Oh! It's me.

--Nomi

A: You just said it!! 彡 That's my face on the right!!

Q: Take this, Odacchi!
Land of Nothing!
--I'm the Master

A: Urk!! I...I can't...!!
Hrg...can't...breathe...!! I...can breathe?
Okay, next question.

Q: Um...I have a problem. My *One Piece*-loving friend keeps telling me that I look just like Koby. What should I do about this? (cries)
You have to take responsibility!)↙ (angry)
--Yuminami Kobayashi Pigeon

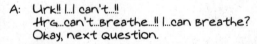

A: What?!彡 Wow, you're really angry!彡 What's so bad about that? Koby's gotten so much cooler lately! I just... can't take responsibility for this. I mean, who's saying this to you?

Q: Odacchi!! Hey, Odacchi! One of my friends totally looks like Koby!!! But he's really angry at you because of it, so watch out!!! Anyway, here's my question.♪ In Chapter 653…
--Yuminami Kobayashi Cat

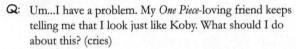

A: Wait a second!! It's you!!彡
I was totally getting chewed out because you keep teasing the kid in the previous letter!! What's the big idea?! And looking at your pen names...you two seem to get along just fine!

Chapter 694:
THE MOST DANGEROUS MAN

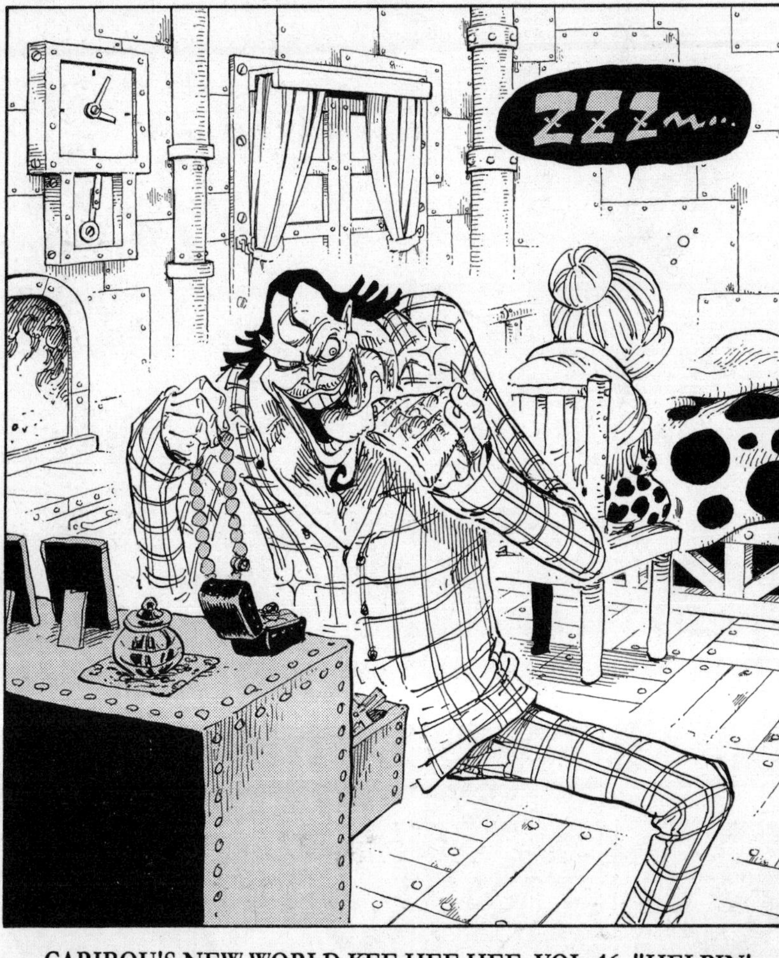
ZZZm...

CARIBOU'S NEW WORLD KEE HEE HEE, VOL. 16: "HELPIN' HIMSELF TO THE OLD HAG'S MEAT PIE AND CHEAP JEWELRY"

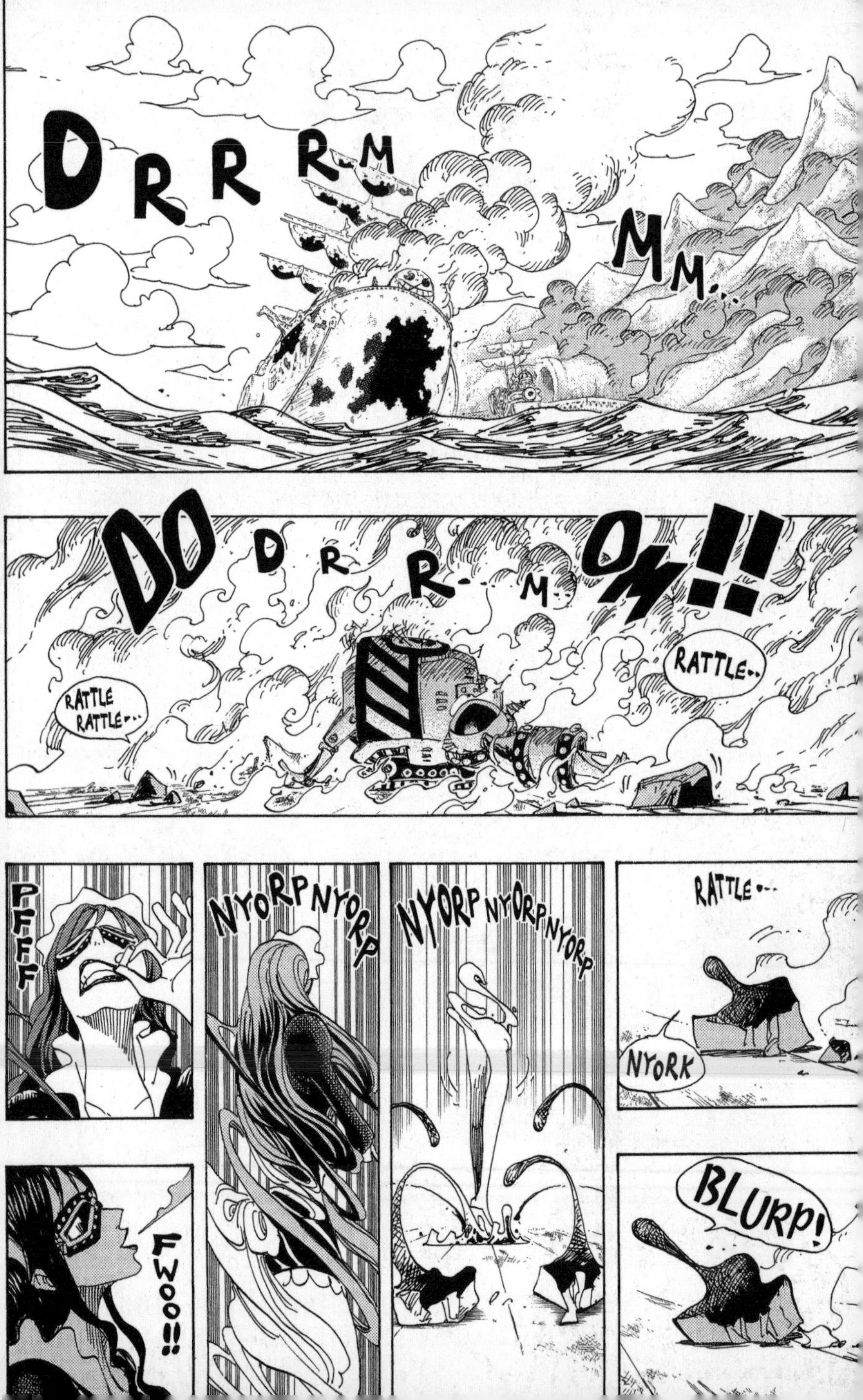
DRRRMMM..
DODRRMOM!!
RATTLE..
RATTLE RATTLE...
RATTLE...
NYORK
BLURP!
NYORPNYORPNYORPNYORP
NYORPNYORP
PFFF
FWOO!!

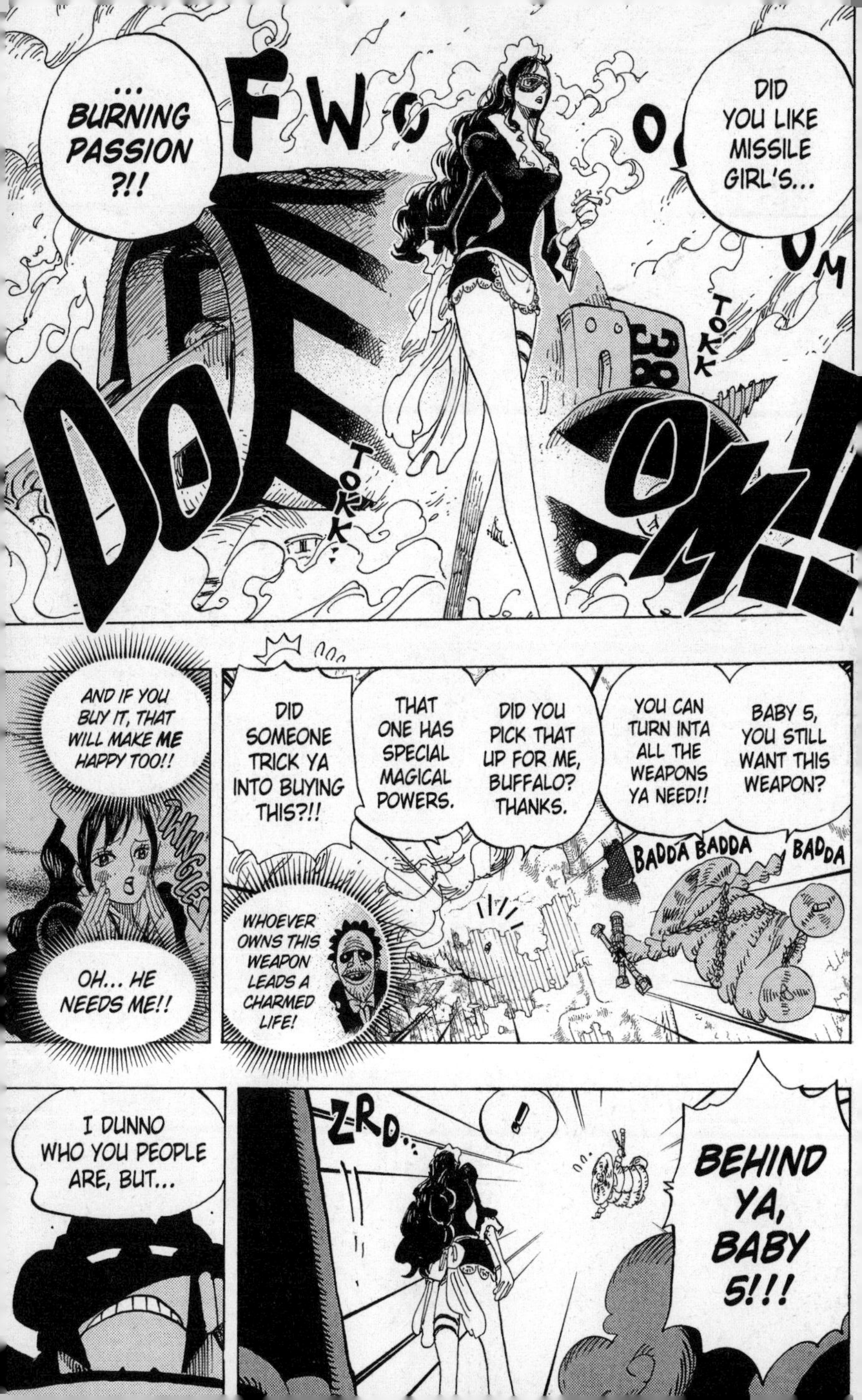
DID YOU LIKE MISSILE GIRL'S...
... BURNING PASSION ?!!
FWOOOM
TOKK
TOKK
DOOM!!
BABY 5, YOU STILL WANT THIS WEAPON?
YOU CAN TURN INTA ALL THE WEAPONS YA NEED!!
DID YOU PICK THAT UP FOR ME, BUFFALO? THANKS.
THAT ONE HAS SPECIAL MAGICAL POWERS.
DID SOMEONE TRICK YA INTO BUYING THIS?!!
BADDA BADDA
BADDA
WHOEVER OWNS THIS WEAPON LEADS A CHARMED LIFE!
AND IF YOU BUY IT, THAT WILL MAKE ME HAPPY TOO!!
THINGLE
OH... HE NEEDS ME!!
BEHIND YA, BABY 5!!!
!
ZRD...
I DUNNO WHO YOU PEOPLE ARE, BUT...

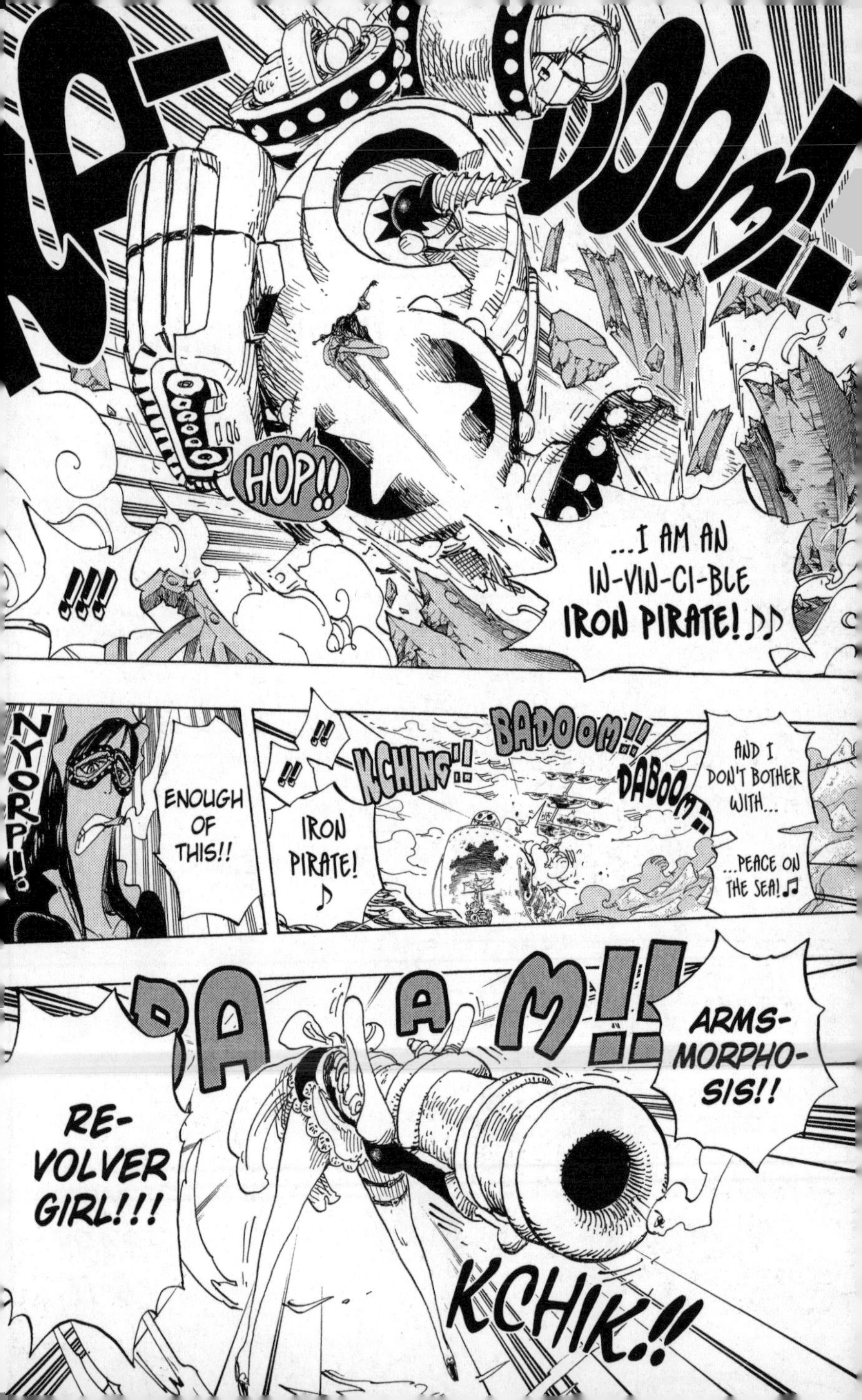
BA-DOOM!!
HOP!!
!!!
...I AM AN IN-VIN-CI-BLE IRON PIRATE! ♪♪
AND I DON'T BOTHER WITH...
BADOOM!!
DABOOM!!
...PEACE ON THE SEA! ♫
KCHING!!
!!
IRON PIRATE! ♪
!!
ENOUGH OF THIS!!
NYORP!!
BAAM!!
ARMS-MORPHOSIS!!
RE-VOLVER GIRL!!!
KCHIK!!

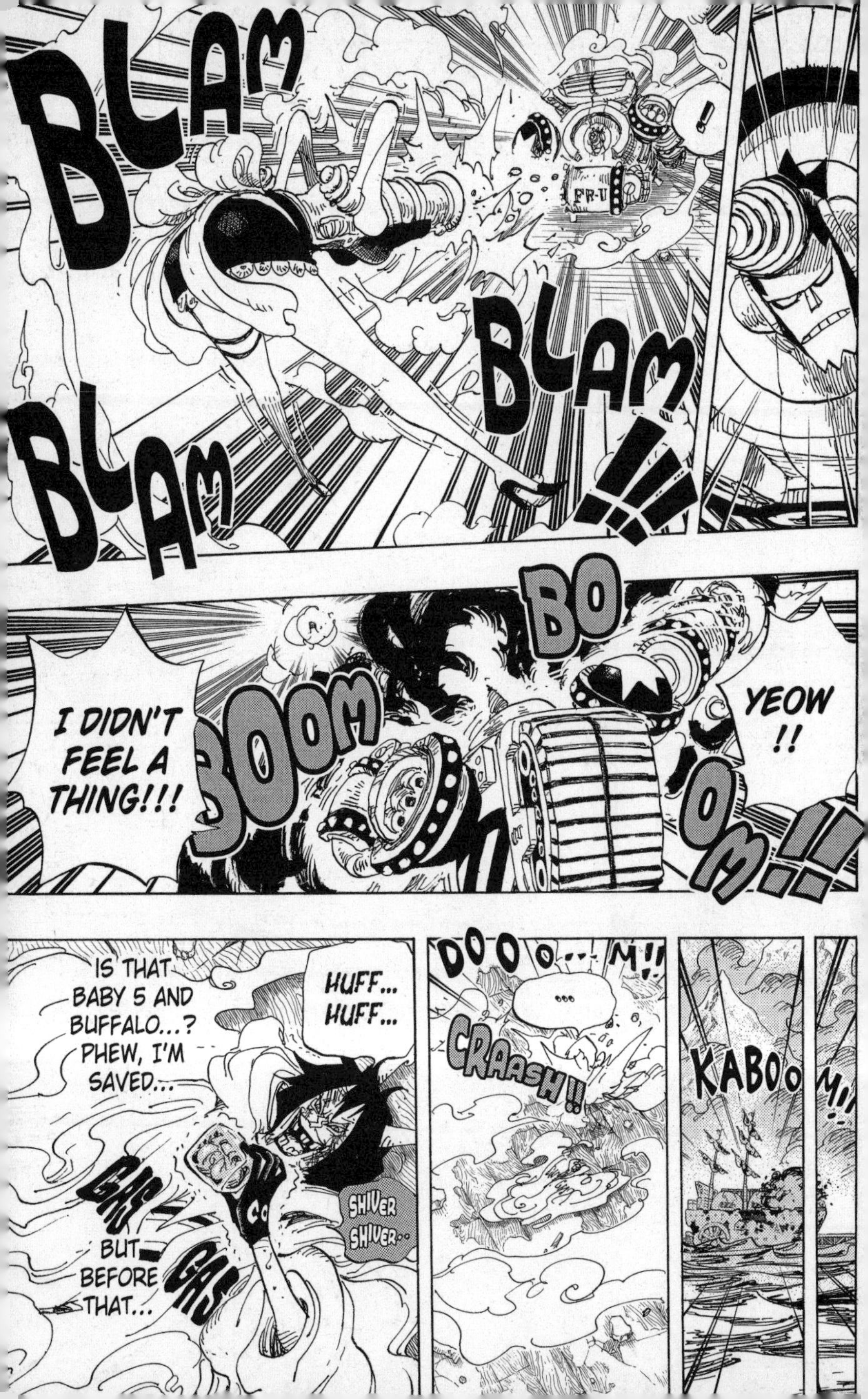
BLAM
!
FR-U
BLAM
BLAM!!!
BO
BOOM
I DIDN'T FEEL A THING!!!
YEOW!!
OM!!
KABOOM!!
DOOO...M!!
...
CRAASH!!
HUFF... HUFF...
IS THAT BABY 5 AND BUFFALO...? PHEW, I'M SAVED...
BUT BEFORE THAT...
GAS GAS
SHIVER SHIVER..

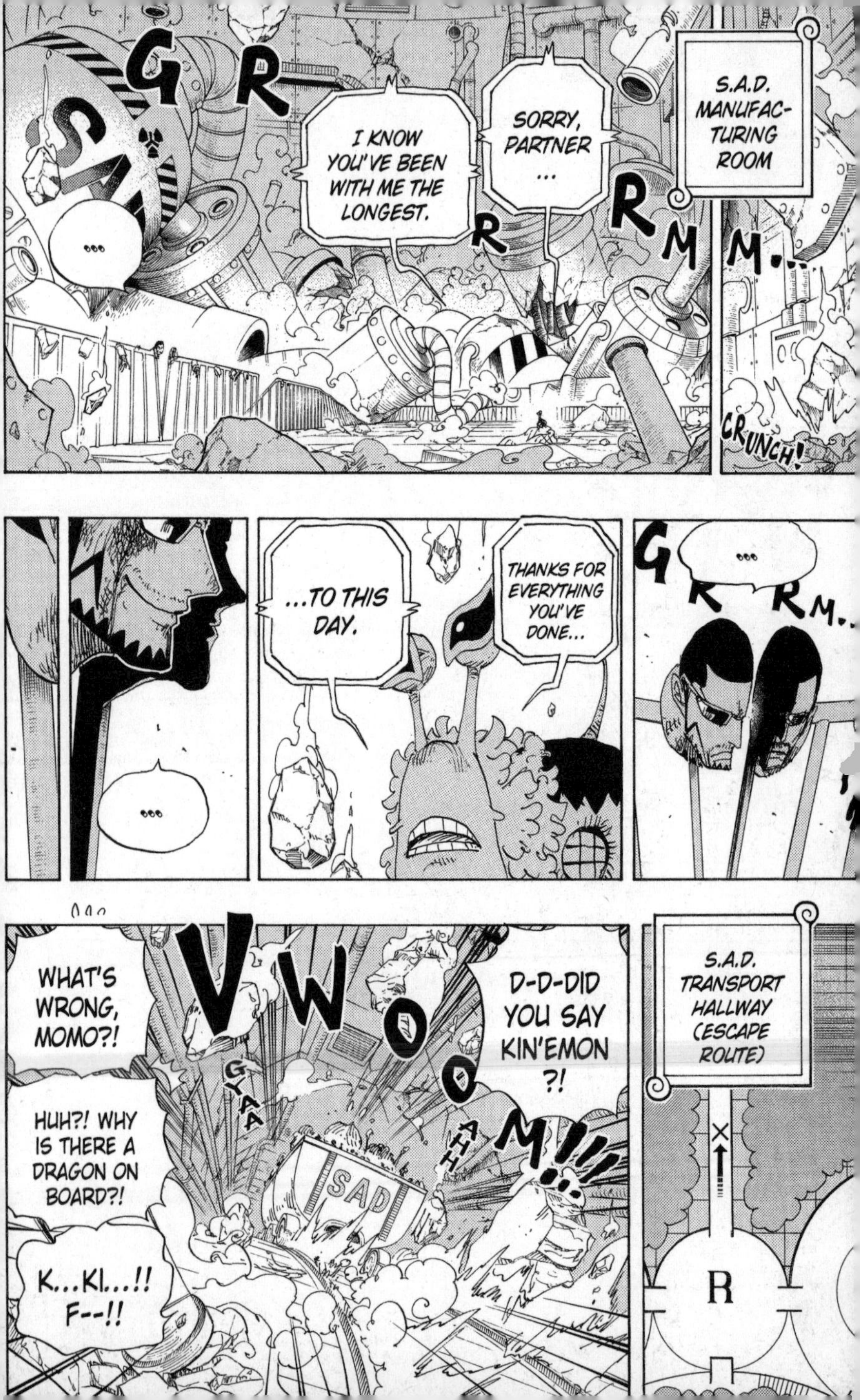
S.A.D. MANUFACTURING ROOM
CRUNCH!
SORRY, PARTNER...
I KNOW YOU'VE BEEN WITH ME THE LONGEST.
GRRRRMM...
...
GRRM...
...
THANKS FOR EVERYTHING YOU'VE DONE...
...TO THIS DAY.
...
S.A.D. TRANSPORT HALLWAY (ESCAPE ROUTE)
R
D-D-DID YOU SAY KIN'EMON?!
VWOOOM!!!
GYAAAHH
SAD
WHAT'S WRONG, MOMO?!
HUH?! WHY IS THERE A DRAGON ON BOARD?!
K...KI...!! F--!!

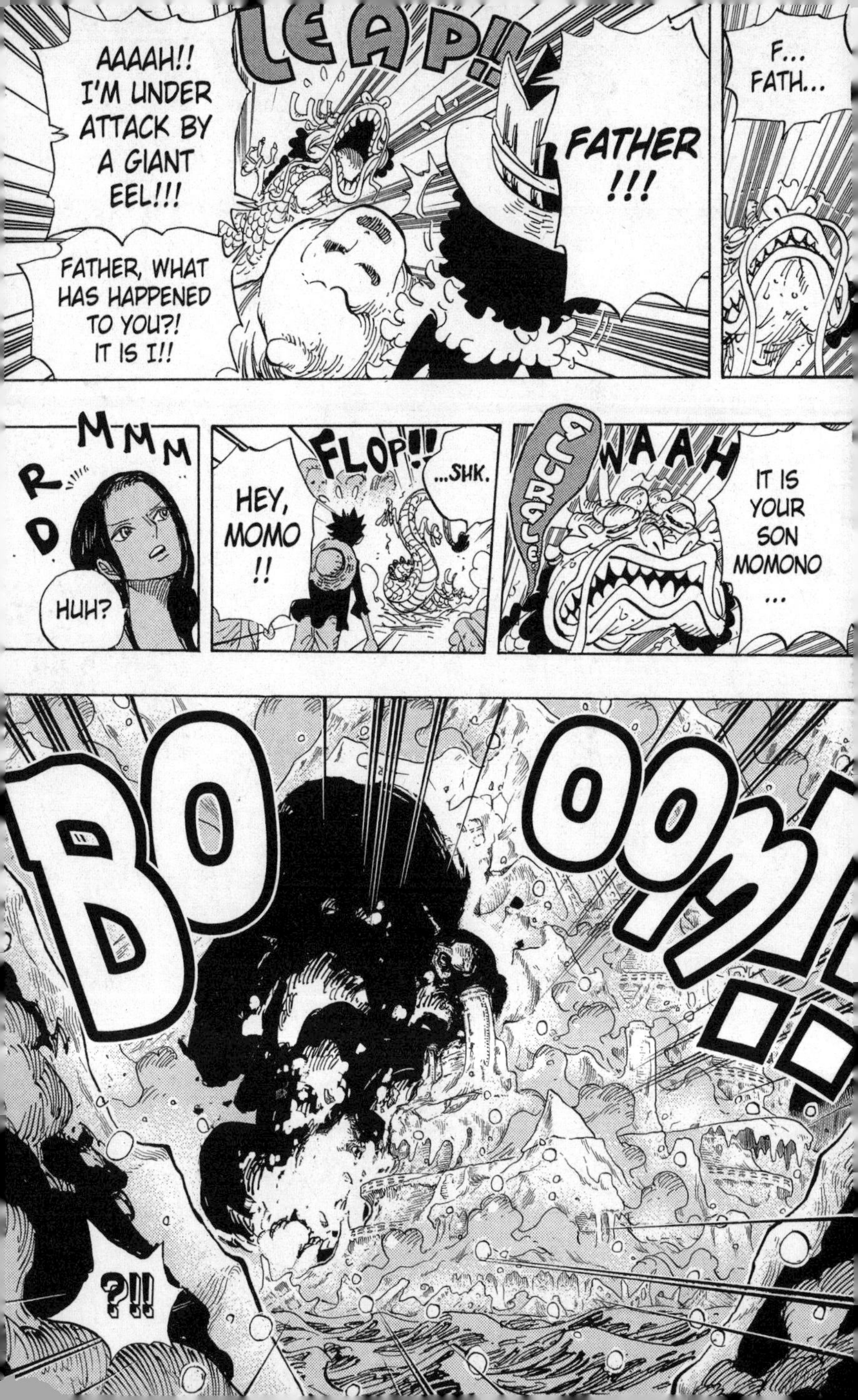
F... FATH...
LEAP!!
FATHER!!!
AAAAH!! I'M UNDER ATTACK BY A GIANT EEL!!!
FATHER, WHAT HAS HAPPENED TO YOU?! IT IS I!!
WAAAH
GURGLE
IT IS YOUR SON MOMONO...
FLOP!!
...SHK.
HEY, MOMO!!
RMMM
RD
HUH?
BOOOM!!
?!!

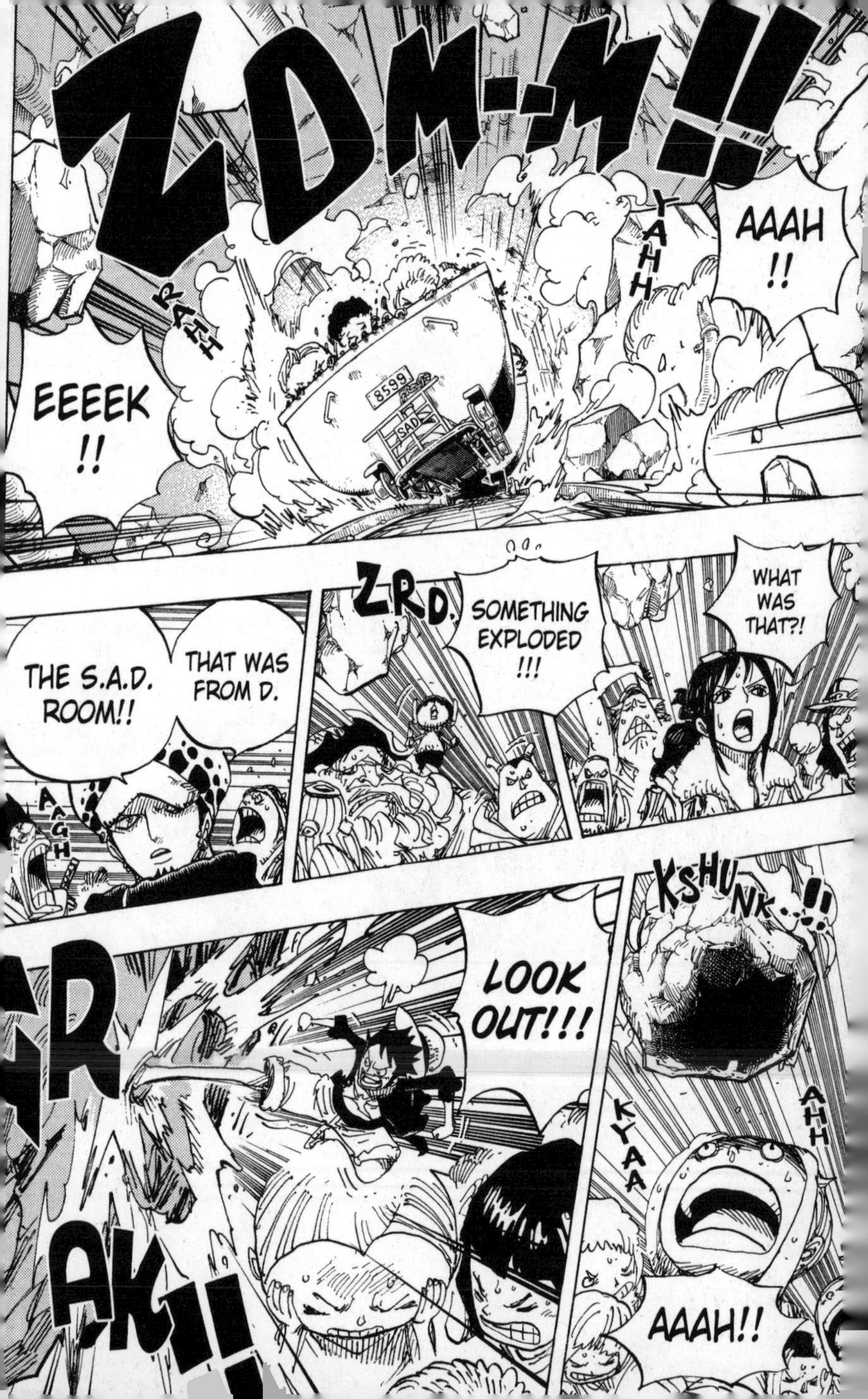
ZDM-M!!
AAAH!!
YAHH
RAHH
EEEEK!!
WHAT WAS THAT?!
ZRD.
SOMETHING EXPLODED!!!
THAT WAS FROM D.
THE S.A.D. ROOM!!
AAGH
KSHUNK..!!
AHH
KYAAA
AAAH!!
LOOK OUT!!!
AK!!

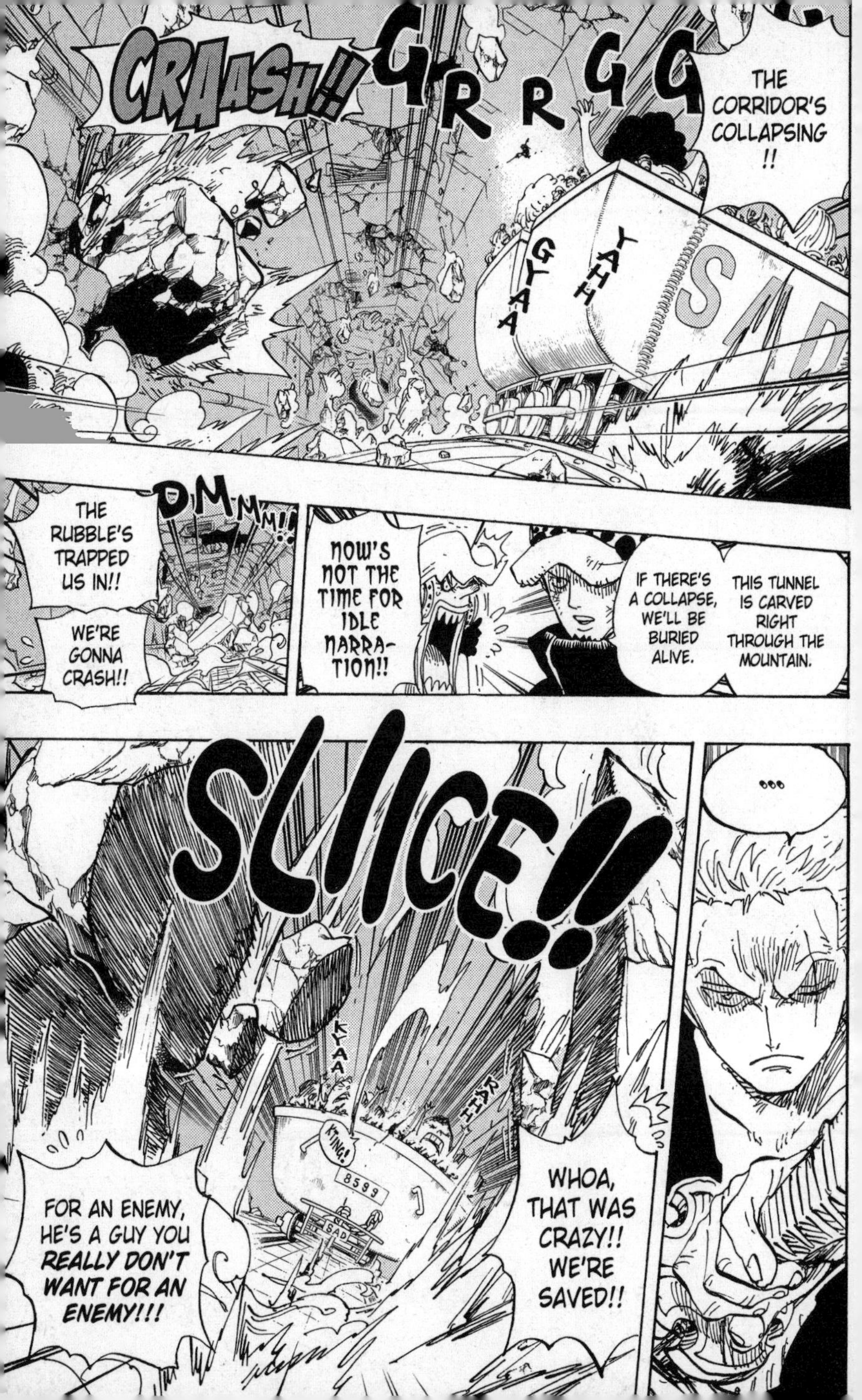
THE CORRIDOR'S COLLAPSING!!
YAHH
GYAA
SAD
GRRGG
CRAASH!!
THIS TUNNEL IS CARVED RIGHT THROUGH THE MOUNTAIN.
IF THERE'S A COLLAPSE, WE'LL BE BURIED ALIVE.
NOW'S NOT THE TIME FOR IDLE NARRATION!!
DMMM!!
THE RUBBLE'S TRAPPED US IN!!
WE'RE GONNA CRASH!!
...
SLIICE!!
KYAA
RAHH
KTING!
8599
SAD
WHOA, THAT WAS CRAZY!! WE'RE SAVED!!
FOR AN ENEMY, HE'S A GUY YOU ***REALLY DON'T WANT FOR AN ENEMY!!!***

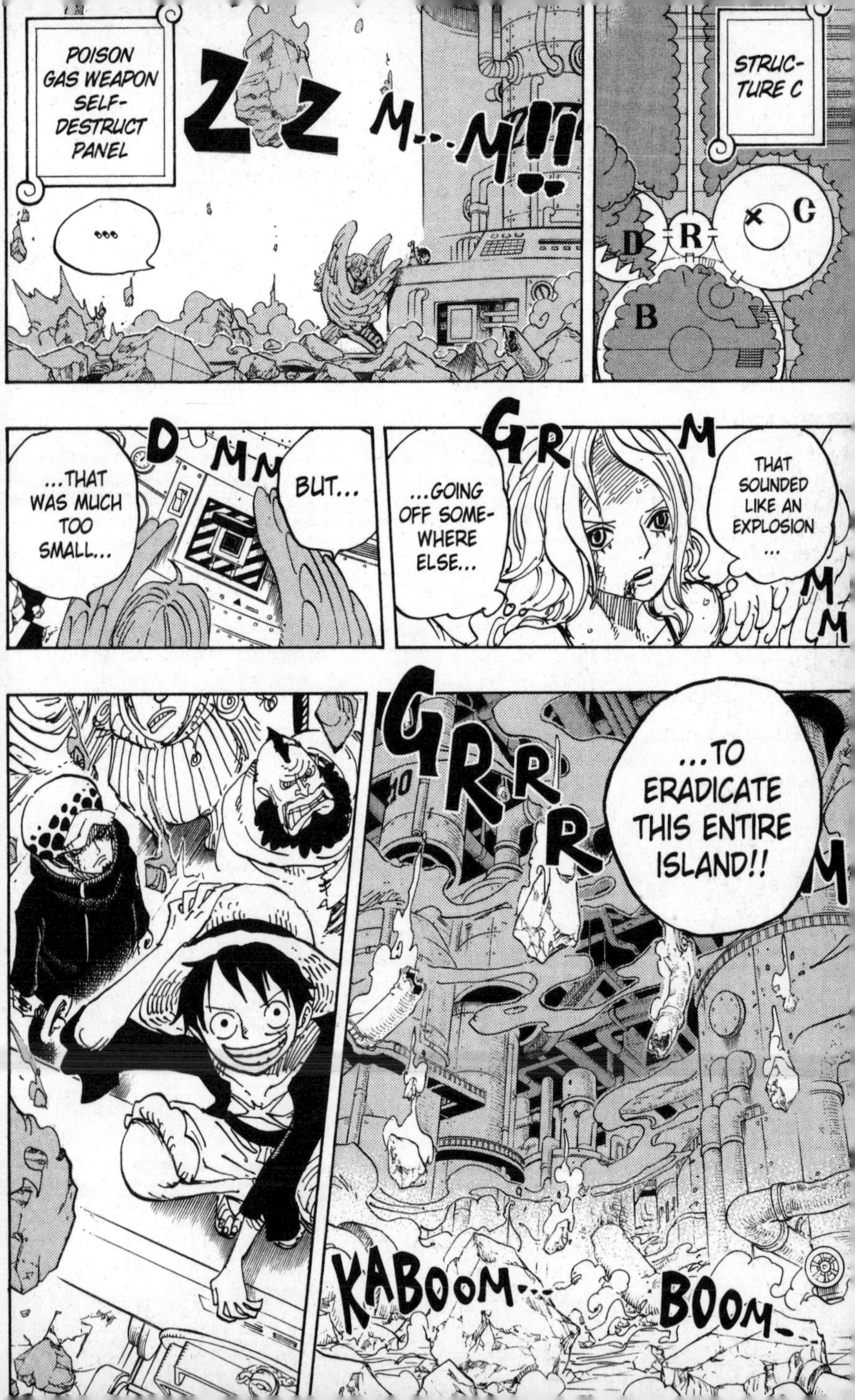
STRUC-
TURE C
D
R
C
B
POISON GAS WEAPON SELF-DESTRUCT PANEL
ZZ
M...M!!!
...
GRM
THAT SOUNDED LIKE AN EXPLOSION...
...GOING OFF SOME-WHERE ELSE...
MM
DMN
BUT...
...THAT WAS MUCH TOO SMALL...
GRRR
...TO ERADICATE THIS ENTIRE ISLAND!!
M
KABOOM...
BOOM...

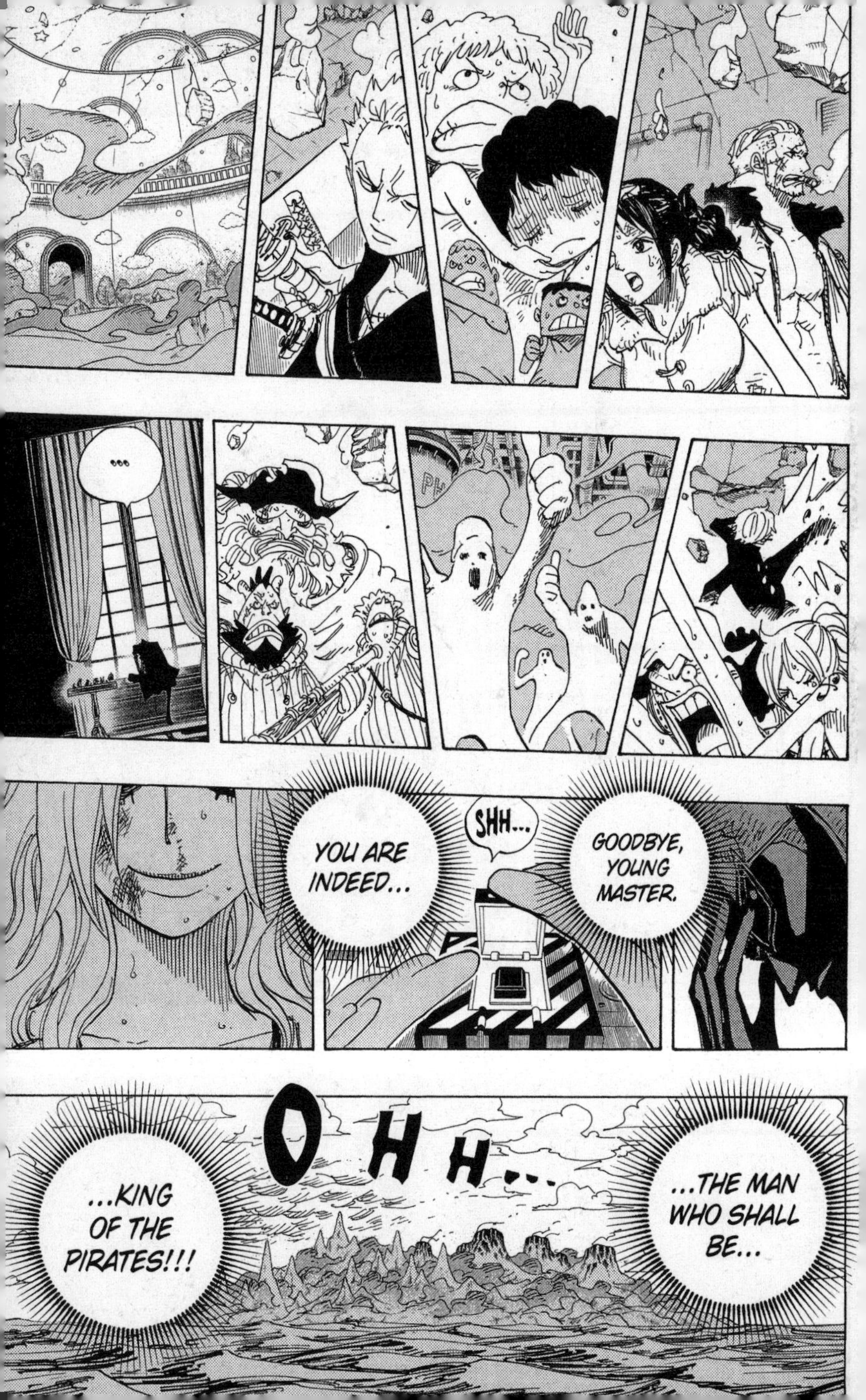
...
GOODBYE, YOUNG MASTER.
SHH...
YOU ARE INDEED...
...THE MAN WHO SHALL BE...
OHH...
...KING OF THE PIRATES!!!

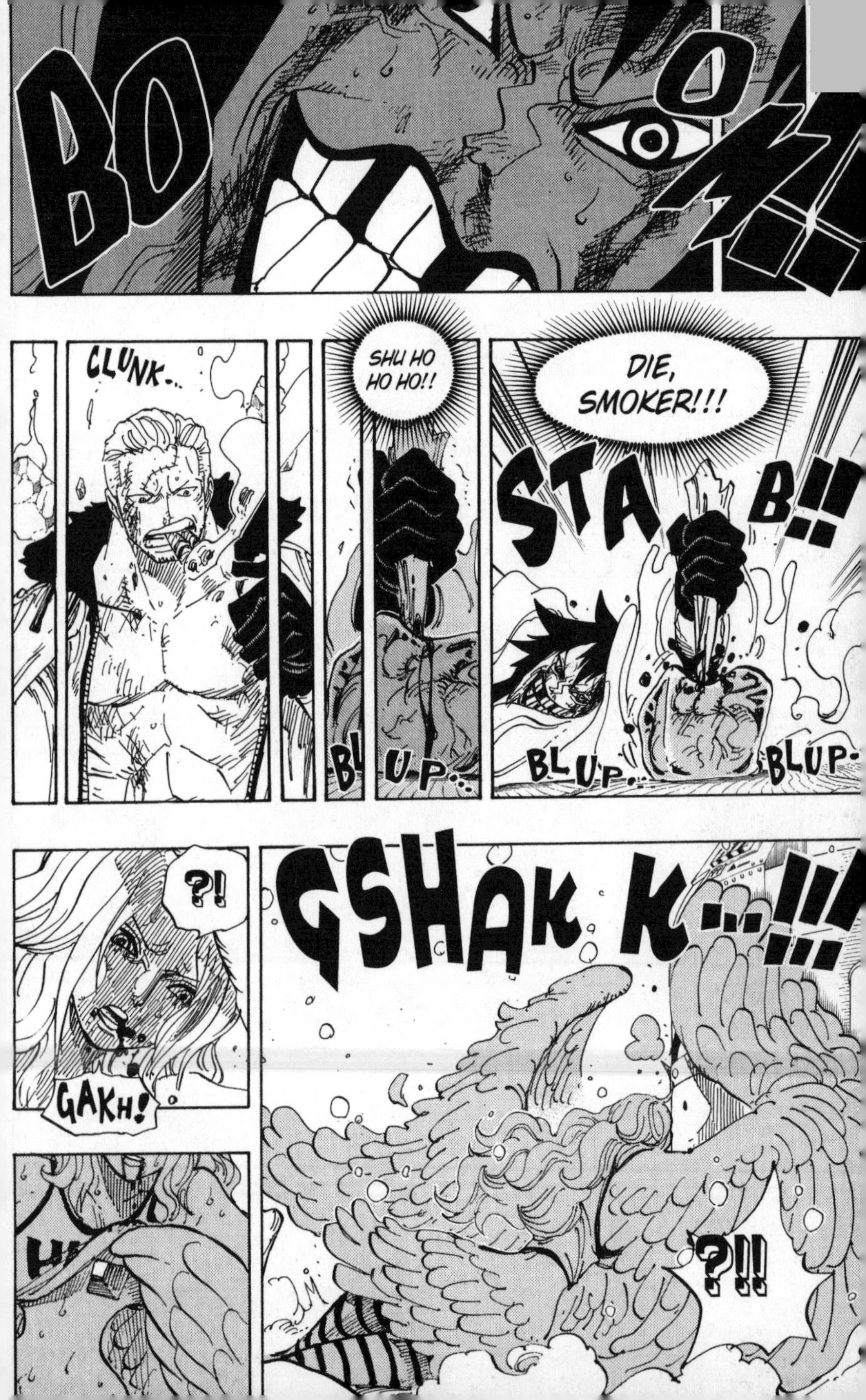
BOOM!!
DIE, SMOKER!!!
STAB!!
BLUP-
BLUP...
SHU HO HO HO!!
BLUP...
CLUNK...
GSHAKK...!!!
?!!
?!
GAKH!

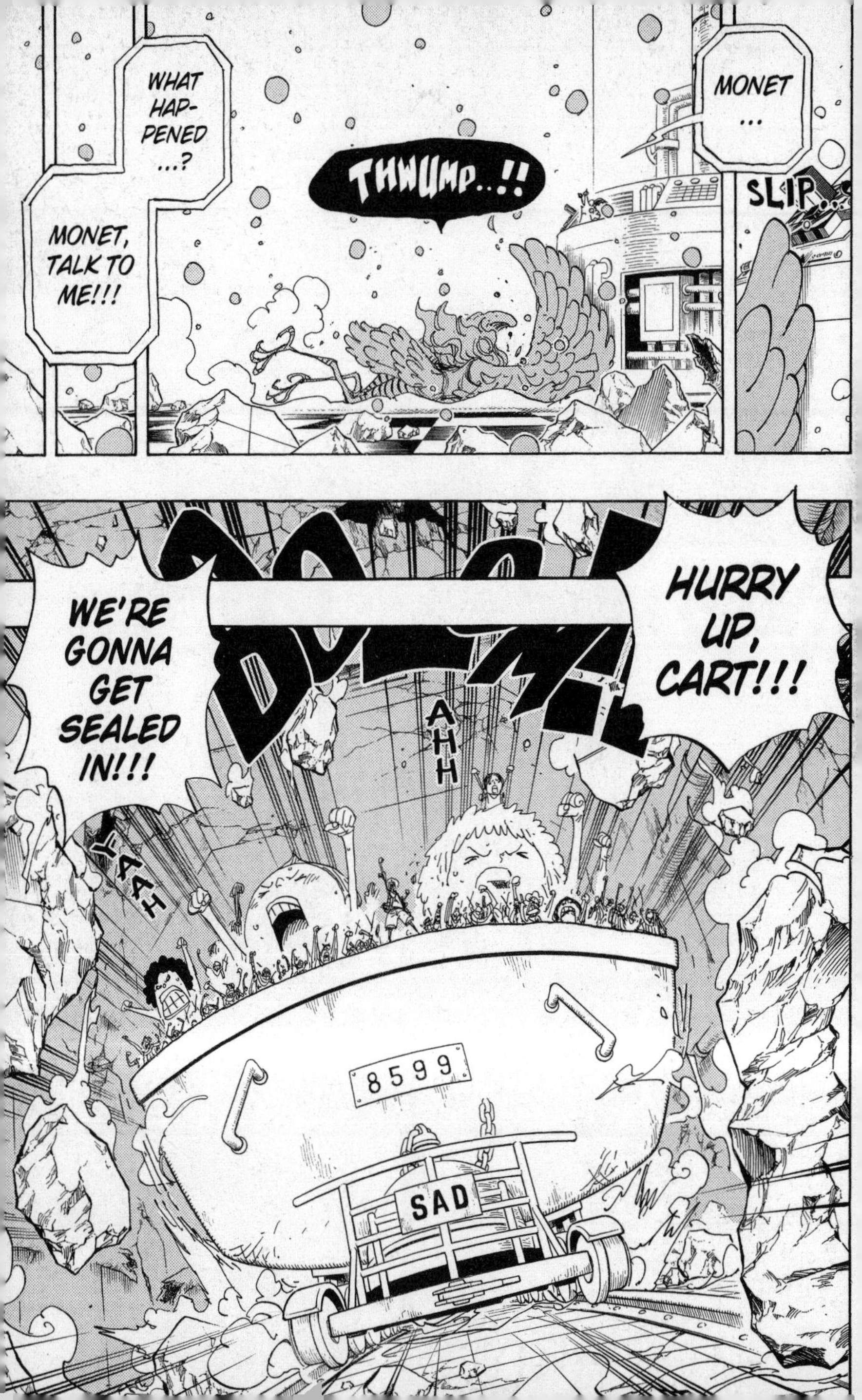
MONET ...
SLIP
THWUMP..!!
WHAT HAP-PENED ...?
MONET, TALK TO ME!!!
HURRY UP, CART!!!
AHH
WE'RE GONNA GET SEALED IN!!!
YAAH
8599
SAD

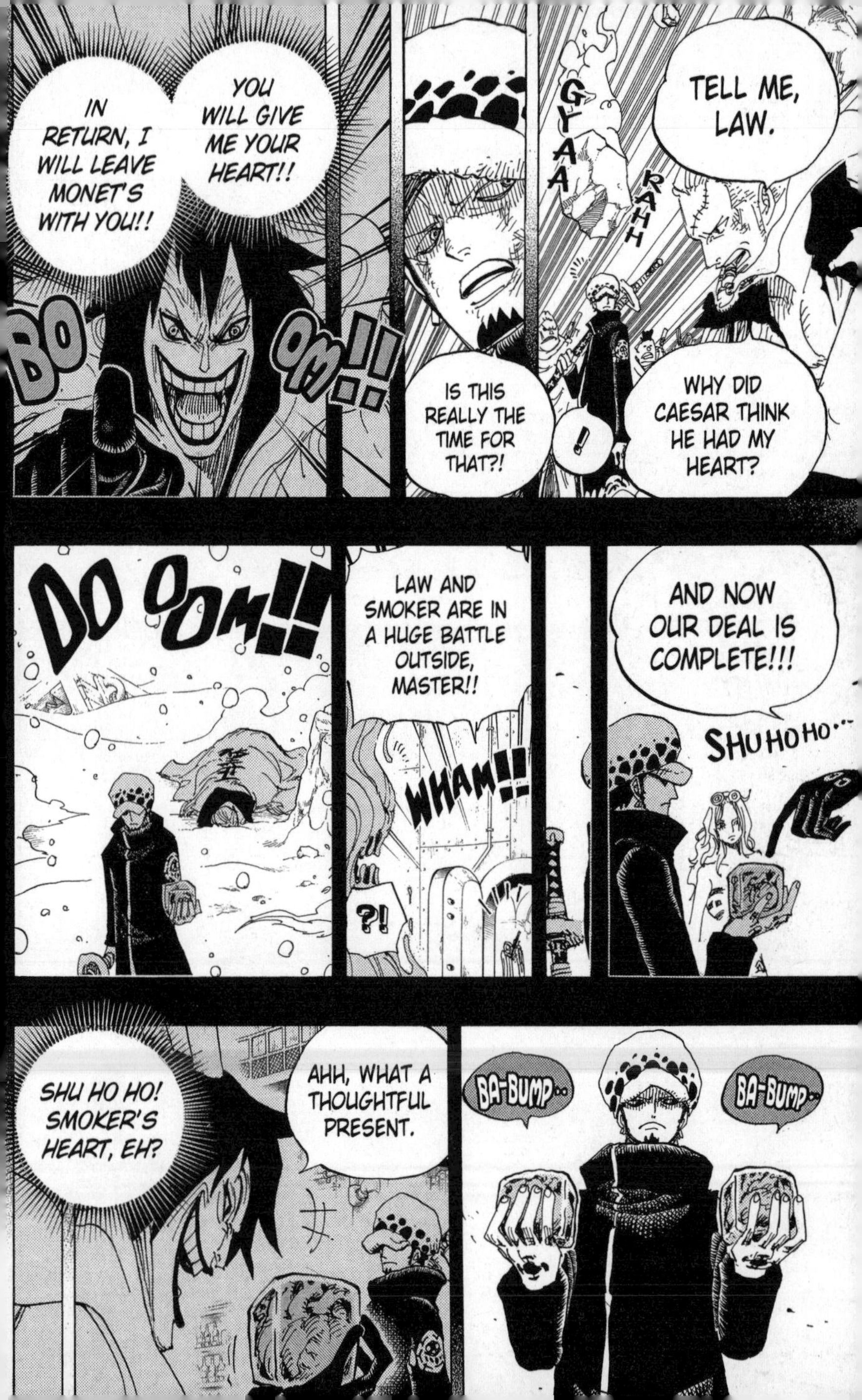
TELL ME, LAW.
GYAAA
RAHH
WHY DID CAESAR THINK HE HAD MY HEART?
!
IS THIS REALLY THE TIME FOR THAT?!
YOU WILL GIVE ME YOUR HEART!!
IN RETURN, I WILL LEAVE MONET'S WITH YOU!!
BOOM!!
AND NOW OUR DEAL IS COMPLETE!!!
SHUHOHO...
LAW AND SMOKER ARE IN A HUGE BATTLE OUTSIDE, MASTER!!
WHAM!!
?!
DOOOM!!
BA-BUMP..
BA-BUMP..
AHH, WHAT A THOUGHTFUL PRESENT.
SHU HO HO! SMOKER'S HEART, EH?

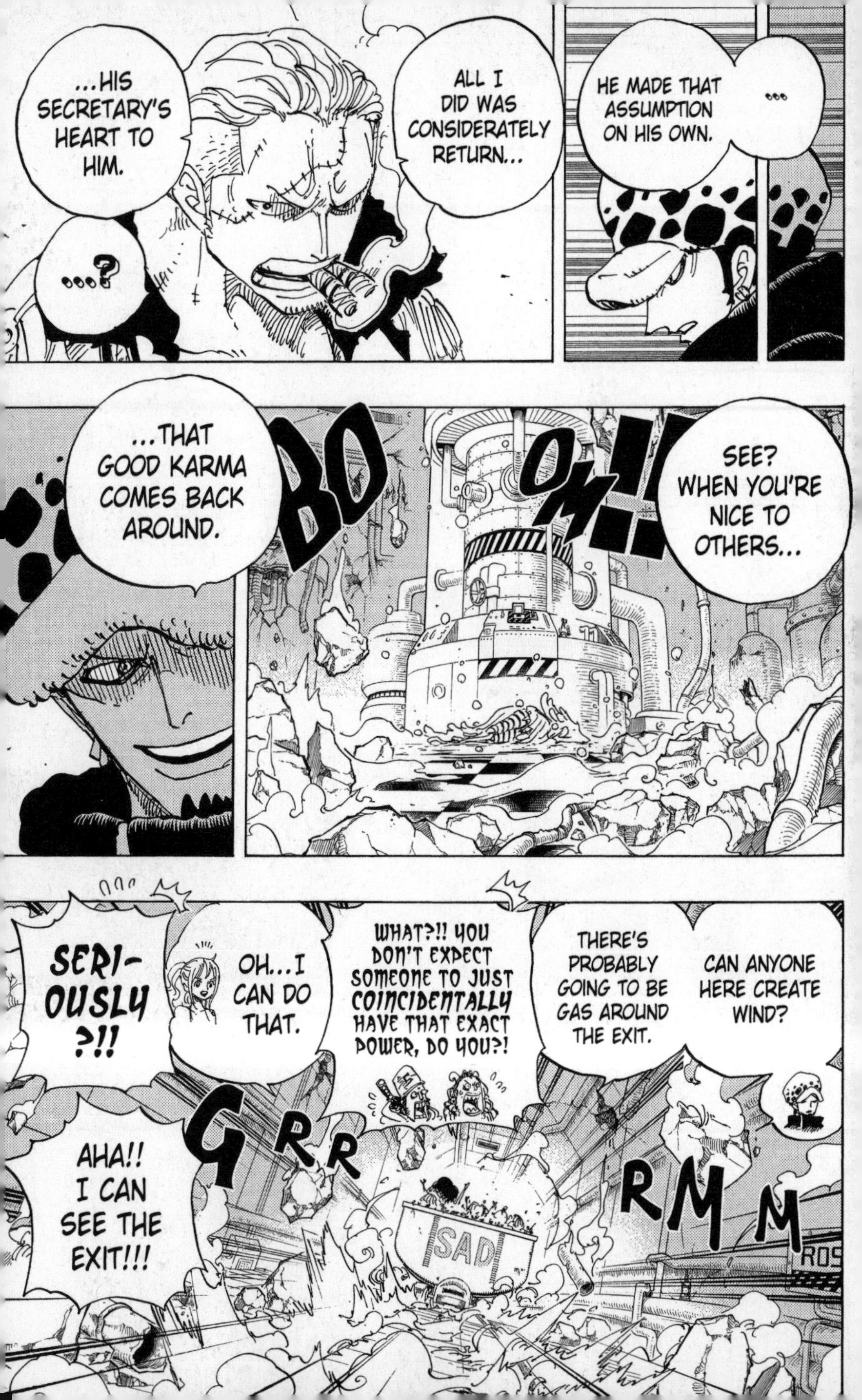

...
HE MADE THAT ASSUMPTION ON HIS OWN.
ALL I DID WAS CONSIDERATELY RETURN...
...HIS SECRETARY'S HEART TO HIM.
...?
SEE? WHEN YOU'RE NICE TO OTHERS...
BOOM!!
...THAT GOOD KARMA COMES BACK AROUND.
CAN ANYONE HERE CREATE WIND?
THERE'S PROBABLY GOING TO BE GAS AROUND THE EXIT.
WHAT?!! YOU DON'T EXPECT SOMEONE TO JUST COINCIDENTALLY HAVE THAT EXACT POWER, DO YOU?!
OH...I CAN DO THAT.
SERI-OUSLY?!!
RMMM
GRR
SAD
AHA!! I CAN SEE THE EXIT!!!

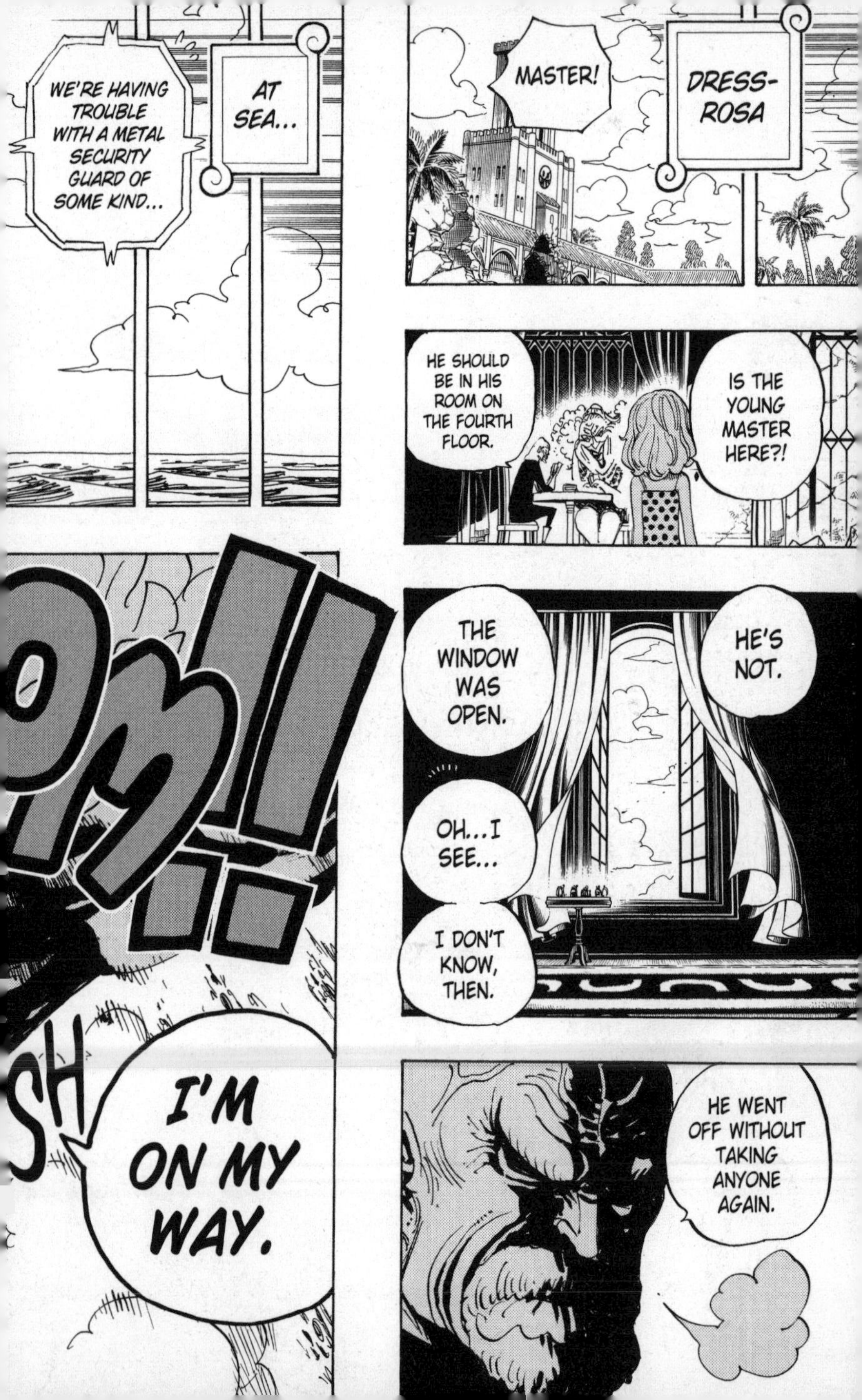
DRESS-ROSA
MASTER!
IS THE YOUNG MASTER HERE?!
HE SHOULD BE IN HIS ROOM ON THE FOURTH FLOOR.
HE'S NOT.
THE WINDOW WAS OPEN.
OH...I SEE...
I DON'T KNOW, THEN.
HE WENT OFF WITHOUT TAKING ANYONE AGAIN.
AT SEA...
WE'RE HAVING TROUBLE WITH A METAL SECURITY GUARD OF SOME KIND...
SH
I'M ON MY WAY.

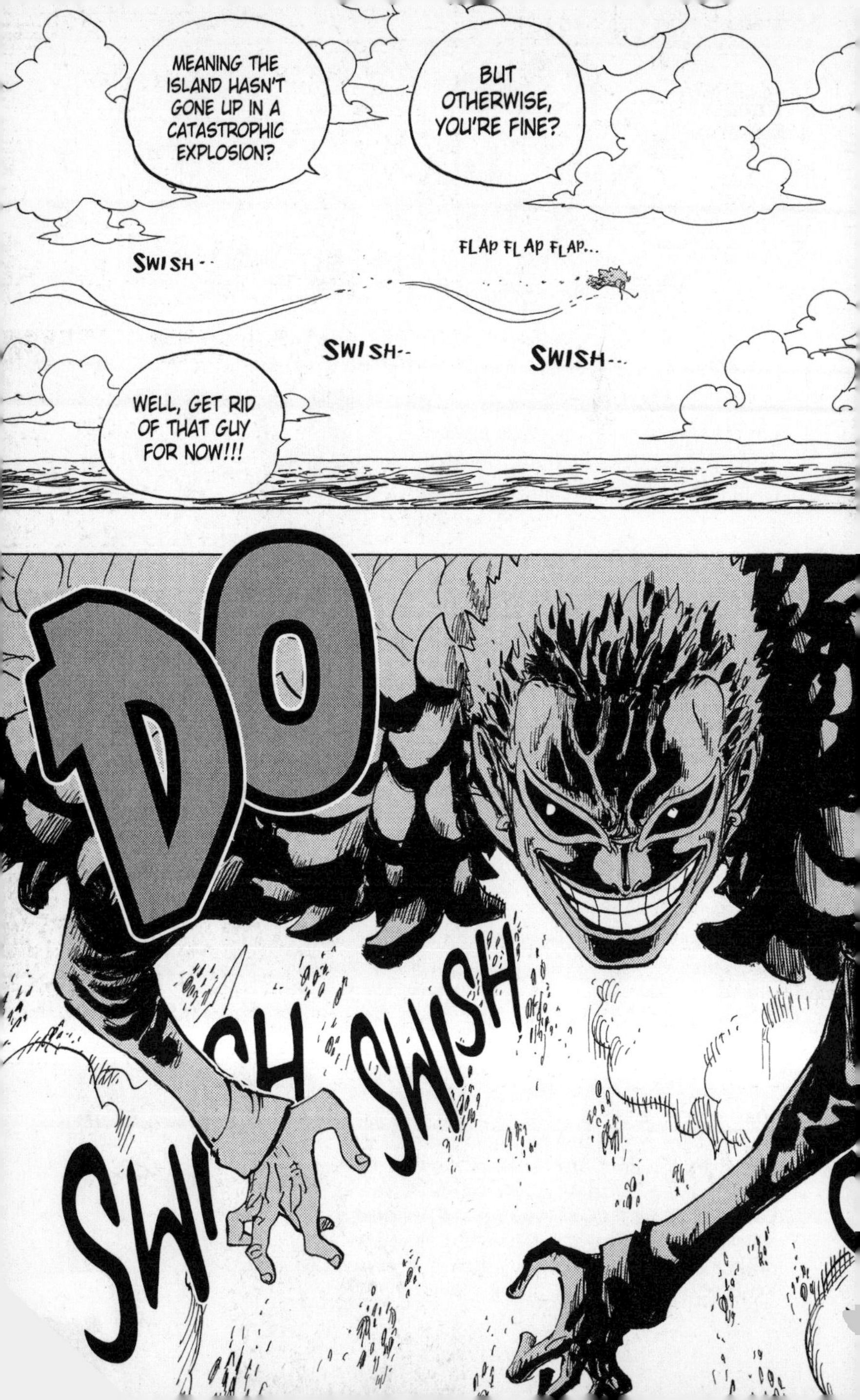
MEANING THE ISLAND HASN'T GONE UP IN A CATASTROPHIC EXPLOSION?
BUT OTHERWISE, YOU'RE FINE?
FLAP FLAP FLAP...
SWISH...
SWISH...
SWISH...
WELL, GET RID OF THAT GUY FOR NOW!!!
DO
SWISH
SWISH

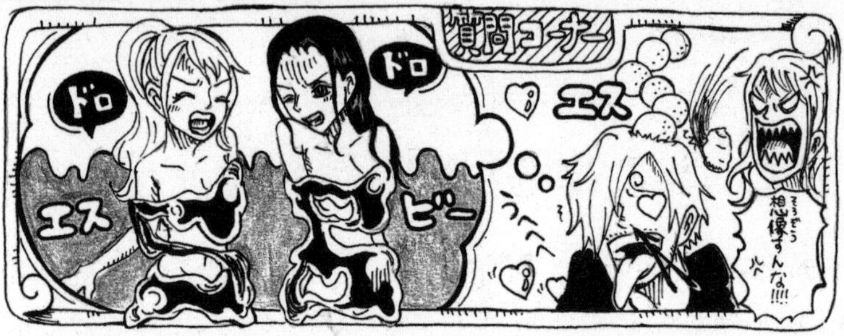
質問コーナー
ドロ
ドロ
エス
ビー
エス
うへへへ
想像すんな!!!

(Potofu, Tokyo)

A: Well, since I didn't answer the last question from the previous section, let's start with that.

Q: In Chapter 653, when Shirahoshi and the crew promised to go on a walk in a real forest the next time they met, why did Zolo and Franky not do the pinky promise?!

--Yuminami Kobayashi Cat

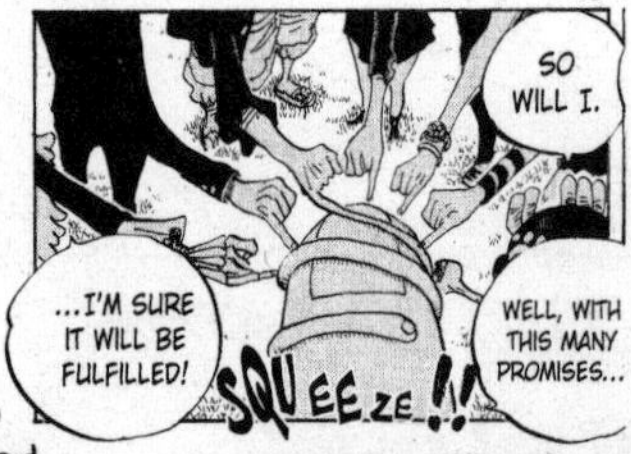
SO WILL I.
WELL, WITH THIS MANY PROMISES...
...I'M SURE IT WILL BE FULFILLED!
SQUEEZE!!

A: Hmm. Seems like many people were bothered by this. There's no real deep meaning to this, but based on the path the story traveled and the individual characters' actions, it seemed like maybe those two in particular hadn't had much interaction with Shirahoshi, so why would they feel the need to hold out their pinkies? Of course, given that their captain and crewmates made that promise, I'm sure Zolo and Franky felt just like the rest of them. Don't worry.

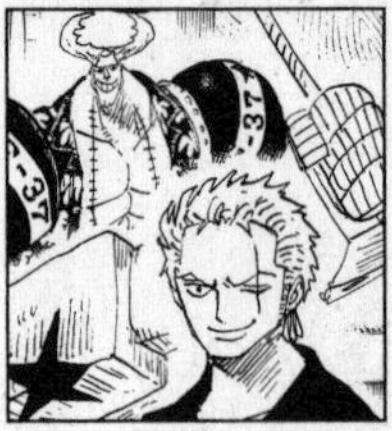

Q: In Chapter 692, there's a scene where Nami and Luffy reunite. You can see a stocky-looking sailor who appears to be carrying Tashigi on his shoulder. That's her, right?! Why is she riding him? She told Zolo, "Let me down when we find my men." Is Zolo really that worried about her health? Heehee.

--Someta

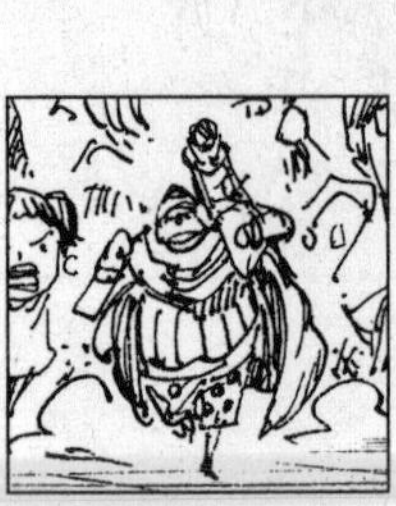

A: Well spotted. Yes, that is Tashigi. But that wasn't on Zolo's orders. I think Tashigi being embarrassed by Zolo was simply that she didn't want her subordinates to see her being helped by a pirate. But being carried by her own men is different. I suppose she might be embarrassed in a different way, though. I don't really know how young women think.

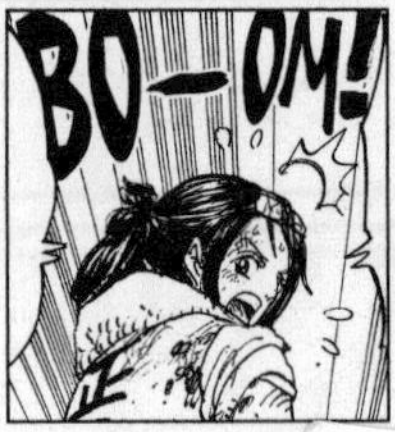
BO—OM!

Chapter 695:

LEAVE IT TO US!!!

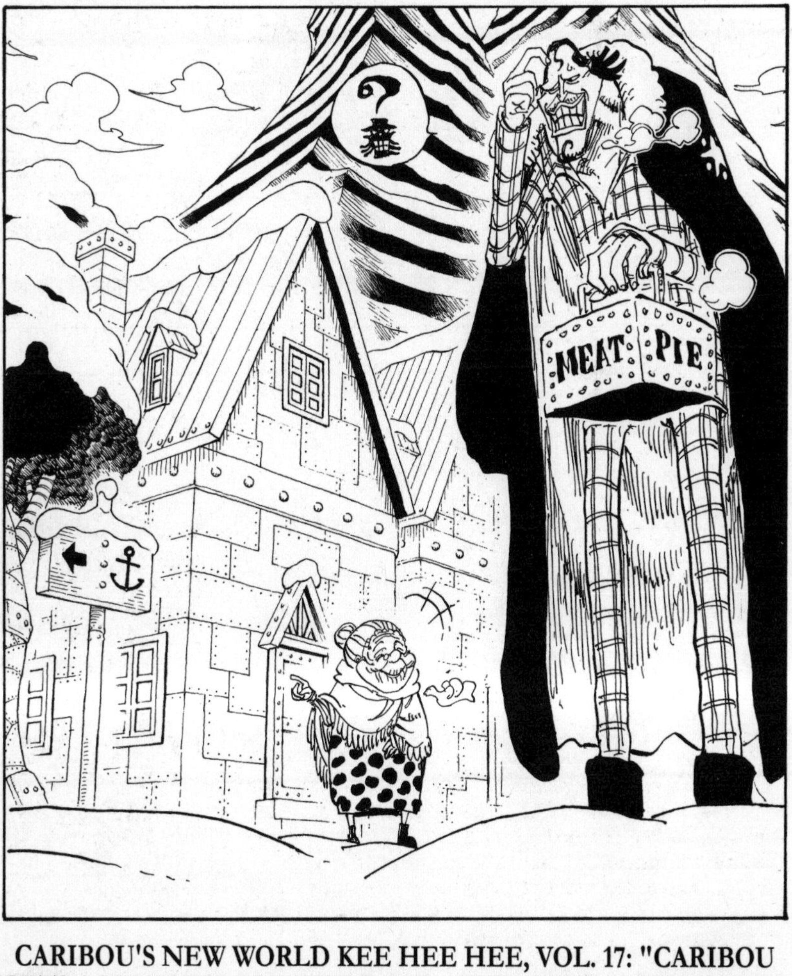
MEAT PIE

CARIBOU'S NEW WORLD KEE HEE HEE, VOL. 17: "CARIBOU GETS A MEAT PIE FOR THE ROAD—THE PORT IS THAT WAY"

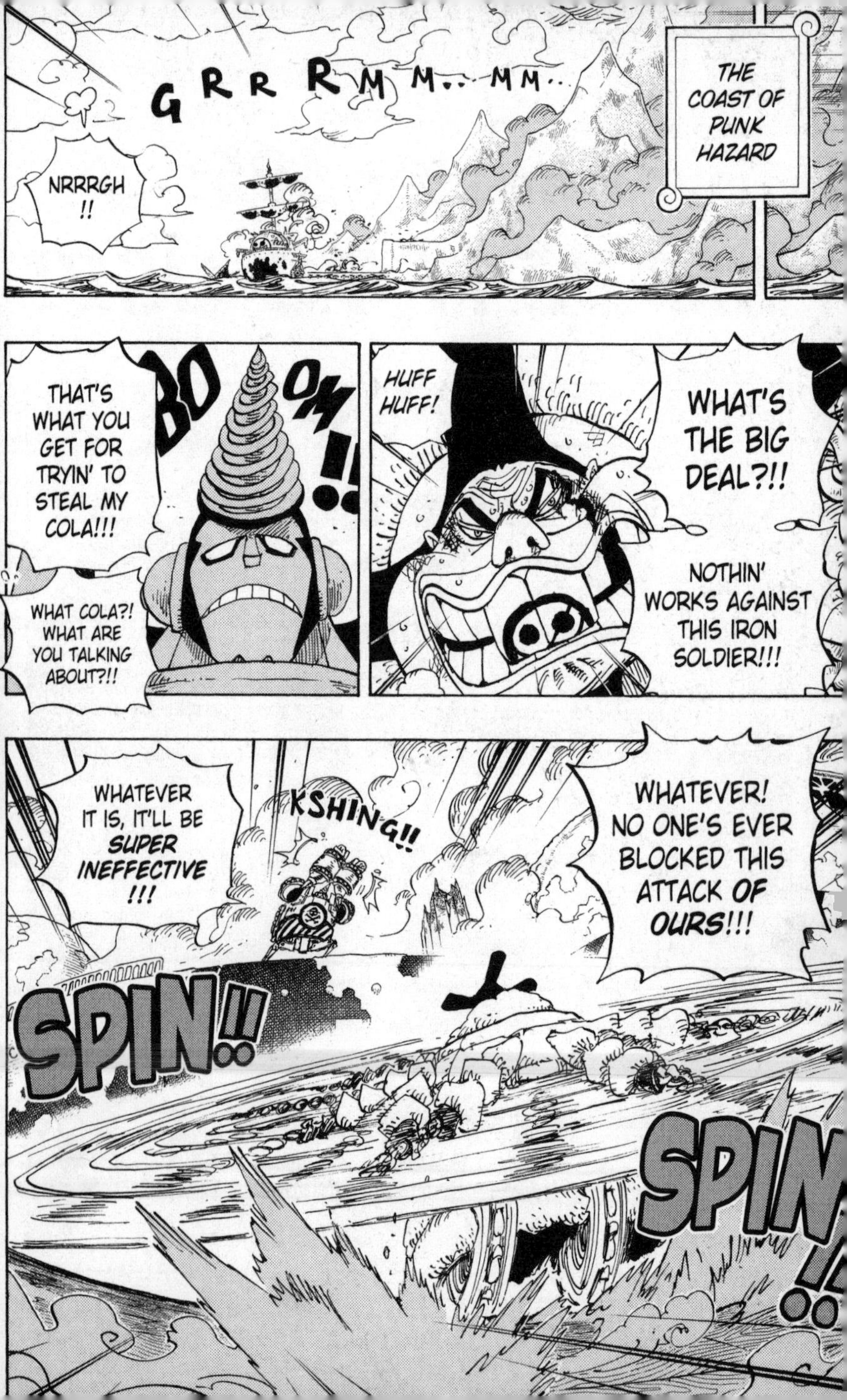
THE COAST OF PUNK HAZARD
GRRRMM... MM...
NRRRGH!!
WHAT'S THE BIG DEAL?!!
HUFF HUFF!
NOTHIN' WORKS AGAINST THIS IRON SOLDIER!!!
THAT'S WHAT YOU GET FOR TRYIN' TO STEAL MY COLA!!!
BOOM!!
WHAT COLA?! WHAT ARE YOU TALKING ABOUT?!!
WHATEVER! NO ONE'S EVER BLOCKED THIS ATTACK OF OURS!!!
KSHING!!
WHATEVER IT IS, IT'LL BE SUPER INEFFECTIVE!!!
SPIN!!
SPIN!!

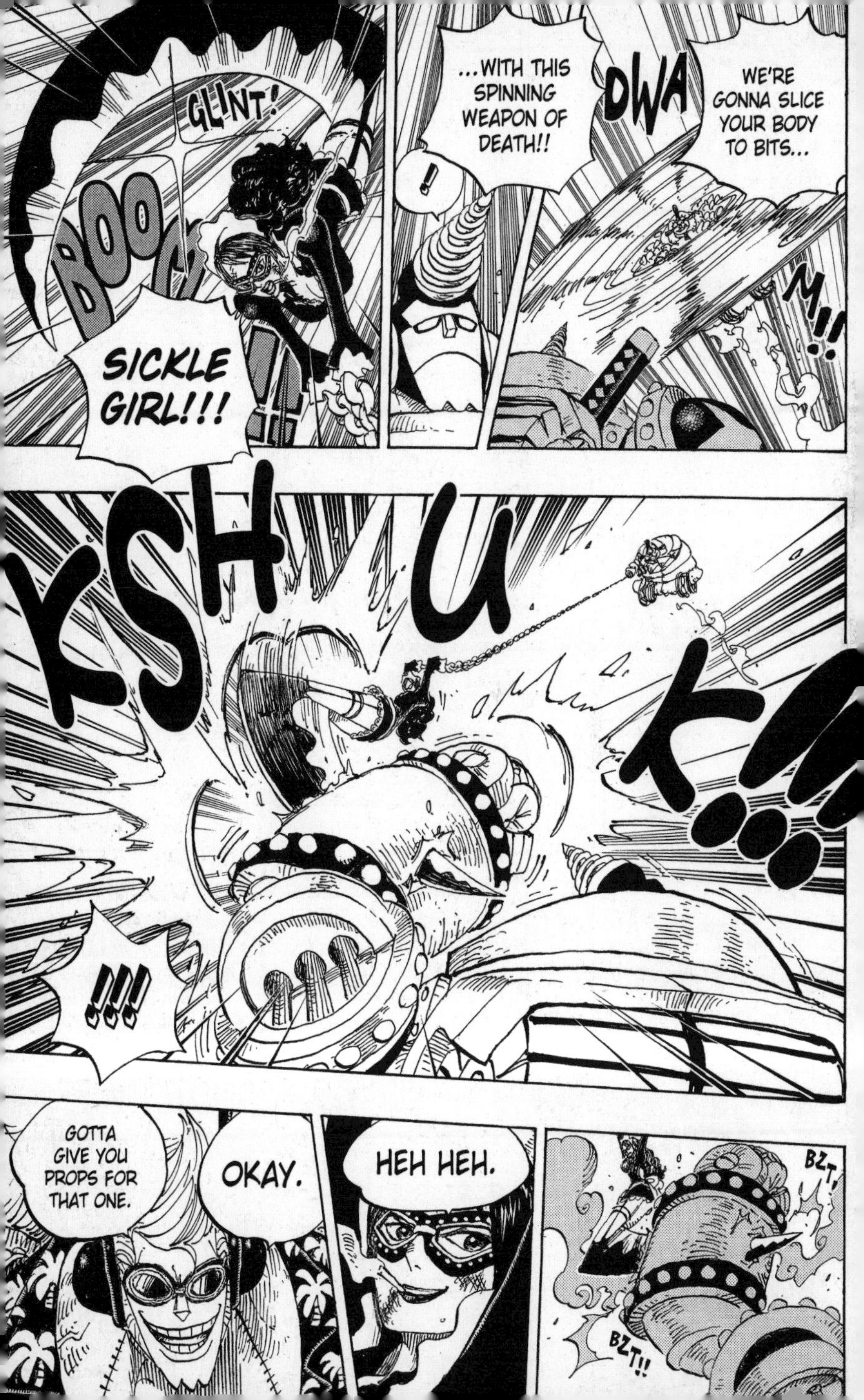
WE'RE GONNA SLICE YOUR BODY TO BITS...
DWA
...WITH THIS SPINNING WEAPON OF DEATH!!
!
GLINT!
SICKLE GIRL!!!
KSHUK!!
!!!
BZT,
BZT!!
HEH HEH.
OKAY.
GOTTA GIVE YOU PROPS FOR THAT ONE.

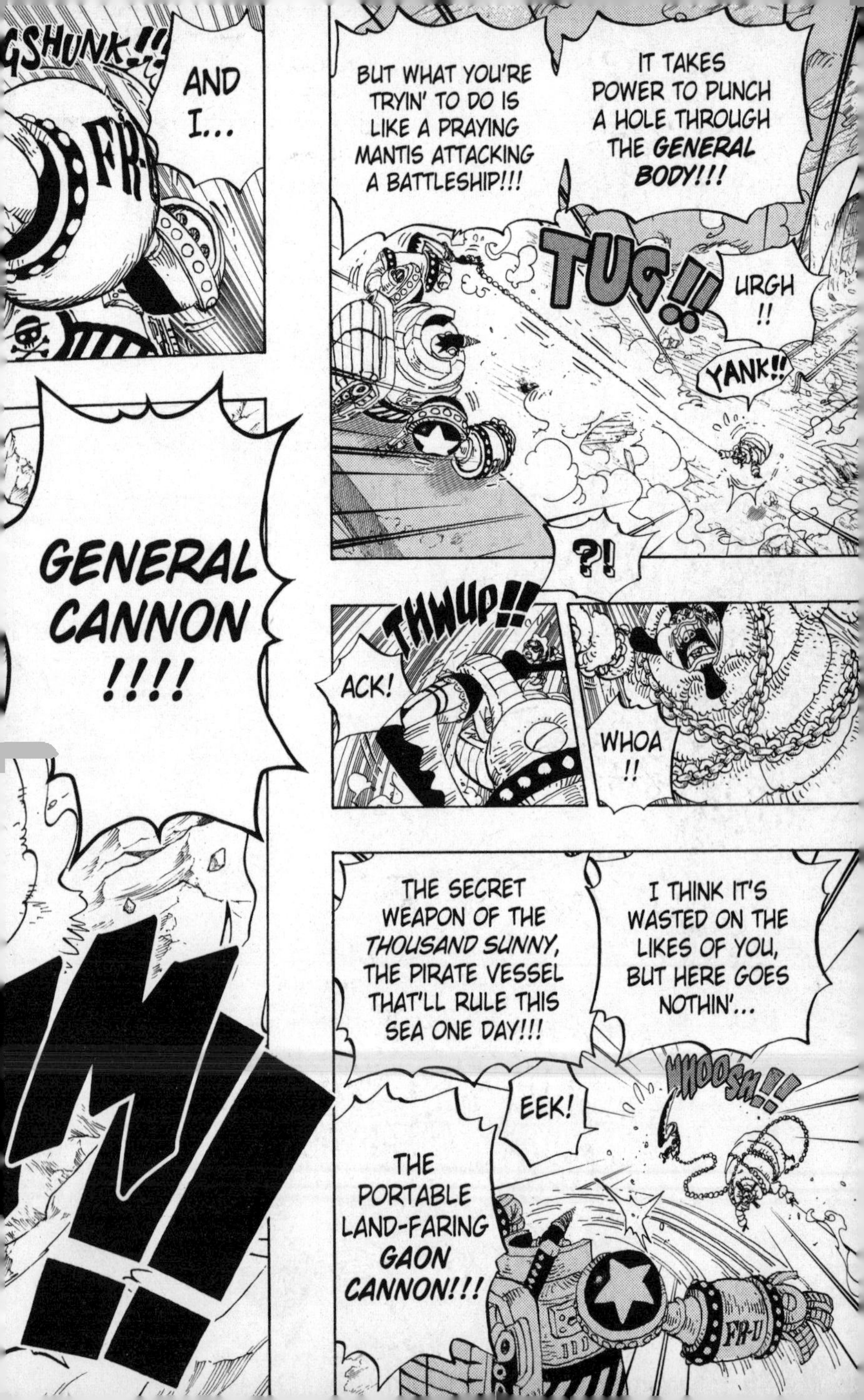
IT TAKES POWER TO PUNCH A HOLE THROUGH THE GENERAL BODY!!!
BUT WHAT YOU'RE TRYIN' TO DO IS LIKE A PRAYING MANTIS ATTACKING A BATTLESHIP!!!
TUG!!
URGH !!
YANK!!
?!
WHOA !!
THWUP!!
ACK!
I THINK IT'S WASTED ON THE LIKES OF YOU, BUT HERE GOES NOTHIN'...
THE SECRET WEAPON OF THE THOUSAND SUNNY, THE PIRATE VESSEL THAT'LL RULE THIS SEA ONE DAY!!!
WHOOSH!!
EEK!
THE PORTABLE LAND-FARING GAON CANNON!!!
GSHUNK!!
AND I...
GENERAL CANNON !!!!

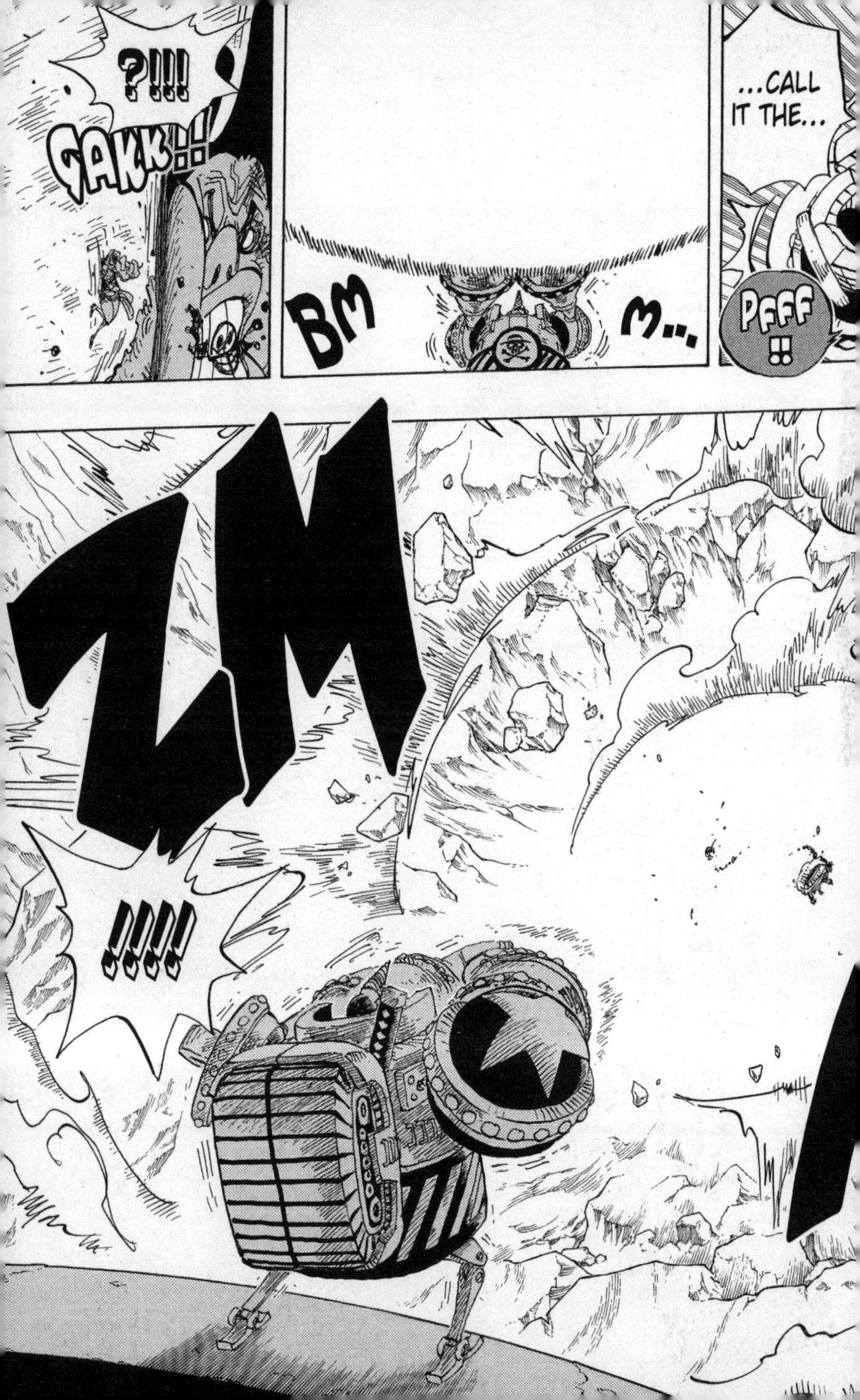
...CALL IT THE...
PFFF !!
BM
M...
?!!!
GAKK!!
ZM
!!!!

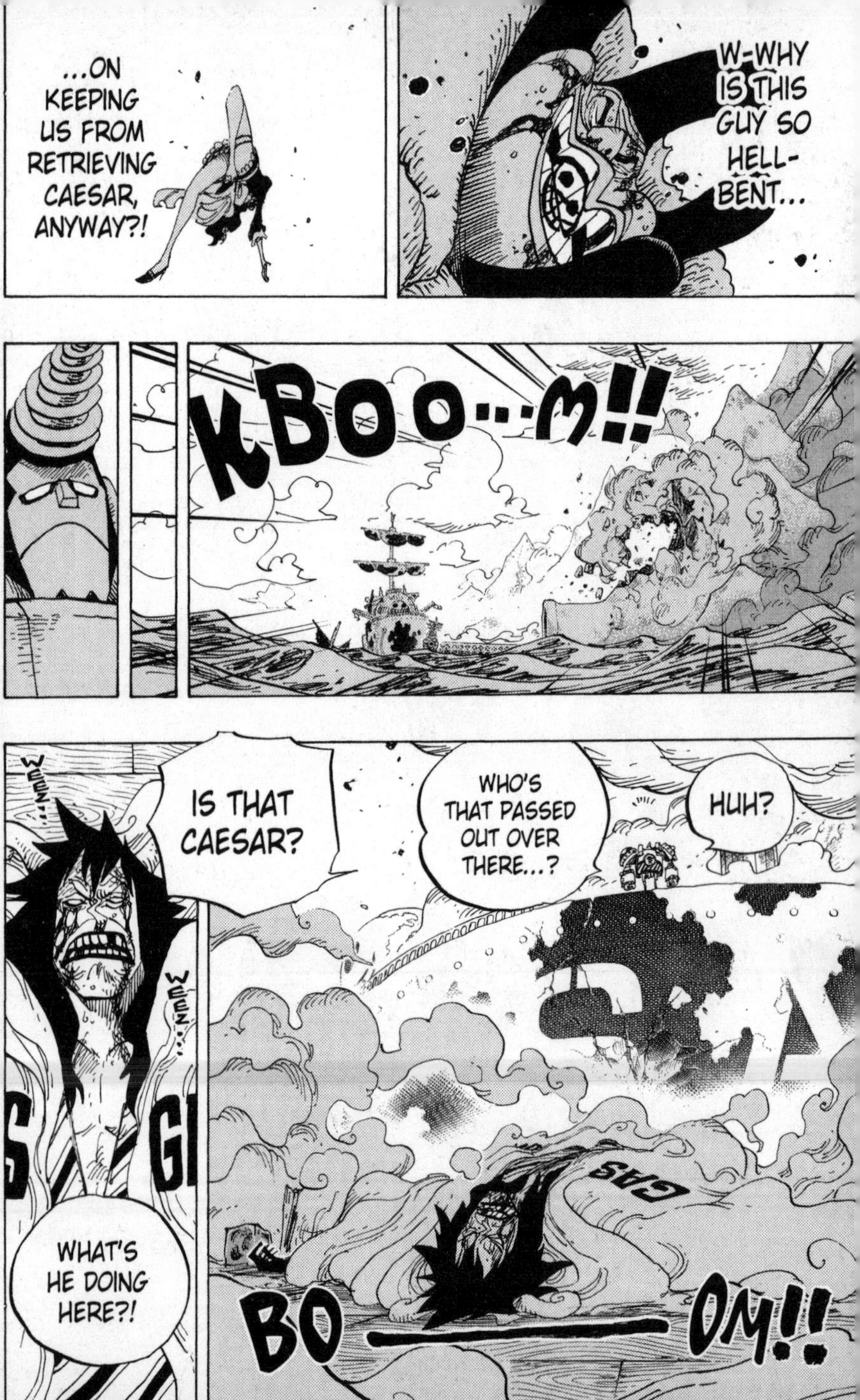
W-WHY IS THIS GUY SO HELL-BENT...
...ON KEEPING US FROM RETRIEVING CAESAR, ANYWAY?!
KBOO...M!!
HUH?
WHO'S THAT PASSED OUT OVER THERE...?
IS THAT CAESAR?
GAS
BO——OM!!
WEEZ...
WEEZ...
WHAT'S HE DOING HERE?!

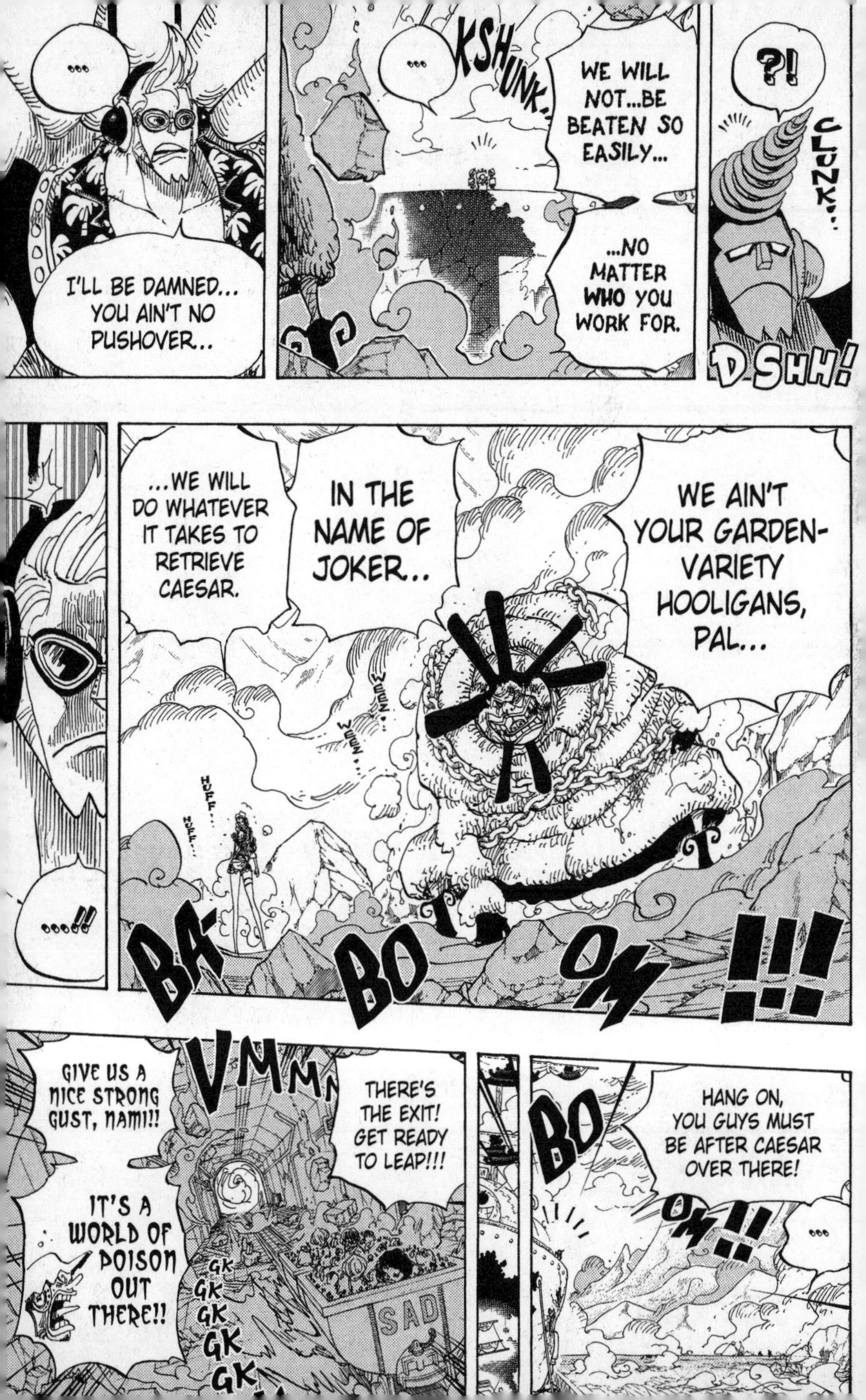
?!
CLUNK...
D-SHH!
KSHUNK...
...
WE WILL NOT...BE BEATEN SO EASILY...
...NO MATTER WHO YOU WORK FOR.
...
I'LL BE DAMNED... YOU AIN'T NO PUSHOVER...
WE AIN'T YOUR GARDEN-VARIETY HOOLIGANS, PAL...
IN THE NAME OF JOKER...
...WE WILL DO WHATEVER IT TAKES TO RETRIEVE CAESAR.
WEEN...
WEEN...
HUFF...
HUFF...
BA-BOOM!!!
...!!
HANG ON, YOU GUYS MUST BE AFTER CAESAR OVER THERE!
BO
OM!!
...
VMMN
THERE'S THE EXIT! GET READY TO LEAP!!!
GIVE US A NICE STRONG GUST, NAMI!!
IT'S A WORLD OF POISON OUT THERE!!
GK GK GK GK GK GK
SAD

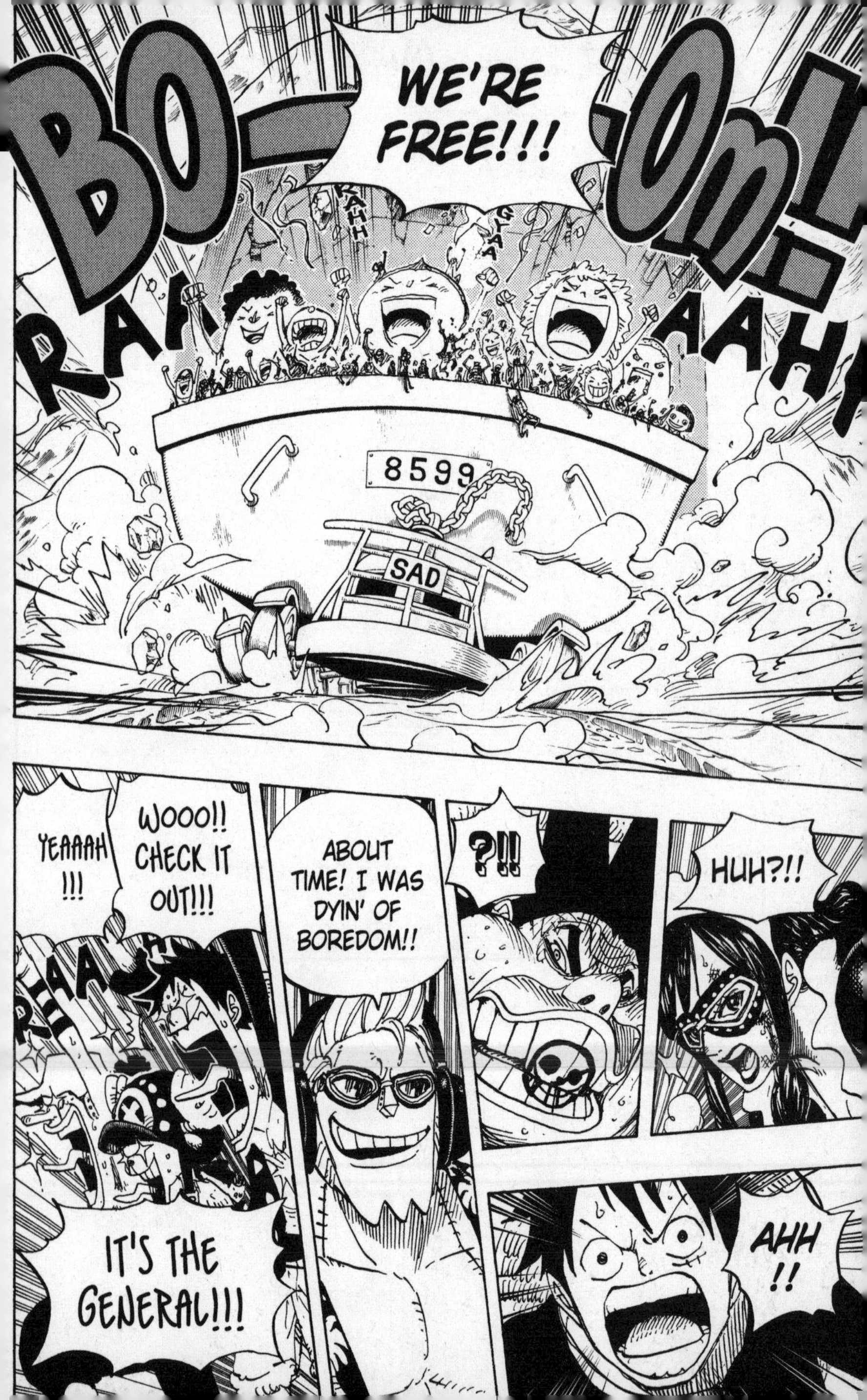
BO—
—OM!!
WE'RE FREE!!!
GYAA
RAHH
AAH
RAA
HUH?!!
?!!
AHH !!
ABOUT TIME! I WAS DYIN' OF BOREDOM!!
WOOO!! CHECK IT OUT!!!
YEAAAH !!!
IT'S THE GENERAL!!!

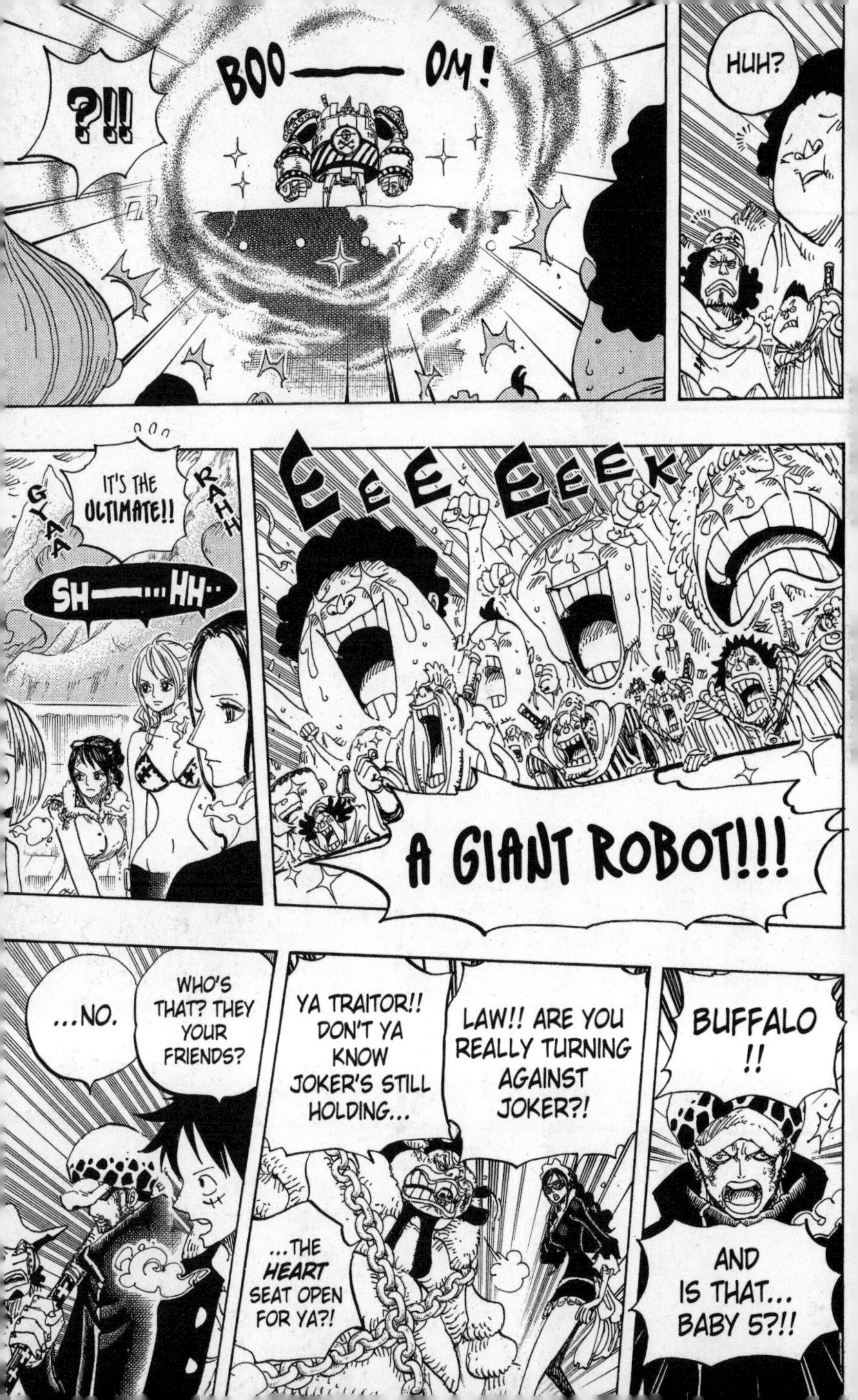
HUH?
?!!
BOO——OM!
EEEEEEK
A GIANT ROBOT!!!
IT'S THE ULTIMATE!!
RAHH
GYAA
SH—...HH..
BUFFALO !!
AND IS THAT... BABY 5?!!
LAW!! ARE YOU REALLY TURNING AGAINST JOKER?!
YA TRAITOR!! DON'T YA KNOW JOKER'S STILL HOLDING...
...THE HEART SEAT OPEN FOR YA?!
WHO'S THAT? THEY YOUR FRIENDS?
...NO.

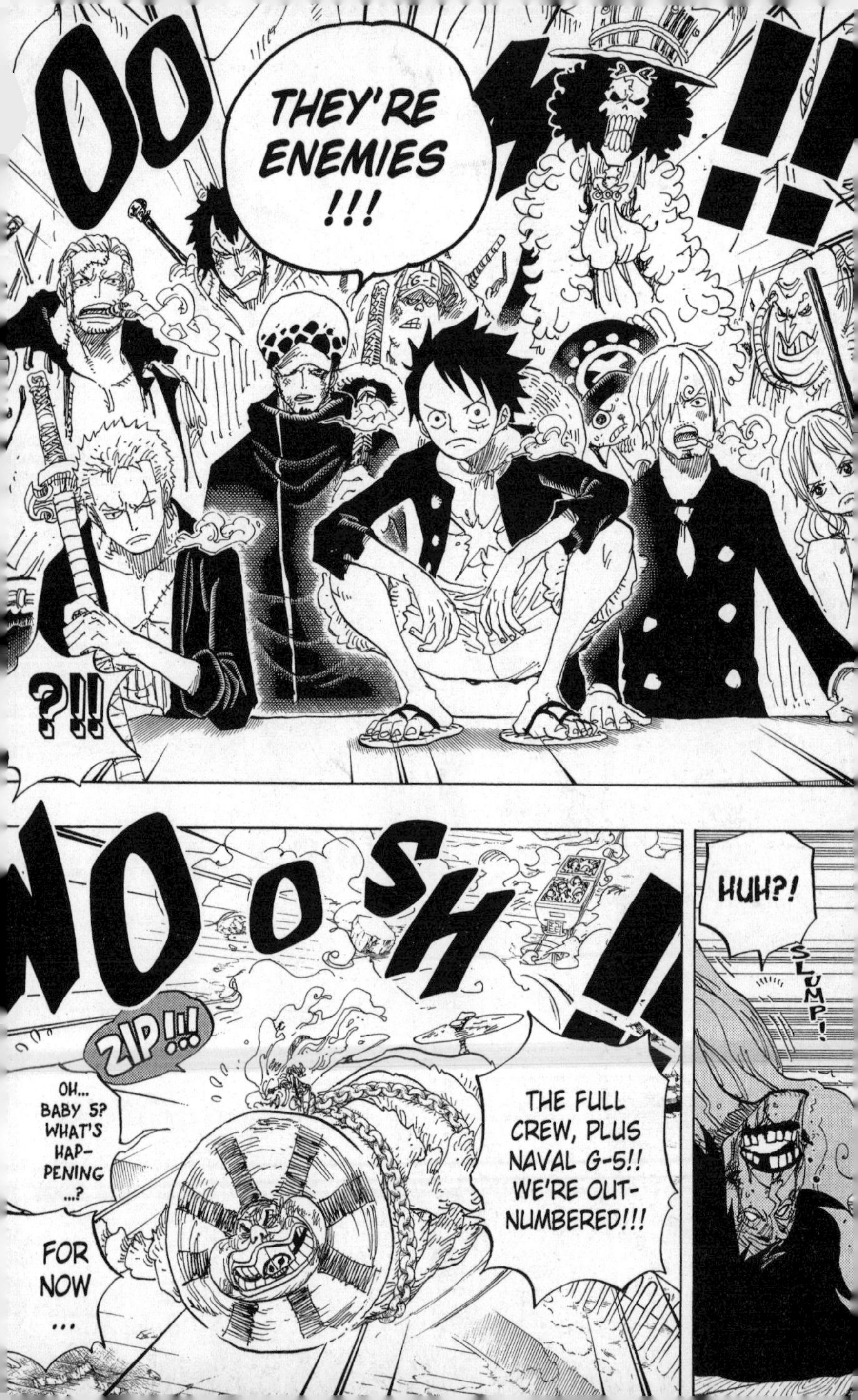

THEY'RE ENEMIES !!!
?!!
HUH?!
SLUMP!
ZIP!!!
THE FULL CREW, PLUS NAVAL G-5!! WE'RE OUT-NUMBERED!!!
OH... BABY 5? WHAT'S HAP-PENING ...?
FOR NOW ...

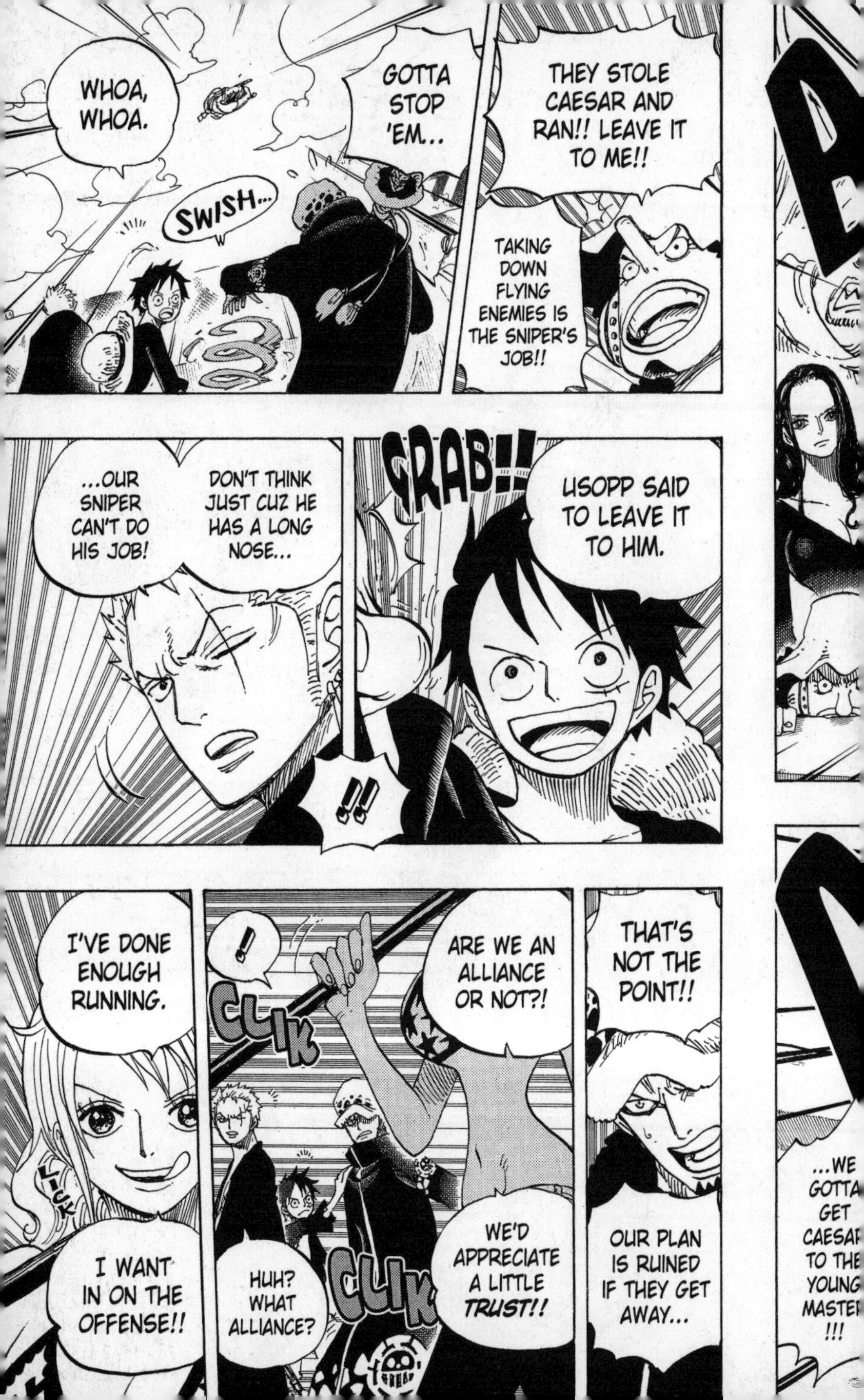
THEY STOLE CAESAR AND RAN!! LEAVE IT TO ME!!
TAKING DOWN FLYING ENEMIES IS THE SNIPER'S JOB!!
GOTTA STOP 'EM...
WHOA, WHOA.
SWISH...
GRAB!!
USOPP SAID TO LEAVE IT TO HIM.
!!
DON'T THINK JUST CUZ HE HAS A LONG NOSE...
...OUR SNIPER CAN'T DO HIS JOB!
THAT'S NOT THE POINT!!
OUR PLAN IS RUINED IF THEY GET AWAY...
ARE WE AN ALLIANCE OR NOT?!
!
CLIK
WE'D APPRECIATE A LITTLE *TRUST!!*
CLIK
HUH? WHAT ALLIANCE?
I'VE DONE ENOUGH RUNNING.
LICK
I WANT IN ON THE OFFENSE!!

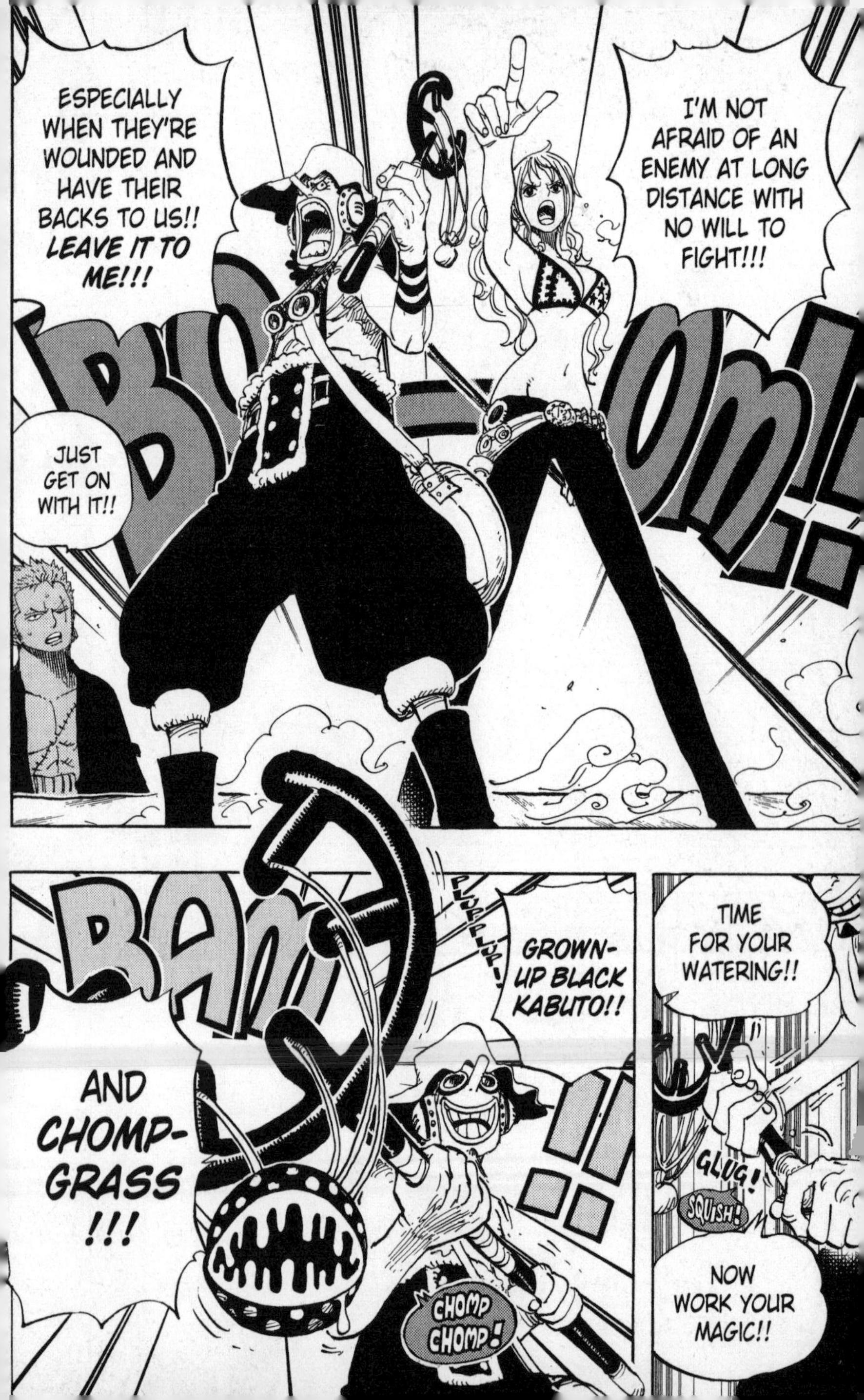
I'M NOT AFRAID OF AN ENEMY AT LONG DISTANCE WITH NO WILL TO FIGHT!!!
ESPECIALLY WHEN THEY'RE WOUNDED AND HAVE THEIR BACKS TO US!! *LEAVE IT TO ME!!!*
BOOM!!
JUST GET ON WITH IT!!
TIME FOR YOUR WATERING!!
GLUG!
SQUISH!
NOW WORK YOUR MAGIC!!
GROWN-UP BLACK KABUTO!!
PLUP PLUP!
BAM!!
AND CHOMP-GRASS!!!
CHOMP CHOMP!

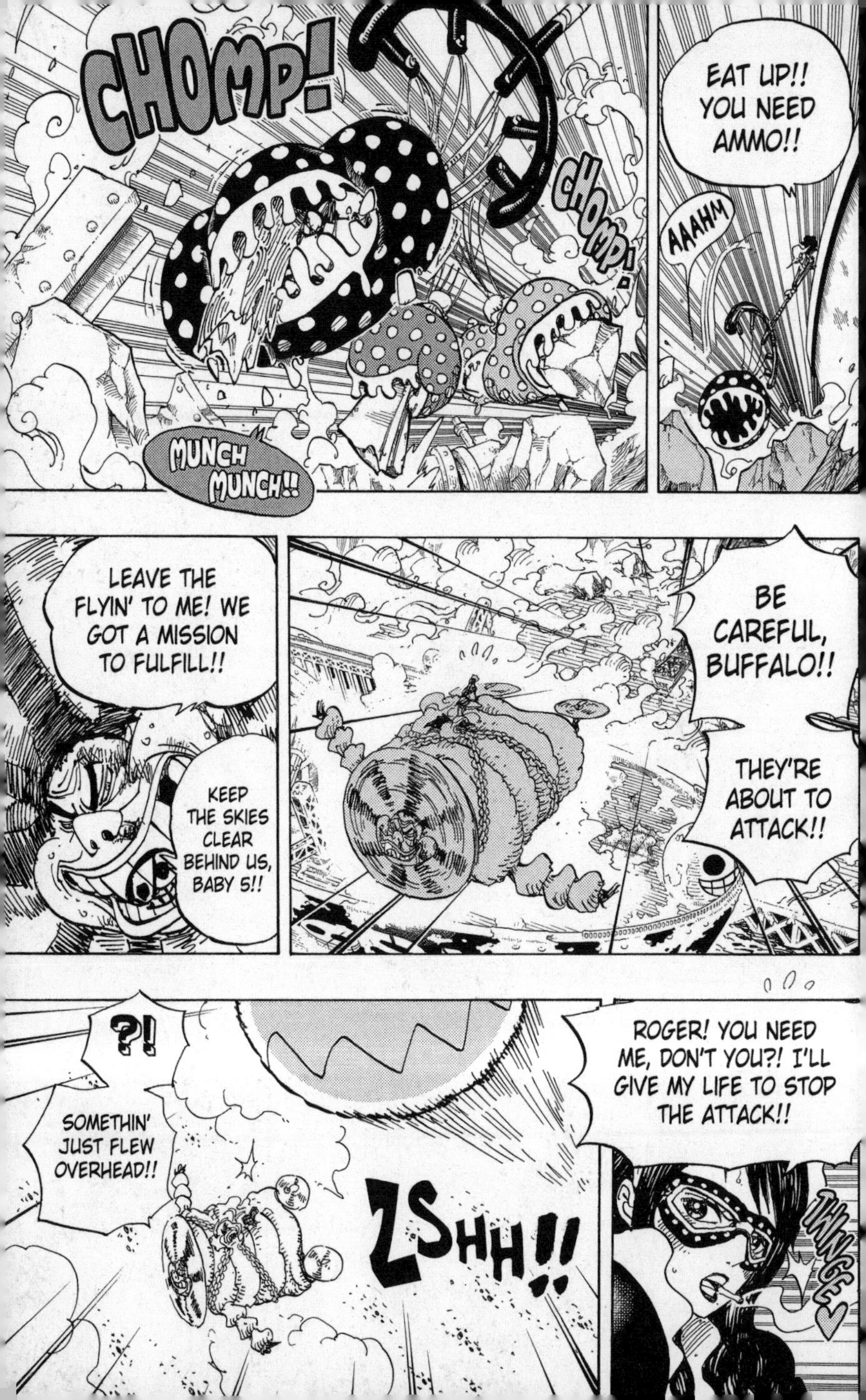
EAT UP!! YOU NEED AMMO!!
AAAHM
CHOMP!
CHOMP!
MUNCH MUNCH!!
BE CAREFUL, BUFFALO!!
THEY'RE ABOUT TO ATTACK!!
LEAVE THE FLYIN' TO ME! WE GOT A MISSION TO FULFILL!!
KEEP THE SKIES CLEAR BEHIND US, BABY 5!!
ROGER! YOU NEED ME, DON'T YOU?! I'LL GIVE MY LIFE TO STOP THE ATTACK!!
TWINGE
?!
SOMETHIN' JUST FLEW OVERHEAD!!
ZSHH!!

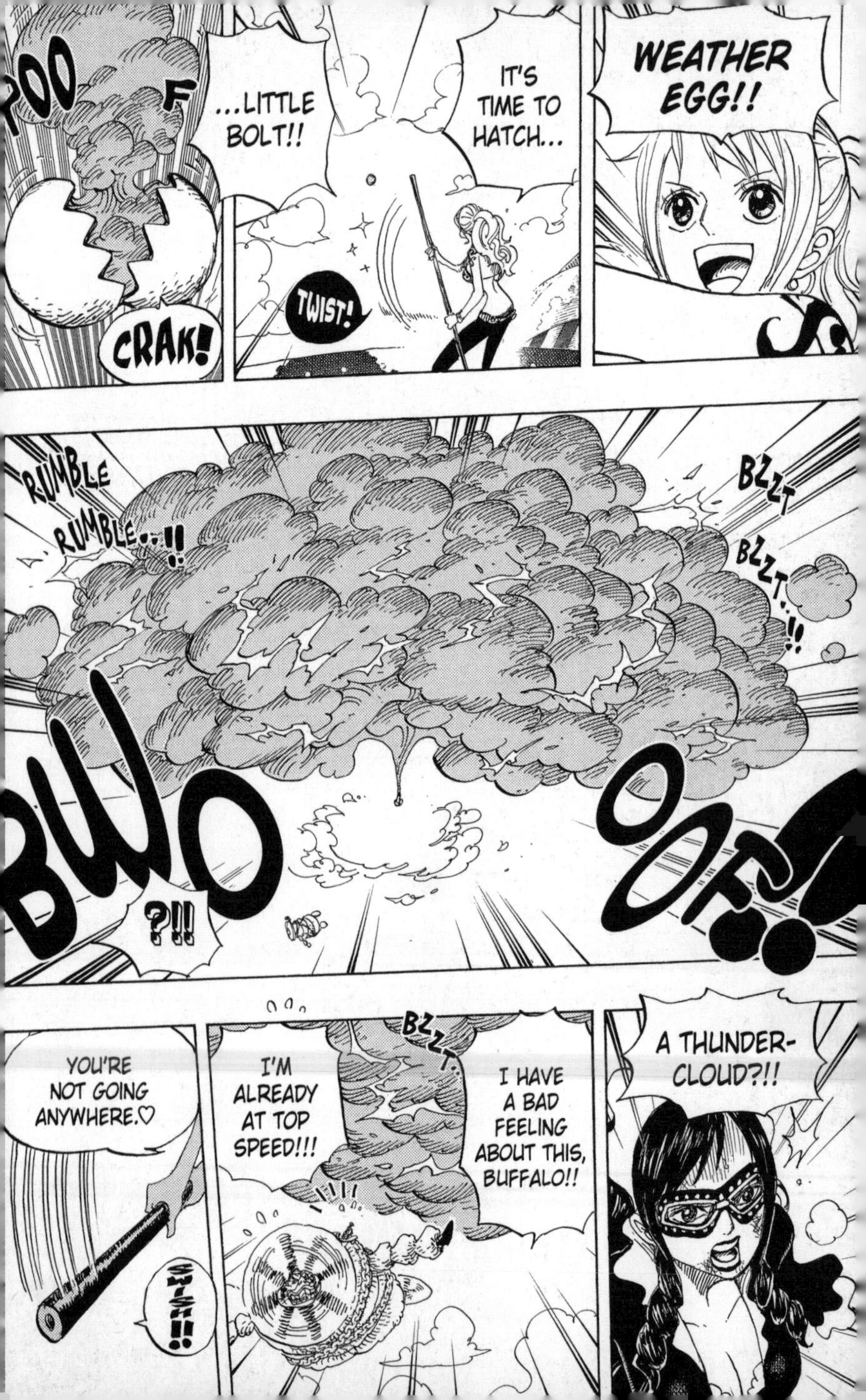
WEATHER EGG!!
IT'S TIME TO HATCH...
...LITTLE BOLT!!
TWIST!
POOF
CRAK!
BZZT
BZZT..!!
RUMBLE RUMBLE..!!
BUO
OOF!
?!!
A THUNDER-CLOUD?!!
BZZT
I HAVE A BAD FEELING ABOUT THIS, BUFFALO!!
I'M ALREADY AT TOP SPEED!!!
YOU'RE NOT GOING ANYWHERE.♡
SWISH!!

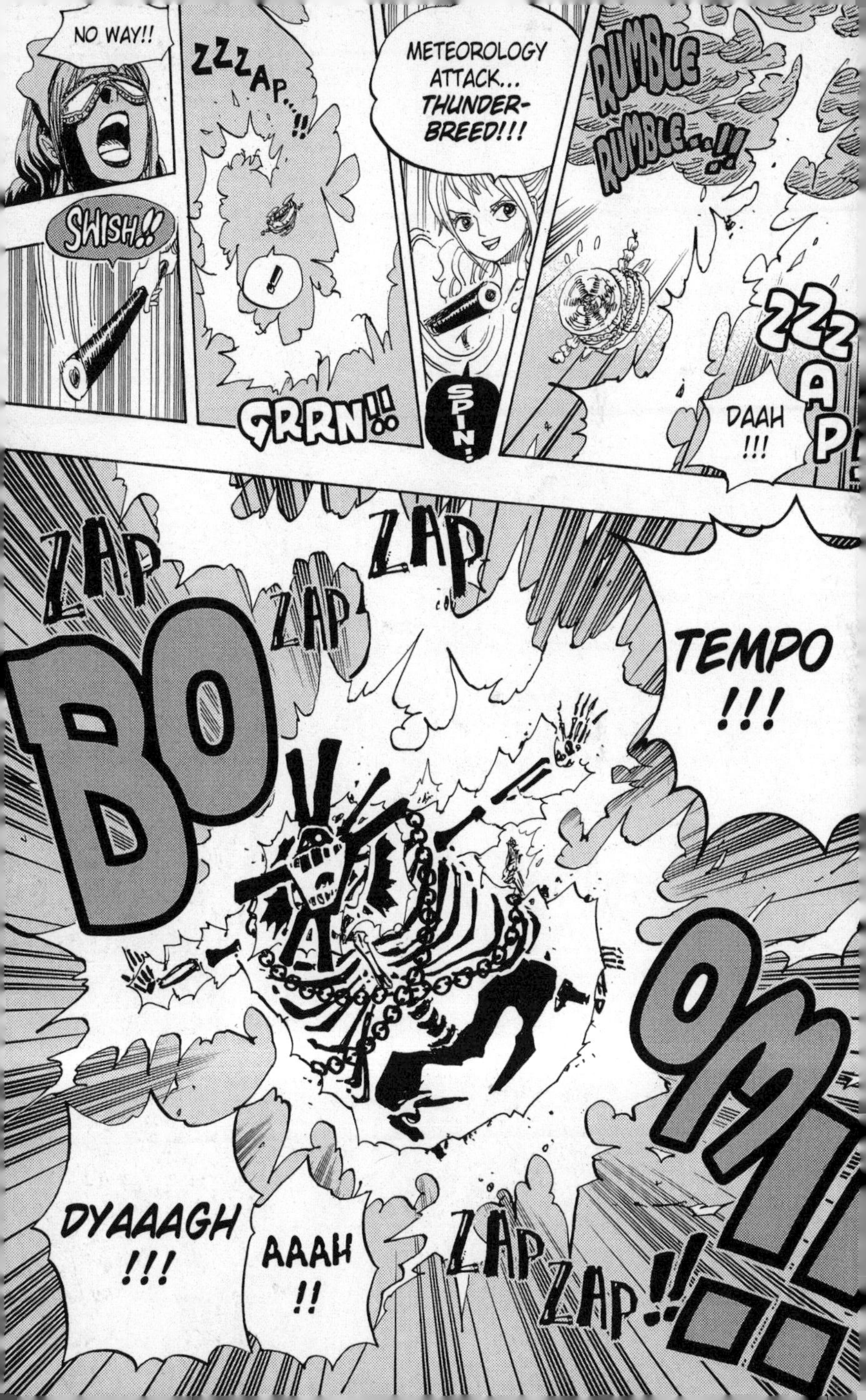
RUMBLE RUMBLE...!!
ZZZAP!
DAAH!!!
METEOROLOGY ATTACK... THUNDER-BREED!!!
SPIN!
ZZZAP...!!
!
GRRN!!
NO WAY!!
SWISH!!
TEMPO!!!
ZAP
ZAP
ZAP
BOOM!!
ZAP ZAP!!
AAAH!!
DYAAAGH!!!

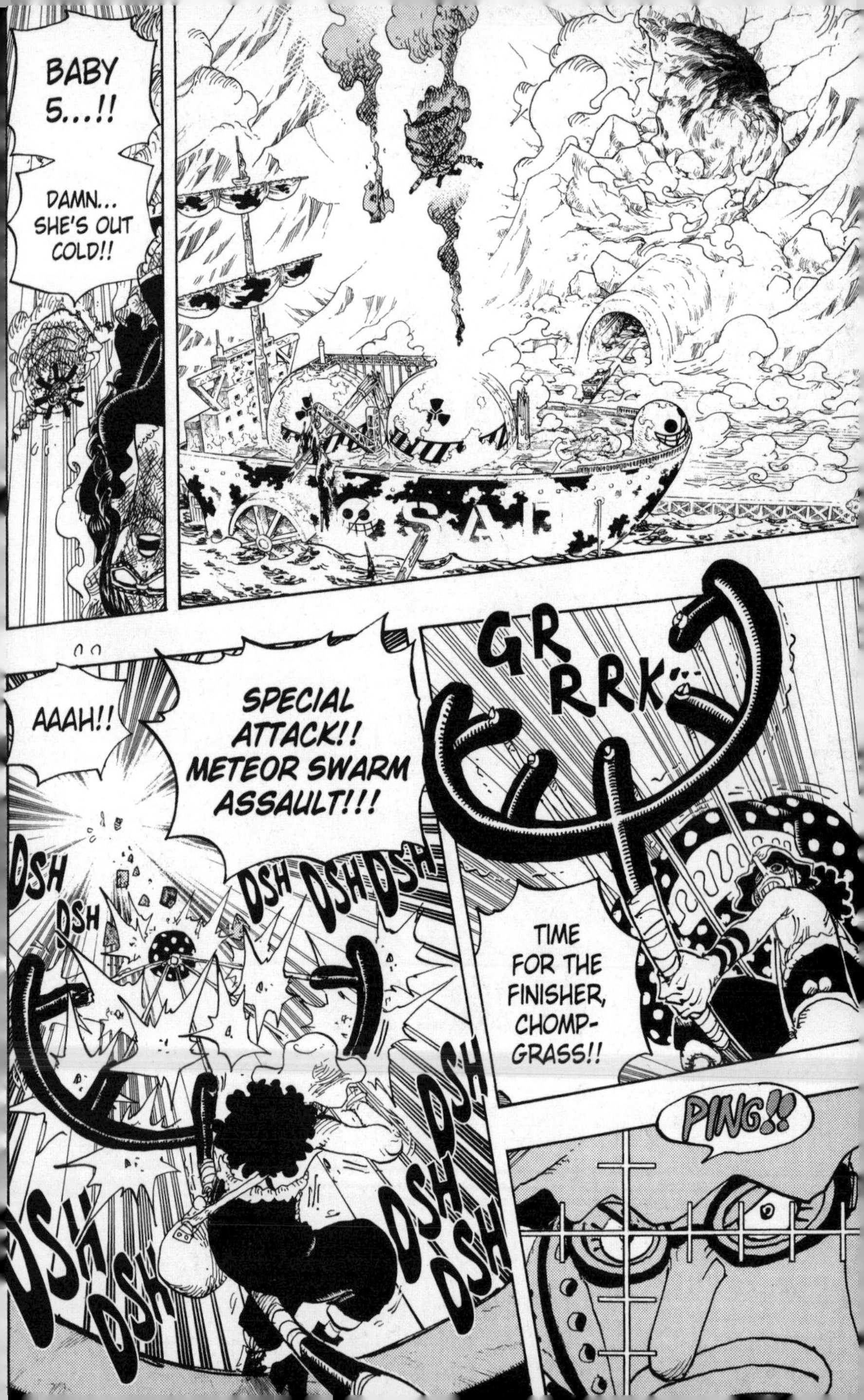
BABY 5...!!
DAMN... SHE'S OUT COLD!!
GR RRK
TIME FOR THE FINISHER, CHOMP-GRASS!!
PING!!
SPECIAL ATTACK!! METEOR SWARM ASSAULT!!!
AAAH!!
DSH DSH DSH
DSH DSH
DSH DSH DSH
DSH DSH
DSH DSH

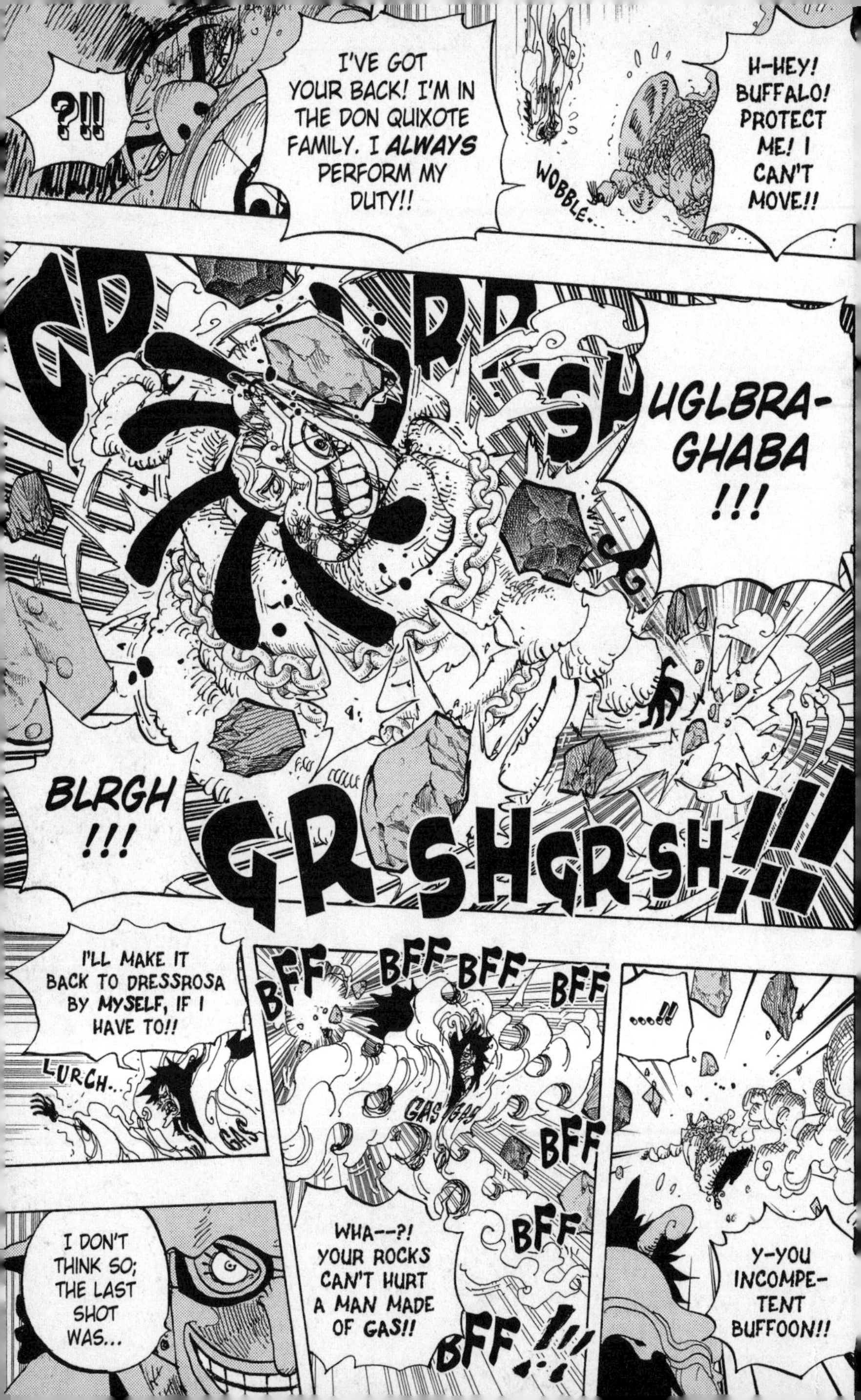
H-HEY! BUFFALO! PROTECT ME! I CAN'T MOVE!!
WOBBLE...
I'VE GOT YOUR BACK! I'M IN THE DON QUIXOTE FAMILY. I ALWAYS PERFORM MY DUTY!!
?!!
UGLBRA-GHABA!!!
BLRGH!!!
GRSHGRSH!!!
....!!
Y-YOU INCOMPE-TENT BUFFOON!!
BFF BFF BFF BFF
GAS GAS
BFF
BFF
WHA--?! YOUR ROCKS CAN'T HURT A MAN MADE OF GAS!!
BFF!!!
I'LL MAKE IT BACK TO DRESSROSA BY MYSELF, IF I HAVE TO!!
LURCH...
GAS
I DON'T THINK SO; THE LAST SHOT WAS...

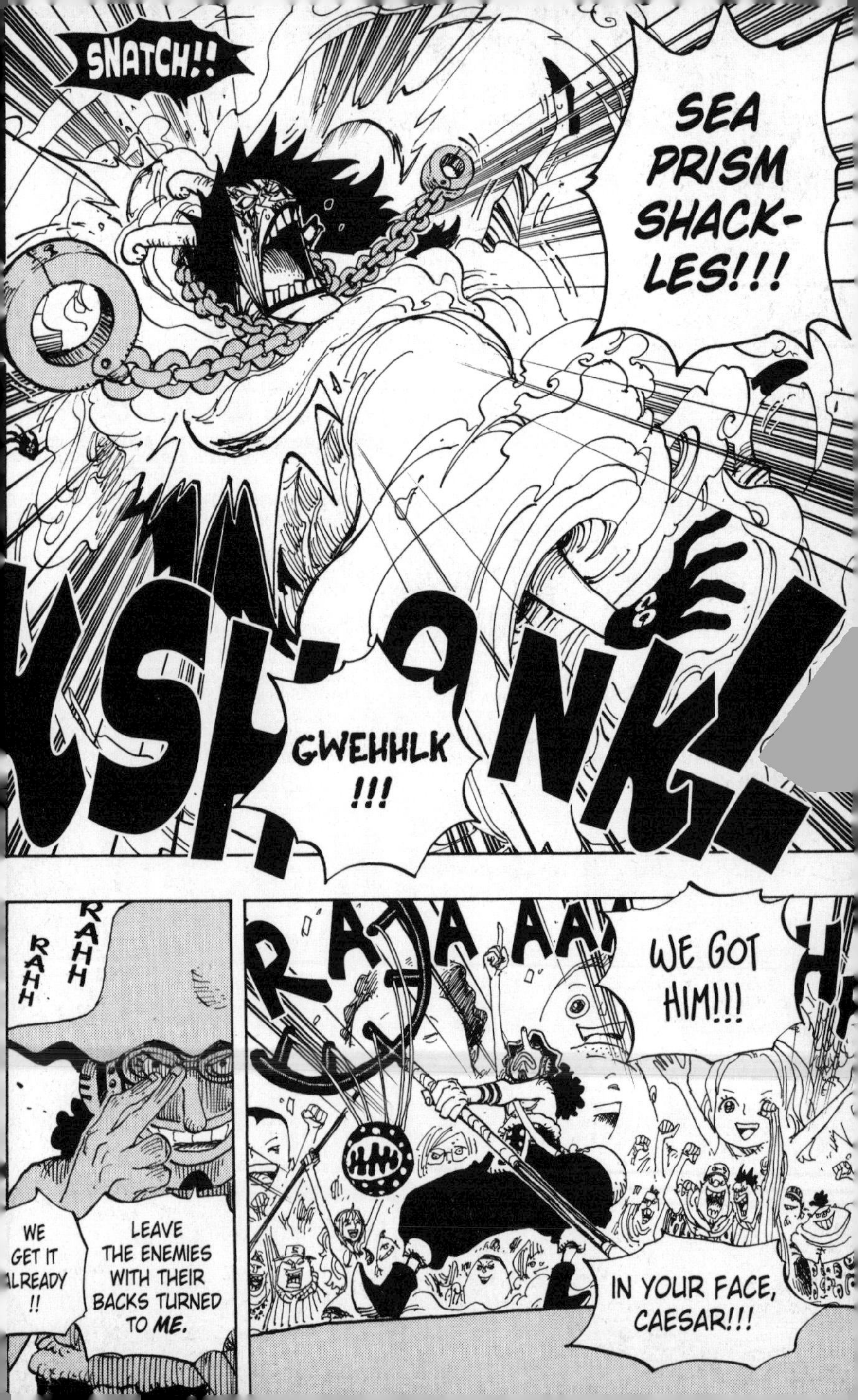
SEA PRISM SHACK-LES!!!
SNATCH!!
KSHANK!!
GWEHHLK !!!
RAAAA
WE GOT HIM!!!
IN YOUR FACE, CAESAR!!!
RAHH RAHH
LEAVE THE ENEMIES WITH THEIR BACKS TURNED TO *ME.*
WE GET IT ALREADY !!

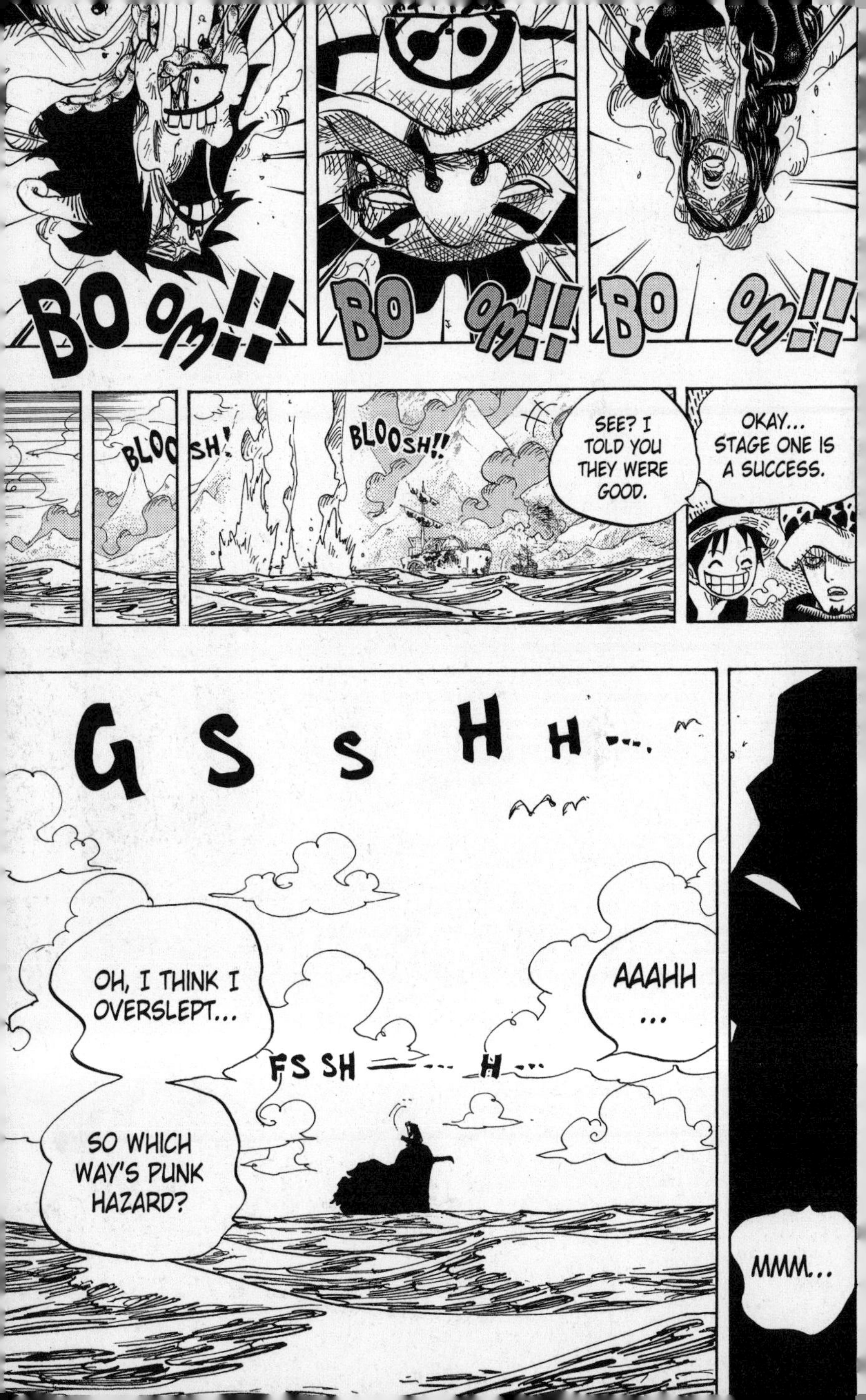
BOOM!!
BOOM!!
BOOM!!
OKAY... STAGE ONE IS A SUCCESS.
SEE? I TOLD YOU THEY WERE GOOD.
BLOOSH!!
BLOOSH!
MMM...
GSSHH...
AAAHH ...
OH, I THINK I OVERSLEPT...
FSSH—...H...
SO WHICH WAY'S PUNK HAZARD?

SBS Question Corner

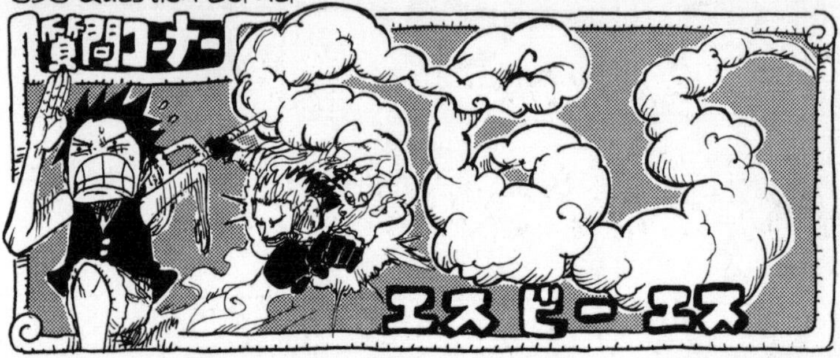
質問コーナー
エスビーエス

(Ponio, Aichi)

Q: In the last panel of the tenth page of Chapter 602 (Volume 61), she says, "Creatures I've never seen before! One, two, three, four..." So that would be Brook, Franky, Chopper, and who?

--Chopper's Friend's Owner

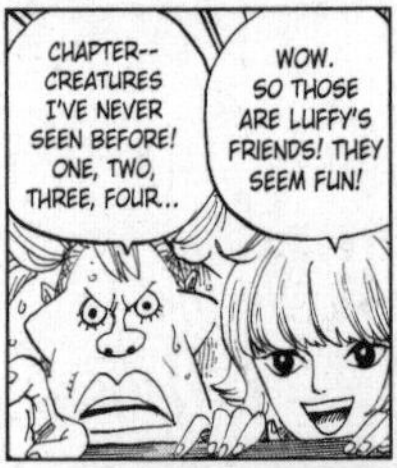
WOW. SO THOSE ARE LUFFY'S FRIENDS! THEY SEEM FUN!
CHAPTER-- CREATURES I'VE NEVER SEEN BEFORE! ONE, TWO, THREE, FOUR...

A: I'm assuming it'sSanji with a bizarre look on his face.

Q: Hello! I'm usually a graphic-novel-only reader, but I heard about how incredible this color chapter cover was, and rushed out to buy the issue of Jump with Chapter 691 (^_^). And I just so happened to spot, on the right edge over Brook's shoulder, among all the younger versions of the Naval officers, what appears to be the same person who was to the right of Ivankov on the page after Whitebeard's order to "back up Luffy with all you've got." Is that really the same person?!! Did he go from the Navy to being a pirate?!!

--Anri

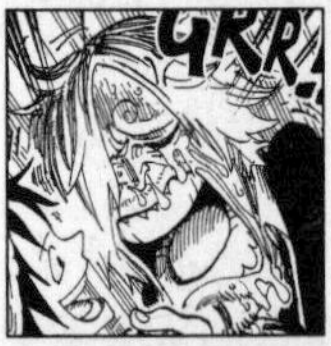
GRR!

A: That's very well spotted. So how does the same face show up in both the Navy and a pirate crew? Well, there was a fellow originally introduced in the book One Piece Green (in Japan) as "Pirate Captain Andre," a member of Whitebeard's fleet. But the people I drew in the Chapter 691 cover illustration are all past versions of Navy officers. The guy with the same face shown here is actually still in the Navy, and his name is Kandre. A few years ago during the Paramount War arc, I'm pretty sure I drew Kandre as well, fighting on the side of the Navy--search for him if you're bored sometime! You see, the twin brothers Andre and Kandre were forced to fight against each other in the big war!!
It's a very boring and pointless story!!
But thanks for spotting them!

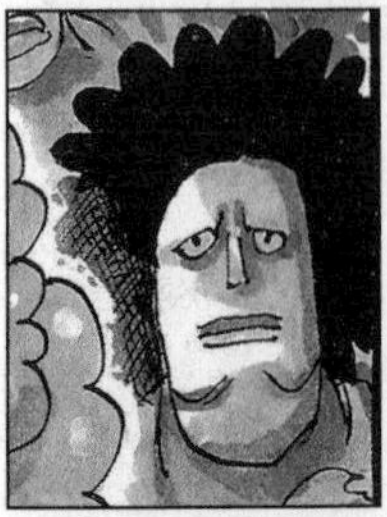

Chapter 691, cover

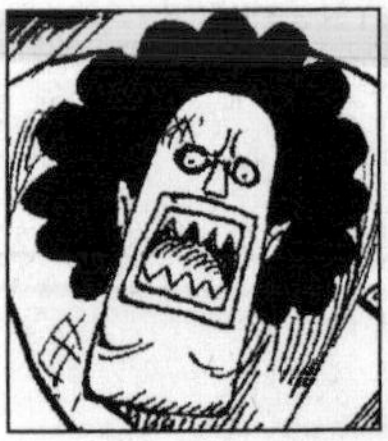

Volume 58, p.138

Chapter 696:

ALIGNMENT OF INTERESTS

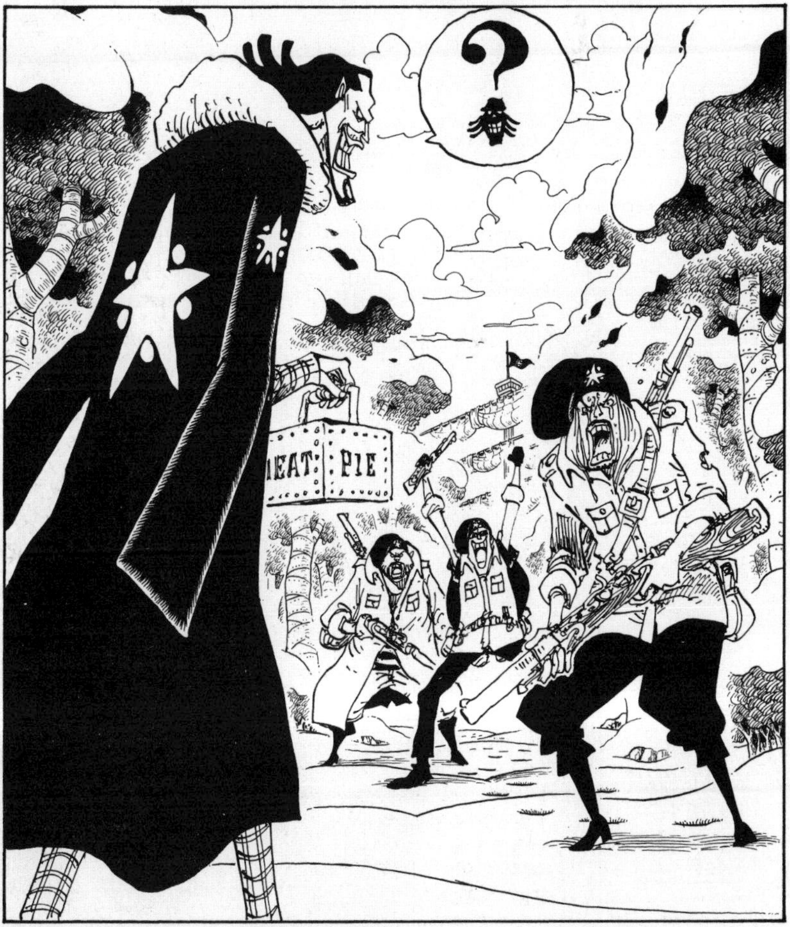
?
MEAT PIE

CARIBOU'S NEW WORLD KEE HEE HEE, VOL. 18: "ON THE ROAD TO PORT, A VOICE CALLS OUT, "CAPTAIN GOBBLE!!""

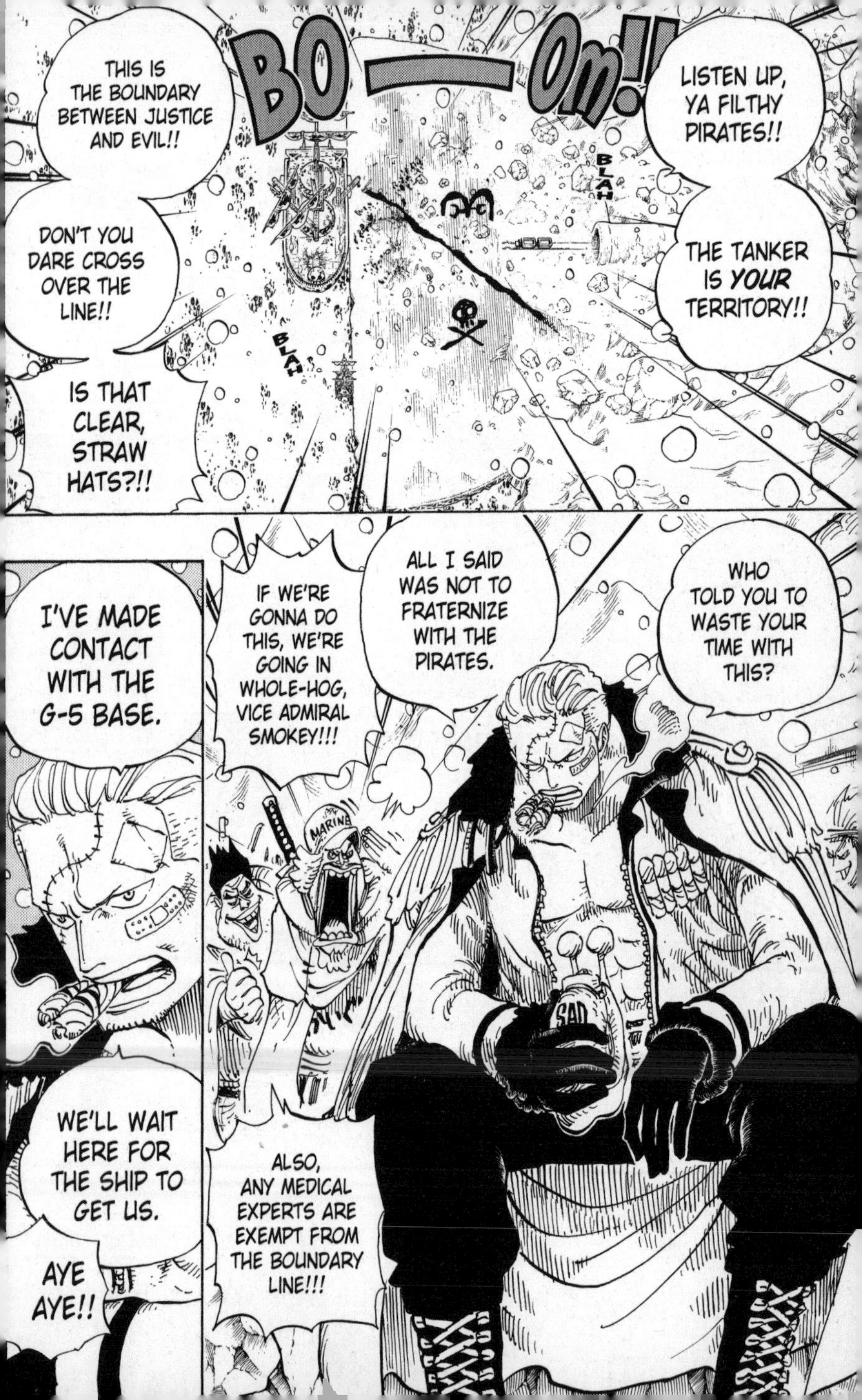
LISTEN UP, YA FILTHY PIRATES!!
THE TANKER IS YOUR TERRITORY!!
BO——Om!!
BLAH
BLAH
THIS IS THE BOUNDARY BETWEEN JUSTICE AND EVIL!!
DON'T YOU DARE CROSS OVER THE LINE!!
IS THAT CLEAR, STRAW HATS?!!
WHO TOLD YOU TO WASTE YOUR TIME WITH THIS?
ALL I SAID WAS NOT TO FRATERNIZE WITH THE PIRATES.
IF WE'RE GONNA DO THIS, WE'RE GOING IN WHOLE-HOG, VICE ADMIRAL SMOKEY!!!
MARINE
SAD
ALSO, ANY MEDICAL EXPERTS ARE EXEMPT FROM THE BOUNDARY LINE!!!
I'VE MADE CONTACT WITH THE G-5 BASE.
WE'LL WAIT HERE FOR THE SHIP TO GET US.
AYE AYE!!

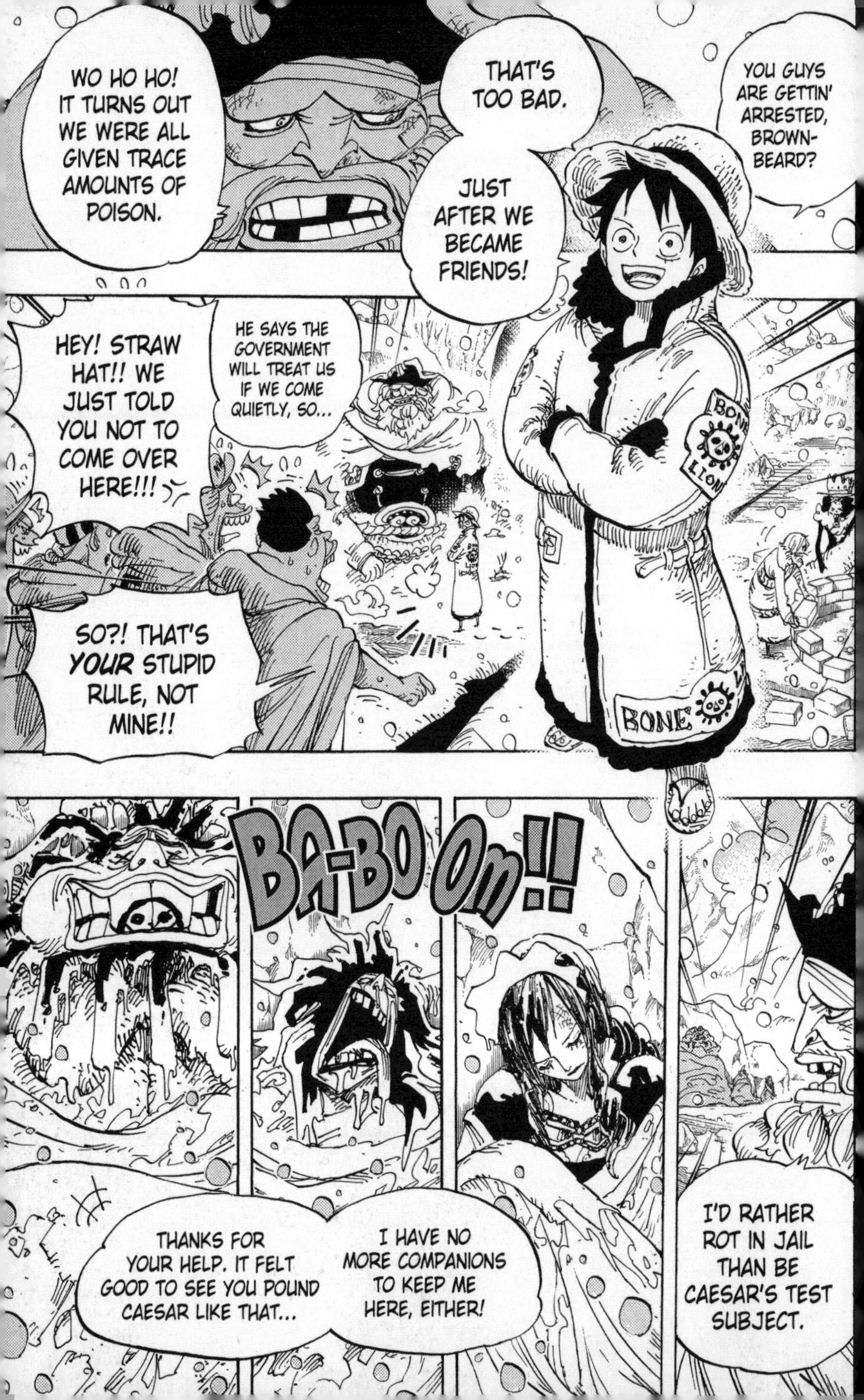
YOU GUYS ARE GETTIN' ARRESTED, BROWN-BEARD?
THAT'S TOO BAD.
JUST AFTER WE BECAME FRIENDS!
WO HO HO! IT TURNS OUT WE WERE ALL GIVEN TRACE AMOUNTS OF POISON.
BONE
LION
BONE
HE SAYS THE GOVERNMENT WILL TREAT US IF WE COME QUIETLY, SO...
HEY! STRAW HAT!! WE JUST TOLD YOU NOT TO COME OVER HERE!!!
SO?! THAT'S *YOUR* STUPID RULE, NOT MINE!!
I'D RATHER ROT IN JAIL THAN BE CAESAR'S TEST SUBJECT.
BA-BOOM!!
I HAVE NO MORE COMPANIONS TO KEEP ME HERE, EITHER!
THANKS FOR YOUR HELP. IT FELT GOOD TO SEE YOU POUND CAESAR LIKE THAT...

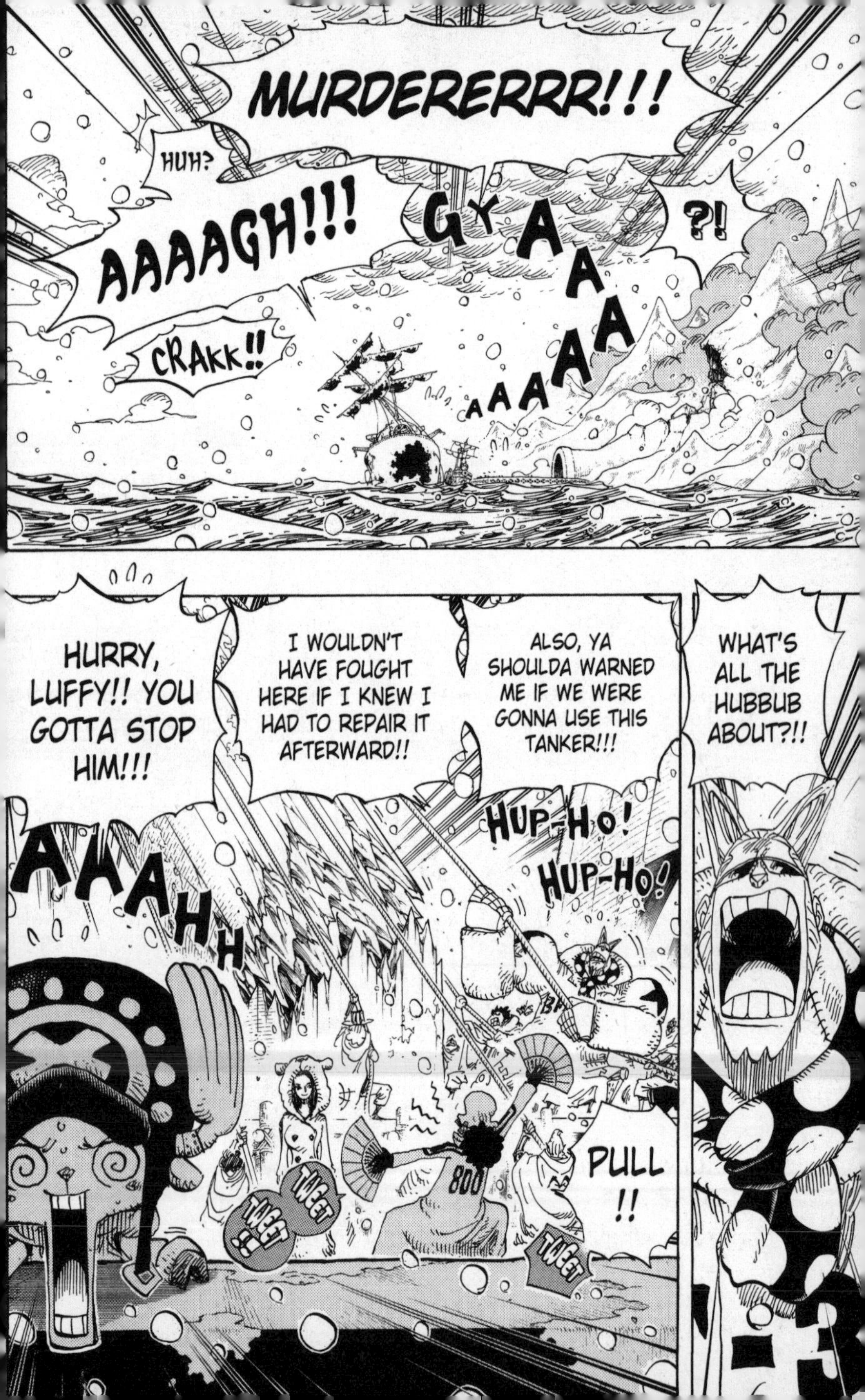
MURDERERRR!!!
?!
GYAAAAAAA
HUH?
AAAAGH!!!
CRAKK!!
WHAT'S ALL THE HUBBUB ABOUT?!!
ALSO, YA SHOULDA WARNED ME IF WE WERE GONNA USE THIS TANKER!!!
I WOULDN'T HAVE FOUGHT HERE IF I KNEW I HAD TO REPAIR IT AFTERWARD!!
HURRY, LUFFY!! YOU GOTTA STOP HIM!!!
HUP-HO!
HUP-HO!
AAAHHH
PULL !!
800
TWEET
TWEET
TWEET

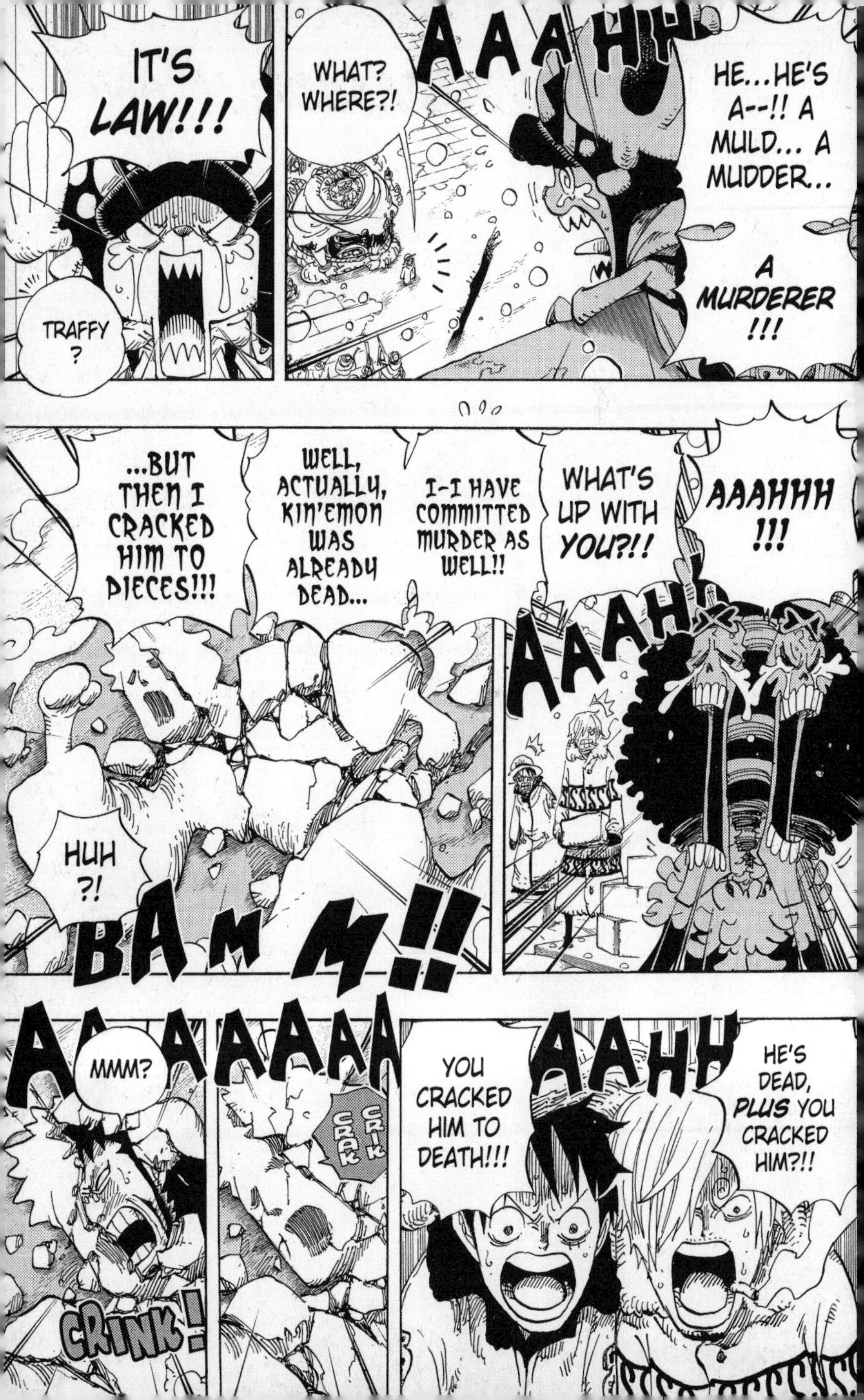
AAAHH
HE...HE'S A--!! A MULD... A MUDDER...
A MURDERER!!!
WHAT? WHERE?!
IT'S LAW!!!
TRAFFY?
AAAHHH!!!
WHAT'S UP WITH YOU?!!
AAAH
I-I HAVE COMMITTED MURDER AS WELL!!
WELL, ACTUALLY, KIN'EMON WAS ALREADY DEAD...
...BUT THEN I CRACKED HIM TO PIECES!!!
HUH?!
BAMM!!
AAHH
HE'S DEAD, PLUS YOU CRACKED HIM?!!
YOU CRACKED HIM TO DEATH!!!
CRIK CRAK
AAAAA
AA
MMM?
CRINK!

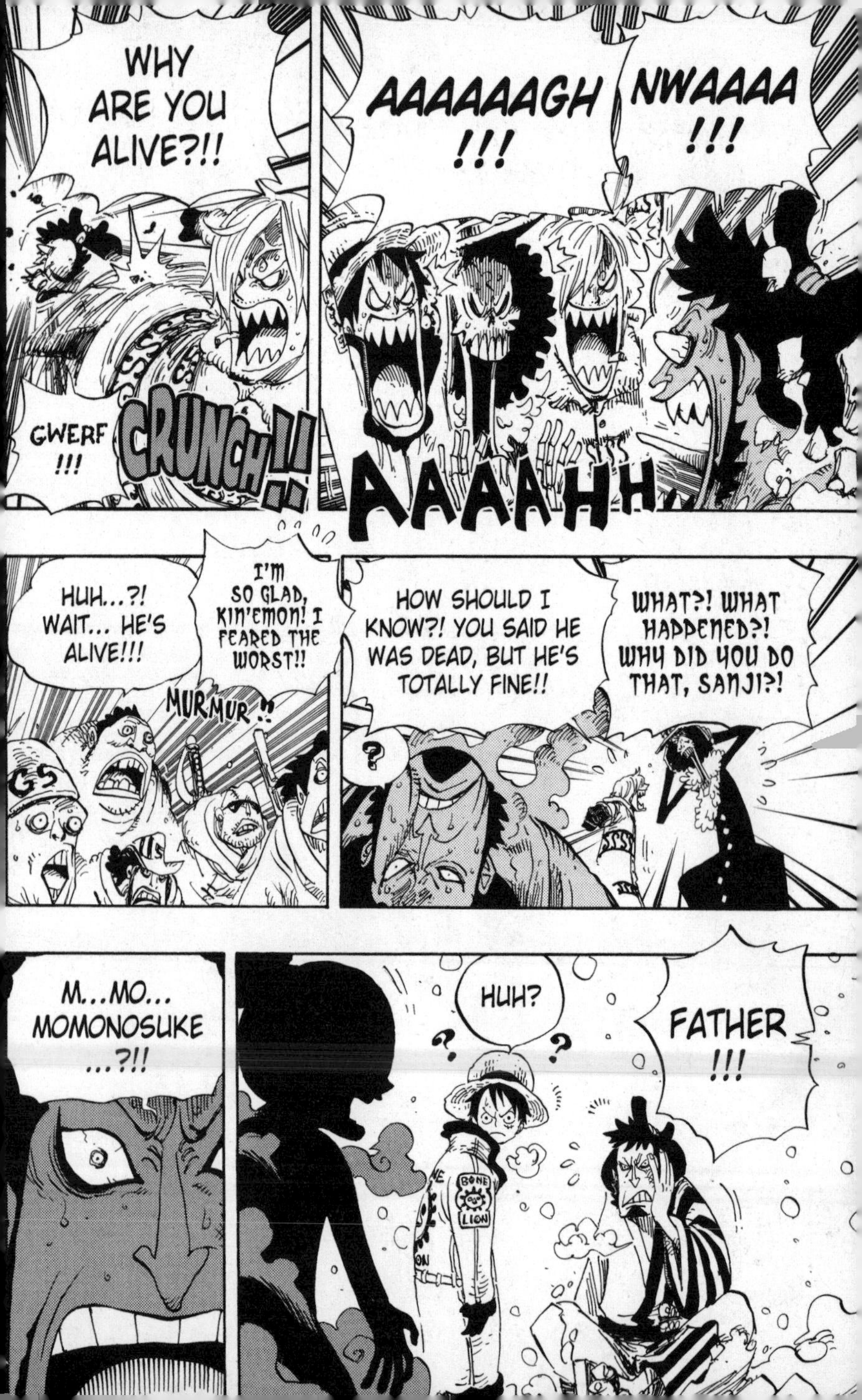
NWAAAA !!!
AAAAAAGH !!!
AAAAHH
WHY ARE YOU ALIVE?!!
CRUNCH!!!
GWERF !!!
WHAT?! WHAT HAPPENED?! WHY DID YOU DO THAT, SANJI?!
HOW SHOULD I KNOW?! YOU SAID HE WAS DEAD, BUT HE'S TOTALLY FINE!!
?
I'M SO GLAD, KIN'EMON! I FEARED THE WORST!!
HUH...?! WAIT... HE'S ALIVE!!!
MURMUR!!
FATHER !!!
HUH?
? ?
M...MO... MOMONOSUKE ...?!!

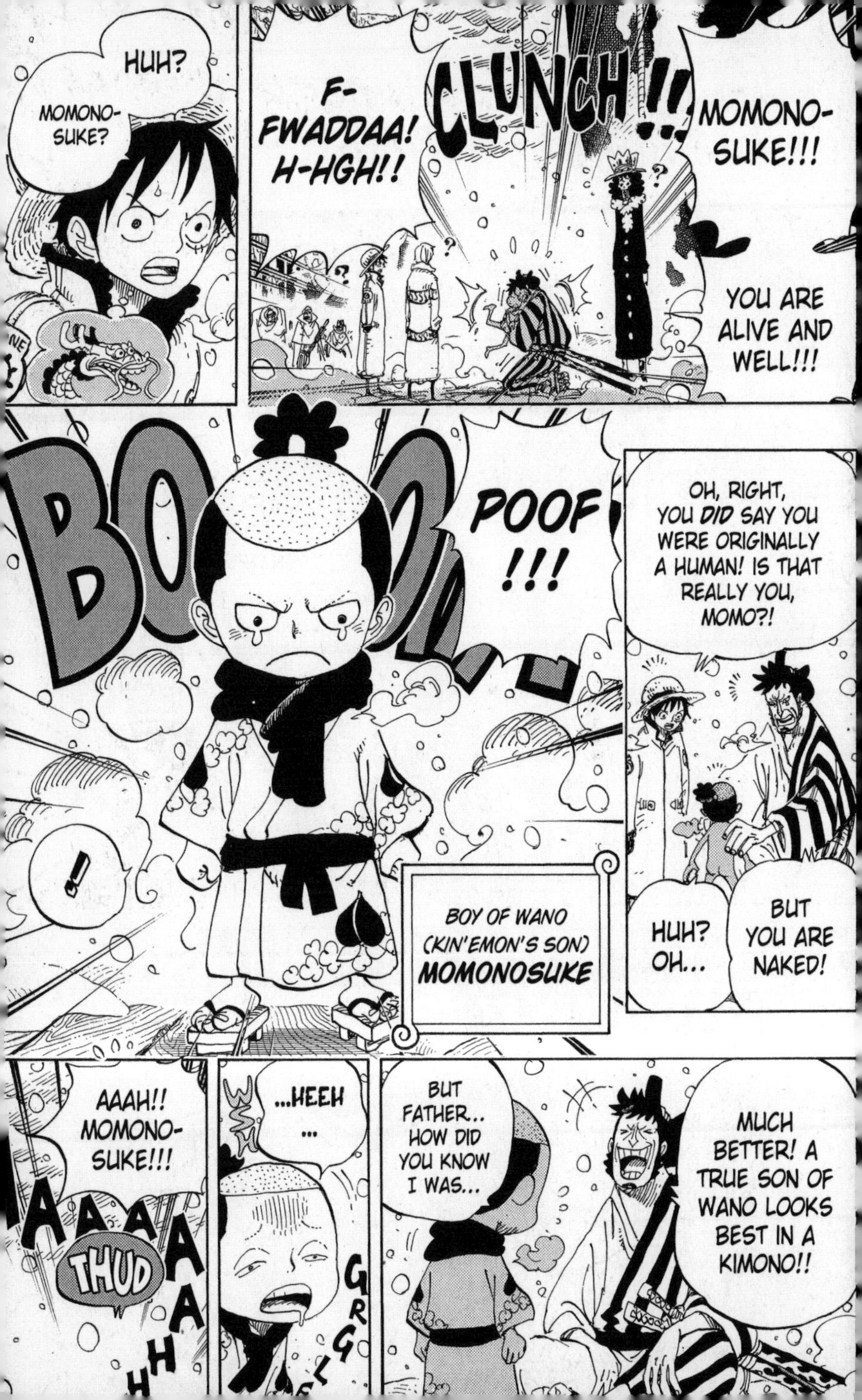
MOMONO-SUKE!!!
CLUNCH!!!
F-FWADDAA! H-HGH!!
YOU ARE ALIVE AND WELL!!!
HUH?
MOMONO-SUKE?
OH, RIGHT, YOU DID SAY YOU WERE ORIGINALLY A HUMAN! IS THAT REALLY YOU, MOMO?!
BUT YOU ARE NAKED!
HUH? OH...
POOF!!!
!
BOY OF WANO (KIN'EMON'S SON) MOMONOSUKE
MUCH BETTER! A TRUE SON OF WANO LOOKS BEST IN A KIMONO!!
BUT FATHER... HOW DID YOU KNOW I WAS...
WSH
...HEEH ...
GRGL
AAAH!! MOMONO-SUKE!!!
AAAAAHHH
THUD

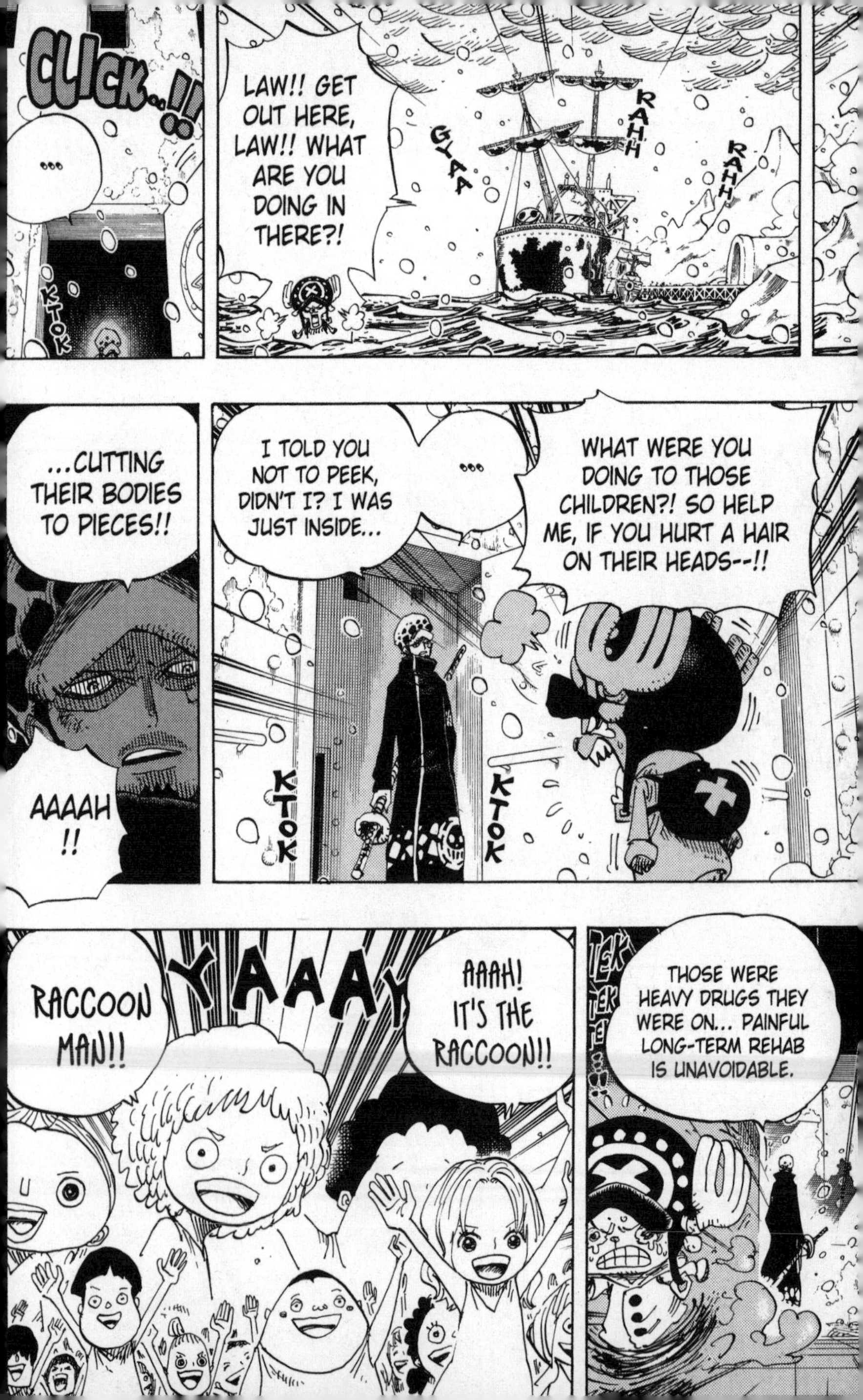
LAW!! GET OUT HERE, LAW!! WHAT ARE YOU DOING IN THERE?!
RAHHH
RAHH
GYAA
CLICK..!!
...
KTOK
WHAT WERE YOU DOING TO THOSE CHILDREN?! SO HELP ME, IF YOU HURT A HAIR ON THEIR HEADS--!!
...
I TOLD YOU NOT TO PEEK, DIDN'T I? I WAS JUST INSIDE...
KTOK
KTOK
...CUTTING THEIR BODIES TO PIECES!!
AAAAH !!
TEK
TEK
THOSE WERE HEAVY DRUGS THEY WERE ON... PAINFUL LONG-TERM REHAB IS UNAVOIDABLE.
AAAH! IT'S THE RACCOON!!
YAAAY
RACCOON MAN!!

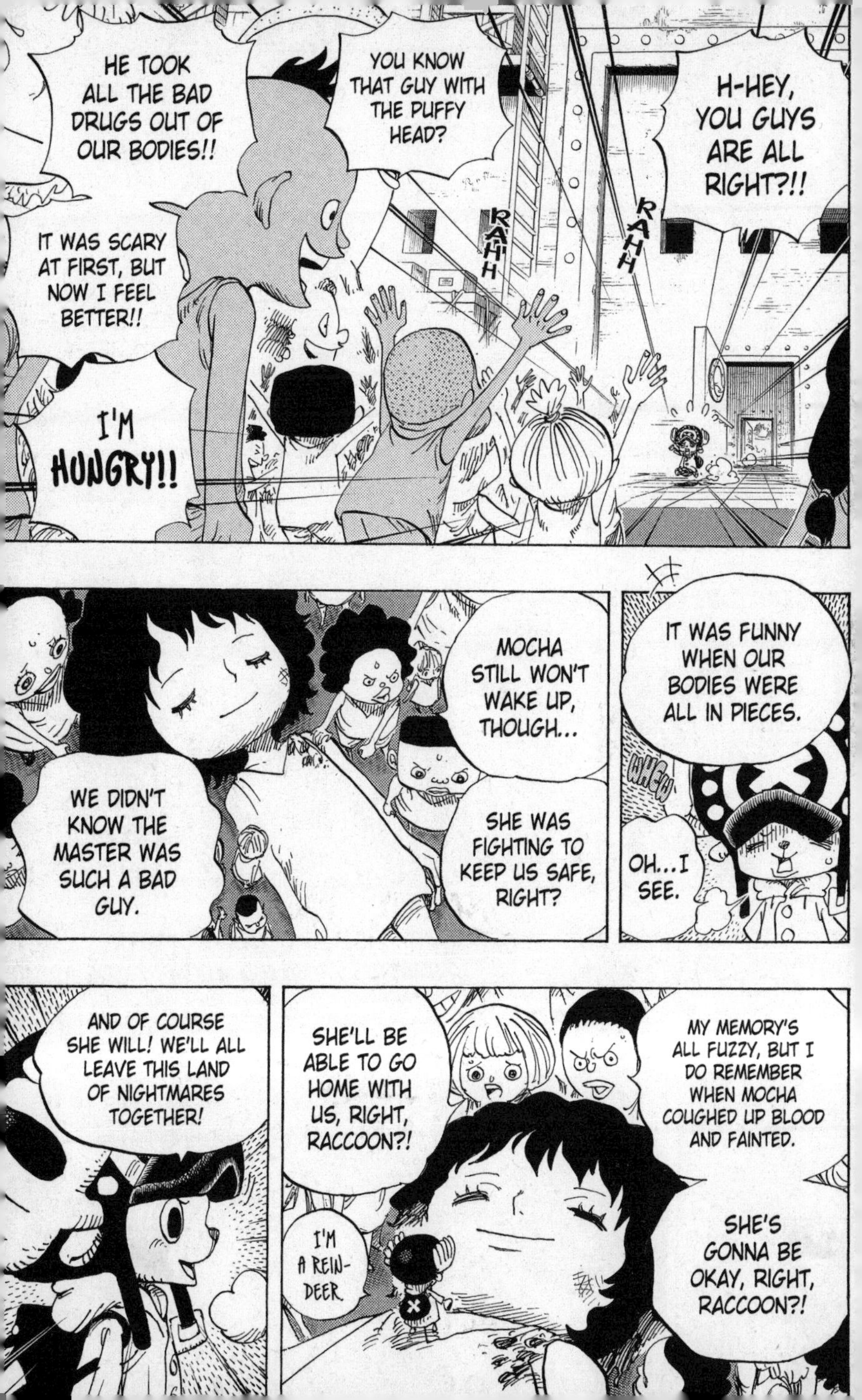
H-HEY, YOU GUYS ARE ALL RIGHT?!!
RAHH
RAHH
YOU KNOW THAT GUY WITH THE PUFFY HEAD?
HE TOOK ALL THE BAD DRUGS OUT OF OUR BODIES!!
IT WAS SCARY AT FIRST, BUT NOW I FEEL BETTER!!
I'M HUNGRY!!
IT WAS FUNNY WHEN OUR BODIES WERE ALL IN PIECES.
OH...I SEE.
MOCHA STILL WON'T WAKE UP, THOUGH...
SHE WAS FIGHTING TO KEEP US SAFE, RIGHT?
WE DIDN'T KNOW THE MASTER WAS SUCH A BAD GUY.
MY MEMORY'S ALL FUZZY, BUT I DO REMEMBER WHEN MOCHA COUGHED UP BLOOD AND FAINTED.
SHE'LL BE ABLE TO GO HOME WITH US, RIGHT, RACCOON?!
SHE'S GONNA BE OKAY, RIGHT, RACCOON?!
I'M A REIN-DEER.
AND OF COURSE SHE WILL! WE'LL ALL LEAVE THIS LAND OF NIGHTMARES TOGETHER!

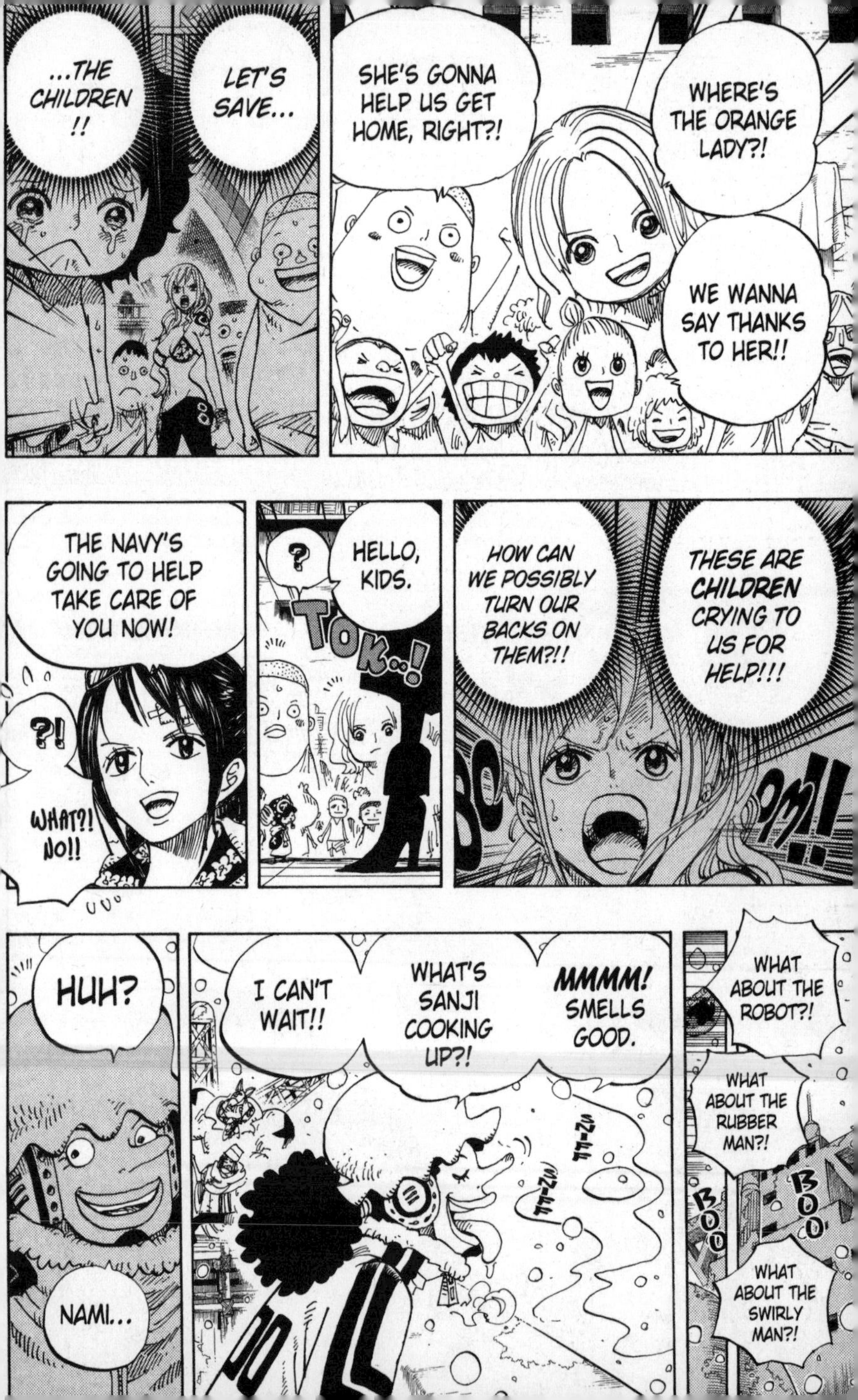
WHERE'S THE ORANGE LADY?!
SHE'S GONNA HELP US GET HOME, RIGHT?!
WE WANNA SAY THANKS TO HER!!
LET'S SAVE...
...THE CHILDREN !!
THESE ARE CHILDREN CRYING TO US FOR HELP!!!
HOW CAN WE POSSIBLY TURN OUR BACKS ON THEM?!!
HELLO, KIDS.
?
TOK..!
THE NAVY'S GOING TO HELP TAKE CARE OF YOU NOW!
?!
WHAT?! NO!!
WHAT ABOUT THE ROBOT?!
WHAT ABOUT THE RUBBER MAN?!
BOO
BOO
WHAT ABOUT THE SWIRLY MAN?!
MMMM! SMELLS GOOD.
WHAT'S SANJI COOKING UP?!
I CAN'T WAIT!!
SNIFF
SNIFF
HUH?
NAMI...

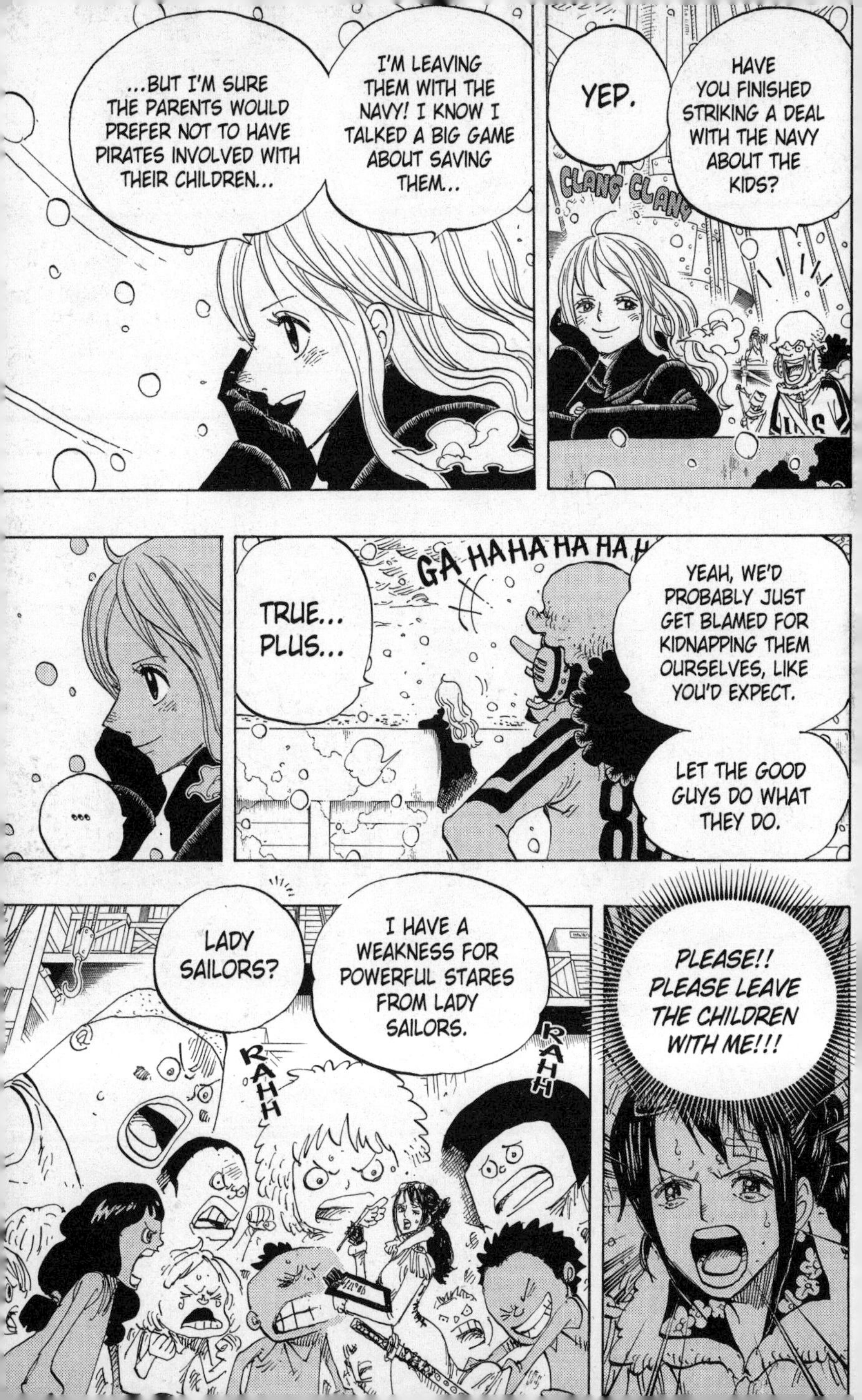
HAVE YOU FINISHED STRIKING A DEAL WITH THE NAVY ABOUT THE KIDS?
YEP.
CLANG CLANG
I'M LEAVING THEM WITH THE NAVY! I KNOW I TALKED A BIG GAME ABOUT SAVING THEM...
...BUT I'M SURE THE PARENTS WOULD PREFER NOT TO HAVE PIRATES INVOLVED WITH THEIR CHILDREN...
GAHAHAHAHAHA
YEAH, WE'D PROBABLY JUST GET BLAMED FOR KIDNAPPING THEM OURSELVES, LIKE YOU'D EXPECT.
LET THE GOOD GUYS DO WHAT THEY DO.
TRUE... PLUS...
...
PLEASE!! PLEASE LEAVE THE CHILDREN WITH ME!!!
I HAVE A WEAKNESS FOR POWERFUL STARES FROM LADY SAILORS.
LADY SAILORS?
RAHH
RAHH

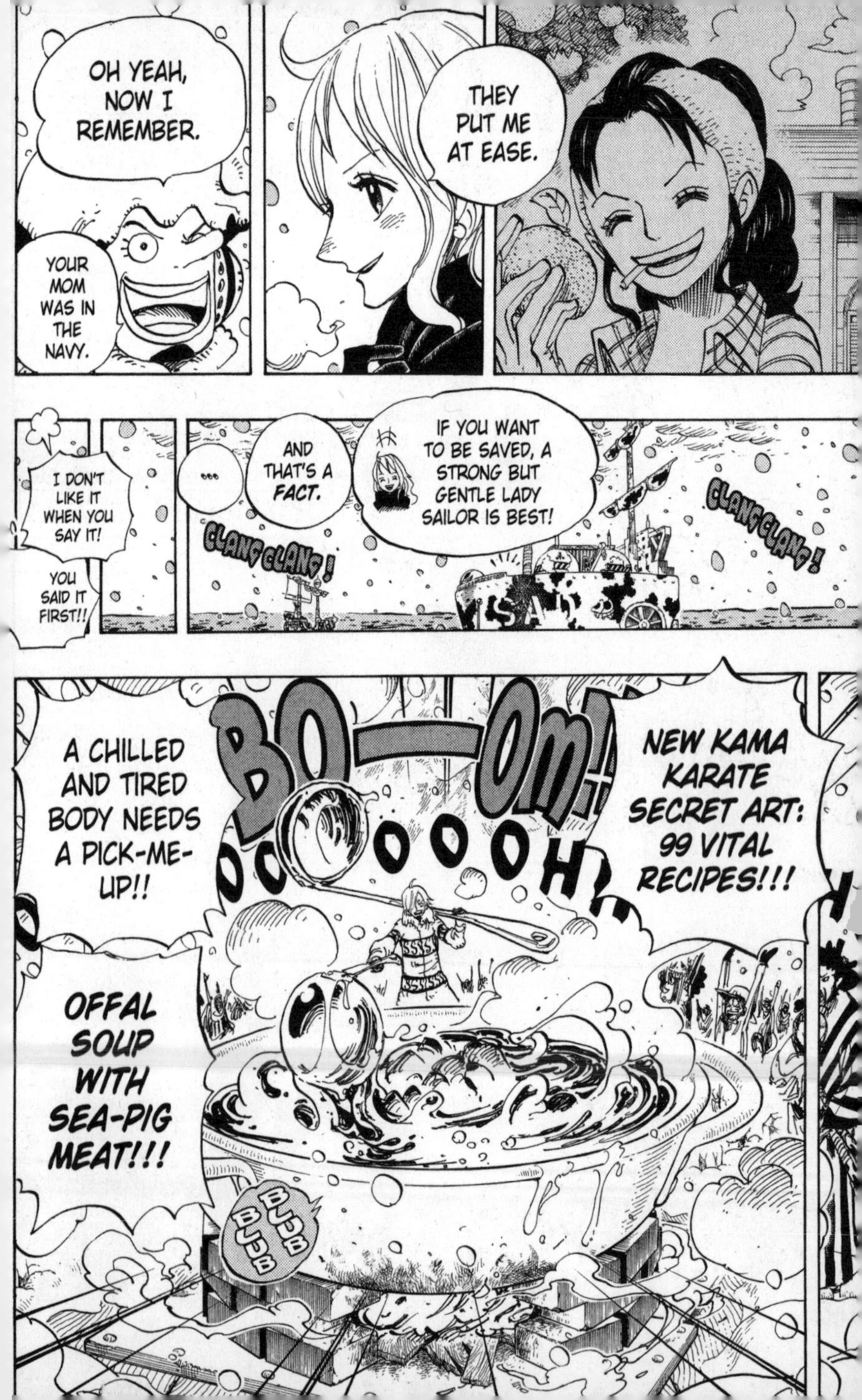
THEY PUT ME AT EASE.
OH YEAH, NOW I REMEMBER.
YOUR MOM WAS IN THE NAVY.
IF YOU WANT TO BE SAVED, A STRONG BUT GENTLE LADY SAILOR IS BEST!
CLANG CLANG!
AND THAT'S A FACT.
CLANG CLANG!
...
I DON'T LIKE IT WHEN YOU SAY IT!
YOU SAID IT FIRST!!
NEW KAMA KARATE SECRET ART: 99 VITAL RECIPES!!!
BO—OM!
OOOOOH!
A CHILLED AND TIRED BODY NEEDS A PICK-ME-UP!!
OFFAL SOUP WITH SEA-PIG MEAT!!!
BLUB BLUB

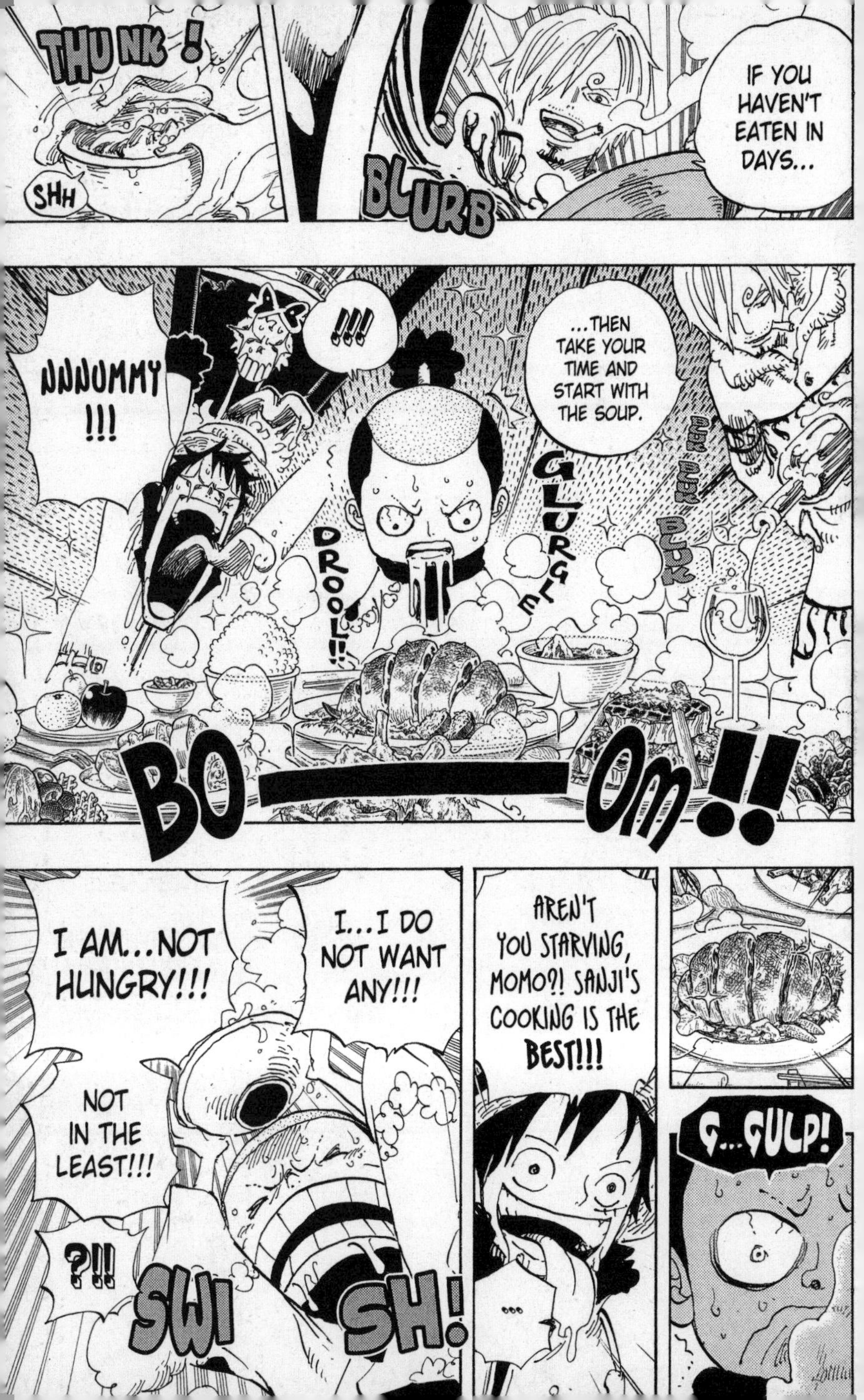

IF YOU HAVEN'T EATEN IN DAYS...
BLURB
THUNK!
SHH
...THEN TAKE YOUR TIME AND START WITH THE SOUP.
BLUK BLUK
GLURGLE
!!!
NNNUMMY!!!
DROOL!!
BO—OM!!
G...GULP!
AREN'T YOU STARVING, MOMO?! SANJI'S COOKING IS THE BEST!!!
...
I...I DO NOT WANT ANY!!!
I AM...NOT HUNGRY!!!
NOT IN THE LEAST!!!
?!!
SWISH!

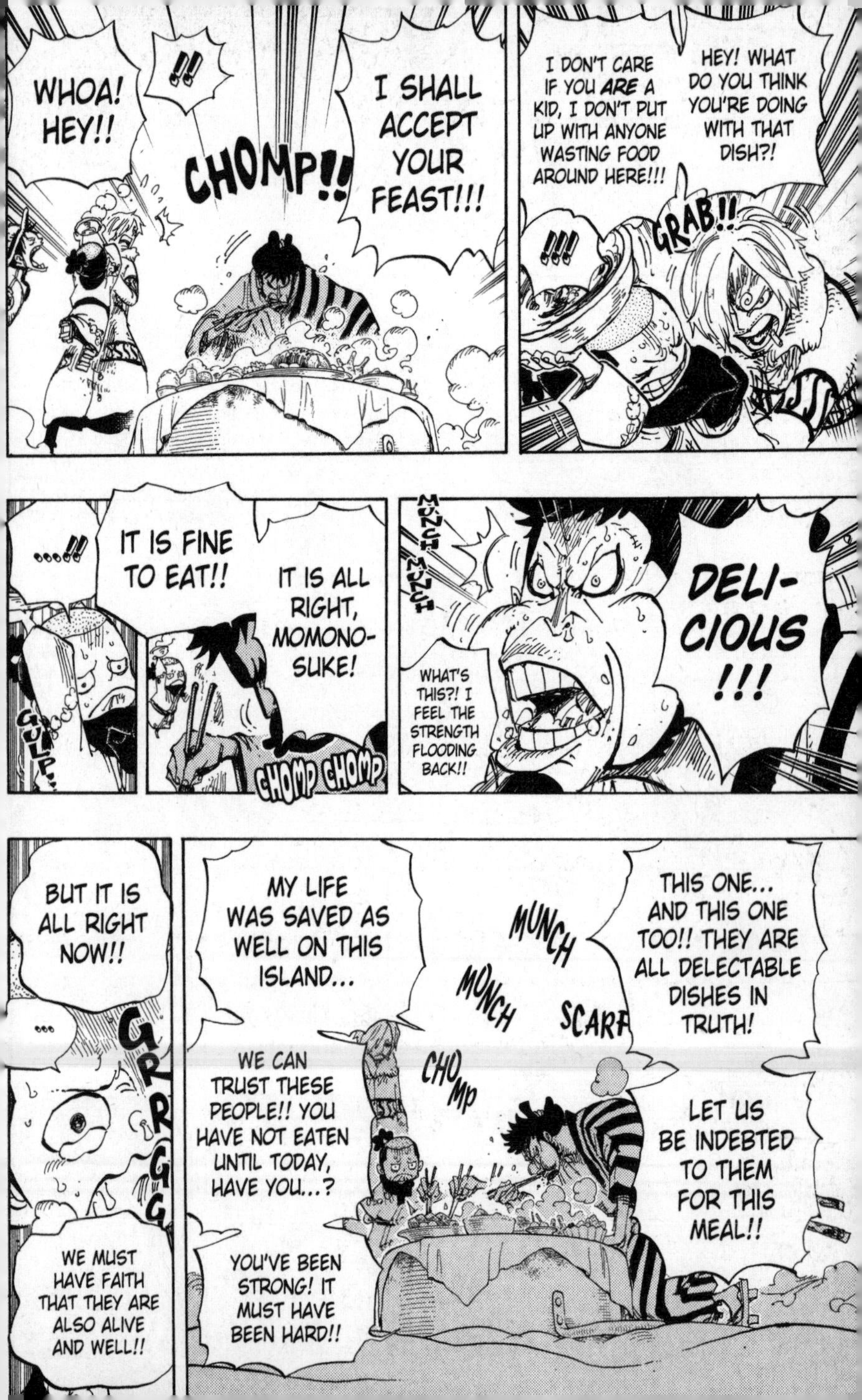
HEY! WHAT DO YOU THINK YOU'RE DOING WITH THAT DISH?!
I DON'T CARE IF YOU *ARE* A KID, I DON'T PUT UP WITH ANYONE WASTING FOOD AROUND HERE!!!
GRAB!!
!!!
I SHALL ACCEPT YOUR FEAST!!!
!!
CHOMP!!
WHOA! HEY!!
DELICIOUS!!!
MUNCH MUNCH
WHAT'S THIS?! I FEEL THE STRENGTH FLOODING BACK!!
IT IS FINE TO EAT!!
IT IS ALL RIGHT, MOMONOSUKE!
CHOMP CHOMP
....!!
GULP...
THIS ONE... AND THIS ONE TOO!! THEY ARE ALL DELECTABLE DISHES IN TRUTH!
MUNCH
MUNCH
SCARF
MY LIFE WAS SAVED AS WELL ON THIS ISLAND...
CHOMP
LET US BE INDEBTED TO THEM FOR THIS MEAL!!
WE CAN TRUST THESE PEOPLE!! YOU HAVE NOT EATEN UNTIL TODAY, HAVE YOU...?
YOU'VE BEEN STRONG! IT MUST HAVE BEEN HARD!!
BUT IT IS ALL RIGHT NOW!!
...
GRRGG
WE MUST HAVE FAITH THAT THEY ARE ALSO ALIVE AND WELL!!

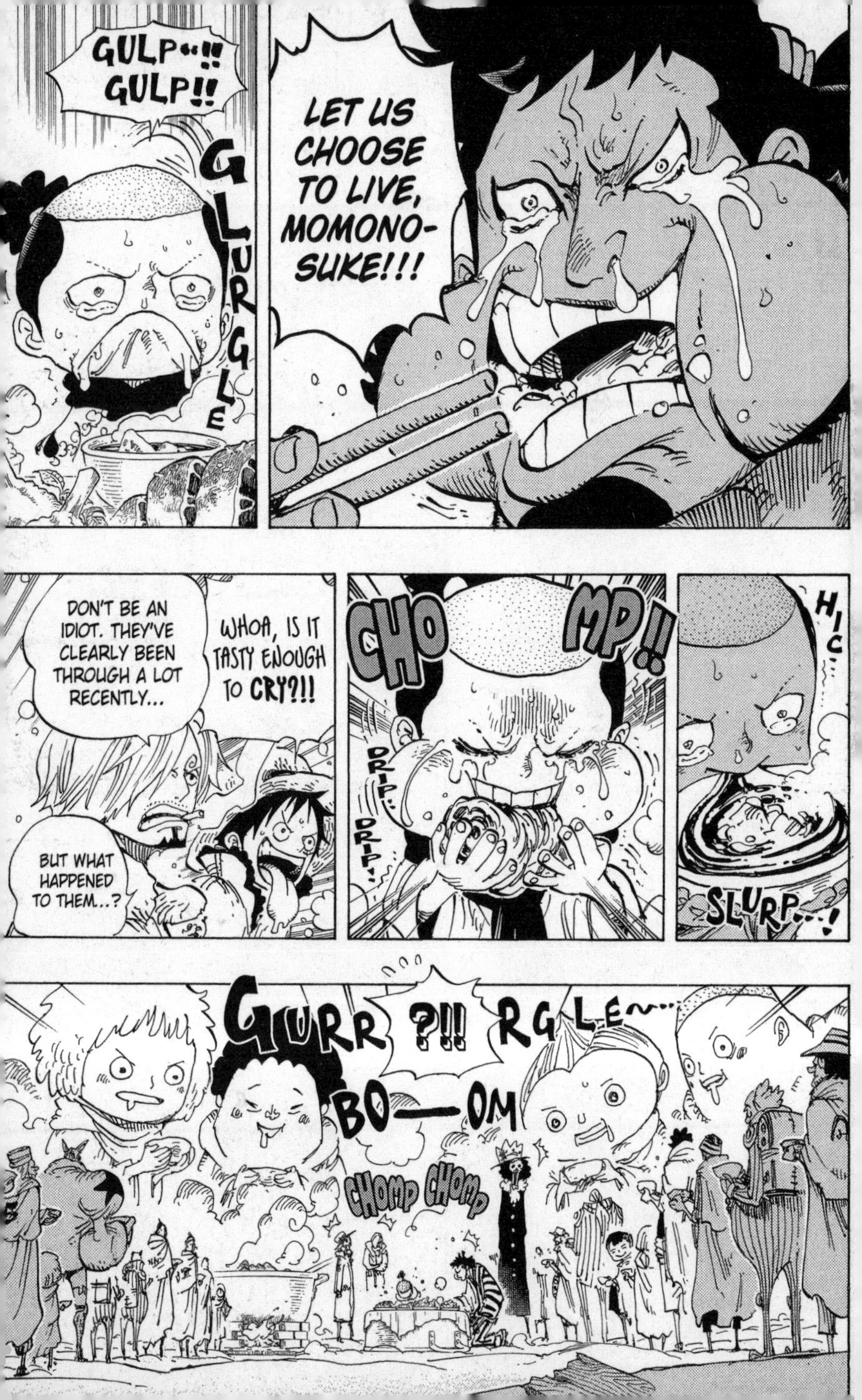
LET US CHOOSE TO LIVE, MOMONOSUKE!!!
GULP...!! GULP!!
GLURGLE
HIC...
SLURP...!
CHOMP!!
DRIP... DRIP...
WHOA, IS IT TASTY ENOUGH TO CRY?!!
DON'T BE AN IDIOT. THEY'VE CLEARLY BEEN THROUGH A LOT RECENTLY...
BUT WHAT HAPPENED TO THEM...?
?!!
GURRRGLE~...
BO—OM
CHOMP CHOMP

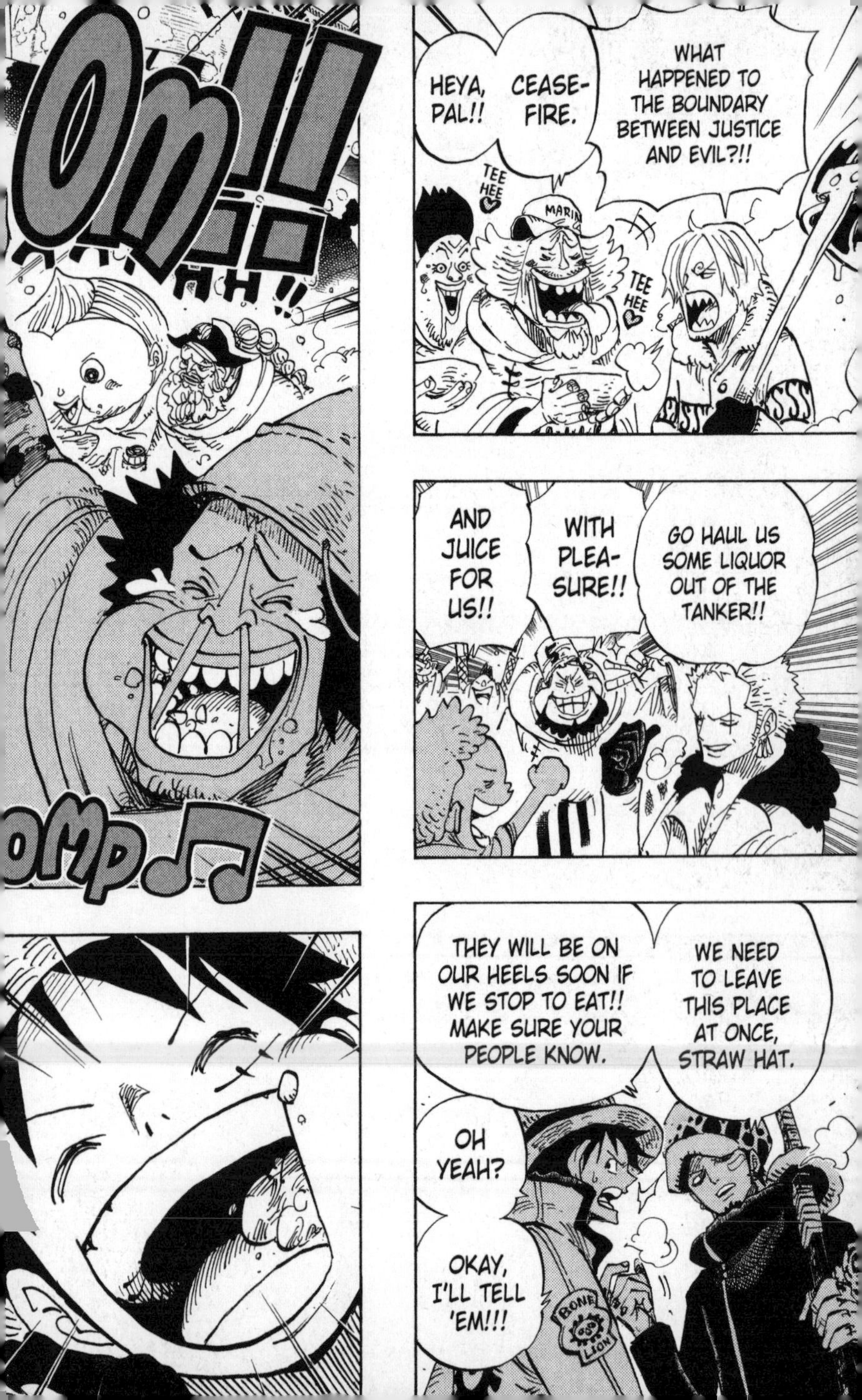
WHAT HAPPENED TO THE BOUNDARY BETWEEN JUSTICE AND EVIL?!!
CEASE-FIRE.
HEYA, PAL!!
TEE HEE
TEE HEE
GO HAUL US SOME LIQUOR OUT OF THE TANKER!!
WITH PLEA-SURE!!
AND JUICE FOR US!!
OM!!
OMP
WE NEED TO LEAVE THIS PLACE AT ONCE, STRAW HAT.
THEY WILL BE ON OUR HEELS SOON IF WE STOP TO EAT!! MAKE SURE YOUR PEOPLE KNOW.
OH YEAH?
OKAY, I'LL TELL 'EM!!!

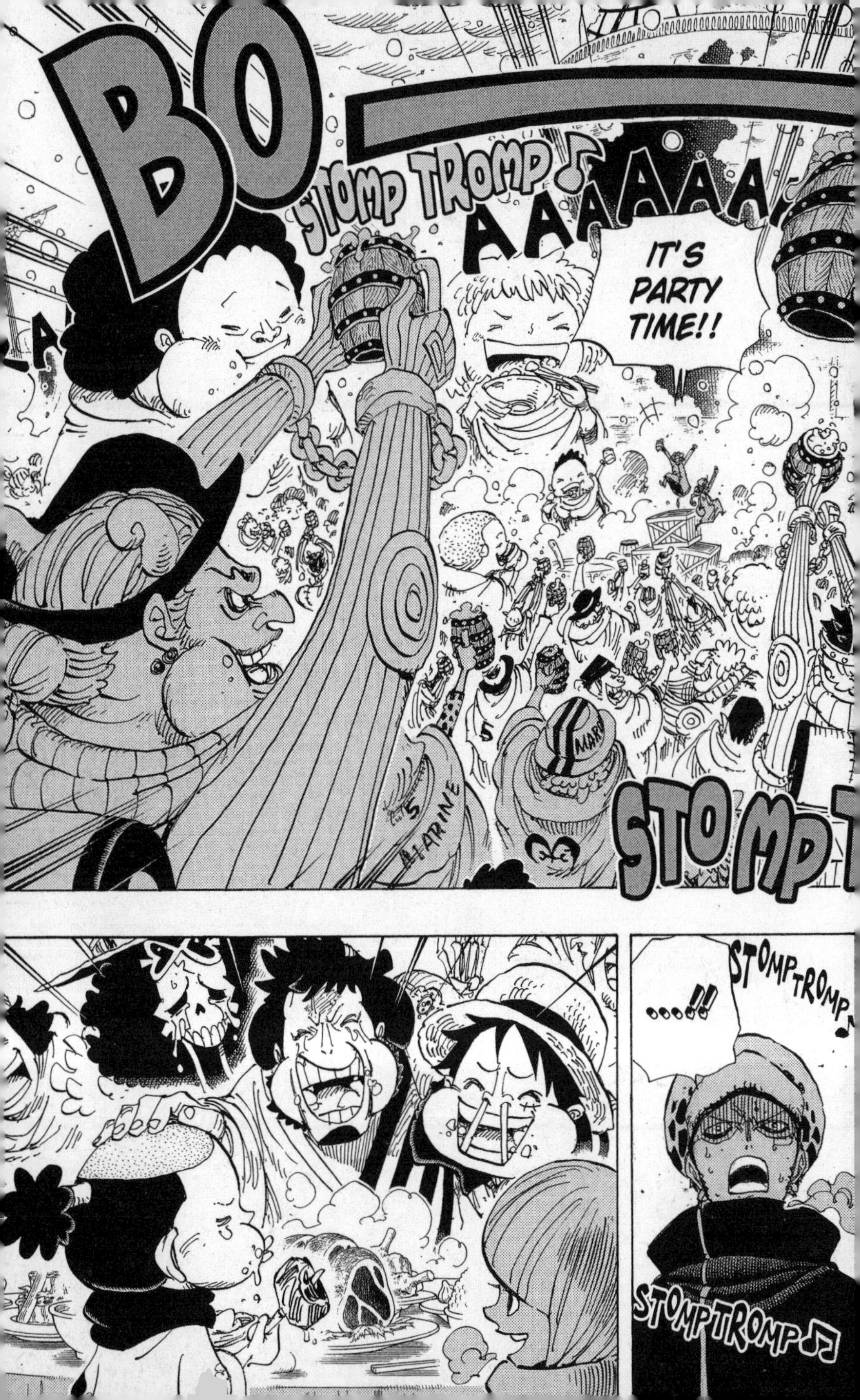
IT'S PARTY TIME!!
BO———AAAAAA
STOMP TROMP♪
STOMP T
STOMPTROMP♪
...!!
STOMPTROMP♫

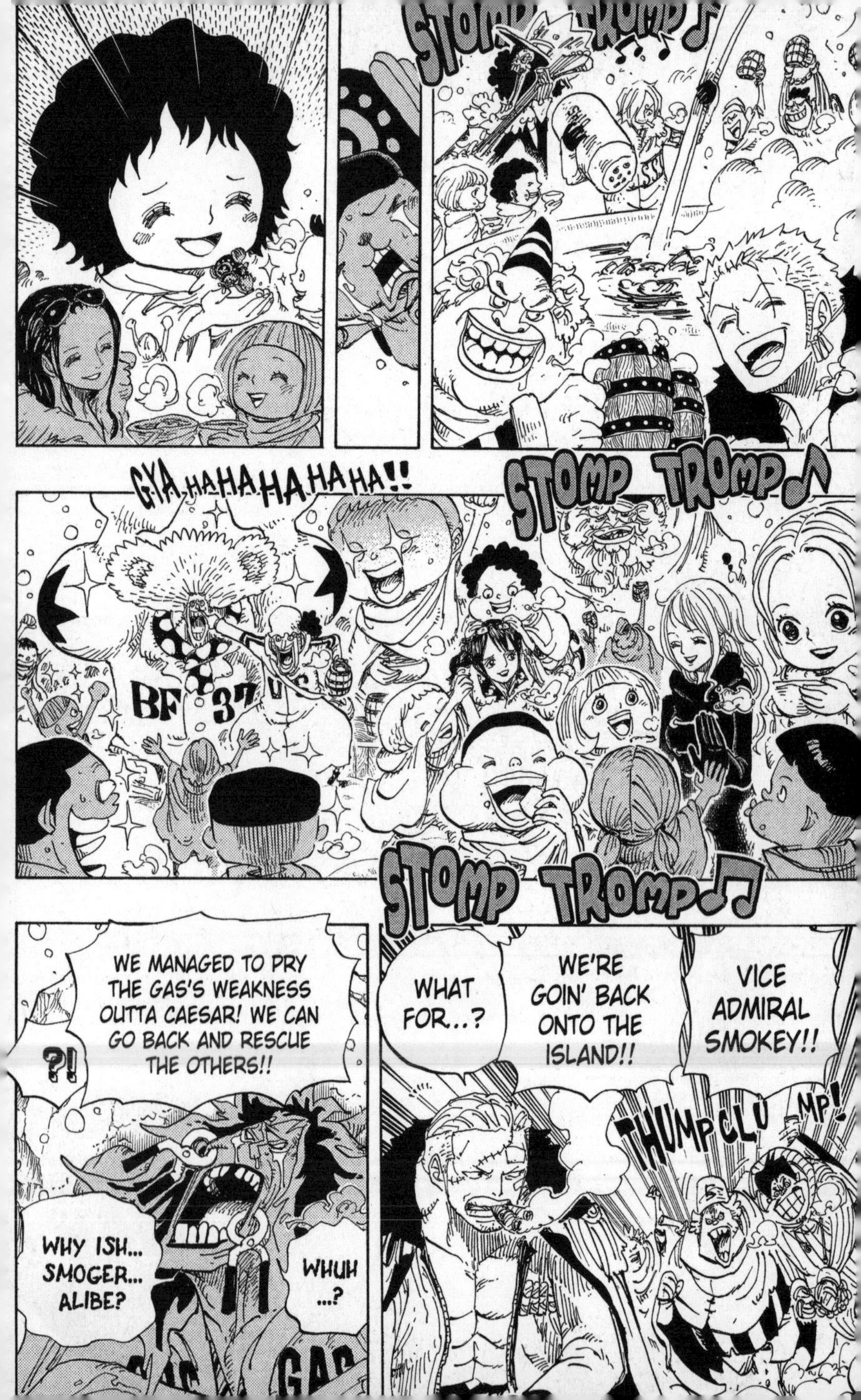
STOM TROMP♪
GYAHAHAHAHAHAHA!!
STOMP TROMP♪
STOMP TROMP♪♫
VICE ADMIRAL SMOKEY!!
WE'RE GOIN' BACK ONTO THE ISLAND!!
WHAT FOR...?
THUMP CLUMP!
WE MANAGED TO PRY THE GAS'S WEAKNESS OUTTA CAESAR! WE CAN GO BACK AND RESCUE THE OTHERS!!
?!
WHY ISH... SMOGER... ALIBE?
WHUH ...?

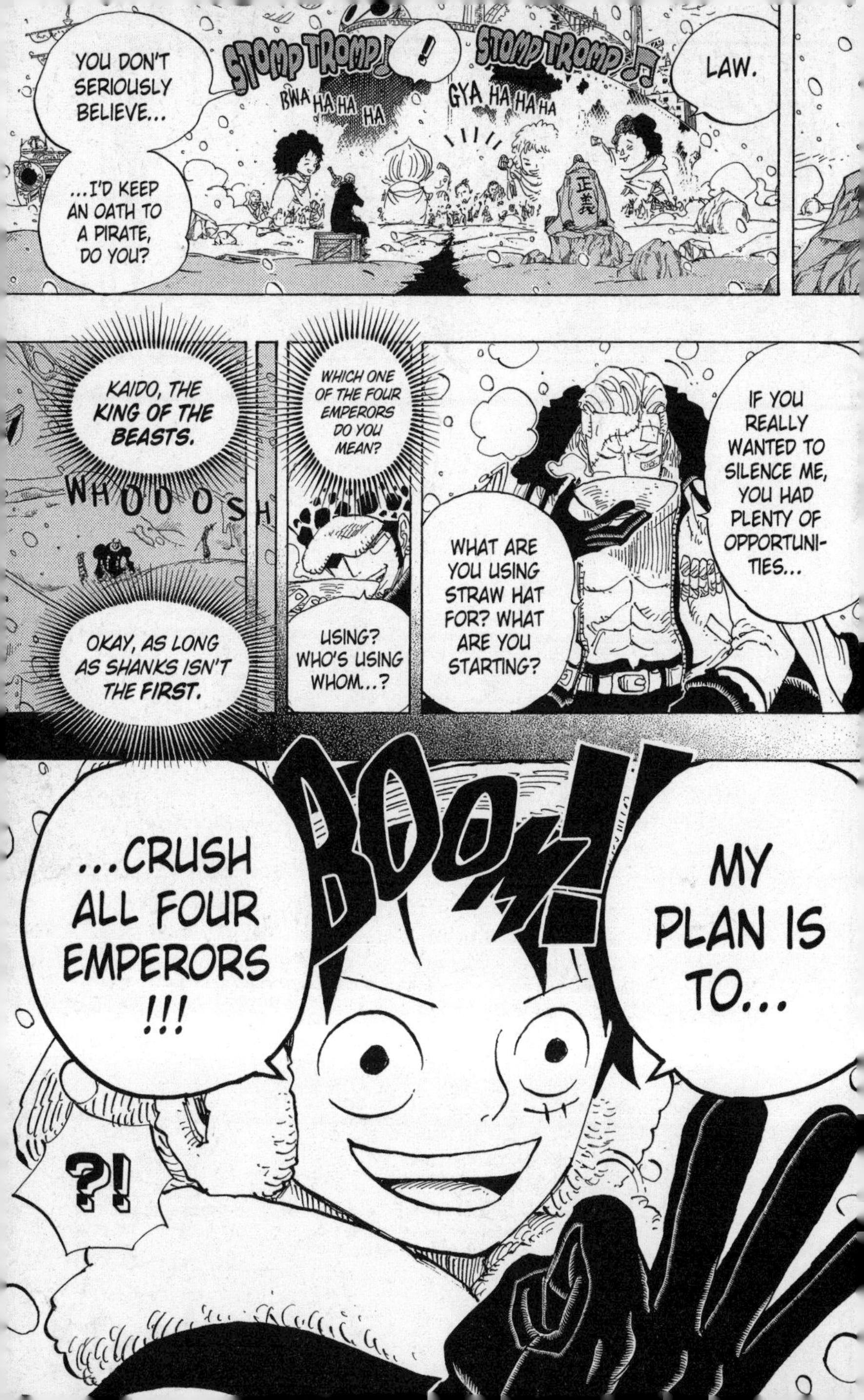
LAW.
STOMP TROMP♫
GYA HA HA HA
!
STOMP TROMP♫
BWA HA HA HA
YOU DON'T SERIOUSLY BELIEVE...
...I'D KEEP AN OATH TO A PIRATE, DO YOU?
IF YOU REALLY WANTED TO SILENCE ME, YOU HAD PLENTY OF OPPORTUNITIES...
WHAT ARE YOU USING STRAW HAT FOR? WHAT ARE YOU STARTING?
WHICH ONE OF THE FOUR EMPERORS DO YOU MEAN?
USING? WHO'S USING WHOM...?
KAIDO, THE KING OF THE BEASTS.
WHOOOSH
OKAY, AS LONG AS SHANKS ISN'T THE FIRST.
MY PLAN IS TO...
BOOM!
...CRUSH ALL FOUR EMPERORS!!!
?!

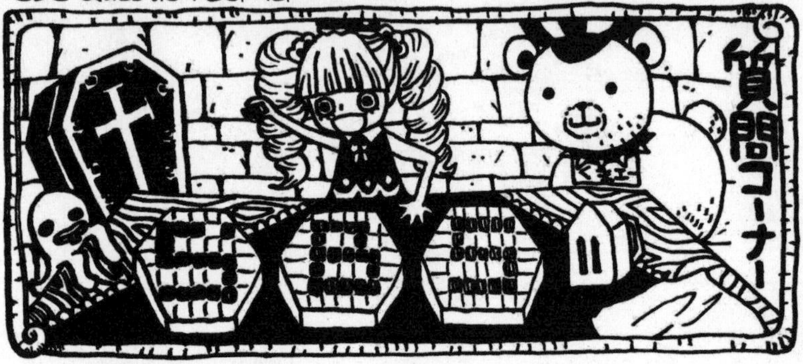
質問コーナー
SBS

(Misapero, Fukui)

Q: Odacchi, speak in Kansai dialect!

--Enoki

A: **Whaaat?** I cain't do that! It's jes' plain impossible, ya jerk! I cain't do it!! Don't make me whupyer behind!!

Q: The crew's hair has to grow out on those long voyages, right? Does someone give the rest haircuts? Nami or Robin, perhaps?

--I Want to be a Hairdresser

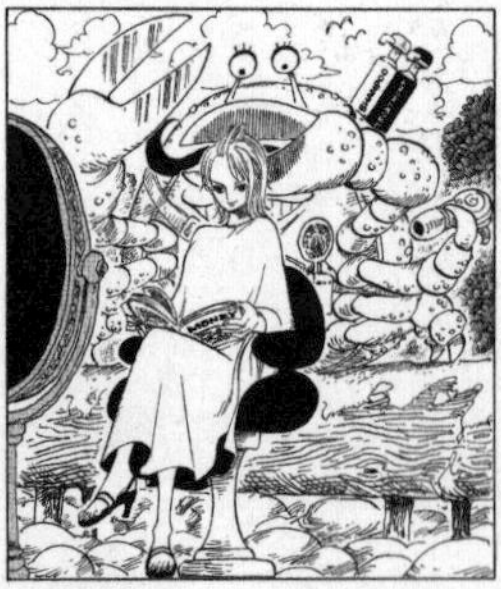

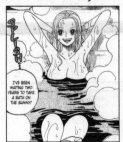

A: True, their hair does grow out. So who gives haircuts on the crew? Why, it's Zolo. He turns on the rest and goes, **"Tiger Trap!!"** Just kidding!! **What the hell, man?!!** I'm gonnawhupyer behind!! Shut yerpiehole!! Why, I oughtta!! The real answer is prolly Usopp or Robin. Maybe I should draw a heart-warmin' picture of a haircut someday.

Q: Can I drink the bath water after Nami's been in it?

--ChageroKiyomizu

A: **What the hell, man?!!** What in tarnation are you thinkin'?! This is a manga for all ages!! Excuse me, officer! This man's a pervert, can ya arrest him for me? Huh? What'm I holding, ya say? Why, it's a pretty lady's flute. What's wrong with lickin' it whiles I walk around plum-naked? What--hey! Not me! He's the pervert, I swear! No, stop! I got deadlines ta meet!

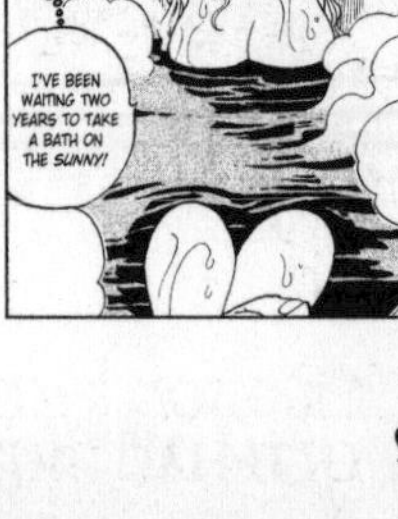
SPLISH...
I'VE BEEN WAITING TWO YEARS TO TAKE A BATH ON THE SUNNY!

What?! Impersonation of a Kansai resident?! What's that s'pose ta mean?! Who cares?! No, look, the readers put me up to it...

Chapter 697:

A DEAL

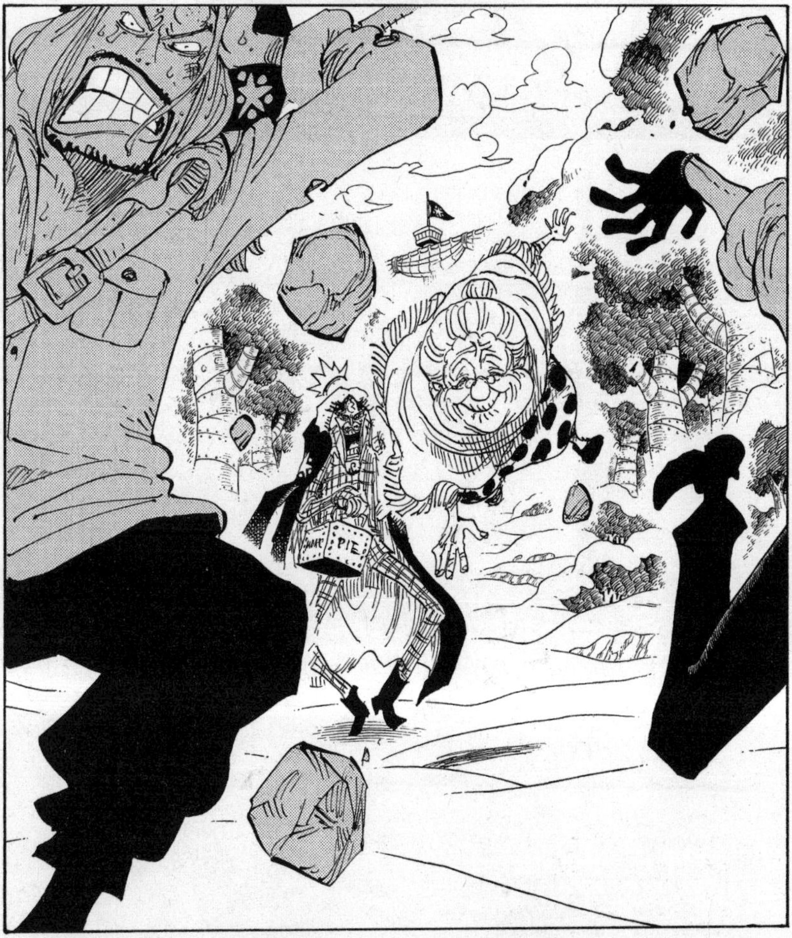
PIE

CARIBOU'S NEW WORLD KEE HEE HEE, VOL. 19: "THE OLD HAG DRIVES OFF THE MYSTERIOUS SOLDIERS"

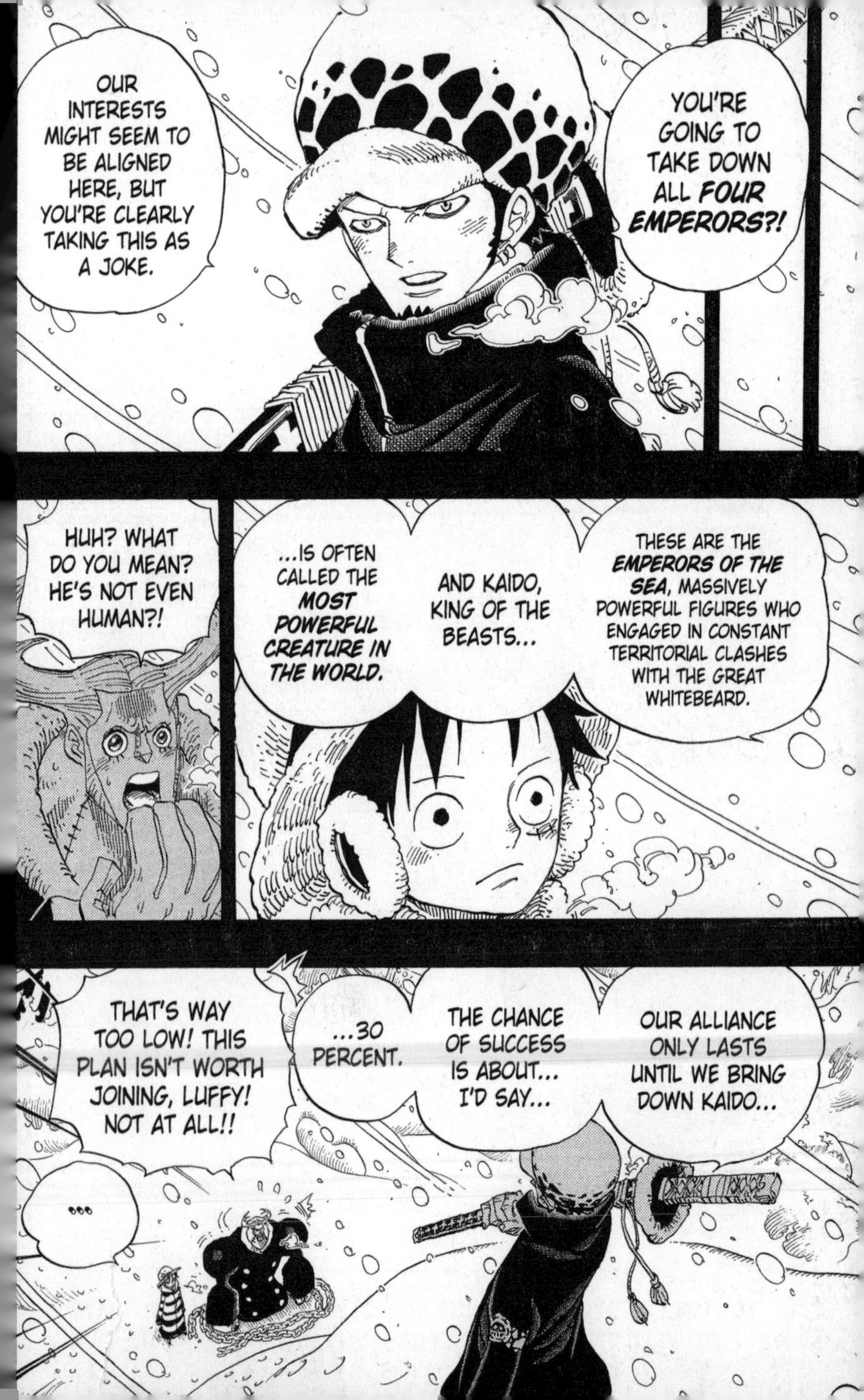

YOU'RE GOING TO TAKE DOWN ALL FOUR EMPERORS?!
OUR INTERESTS MIGHT SEEM TO BE ALIGNED HERE, BUT YOU'RE CLEARLY TAKING THIS AS A JOKE.
THESE ARE THE EMPERORS OF THE SEA, MASSIVELY POWERFUL FIGURES WHO ENGAGED IN CONSTANT TERRITORIAL CLASHES WITH THE GREAT WHITEBEARD.
AND KAIDO, KING OF THE BEASTS...
...IS OFTEN CALLED THE MOST POWERFUL CREATURE IN THE WORLD.
HUH? WHAT DO YOU MEAN? HE'S NOT EVEN HUMAN?!
OUR ALLIANCE ONLY LASTS UNTIL WE BRING DOWN KAIDO...
THE CHANCE OF SUCCESS IS ABOUT... I'D SAY...
...30 PERCENT.
THAT'S WAY TOO LOW! THIS PLAN ISN'T WORTH JOINING, LUFFY! NOT AT ALL!!
...

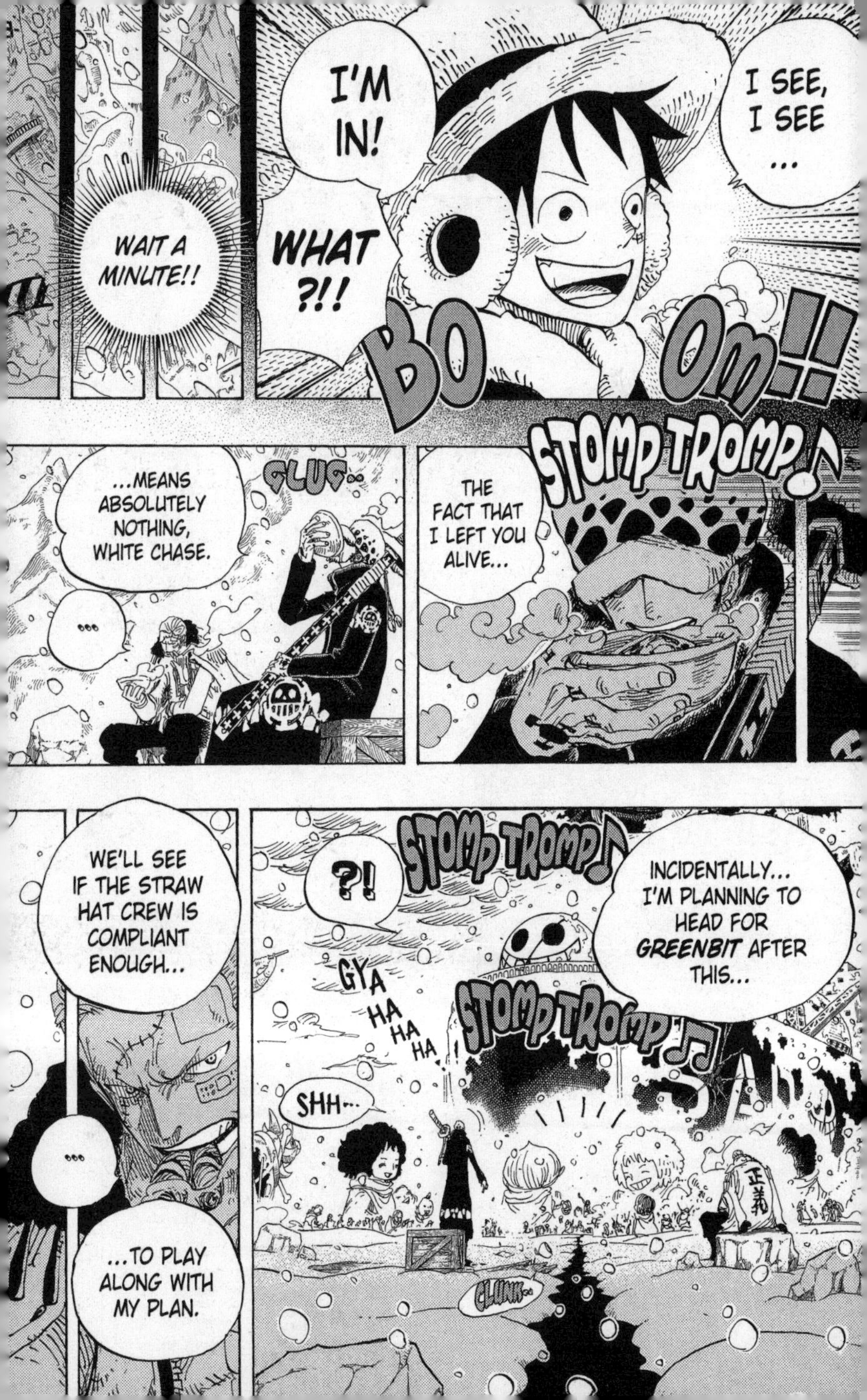
I SEE, I SEE ...
I'M IN!
WHAT ?!!
BOOM!!
WAIT A MINUTE!!
STOMP TROMP♪
THE FACT THAT I LEFT YOU ALIVE...
GLUG
...MEANS ABSOLUTELY NOTHING, WHITE CHASE.
...
INCIDENTALLY... I'M PLANNING TO HEAD FOR *GREENBIT* AFTER THIS...
STOMP TROMP♪
?!
STOMP TROMP♪
GYAHAHAHAHA
SHH...
CLINK
WE'LL SEE IF THE STRAW HAT CREW IS COMPLIANT ENOUGH...
...
...TO PLAY ALONG WITH MY PLAN.

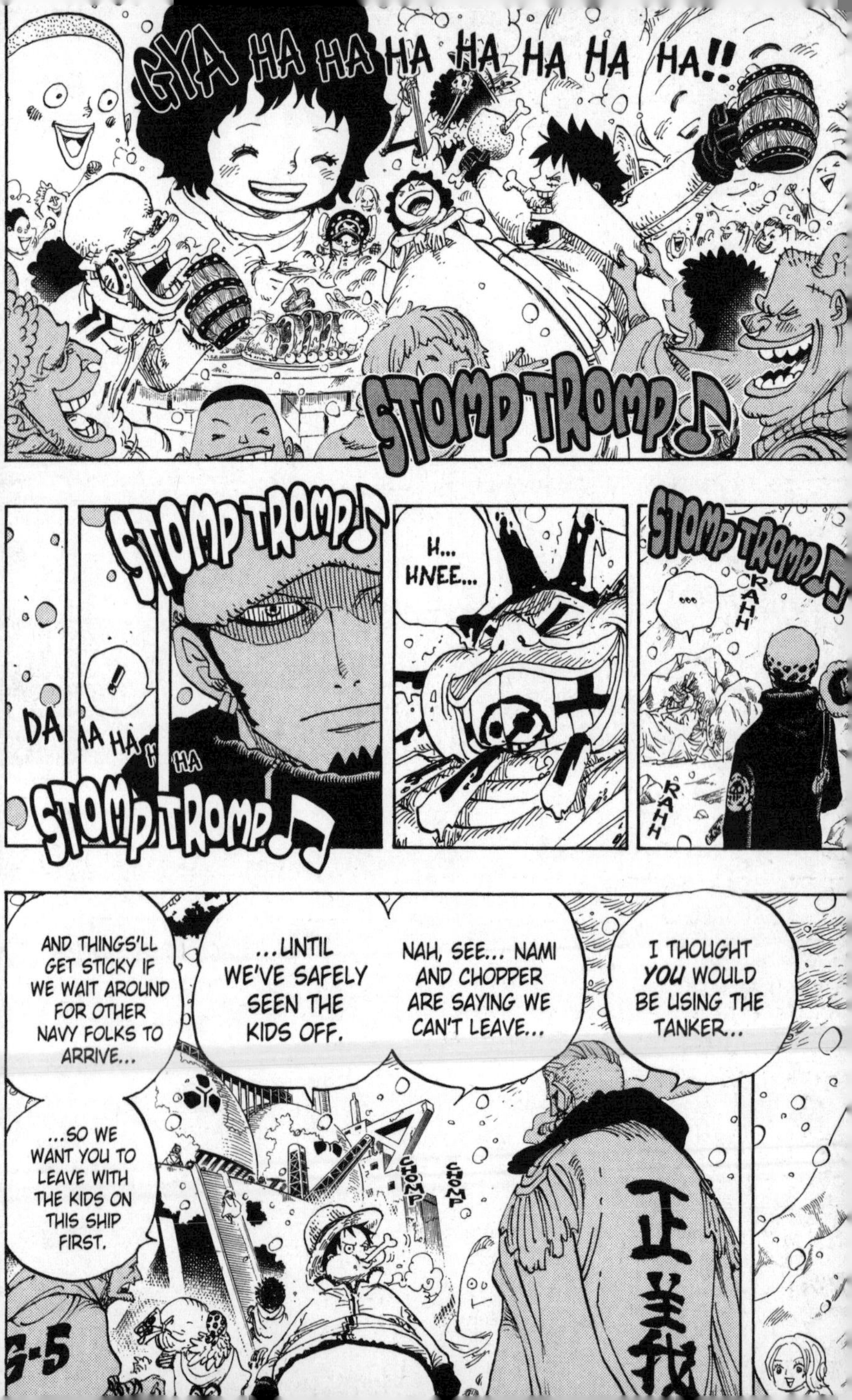
GYA HA HA HA HA HA HA HA!!
STOMP TROMP♪
STOMP TROMP♪
...
RAHH
RAHH
H... HNEE...
STOMP TROMP♪
!
DA HA HA HA HA
STOMP TROMP♪
I THOUGHT YOU WOULD BE USING THE TANKER...
NAH, SEE... NAMI AND CHOPPER ARE SAYING WE CAN'T LEAVE...
...UNTIL WE'VE SAFELY SEEN THE KIDS OFF.
AND THINGS'LL GET STICKY IF WE WAIT AROUND FOR OTHER NAVY FOLKS TO ARRIVE...
...SO WE WANT YOU TO LEAVE WITH THE KIDS ON THIS SHIP FIRST.
CHOMP
CHOMP
正義
G-5

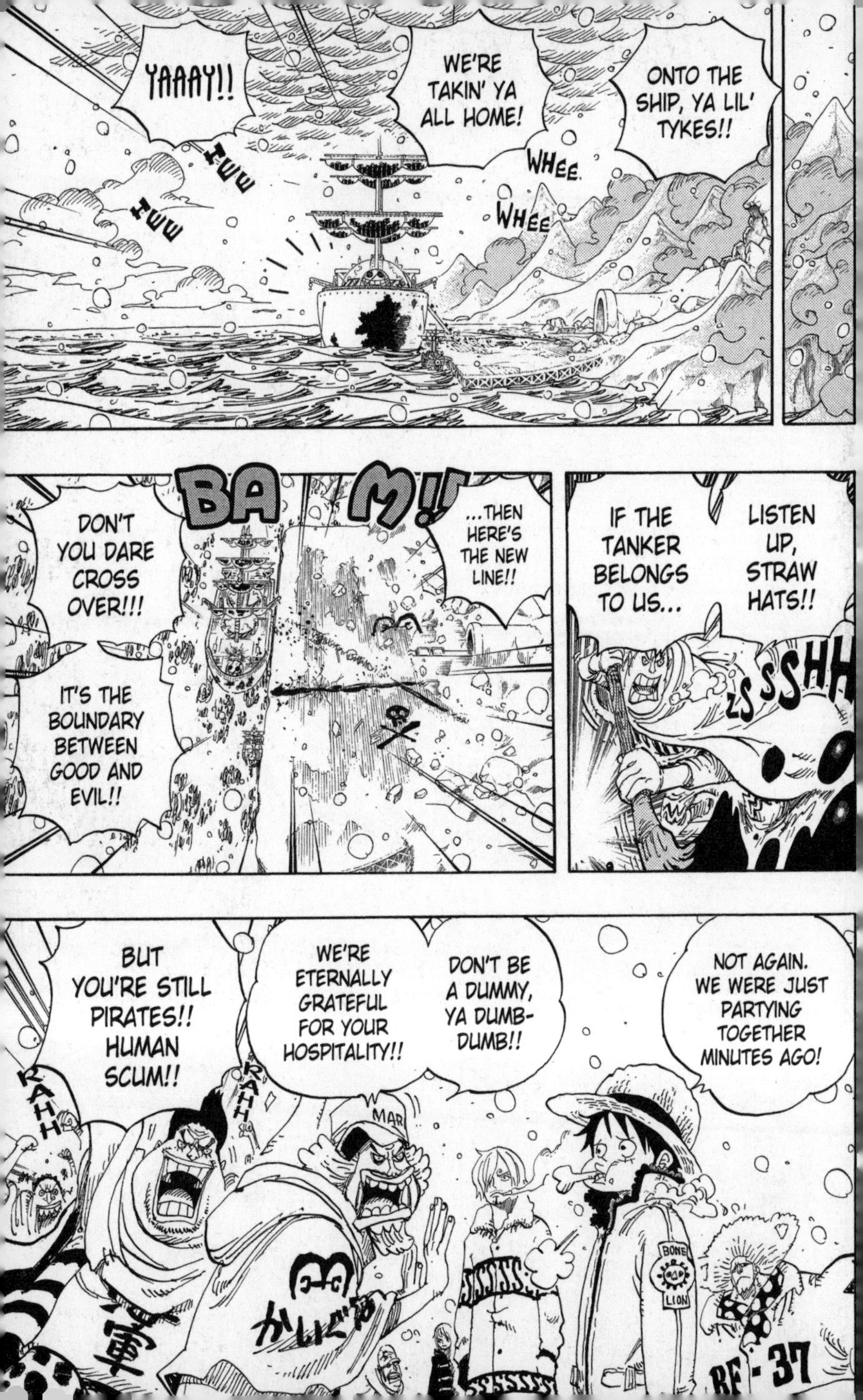

ONTO THE SHIP, YA LIL' TYKES!!
WE'RE TAKIN' YA ALL HOME!
YAAAY!!
WHEE
WHEE
LISTEN UP, STRAW HATS!!
IF THE TANKER BELONGS TO US...
ZSSSHH
...THEN HERE'S THE NEW LINE!!
BAM!!
DON'T YOU DARE CROSS OVER!!!
IT'S THE BOUNDARY BETWEEN GOOD AND EVIL!!
NOT AGAIN. WE WERE JUST PARTYING TOGETHER MINUTES AGO!
DON'T BE A DUMMY, YA DUMB-DUMB!!
WE'RE ETERNALLY GRATEFUL FOR YOUR HOSPITALITY!!
BUT YOU'RE STILL PIRATES!! HUMAN SCUM!!
RAHH
RAHH
MAR
BONE LION
RF-37

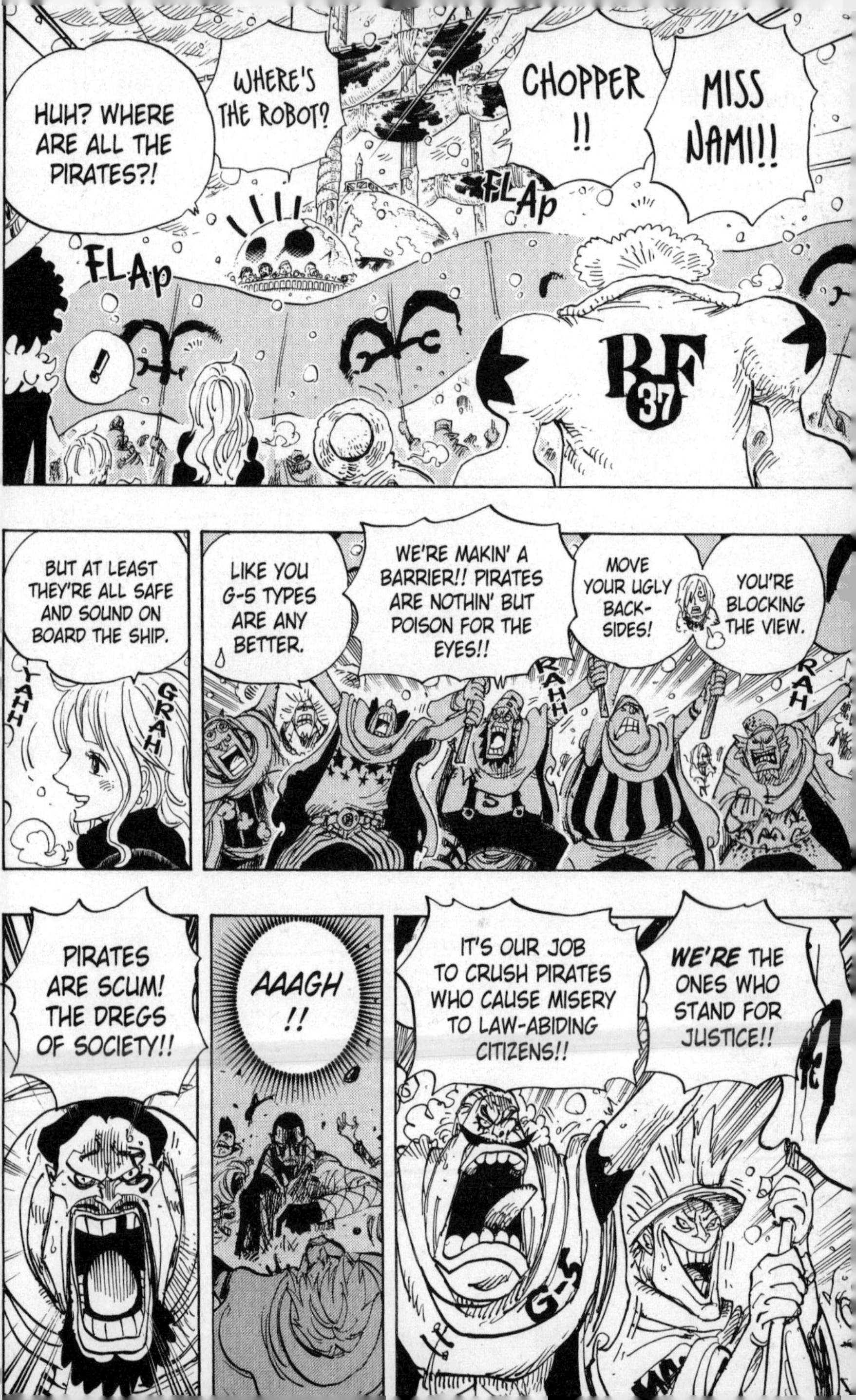
MISS NAMI!!
CHOPPER !!
WHERE'S THE ROBOT?
HUH? WHERE ARE ALL THE PIRATES?!
FLAp
FLAp
!
RAH
YOU'RE BLOCKING THE VIEW.
MOVE YOUR UGLY BACK-SIDES!
RAHH
WE'RE MAKIN' A BARRIER!! PIRATES ARE NOTHIN' BUT POISON FOR THE EYES!!
LIKE YOU G-5 TYPES ARE ANY BETTER.
BUT AT LEAST THEY'RE ALL SAFE AND SOUND ON BOARD THE SHIP.
GRAH
YAHH
WE'RE THE ONES WHO STAND FOR JUSTICE!!
IT'S OUR JOB TO CRUSH PIRATES WHO CAUSE MISERY TO LAW-ABIDING CITIZENS!!
G-5
AAAGH !!
PIRATES ARE SCUM! THE DREGS OF SOCIETY!!

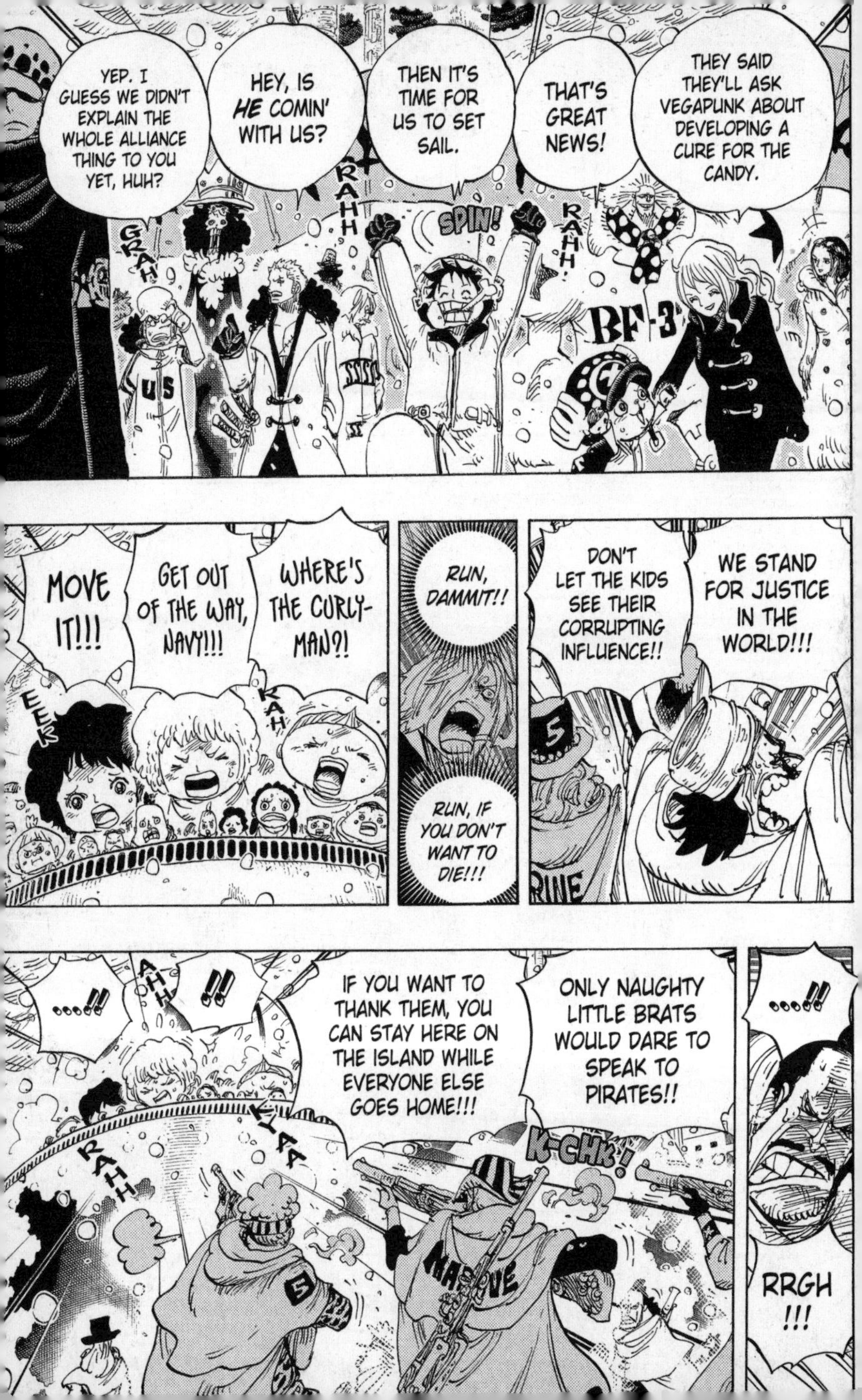
THEY SAID THEY'LL ASK VEGAPUNK ABOUT DEVELOPING A CURE FOR THE CANDY.
THAT'S GREAT NEWS!
RAHH
SPIN!
THEN IT'S TIME FOR US TO SET SAIL.
RAHH
HEY, IS HE COMIN' WITH US?
YEP. I GUESS WE DIDN'T EXPLAIN THE WHOLE ALLIANCE THING TO YOU YET, HUH?
GRAH
WE STAND FOR JUSTICE IN THE WORLD!!!
DON'T LET THE KIDS SEE THEIR CORRUPTING INFLUENCE!!
RUN, DAMMIT!!
RUN, IF YOU DON'T WANT TO DIE!!!
WHERE'S THE CURLY-MAN?!
RAH
GET OUT OF THE WAY, NAVY!!!
MOVE IT!!!
EEEK
...!!
RRGH!!!
ONLY NAUGHTY LITTLE BRATS WOULD DARE TO SPEAK TO PIRATES!!
K-CHK!
IF YOU WANT TO THANK THEM, YOU CAN STAY HERE ON THE ISLAND WHILE EVERYONE ELSE GOES HOME!!!
KYAA
!!
AHH
...!!
RAHH

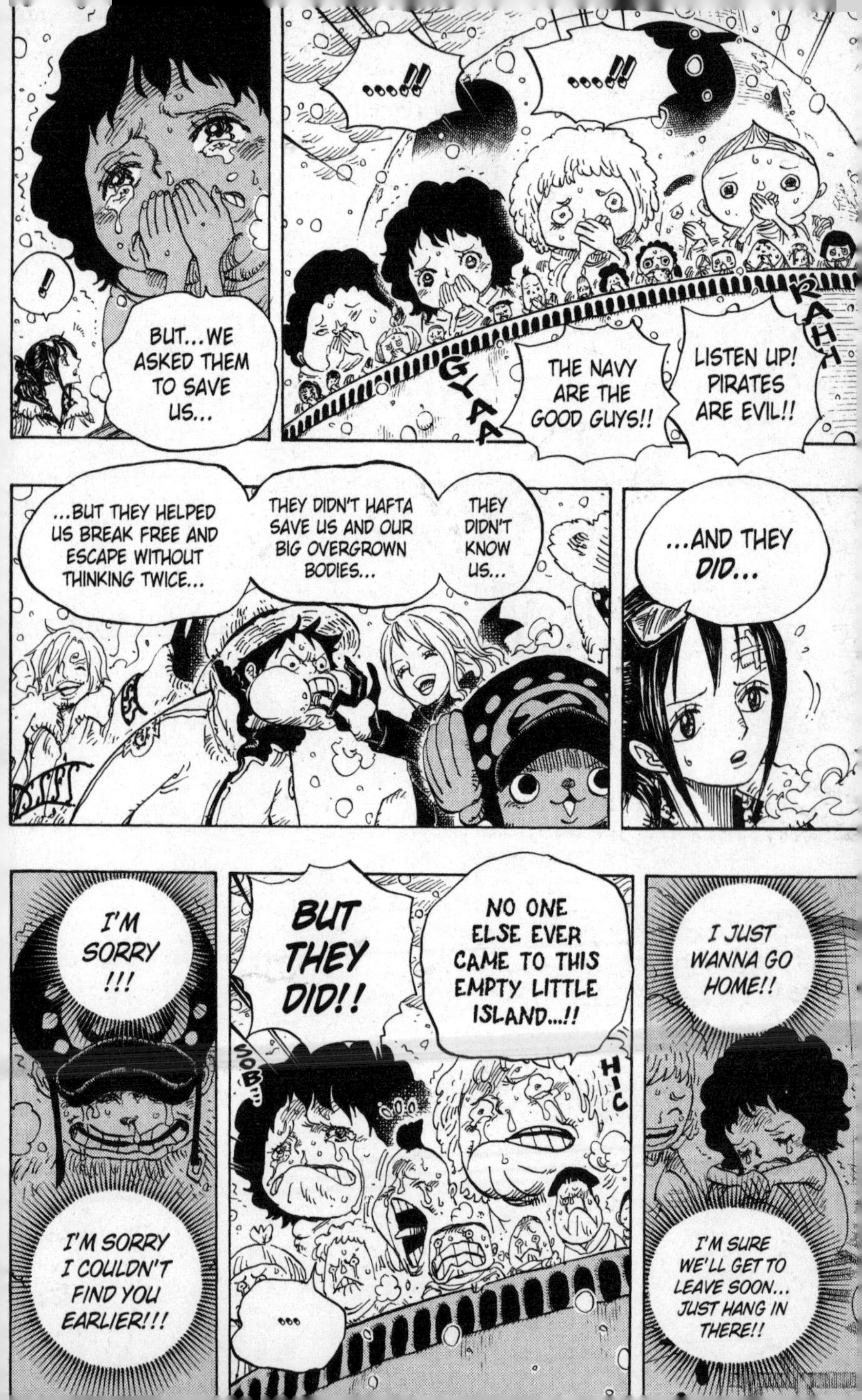
....!!
....!!
RAHH
LISTEN UP! PIRATES ARE EVIL!!
THE NAVY ARE THE GOOD GUYS!!
GYAA
!
BUT...WE ASKED THEM TO SAVE US...
...AND THEY DID...
THEY DIDN'T KNOW US...
THEY DIDN'T HAFTA SAVE US AND OUR BIG OVERGROWN BODIES...
...BUT THEY HELPED US BREAK FREE AND ESCAPE WITHOUT THINKING TWICE...
I JUST WANNA GO HOME!!
I'M SURE WE'LL GET TO LEAVE SOON... JUST HANG IN THERE!!
NO ONE ELSE EVER CAME TO THIS EMPTY LITTLE ISLAND...!!
BUT THEY DID!!
HIC
SOB
...
I'M SORRY!!!
I'M SORRY I COULDN'T FIND YOU EARLIER!!!

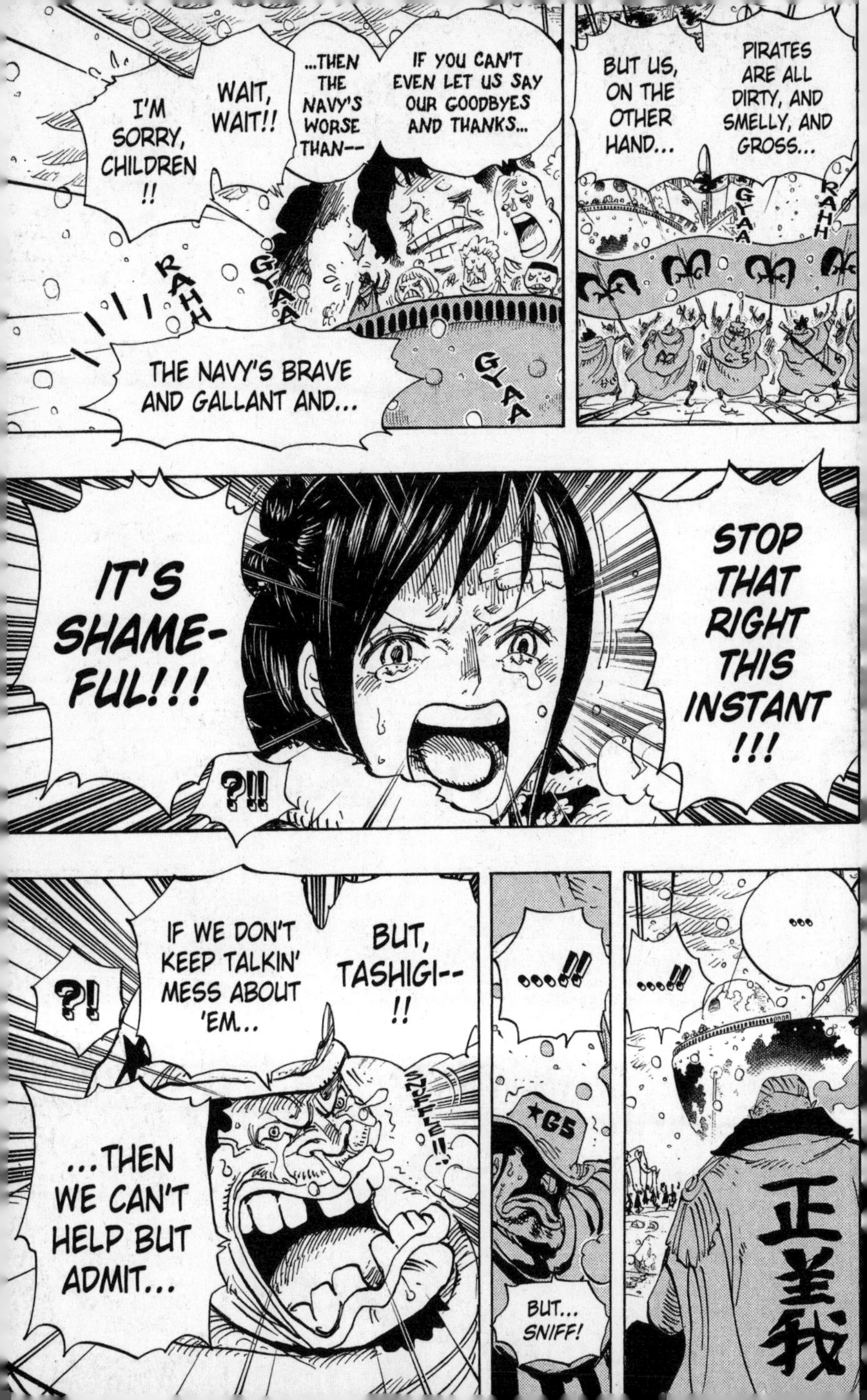
PIRATES ARE ALL DIRTY, AND SMELLY, AND GROSS...
BUT US, ON THE OTHER HAND...
RAHH
GYAA
IF YOU CAN'T EVEN LET US SAY OUR GOODBYES AND THANKS...
...THEN THE NAVY'S WORSE THAN--
WAIT, WAIT!!
I'M SORRY, CHILDREN!!
GYAA
RAHH
THE NAVY'S BRAVE AND GALLANT AND...
GYAA
STOP THAT RIGHT THIS INSTANT!!!
IT'S SHAME-FUL!!!
?!!
...
...!!
正義
...!!
BUT... SNIFF!
BUT, TASHIGI--!!
IF WE DON'T KEEP TALKIN' MESS ABOUT 'EM...
?!
SNIFFLE!!
...THEN WE CAN'T HELP BUT ADMIT...

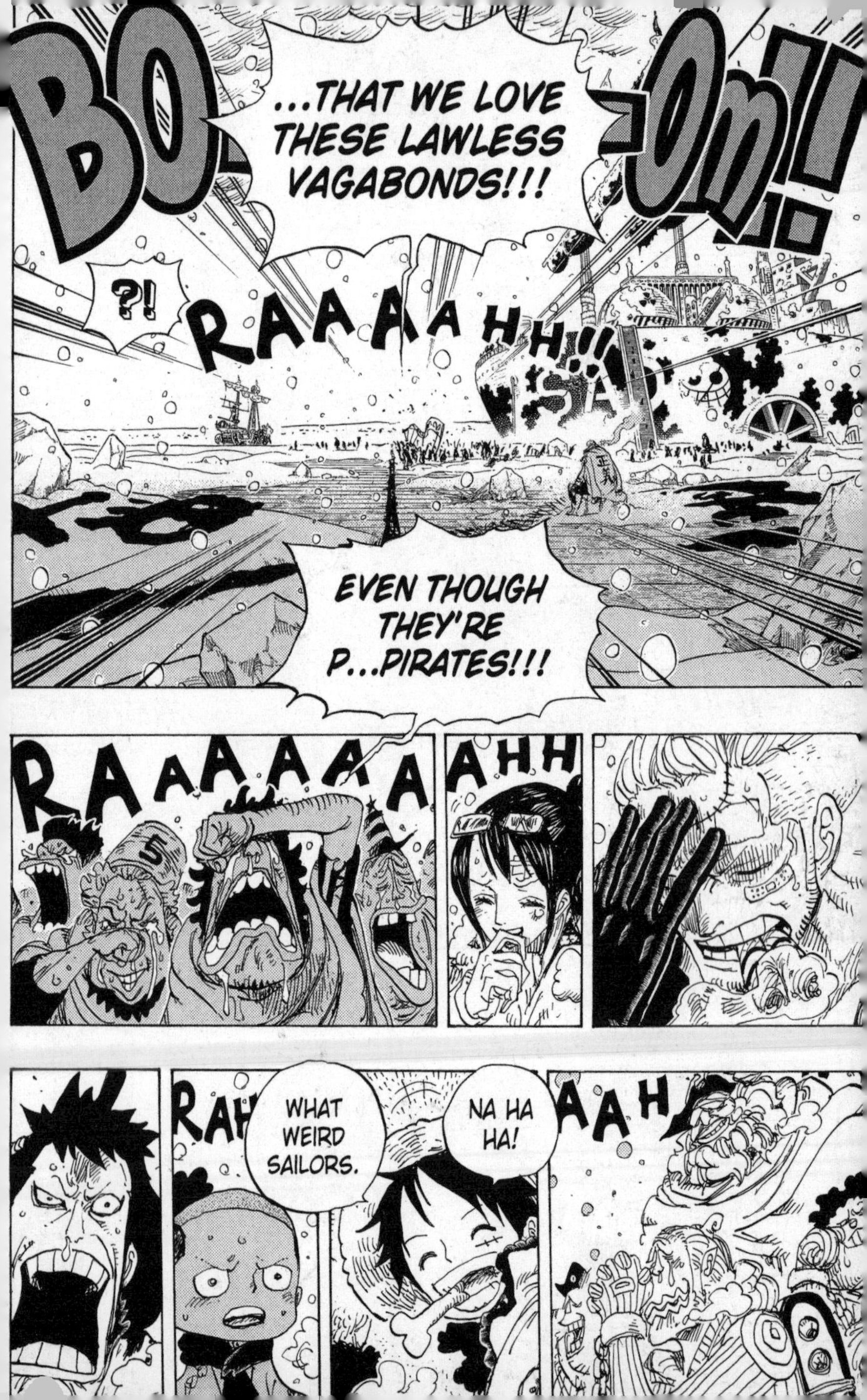
BO-OM!!
...THAT WE LOVE THESE LAWLESS VAGABONDS!!!
?!
RAAAAAHH!!!
EVEN THOUGH THEY'RE P...PIRATES!!!
RAAAAAAAHH
AAH
NA HA HA!
WHAT WEIRD SAILORS.
RAH

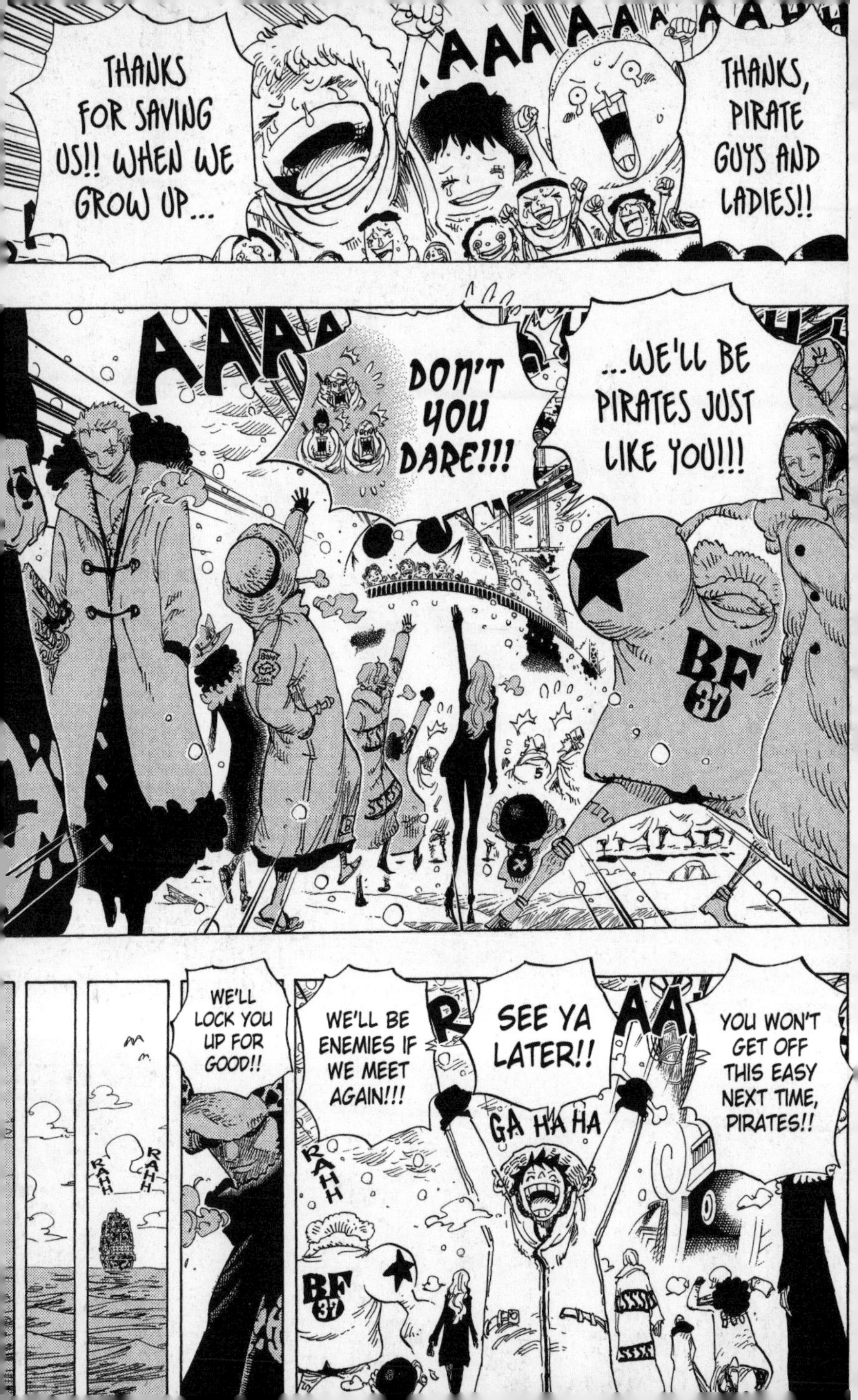
THANKS, PIRATE GUYS AND LADIES!!
THANKS FOR SAVING US!! WHEN WE GROW UP...
...WE'LL BE PIRATES JUST LIKE YOU!!!
DON'T YOU DARE!!!
YOU WON'T GET OFF THIS EASY NEXT TIME, PIRATES!!
SEE YA LATER!!
WE'LL BE ENEMIES IF WE MEET AGAIN!!!
GA HA HA
RAHH
WE'LL LOCK YOU UP FOR GOOD!!
RAHH
RAHH

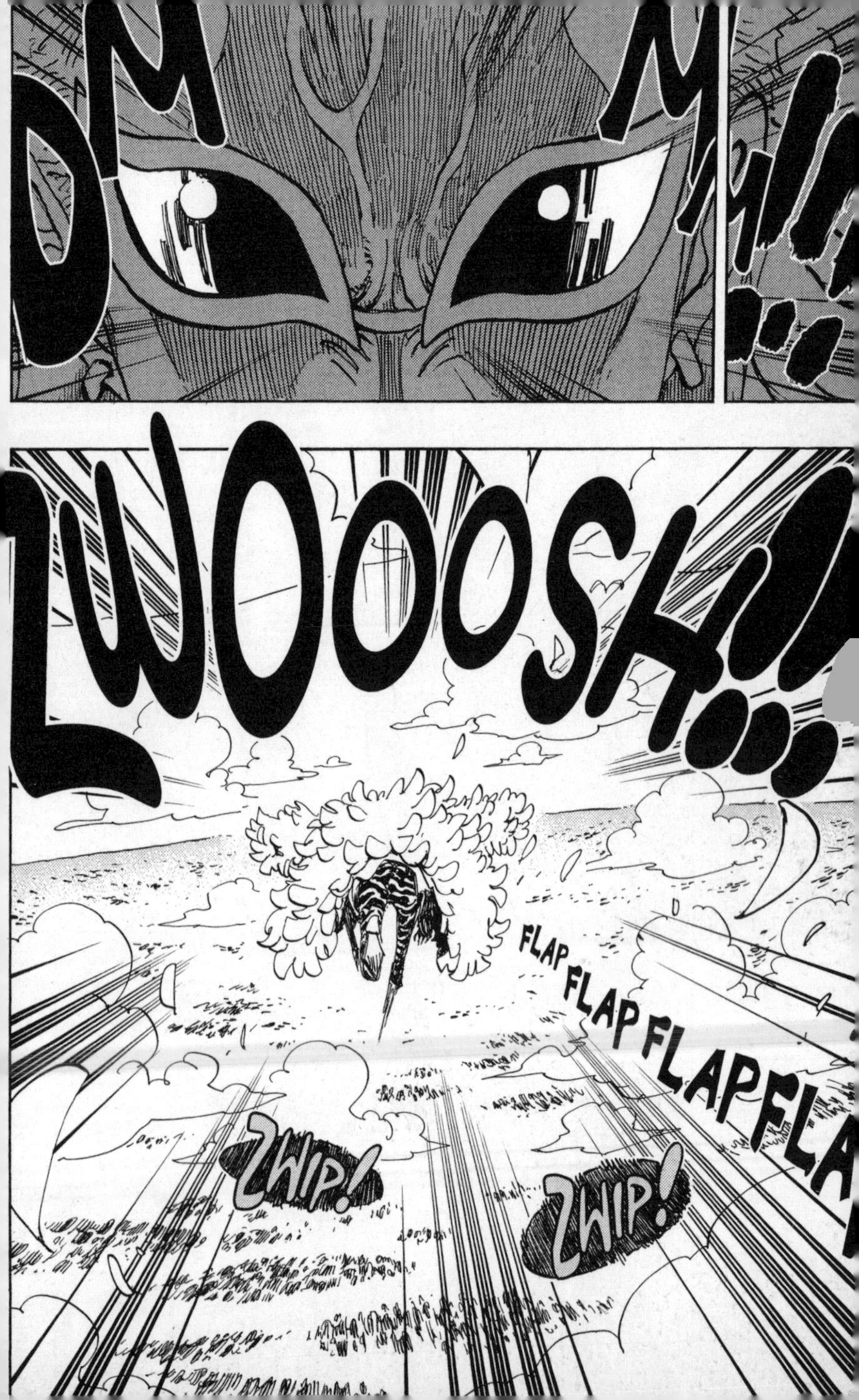
ZWOOOSH!!
FLAP FLAP FLAP FLAP FLA
ZWIP!
ZWIP!

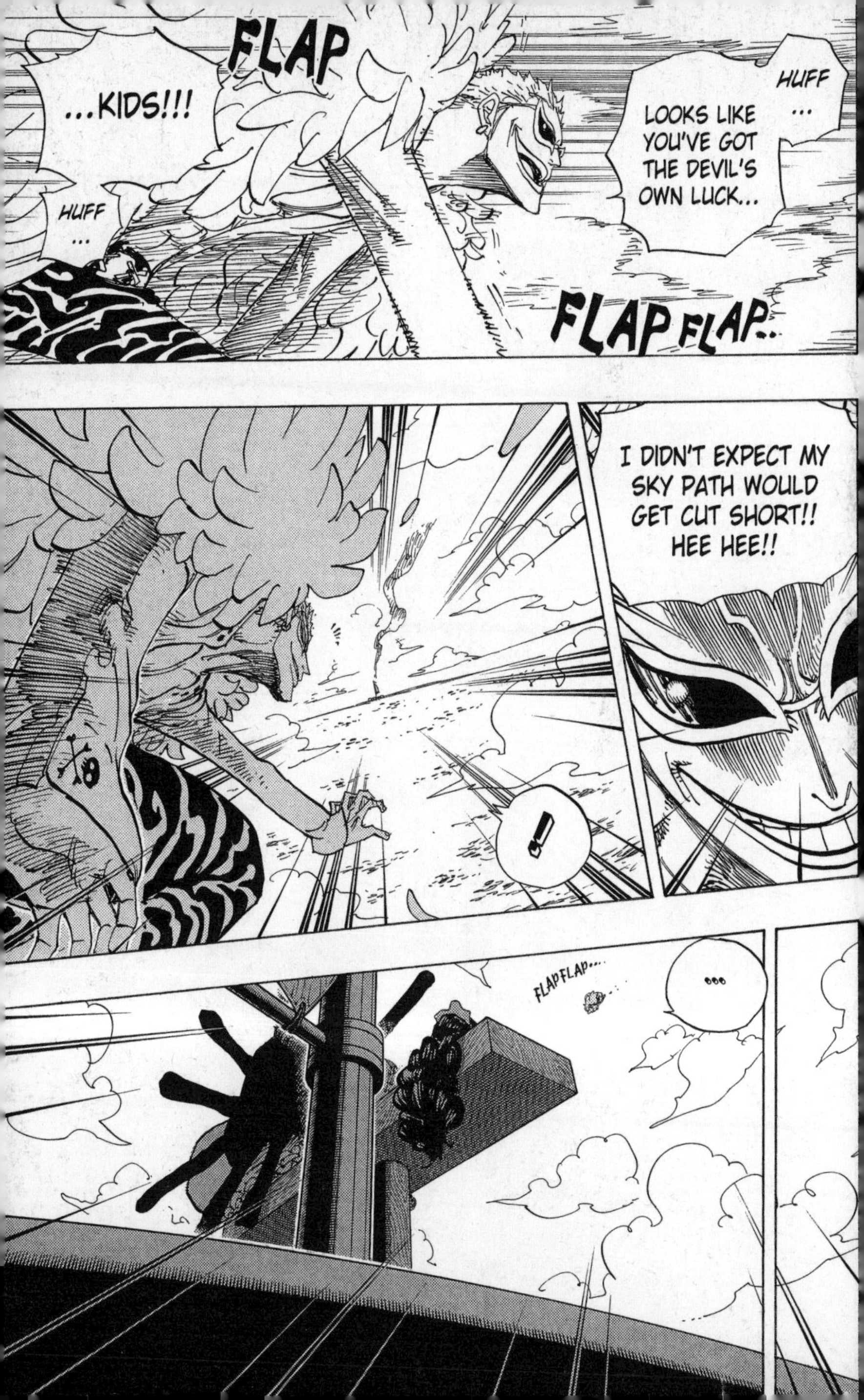
HUFF ...
LOOKS LIKE YOU'VE GOT THE DEVIL'S OWN LUCK...
FLAP
...KIDS!!!
HUFF ...
FLAP FLAP...
I DIDN'T EXPECT MY SKY PATH WOULD GET CUT SHORT!! HEE HEE!!
!
...
FLAPFLAP...

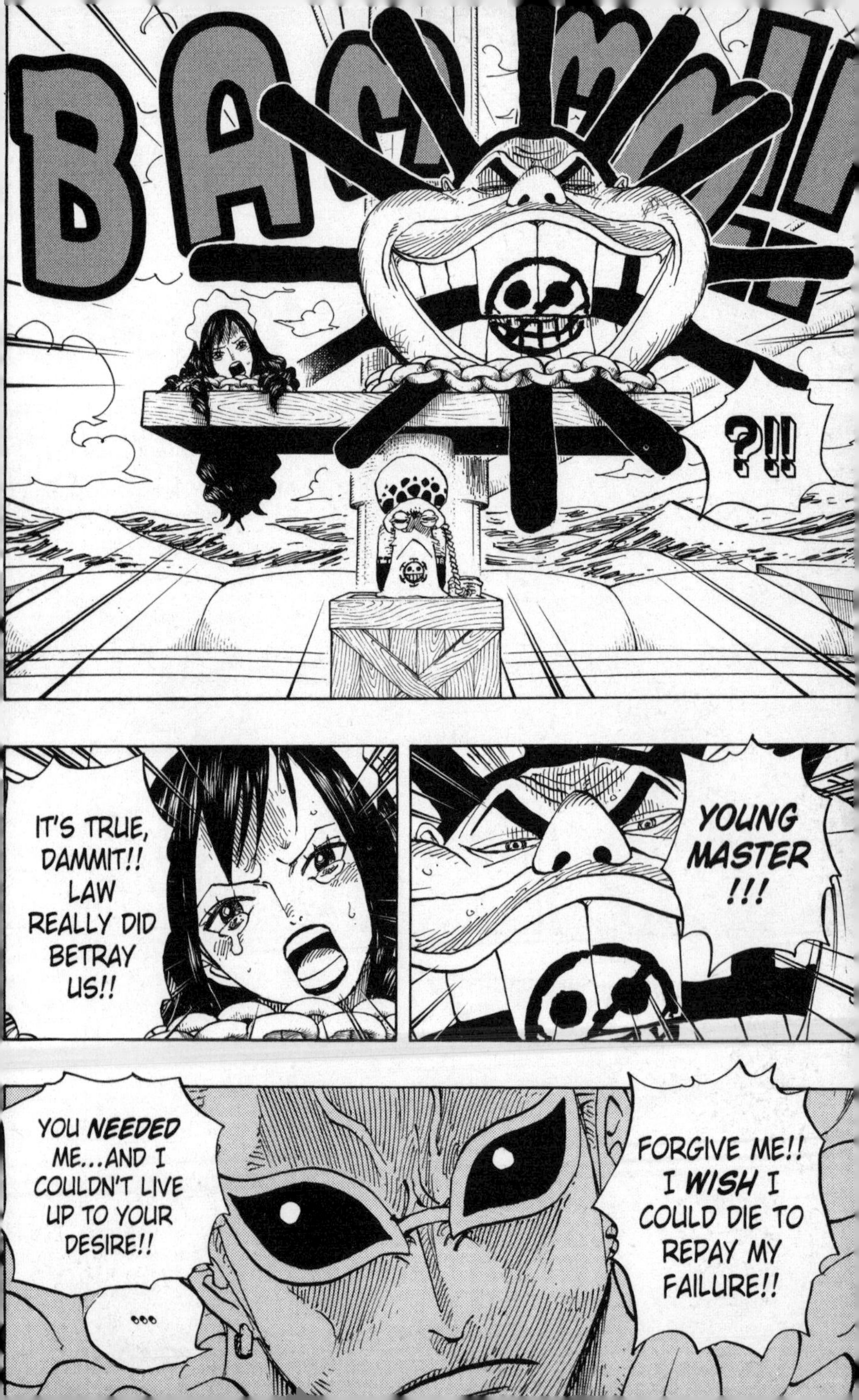
?!!
YOUNG MASTER !!!
IT'S TRUE, DAMMIT!! LAW REALLY DID BETRAY US!!
FORGIVE ME!! I *WISH* I COULD DIE TO REPAY MY FAILURE!!
YOU *NEEDED* ME...AND I COULDN'T LIVE UP TO YOUR DESIRE!!
...

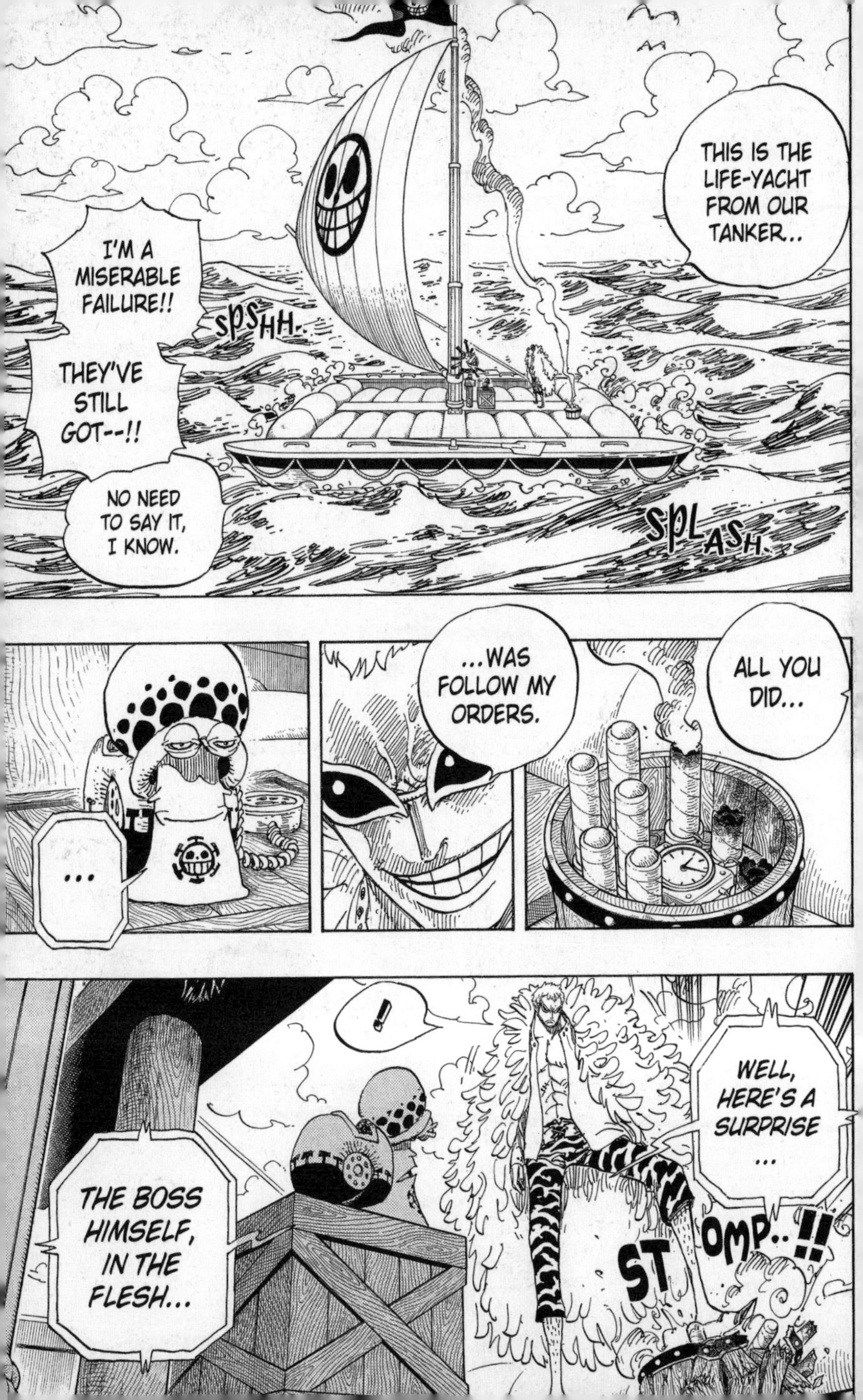
THIS IS THE LIFE-YACHT FROM OUR TANKER...
I'M A MISERABLE FAILURE!!
THEY'VE STILL GOT--!!
SPSHH..
NO NEED TO SAY IT, I KNOW.
SPLASH
ALL YOU DID...
...WAS FOLLOW MY ORDERS.
...
WELL, HERE'S A SURPRISE ...
!
STOMP..!!
THE BOSS HIMSELF, IN THE FLESH...

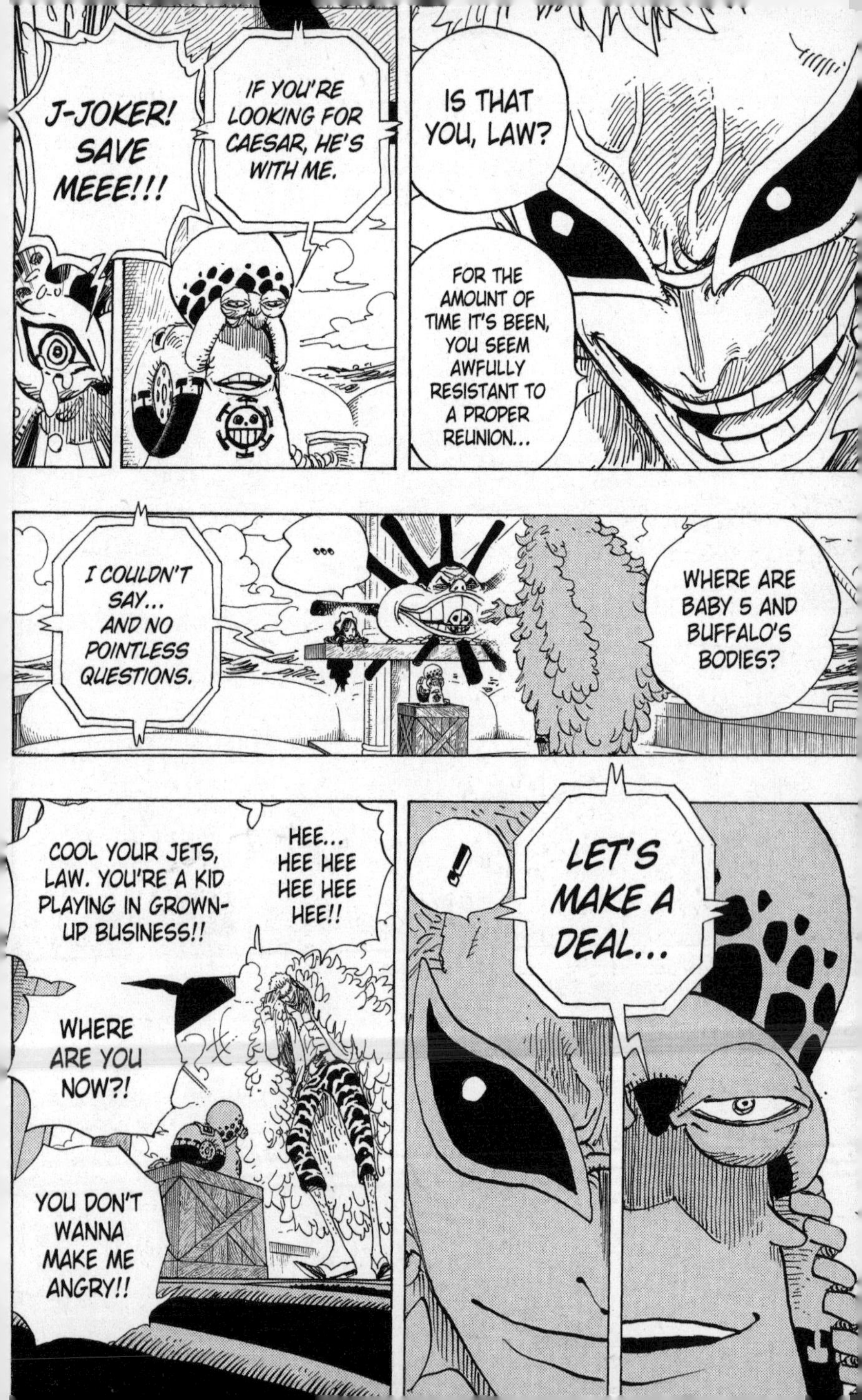
IS THAT YOU, LAW?
FOR THE AMOUNT OF TIME IT'S BEEN, YOU SEEM AWFULLY RESISTANT TO A PROPER REUNION...
IF YOU'RE LOOKING FOR CAESAR, HE'S WITH ME.
J-JOKER! SAVE MEEE!!!
WHERE ARE BABY 5 AND BUFFALO'S BODIES?
...
I COULDN'T SAY... AND NO POINTLESS QUESTIONS.
!
LET'S MAKE A DEAL...
HEE... HEE HEE HEE HEE HEE!!
COOL YOUR JETS, LAW. YOU'RE A KID PLAYING IN GROWN-UP BUSINESS!!
WHERE ARE YOU NOW?!
YOU DON'T WANNA MAKE ME ANGRY!!

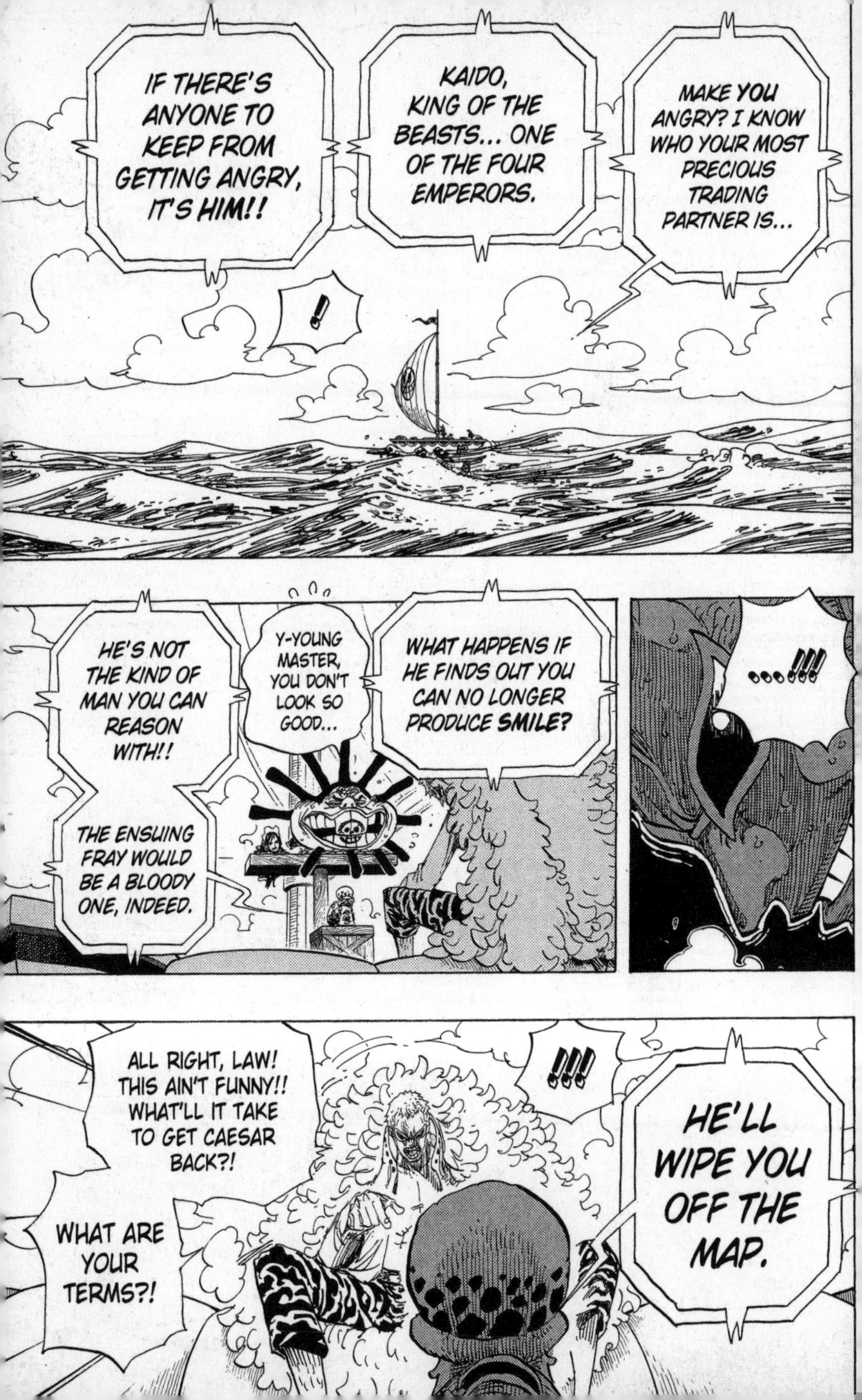
MAKE YOU ANGRY? I KNOW WHO YOUR MOST PRECIOUS TRADING PARTNER IS...
KAIDO, KING OF THE BEASTS... ONE OF THE FOUR EMPERORS.
IF THERE'S ANYONE TO KEEP FROM GETTING ANGRY, IT'S HIM!!
!
...!!!
WHAT HAPPENS IF HE FINDS OUT YOU CAN NO LONGER PRODUCE SMILE?
Y-YOUNG MASTER, YOU DON'T LOOK SO GOOD...
HE'S NOT THE KIND OF MAN YOU CAN REASON WITH!!
THE ENSUING FRAY WOULD BE A BLOODY ONE, INDEED.
HE'LL WIPE YOU OFF THE MAP.
!!!
ALL RIGHT, LAW! THIS AIN'T FUNNY!! WHAT'LL IT TAKE TO GET CAESAR BACK?!
WHAT ARE YOUR TERMS?!

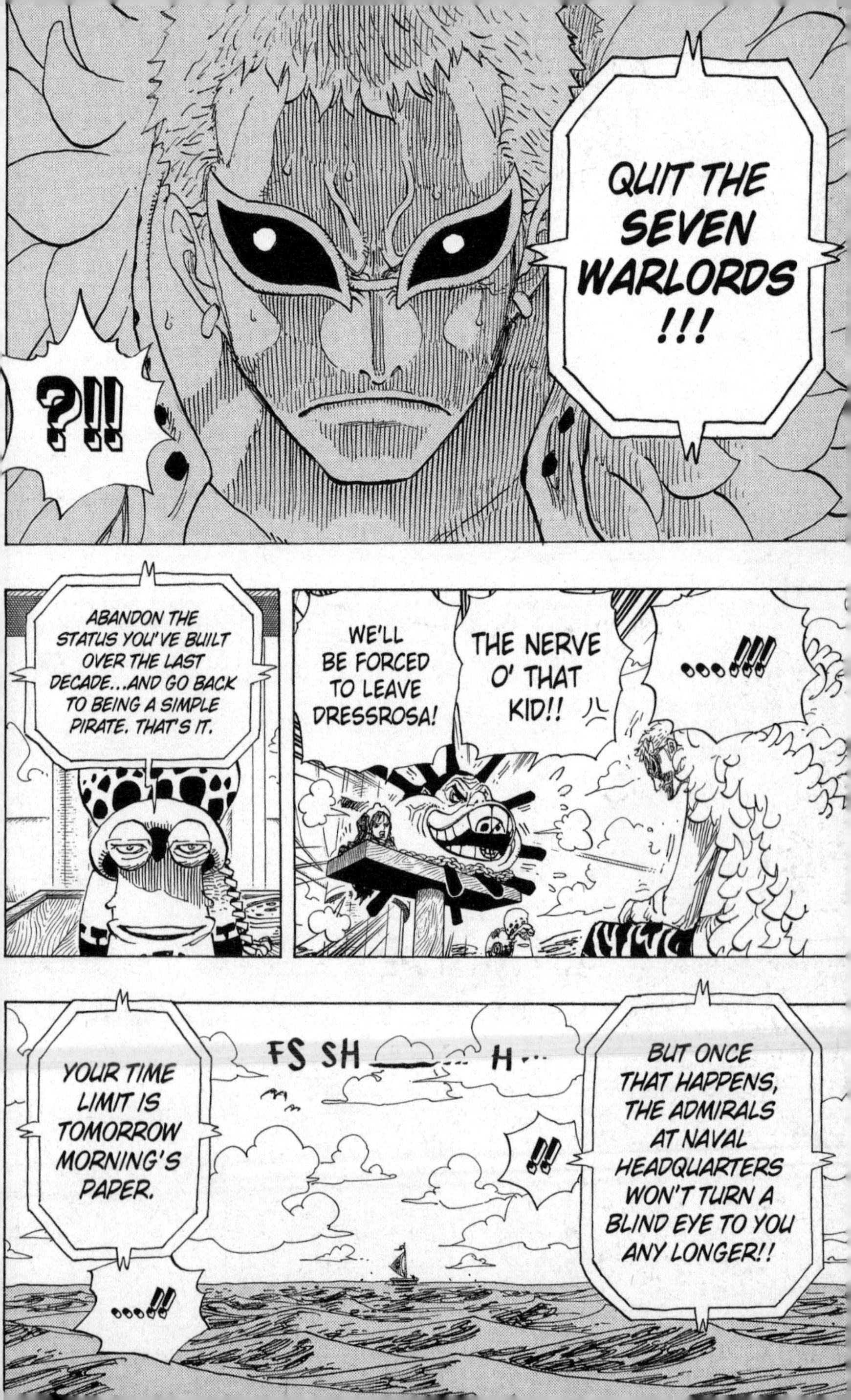
QUIT THE SEVEN WARLORDS!!!
?!!
...!!!
THE NERVE O' THAT KID!!
WE'LL BE FORCED TO LEAVE DRESSROSA!
ABANDON THE STATUS YOU'VE BUILT OVER THE LAST DECADE...AND GO BACK TO BEING A SIMPLE PIRATE. THAT'S IT.
BUT ONCE THAT HAPPENS, THE ADMIRALS AT NAVAL HEADQUARTERS WON'T TURN A BLIND EYE TO YOU ANY LONGER!!
!!
FS SH... H...
YOUR TIME LIMIT IS TOMORROW MORNING'S PAPER.
...!!

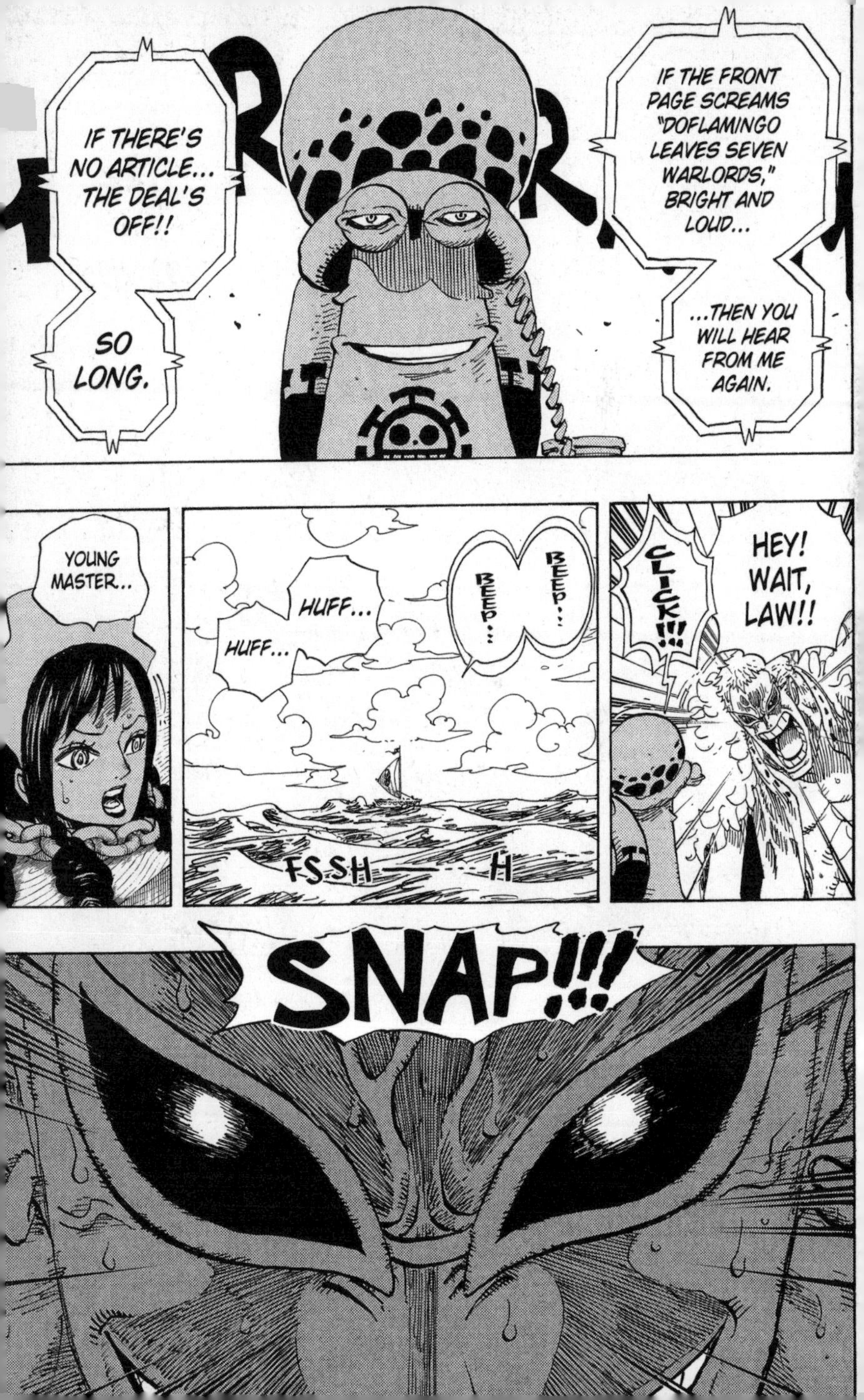
IF THE FRONT PAGE SCREAMS "DOFLAMINGO LEAVES SEVEN WARLORDS," BRIGHT AND LOUD...
...THEN YOU WILL HEAR FROM ME AGAIN.
IF THERE'S NO ARTICLE... THE DEAL'S OFF!!
SO LONG.
HEY! WAIT, LAW!!
CLICK!!!
BEEP...
BEEP...
HUFF...
HUFF...
FSSH—H
YOUNG MASTER...
SNAP!!!

SBS Question Corner

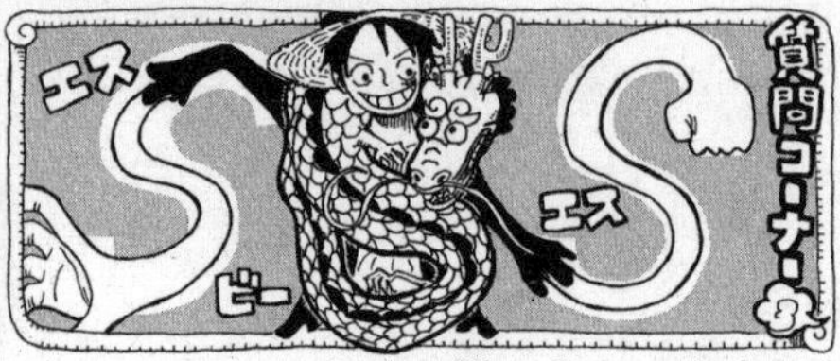
エス
ビー
エス
質問コーナー

(Hiroya Imamura, Kanagawa)

Q: I have a request for Odacchi! I want to see the childhood looks for the following Whitebeard Crew folks: Whitebeard, Marco, Jozu, Vista and Izo!!!

--Arinko

A: Sure thing.

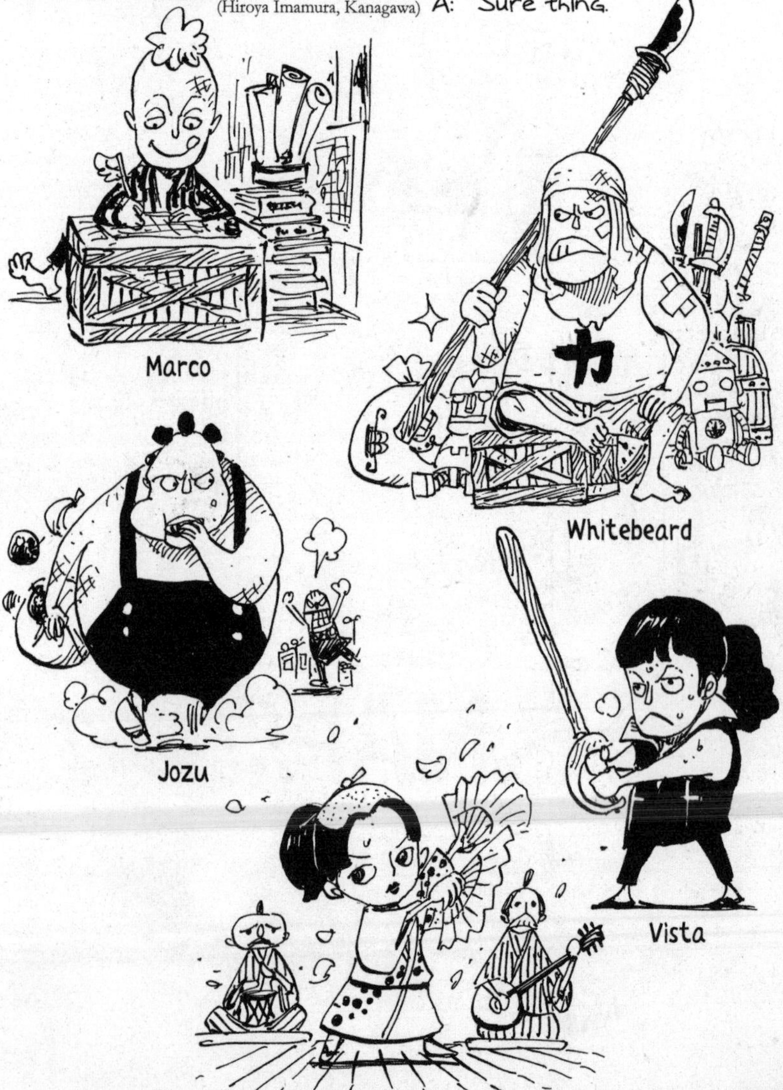
Marco
力
Whitebeard
Jozu
Vista
Izo

Chapter 698:
ENTER DOFLAMINGO

CARIBOU'S NEW WORLD KEE HEE HEE, VOL. 20:
"TO THE PORT"

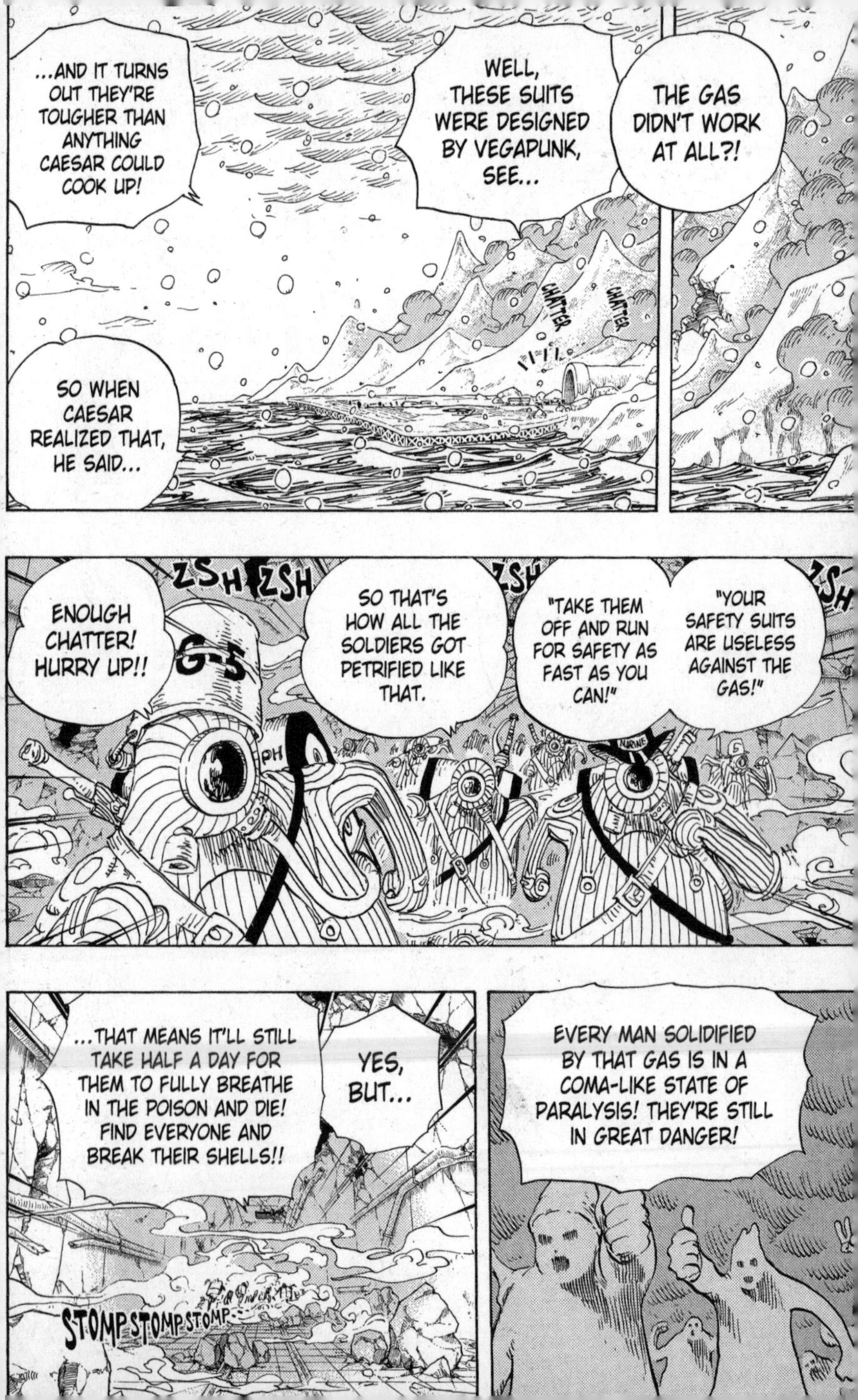
THE GAS DIDN'T WORK AT ALL?!
WELL, THESE SUITS WERE DESIGNED BY VEGAPUNK, SEE...
...AND IT TURNS OUT THEY'RE TOUGHER THAN ANYTHING CAESAR COULD COOK UP!
CHATTER
CHATTER
SO WHEN CAESAR REALIZED THAT, HE SAID...
ZSH
ZSH
"YOUR SAFETY SUITS ARE USELESS AGAINST THE GAS!"
"TAKE THEM OFF AND RUN FOR SAFETY AS FAST AS YOU CAN!"
MARINE
SO THAT'S HOW ALL THE SOLDIERS GOT PETRIFIED LIKE THAT.
ZSH ZSH
ENOUGH CHATTER! HURRY UP!!
G-5
EVERY MAN SOLIDIFIED BY THAT GAS IS IN A COMA-LIKE STATE OF PARALYSIS! THEY'RE STILL IN GREAT DANGER!
YES, BUT...
...THAT MEANS IT'LL STILL TAKE HALF A DAY FOR THEM TO FULLY BREATHE IN THE POISON AND DIE! FIND EVERYONE AND BREAK THEIR SHELLS!!
STOMP STOMP STOMP

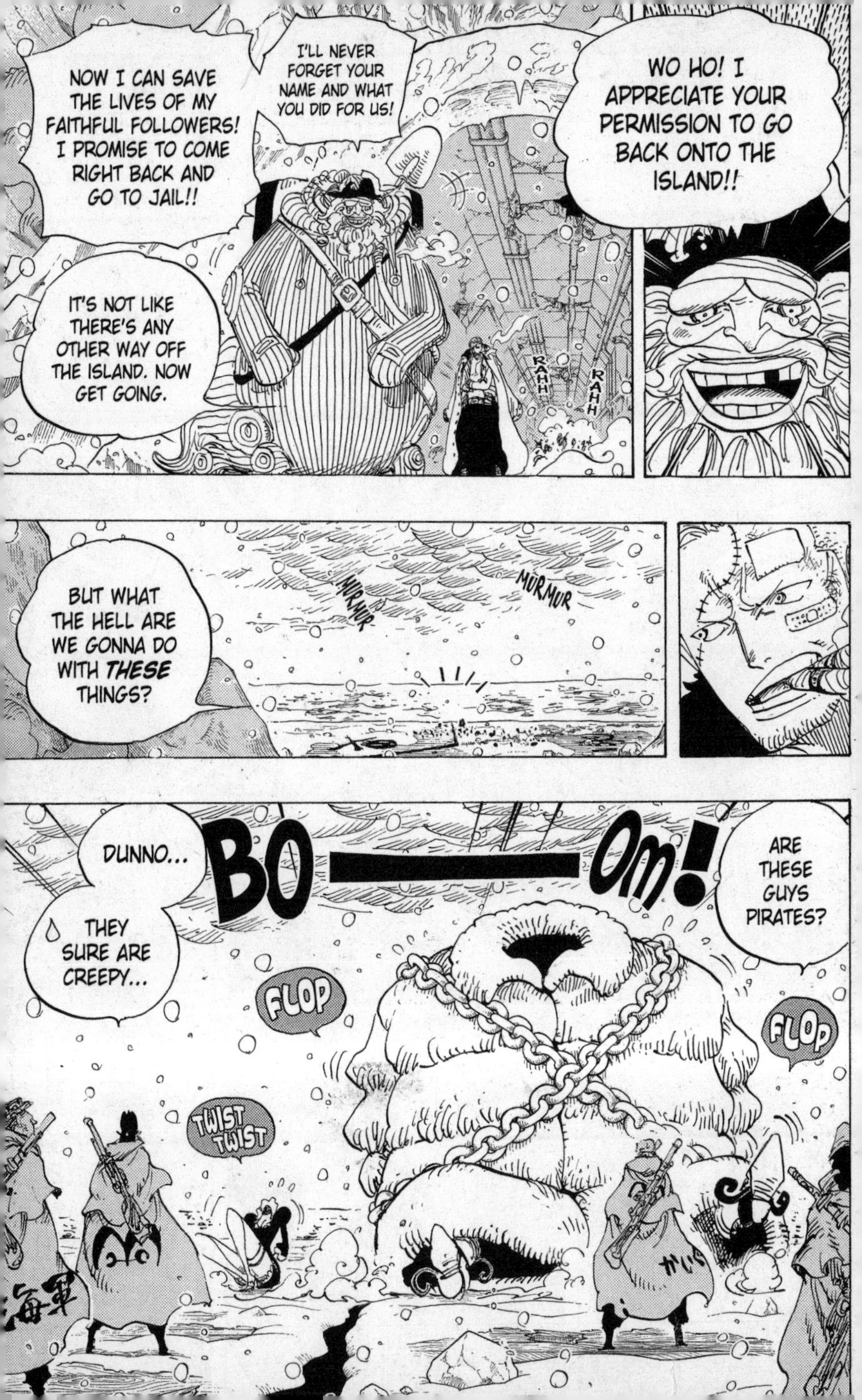
WO HO! I APPRECIATE YOUR PERMISSION TO GO BACK ONTO THE ISLAND!!
I'LL NEVER FORGET YOUR NAME AND WHAT YOU DID FOR US!
NOW I CAN SAVE THE LIVES OF MY FAITHFUL FOLLOWERS! I PROMISE TO COME RIGHT BACK AND GO TO JAIL!!
RAHH
RAHH
IT'S NOT LIKE THERE'S ANY OTHER WAY OFF THE ISLAND. NOW GET GOING.
MURMUR
MURMUR
BUT WHAT THE HELL ARE WE GONNA DO WITH *THESE* THINGS?
ARE THESE GUYS PIRATES?
BO——OM!
DUNNO...
THEY SURE ARE CREEPY...
FLOP
FLOP
TWIST TWIST
海軍

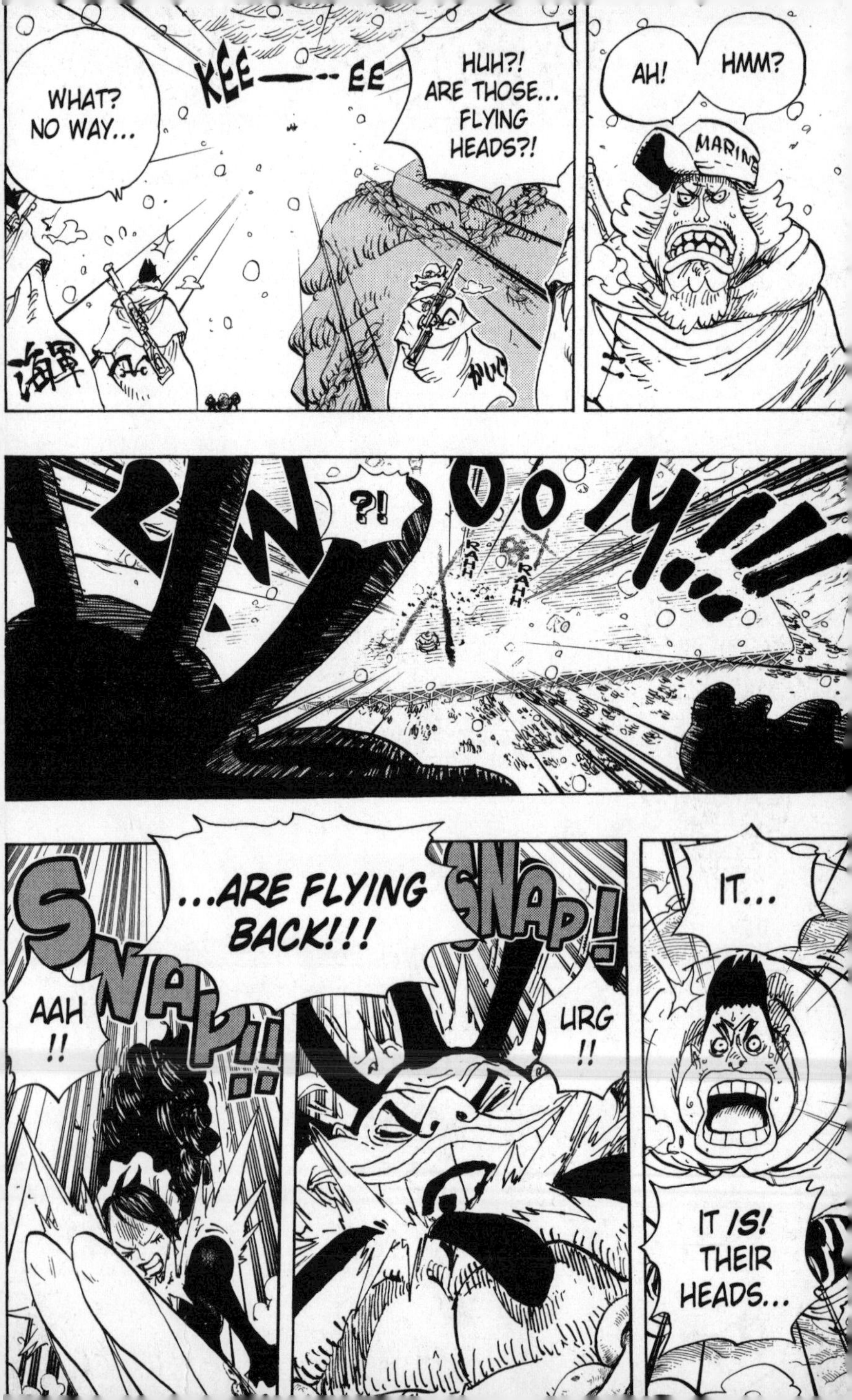

HMM?
AH!
MARINE
HUH?! ARE THOSE... FLYING HEADS?!
KEE———EE
WHAT? NO WAY...
?!
RAHH
RAHH
IT...
IT IS! THEIR HEADS...
...ARE FLYING BACK!!!
SNAP!
URG!!
SNAP!!
AAH!!

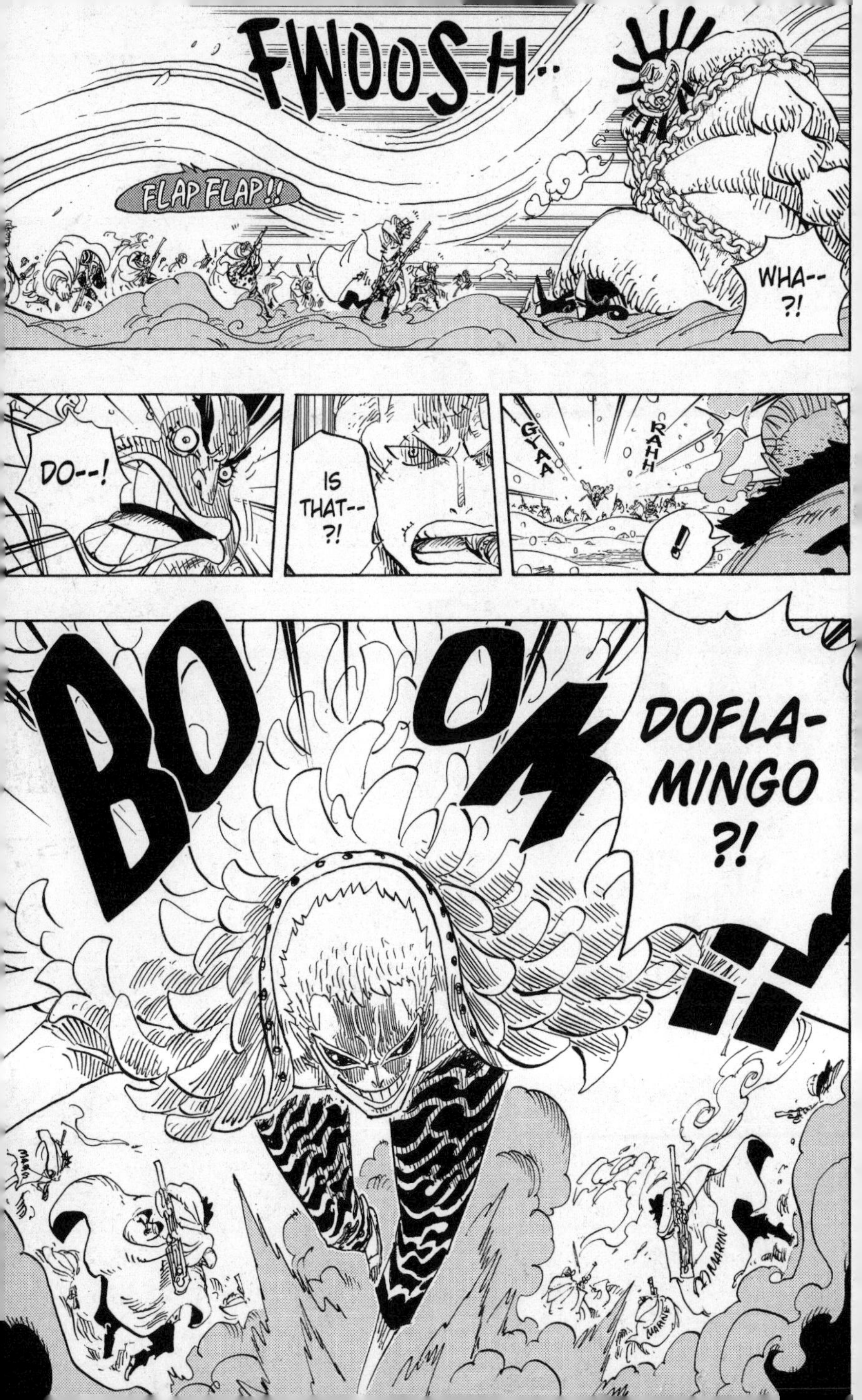
FWOOSH..
WHA-- ?!
FLAP FLAP!!
GYAA
RAHH
!
IS THAT-- ?!
DO--!
DOFLA-
MINGO
?!
BOOM

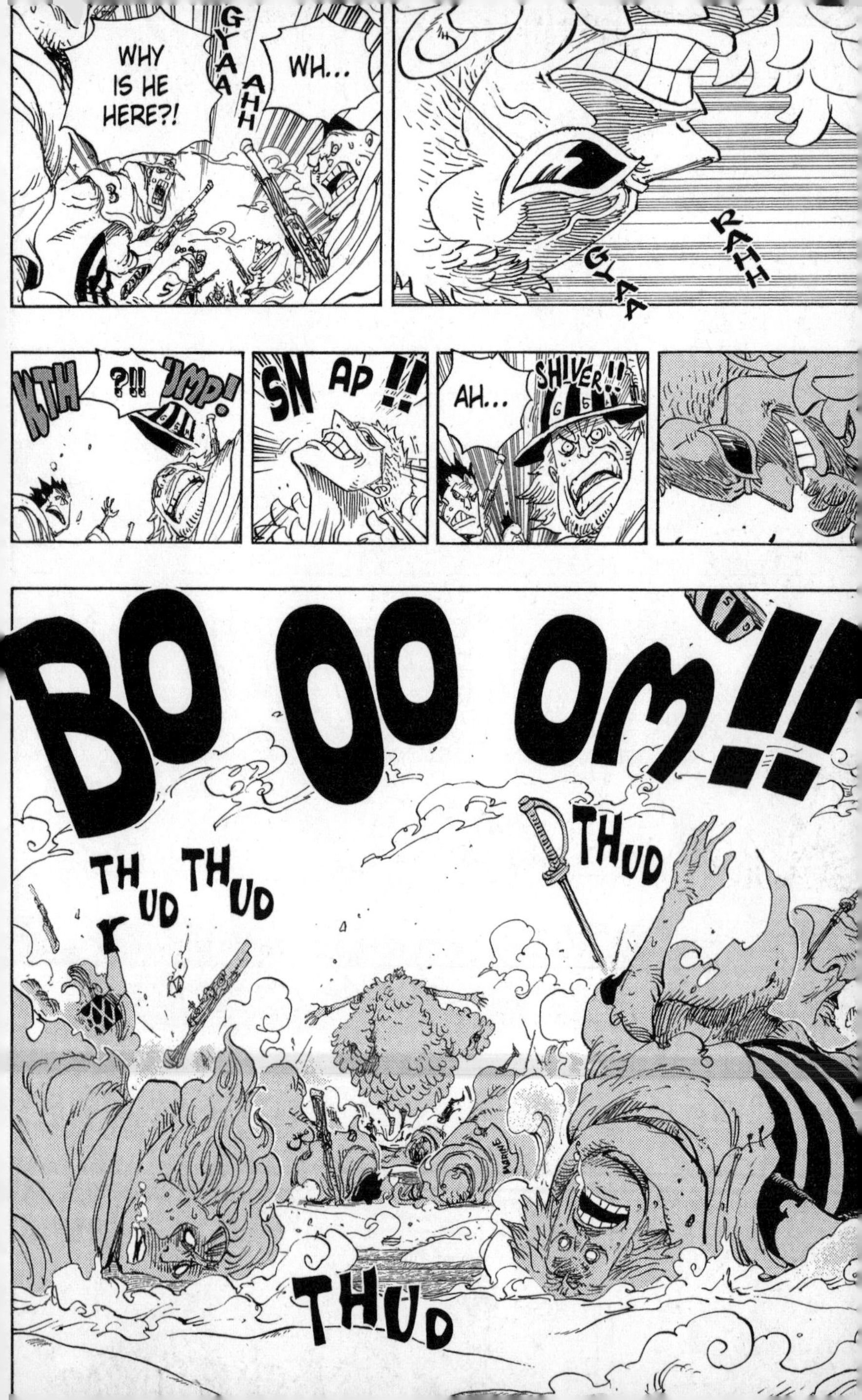
GYAA RAHH
WH...
GYAAAHH
WHY IS HE HERE?!
AH...
SHIVER!!
SNAP!!
?!!
BOOOM!!
THUD
THUD THUD
THUD

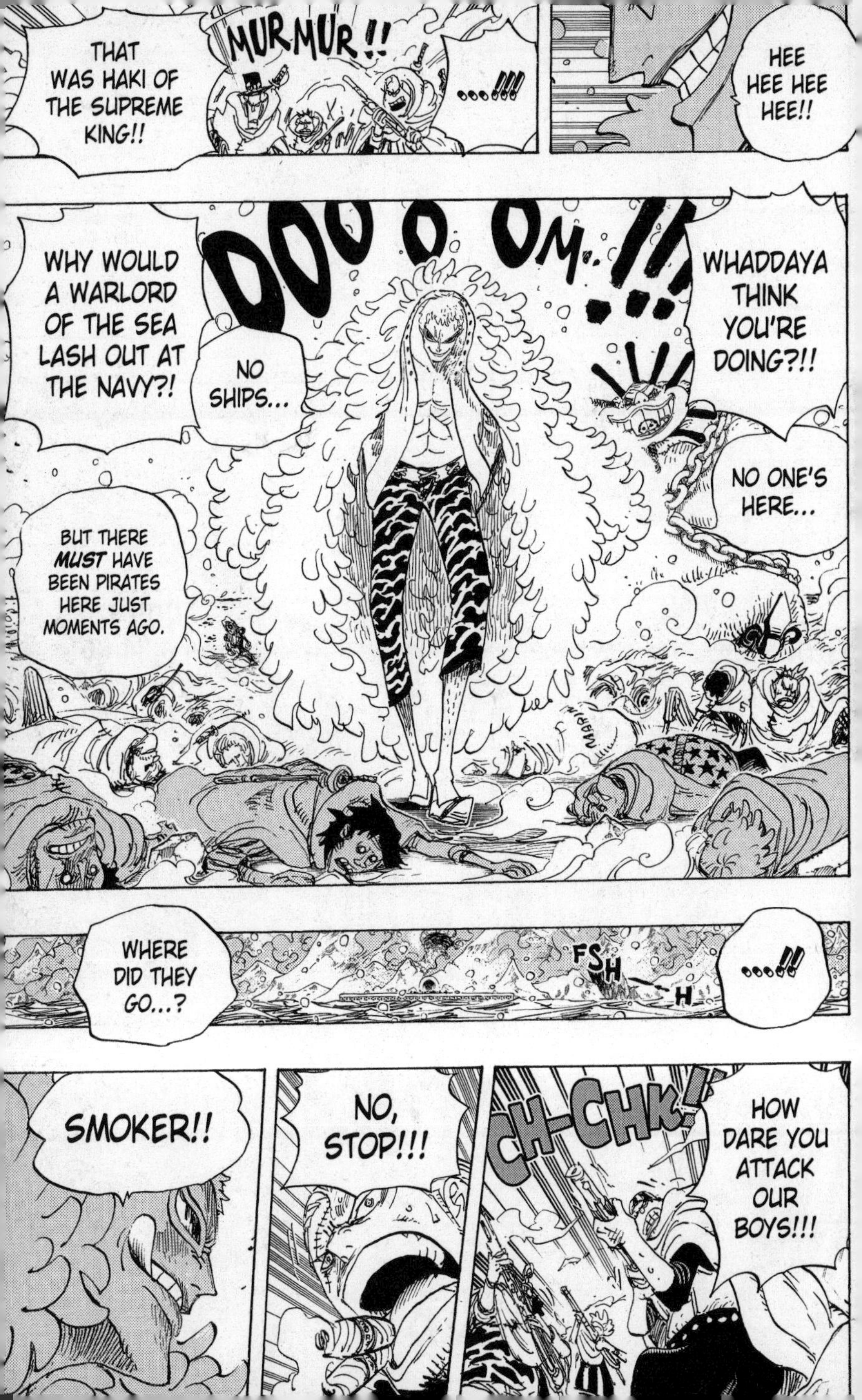
HEE HEE HEE HEE!!
MURMUR!!
...!!!
THAT WAS HAKI OF THE SUPREME KING!!
WHADDAYA THINK YOU'RE DOING?!!
DOOOOM!!
NO ONE'S HERE...
NO SHIPS...
WHY WOULD A WARLORD OF THE SEA LASH OUT AT THE NAVY?!
BUT THERE *MUST* HAVE BEEN PIRATES HERE JUST MOMENTS AGO.
...!!
FSHH
WHERE DID THEY GO...?
HOW DARE YOU ATTACK OUR BOYS!!!
CH-CHK!
NO, STOP!!!
SMOKER!!

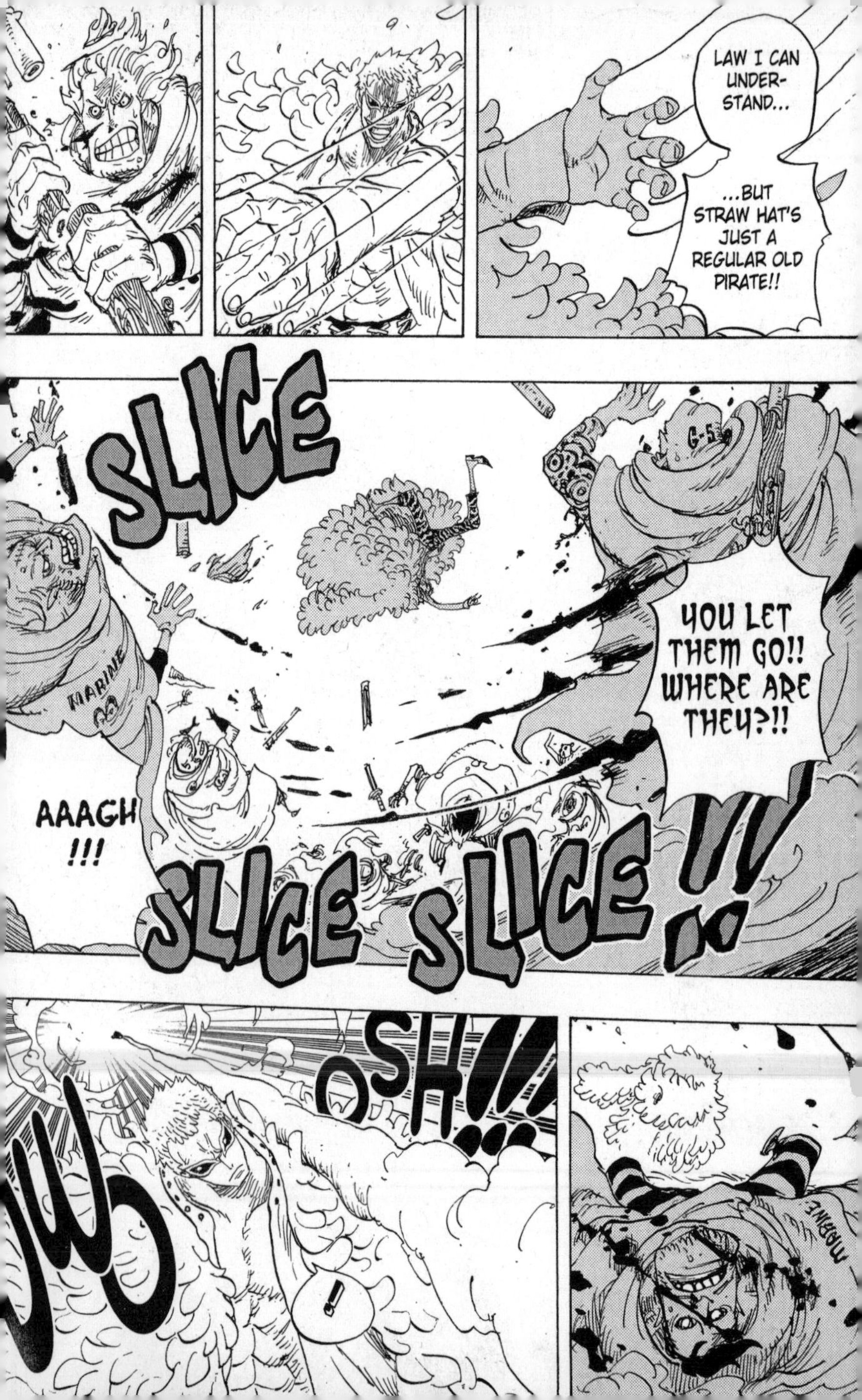
LAW I CAN UNDER-STAND...
...BUT STRAW HAT'S JUST A REGULAR OLD PIRATE!!
G-5
YOU LET THEM GO!! WHERE ARE THEY?!!
SLICE
MARINE
AAAGH !!!
SLICE SLICE !!
OSH!!
!

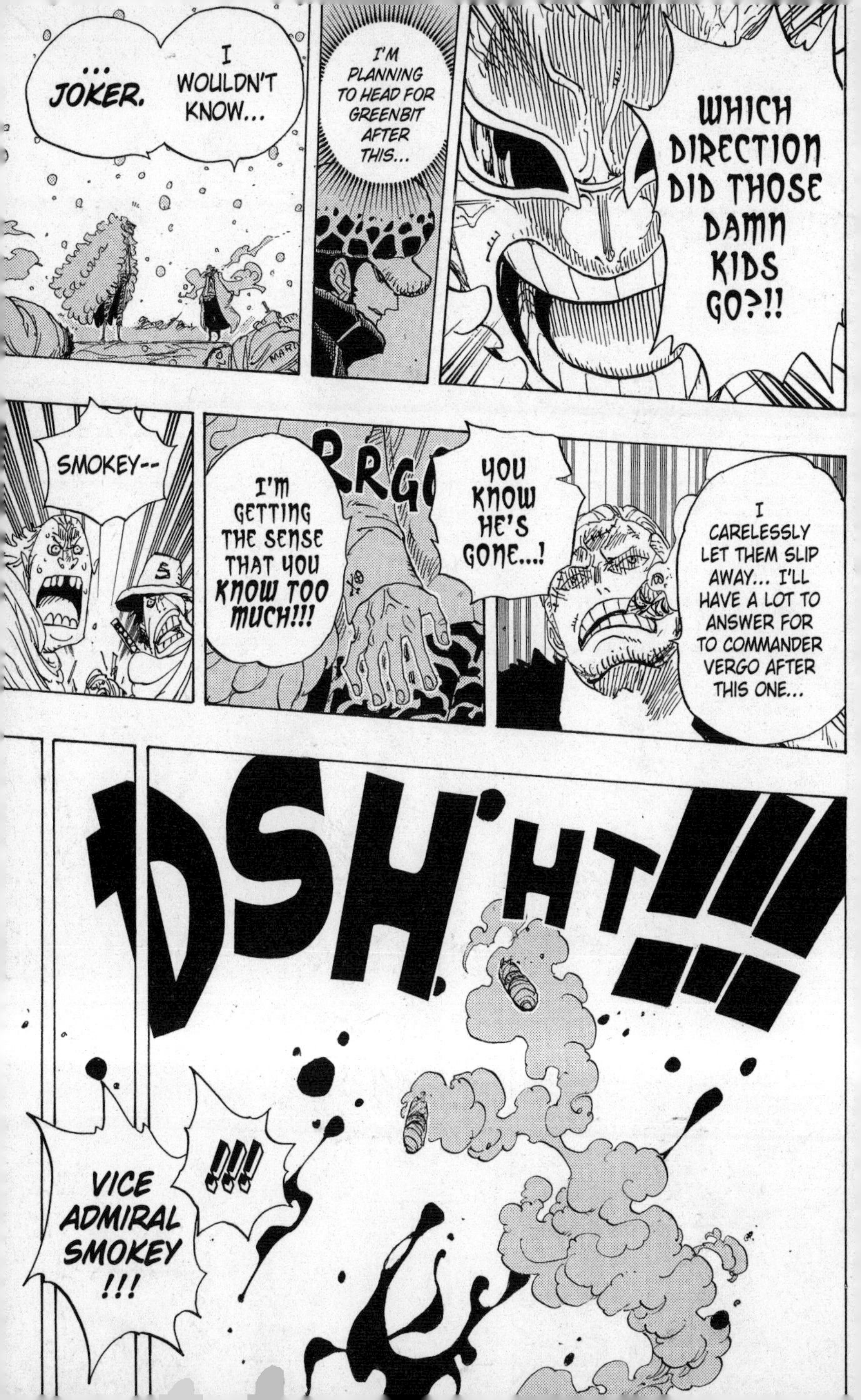

WHICH DIRECTION DID THOSE DAMN KIDS GO?!!
I'M PLANNING TO HEAD FOR GREENBIT AFTER THIS...
I WOULDN'T KNOW...
... JOKER.
I CARELESSLY LET THEM SLIP AWAY... I'LL HAVE A LOT TO ANSWER FOR TO COMMANDER VERGO AFTER THIS ONE...
YOU KNOW HE'S GONE...!
RRG
I'M GETTING THE SENSE THAT YOU KNOW TOO MUCH!!!
SMOKEY--
DSHHT!!!
!!!
VICE ADMIRAL SMOKEY!!!

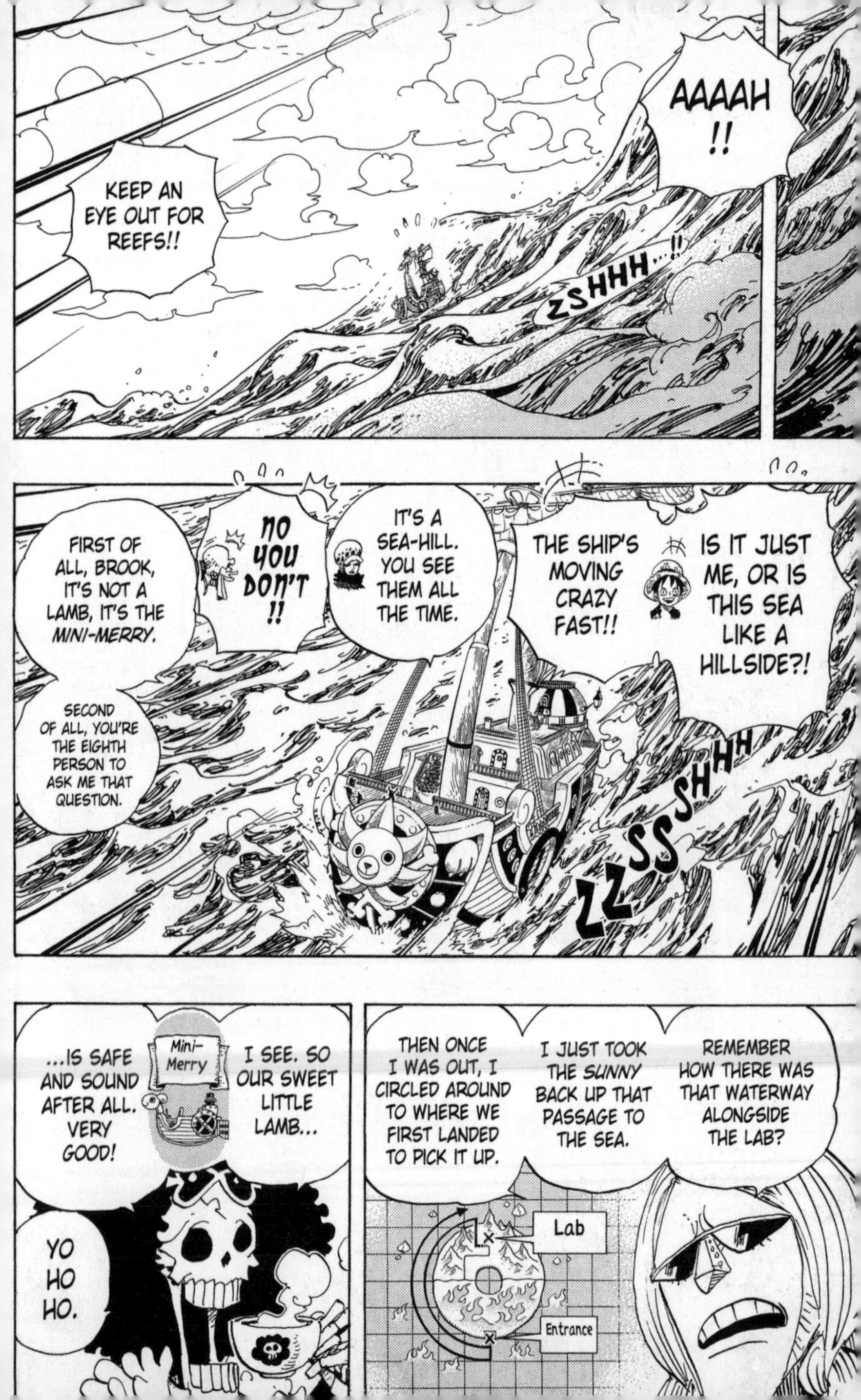
AAAAH!!
KEEP AN EYE OUT FOR REEFS!!
ZSHHH...!!
IS IT JUST ME, OR IS THIS SEA LIKE A HILLSIDE?!
THE SHIP'S MOVING CRAZY FAST!!
IT'S A SEA-HILL. YOU SEE THEM ALL THE TIME.
NO YOU DON'T!!
FIRST OF ALL, BROOK, IT'S NOT A LAMB, IT'S THE *MINI-MERRY*.
SECOND OF ALL, YOU'RE THE EIGHTH PERSON TO ASK ME THAT QUESTION.
ZZSSSHHH
REMEMBER HOW THERE WAS THAT WATERWAY ALONGSIDE THE LAB?
I JUST TOOK THE *SUNNY* BACK UP THAT PASSAGE TO THE SEA.
THEN ONCE I WAS OUT, I CIRCLED AROUND TO WHERE WE FIRST LANDED TO PICK IT UP.
Lab
Entrance
I SEE. SO OUR SWEET LITTLE LAMB...
Mini-Merry
...IS SAFE AND SOUND AFTER ALL. VERY GOOD!
YO HO HO.

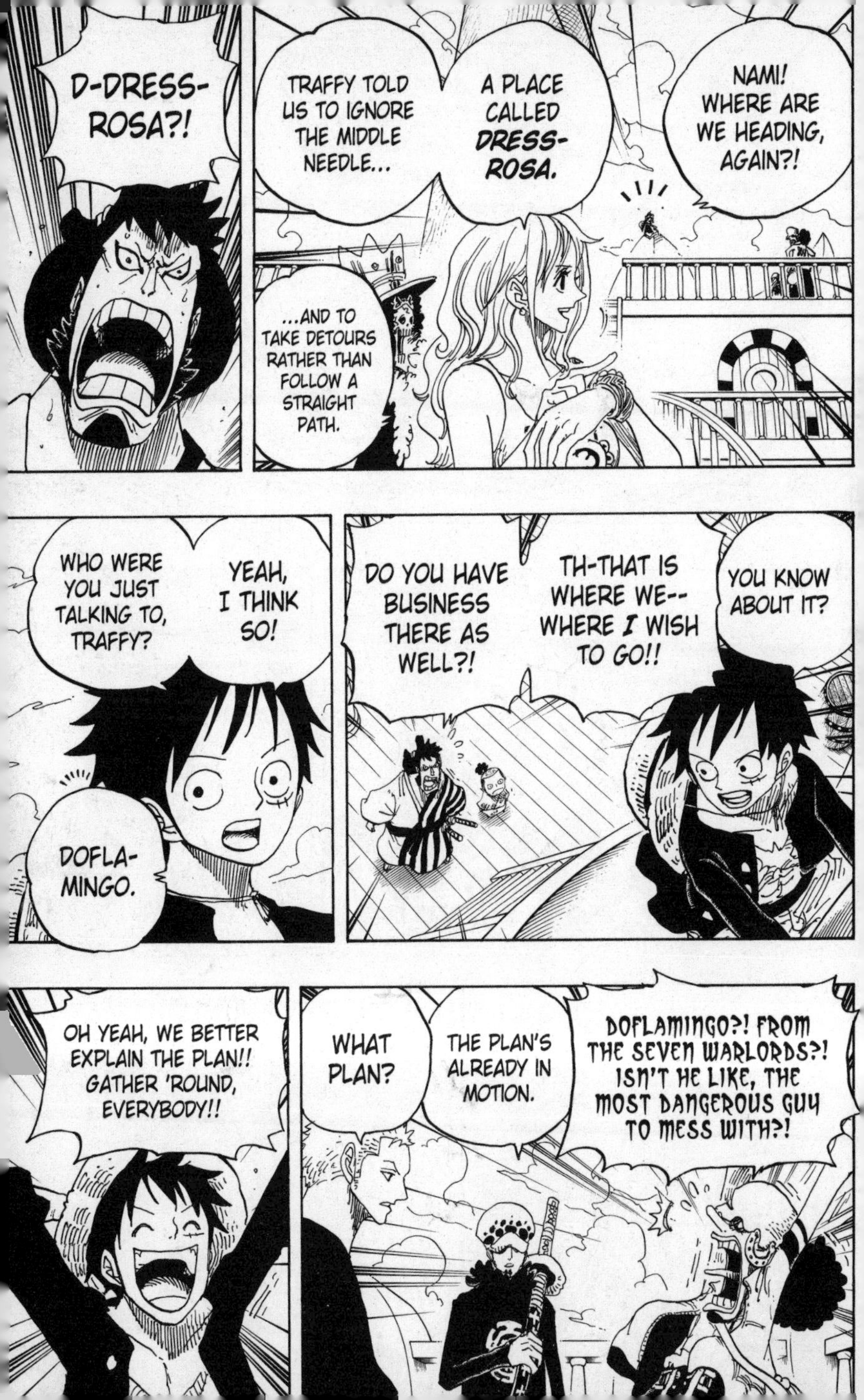
NAMI! WHERE ARE WE HEADING, AGAIN?!
A PLACE CALLED **DRESS-ROSA.**
TRAFFY TOLD US TO IGNORE THE MIDDLE NEEDLE...
...AND TO TAKE DETOURS RATHER THAN FOLLOW A STRAIGHT PATH.
D-DRESS-ROSA?!
YOU KNOW ABOUT IT?
TH-THAT IS WHERE WE-- WHERE *I* WISH TO GO!!
DO YOU HAVE BUSINESS THERE AS WELL?!
YEAH, I THINK SO!
WHO WERE YOU JUST TALKING TO, TRAFFY?
DOFLAMINGO.
DOFLAMINGO?! FROM THE SEVEN WARLORDS?! ISN'T HE LIKE, THE MOST DANGEROUS GUY TO MESS WITH?!
THE PLAN'S ALREADY IN MOTION.
WHAT PLAN?
OH YEAH, WE BETTER EXPLAIN THE PLAN!! GATHER 'ROUND, EVERYBODY!!

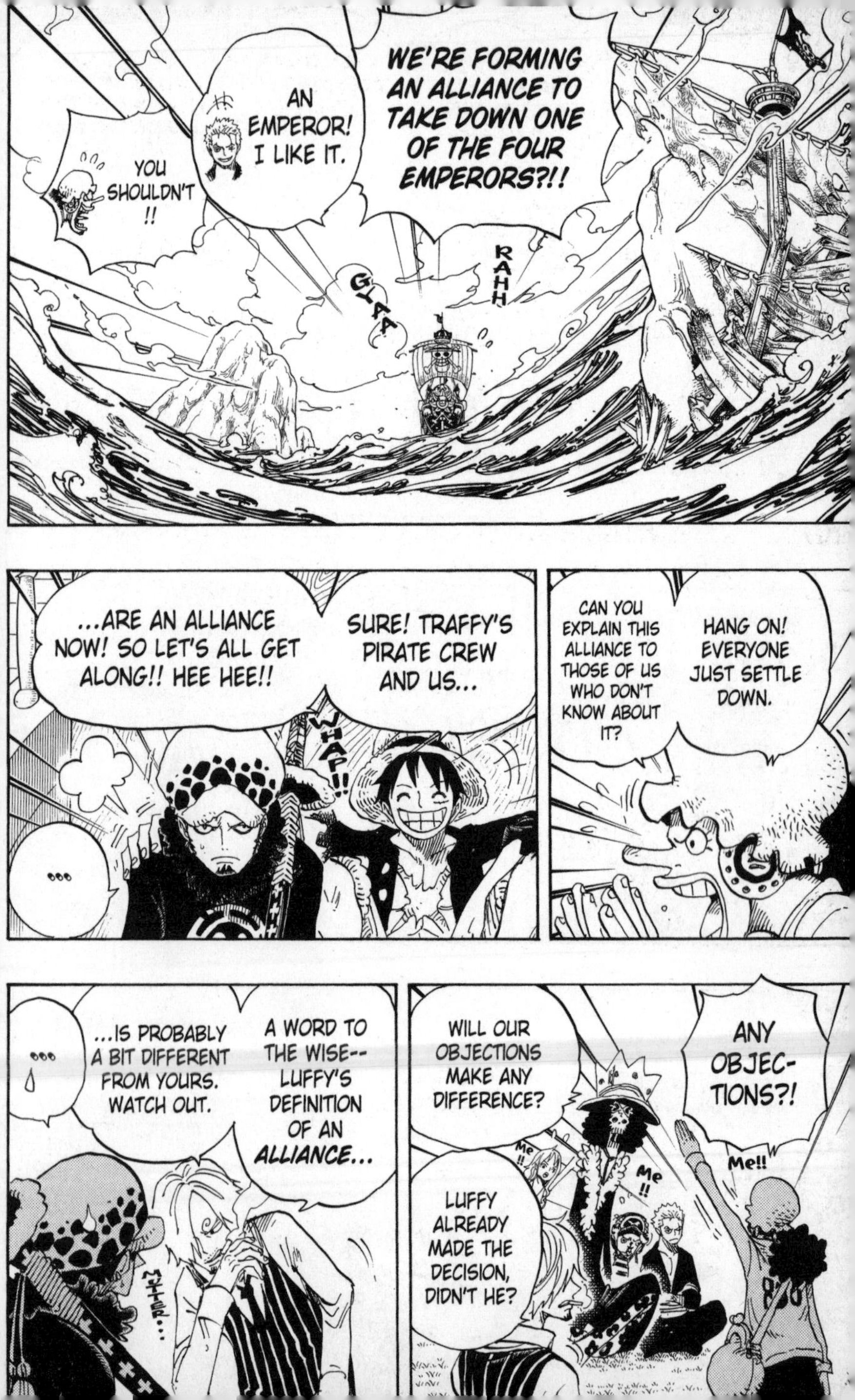
WE'RE FORMING AN ALLIANCE TO TAKE DOWN ONE OF THE FOUR EMPERORS?!!
AN EMPEROR! I LIKE IT.
YOU SHOULDN'T !!
RAHHH
GYAA
HANG ON! EVERYONE JUST SETTLE DOWN.
CAN YOU EXPLAIN THIS ALLIANCE TO THOSE OF US WHO DON'T KNOW ABOUT IT?
SURE! TRAFFY'S PIRATE CREW AND US...
...ARE AN ALLIANCE NOW! SO LET'S ALL GET ALONG!! HEE HEE!!
WHAP!!
...
ANY OBJECTIONS?!
Me!!
WILL OUR OBJECTIONS MAKE ANY DIFFERENCE?
Me !!
Me !!
LUFFY ALREADY MADE THE DECISION, DIDN'T HE?
A WORD TO THE WISE-- LUFFY'S DEFINITION OF AN ALLIANCE...
...IS PROBABLY A BIT DIFFERENT FROM YOURS. WATCH OUT.
...
MUTTER...

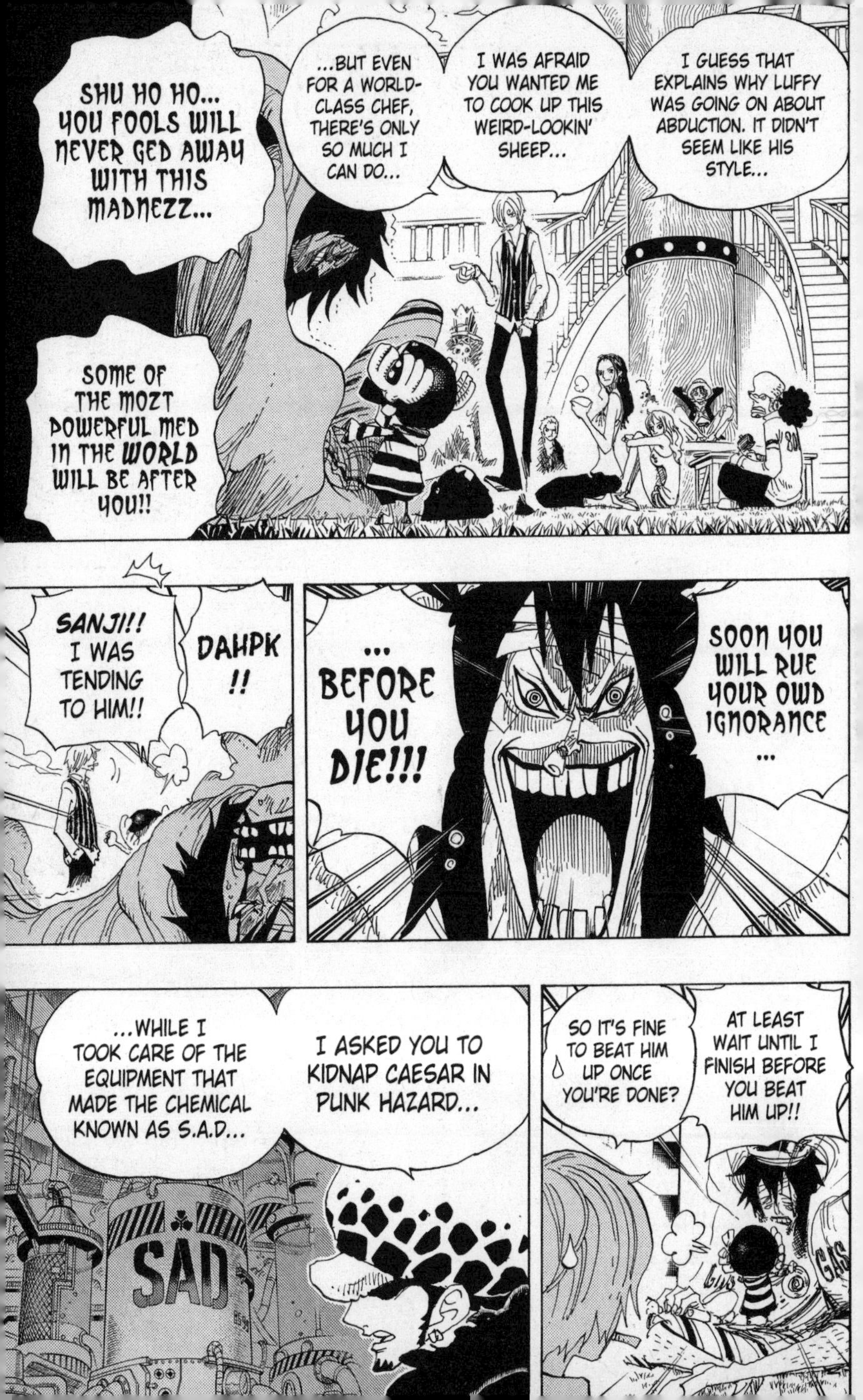
I GUESS THAT EXPLAINS WHY LUFFY WAS GOING ON ABOUT ABDUCTION. IT DIDN'T SEEM LIKE HIS STYLE...
I WAS AFRAID YOU WANTED ME TO COOK UP THIS WEIRD-LOOKIN' SHEEP...
...BUT EVEN FOR A WORLD-CLASS CHEF, THERE'S ONLY SO MUCH I CAN DO...
SHU HO HO... YOU FOOLS WILL NEVER GED AWAY WITH THIS MADNEZZ...
SOME OF THE MOZT POWERFUL MED IN THE WORLD WILL BE AFTER YOU!!
SOON YOU WILL RUE YOUR OWD IGNORANCE...
...BEFORE YOU DIE!!!
DAHPK!!
SANJI!! I WAS TENDING TO HIM!!
AT LEAST WAIT UNTIL I FINISH BEFORE YOU BEAT HIM UP!!
SO IT'S FINE TO BEAT HIM UP ONCE YOU'RE DONE?
GAS
I ASKED YOU TO KIDNAP CAESAR IN PUNK HAZARD...
...WHILE I TOOK CARE OF THE EQUIPMENT THAT MADE THE CHEMICAL KNOWN AS S.A.D...
SAD

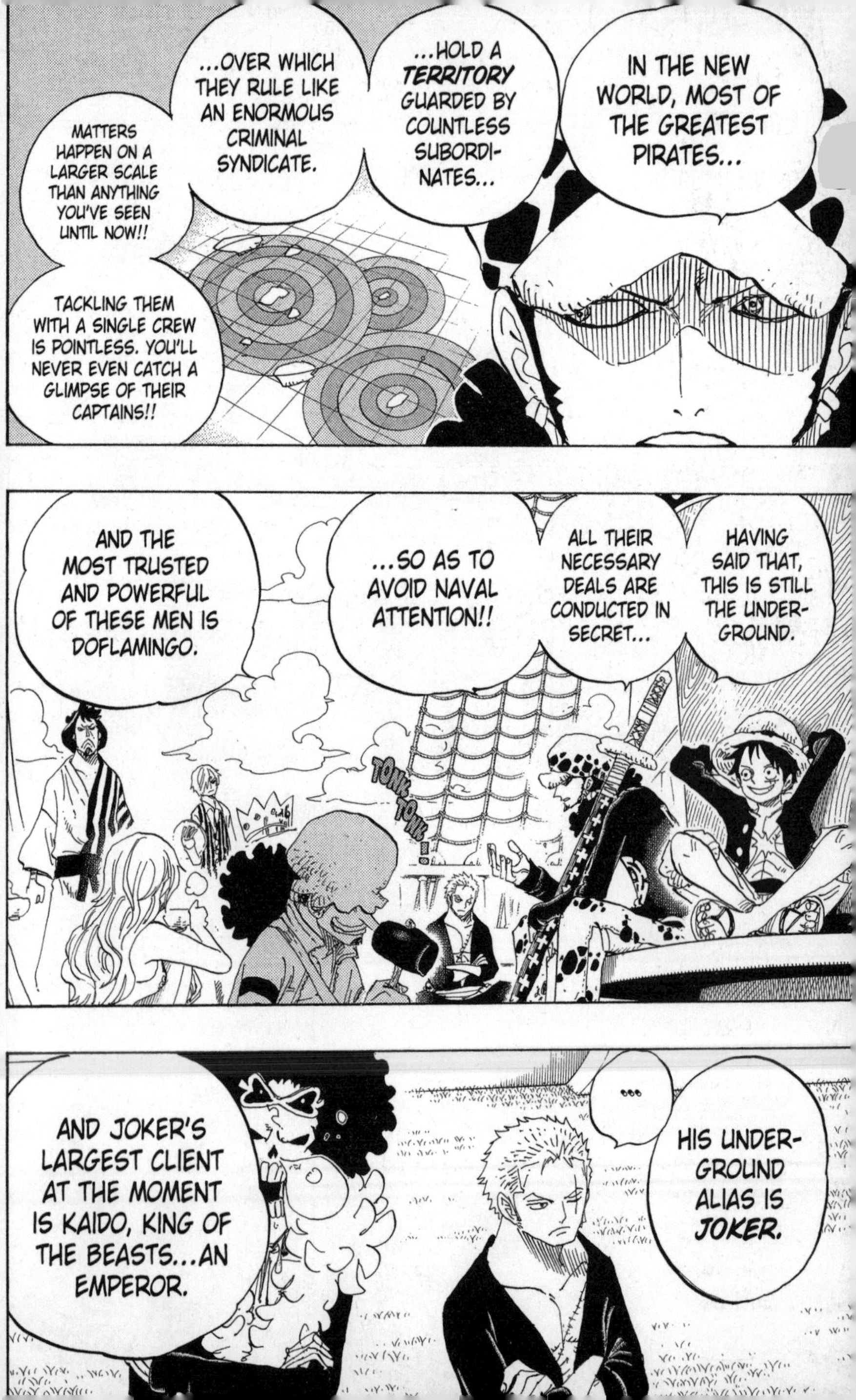
IN THE NEW WORLD, MOST OF THE GREATEST PIRATES...
...HOLD A TERRITORY GUARDED BY COUNTLESS SUBORDI-NATES...
...OVER WHICH THEY RULE LIKE AN ENORMOUS CRIMINAL SYNDICATE.
MATTERS HAPPEN ON A LARGER SCALE THAN ANYTHING YOU'VE SEEN UNTIL NOW!!
TACKLING THEM WITH A SINGLE CREW IS POINTLESS. YOU'LL NEVER EVEN CATCH A GLIMPSE OF THEIR CAPTAINS!!
HAVING SAID THAT, THIS IS STILL THE UNDER-GROUND.
ALL THEIR NECESSARY DEALS ARE CONDUCTED IN SECRET...
...SO AS TO AVOID NAVAL ATTENTION!!
AND THE MOST TRUSTED AND POWERFUL OF THESE MEN IS DOFLAMINGO.
TONK TONK
HIS UNDER-GROUND ALIAS IS JOKER.
...
AND JOKER'S LARGEST CLIENT AT THE MOMENT IS KAIDO, KING OF THE BEASTS...AN EMPEROR.

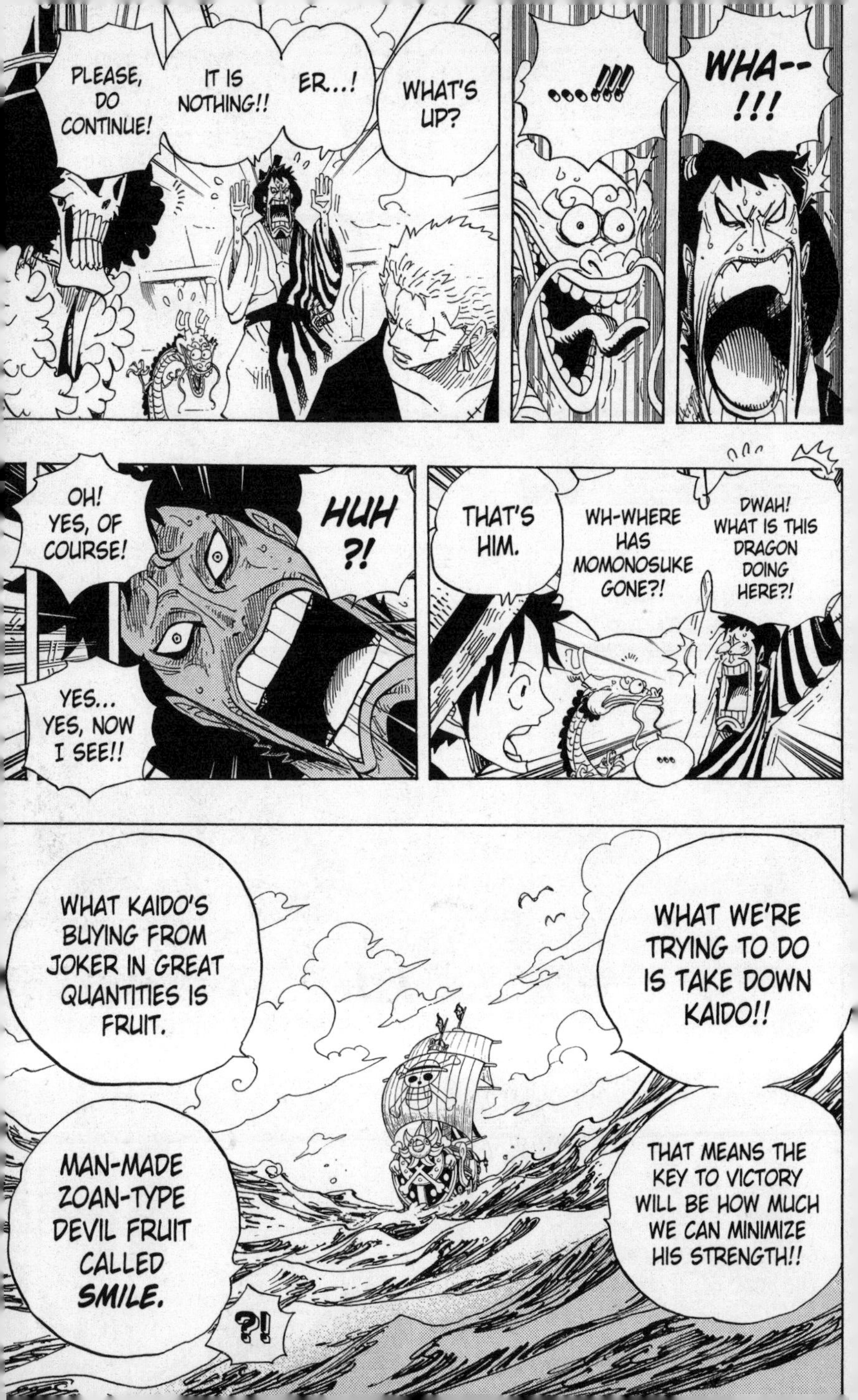
WHA-- !!!
...!!!!
WHAT'S UP?
ER...!
IT IS NOTHING!!
PLEASE, DO CONTINUE!
DWAH! WHAT IS THIS DRAGON DOING HERE?!
WH-WHERE HAS MOMONOSUKE GONE?!
THAT'S HIM.
...
HUH ?!
OH! YES, OF COURSE!
YES... YES, NOW I SEE!!
WHAT WE'RE TRYING TO DO IS TAKE DOWN KAIDO!!
THAT MEANS THE KEY TO VICTORY WILL BE HOW MUCH WE CAN MINIMIZE HIS STRENGTH!!
WHAT KAIDO'S BUYING FROM JOKER IN GREAT QUANTITIES IS FRUIT.
MAN-MADE ZOAN-TYPE DEVIL FRUIT CALLED **SMILE.**
?!

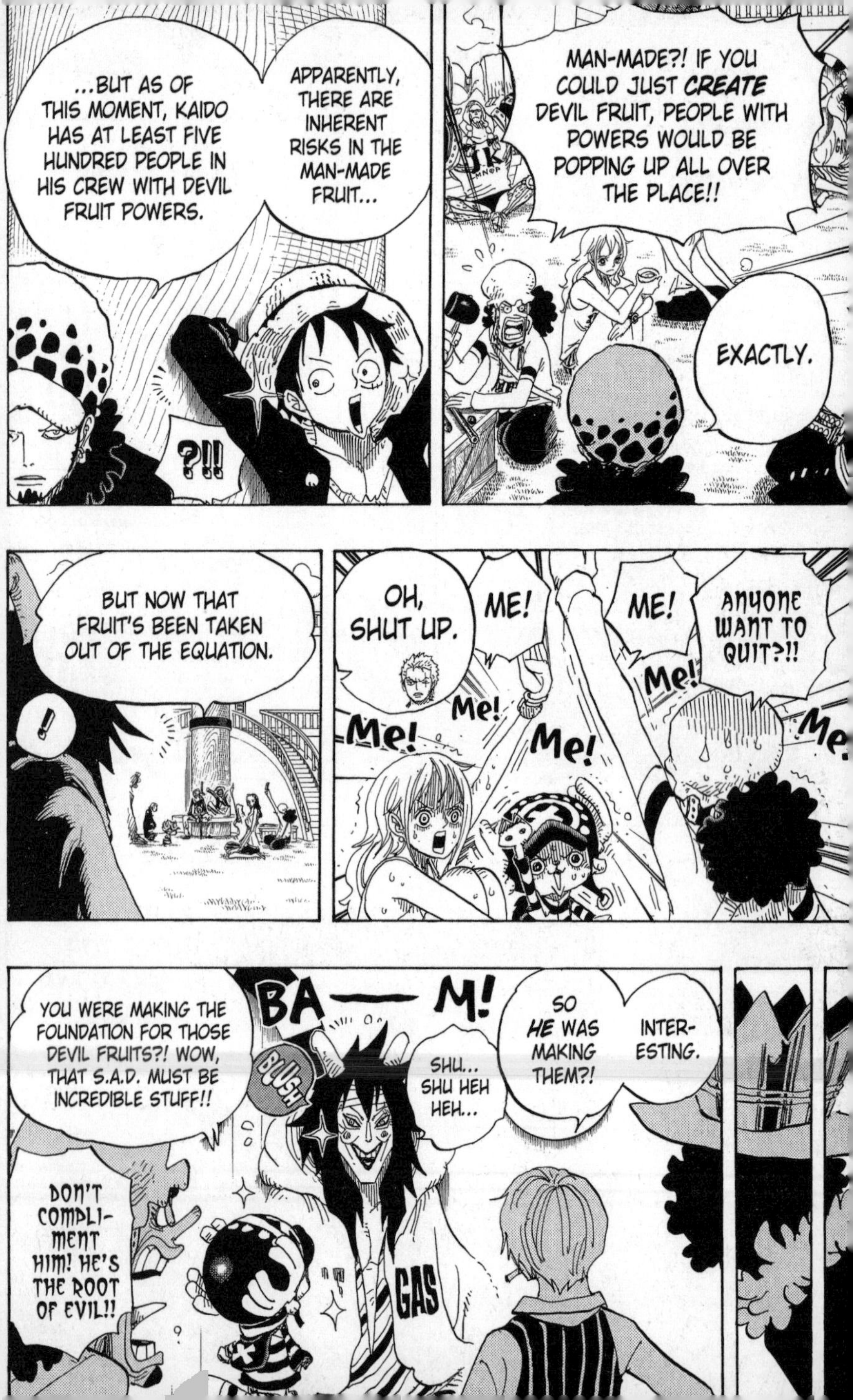

MAN-MADE?! IF YOU COULD JUST *CREATE* DEVIL FRUIT, PEOPLE WITH POWERS WOULD BE POPPING UP ALL OVER THE PLACE!!
EXACTLY.
APPARENTLY, THERE ARE INHERENT RISKS IN THE MAN-MADE FRUIT...
...BUT AS OF THIS MOMENT, KAIDO HAS AT LEAST FIVE HUNDRED PEOPLE IN HIS CREW WITH DEVIL FRUIT POWERS.
?!!
ANYONE WANT TO QUIT?!!
ME!
Me!
ME!
OH, SHUT UP.
Me!
Me!
Me!
Me!
BUT NOW THAT FRUIT'S BEEN TAKEN OUT OF THE EQUATION.
!
INTER-ESTING.
SO *HE* WAS MAKING THEM?!
BA—— M!
SHU... SHU HEH HEH...
YOU WERE MAKING THE FOUNDATION FOR THOSE DEVIL FRUITS?! WOW, THAT S.A.D. MUST BE INCREDIBLE STUFF!!
BLUSH
DON'T COMPLI-MENT HIM! HE'S THE ROOT OF EVIL!!
GAS

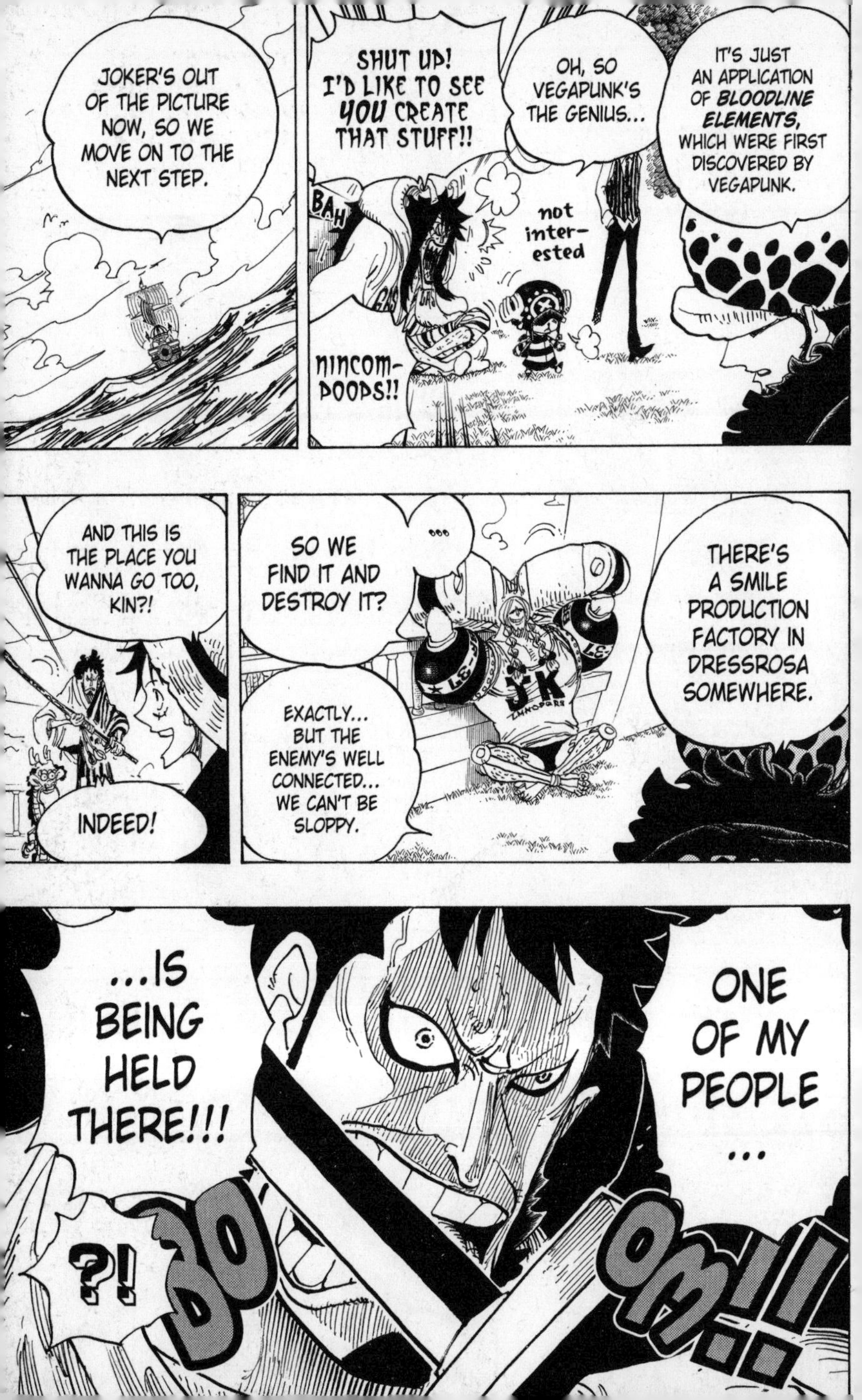
IT'S JUST AN APPLICATION OF BLOODLINE ELEMENTS, WHICH WERE FIRST DISCOVERED BY VEGAPUNK.
OH, SO VEGAPUNK'S THE GENIUS...
SHUT UP! I'D LIKE TO SEE YOU CREATE THAT STUFF!!
BAH
not interested
nincompoops!!
JOKER'S OUT OF THE PICTURE NOW, SO WE MOVE ON TO THE NEXT STEP.
THERE'S A SMILE PRODUCTION FACTORY IN DRESSROSA SOMEWHERE.
...
SO WE FIND IT AND DESTROY IT?
EXACTLY... BUT THE ENEMY'S WELL CONNECTED... WE CAN'T BE SLOPPY.
AND THIS IS THE PLACE YOU WANNA GO TOO, KIN?!
INDEED!
ONE OF MY PEOPLE ...
...IS BEING HELD THERE!!!
?!
BOOM!!

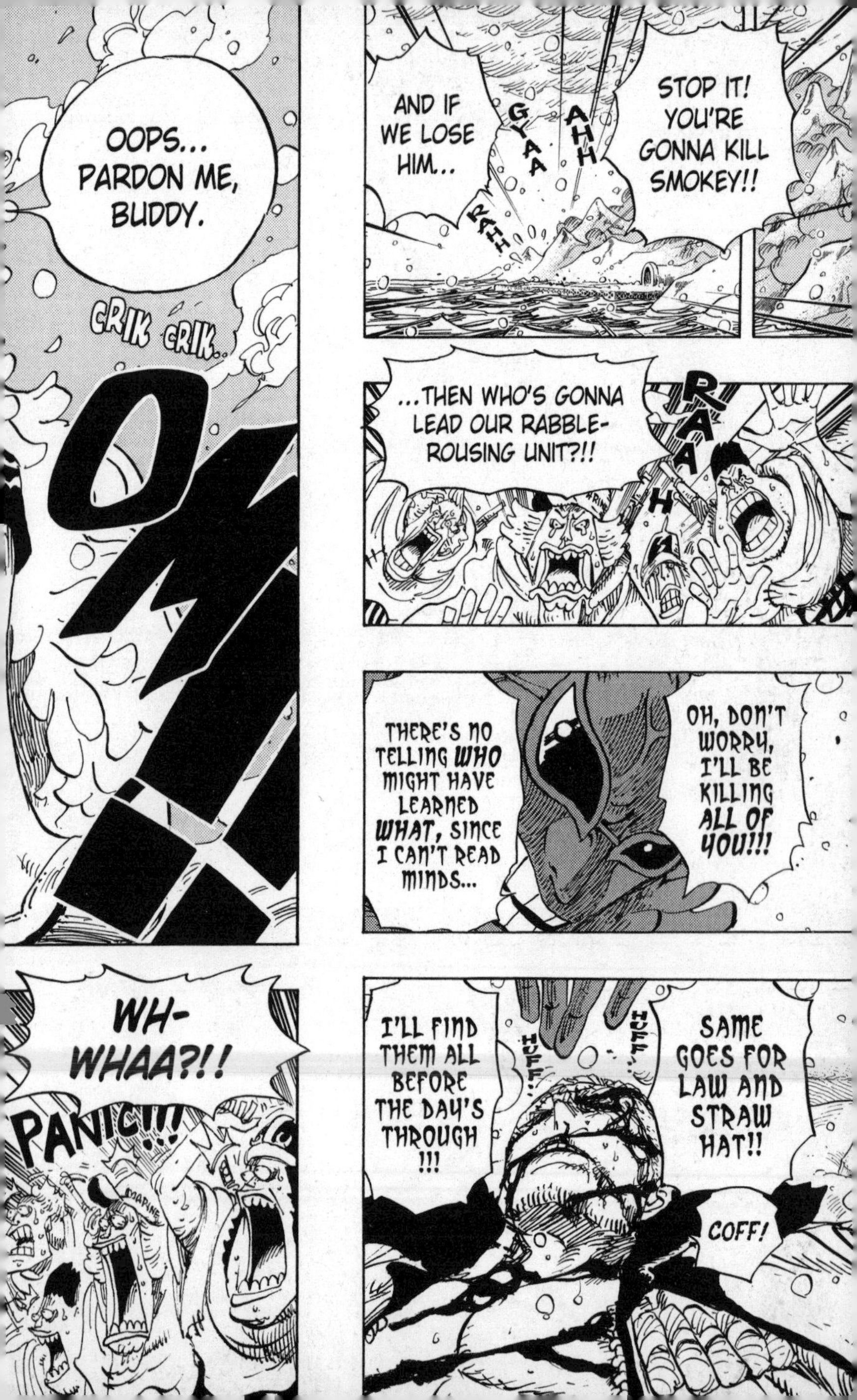
STOP IT! YOU'RE GONNA KILL SMOKEY!!
AHH
GYAA
AND IF WE LOSE HIM...
RAHH
RAAAH
...THEN WHO'S GONNA LEAD OUR RABBLE-ROUSING UNIT?!!
OH, DON'T WORRY, I'LL BE KILLING ALL OF YOU!!!
THERE'S NO TELLING WHO MIGHT HAVE LEARNED WHAT, SINCE I CAN'T READ MINDS...
OOPS... PARDON ME, BUDDY.
CRIK CRIK..
SAME GOES FOR LAW AND STRAW HAT!!
HUFF
HUFF
I'LL FIND THEM ALL BEFORE THE DAY'S THROUGH!!!
COFF!
WH-WHAA?!!
PANIC!!!

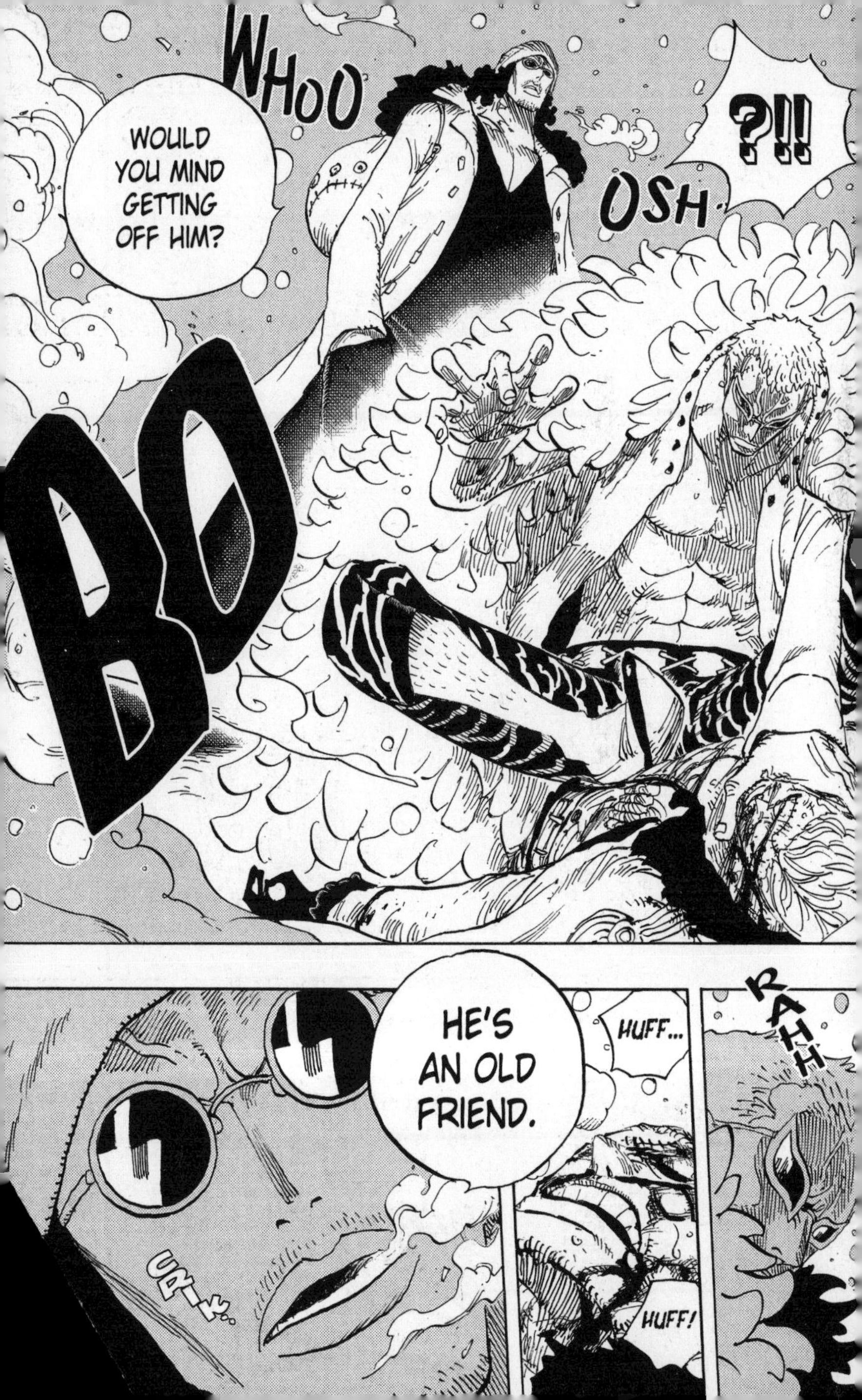
?!!
WHOO
OSH
WOULD YOU MIND GETTING OFF HIM?
BO
RAHH
HUFF...
HUFF!
HE'S AN OLD FRIEND.
URIK...

MORNING EDITION

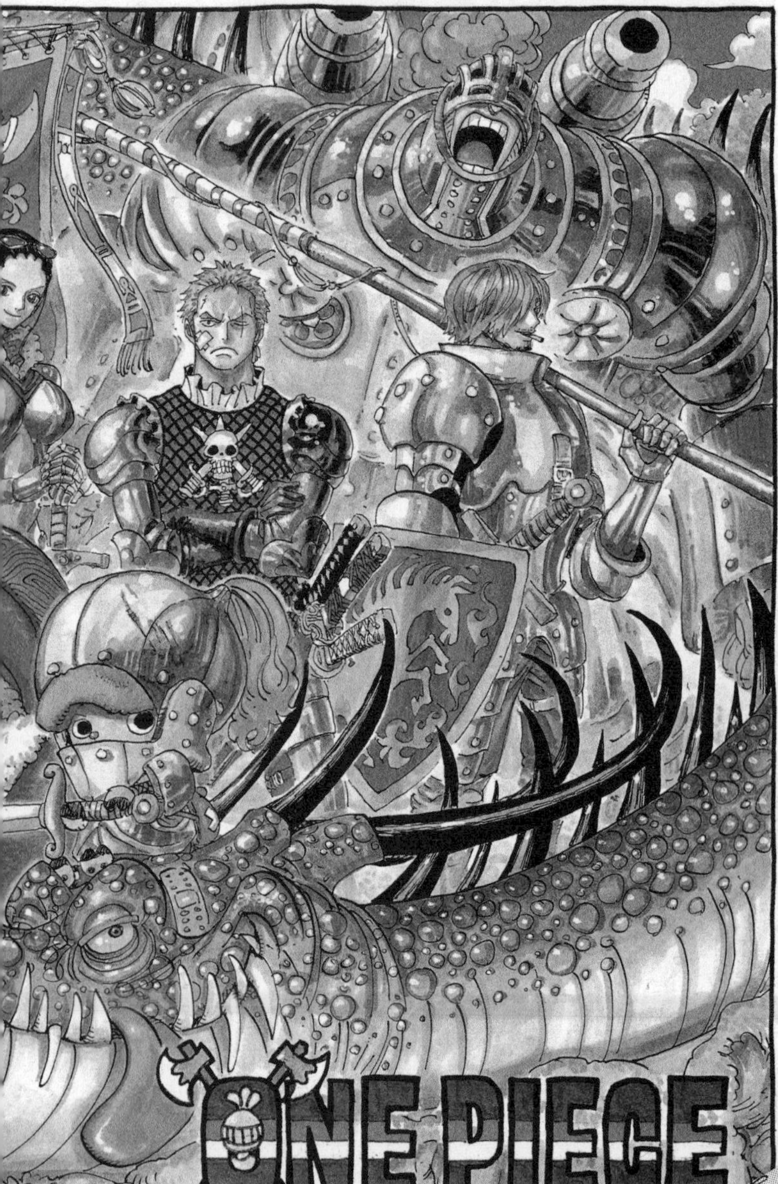
ONE PIECE

Chapter 699:

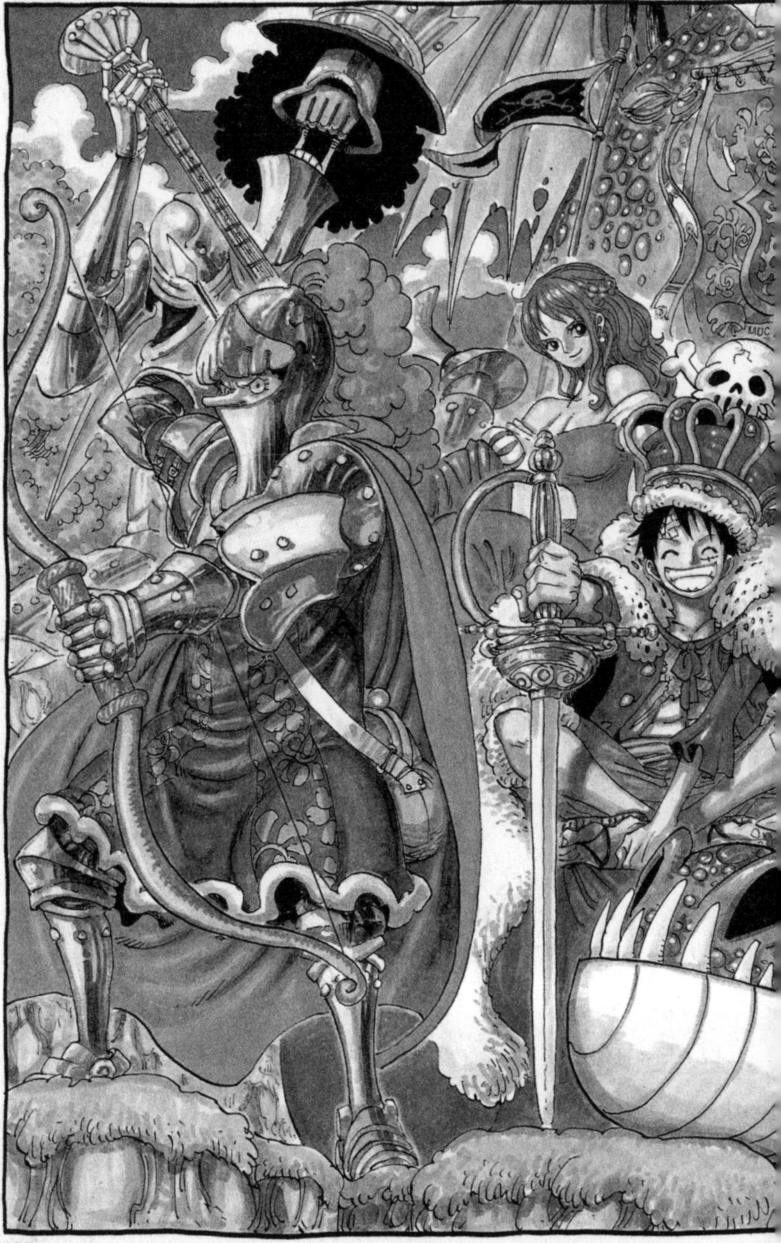

vol. 70
ONE PIECE

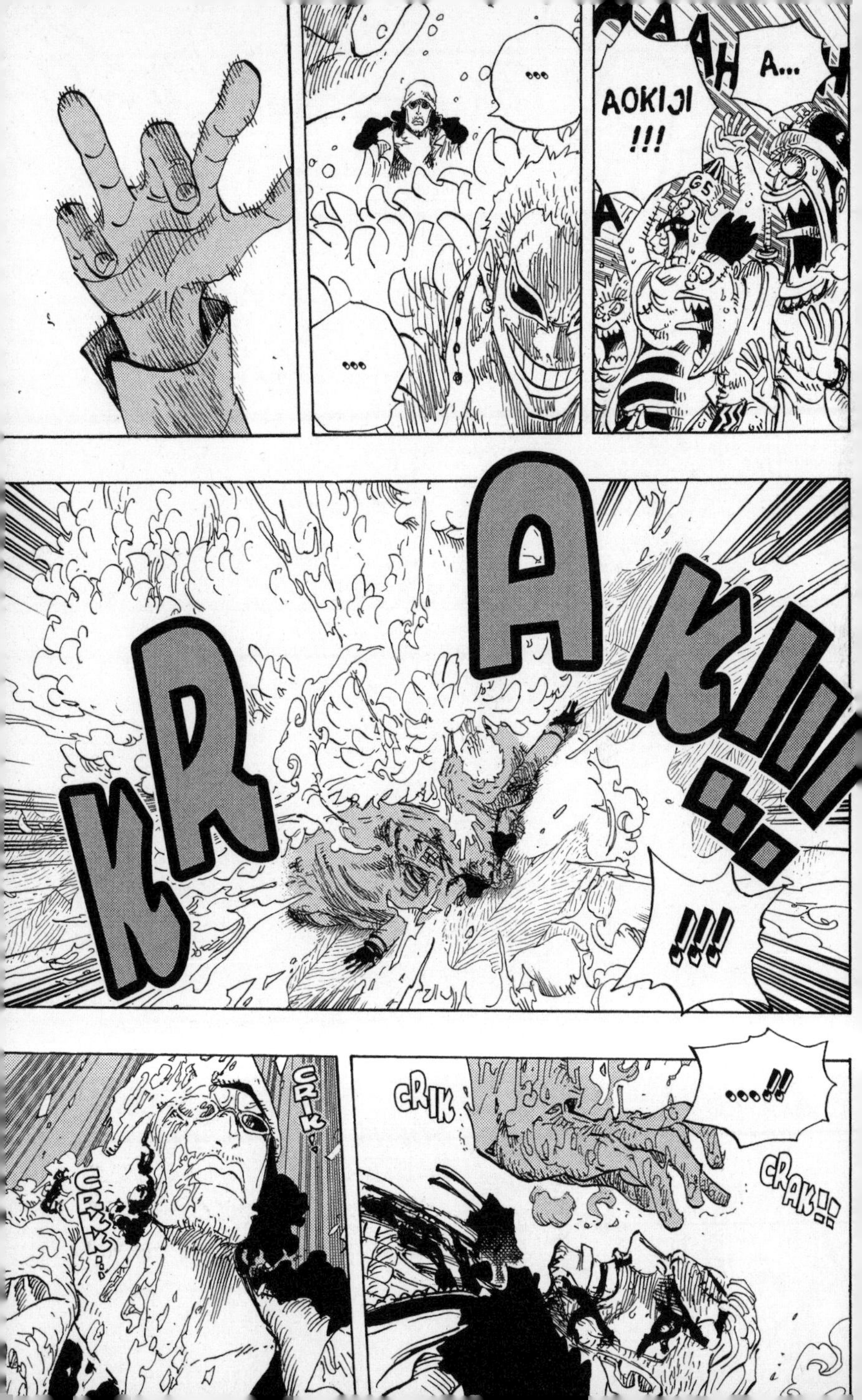
A...
AOKIJI !!!
...
...
KRAKI!!!
!!!
...!!
CRIK
CRAK!!
CRIK!
CRIK!!

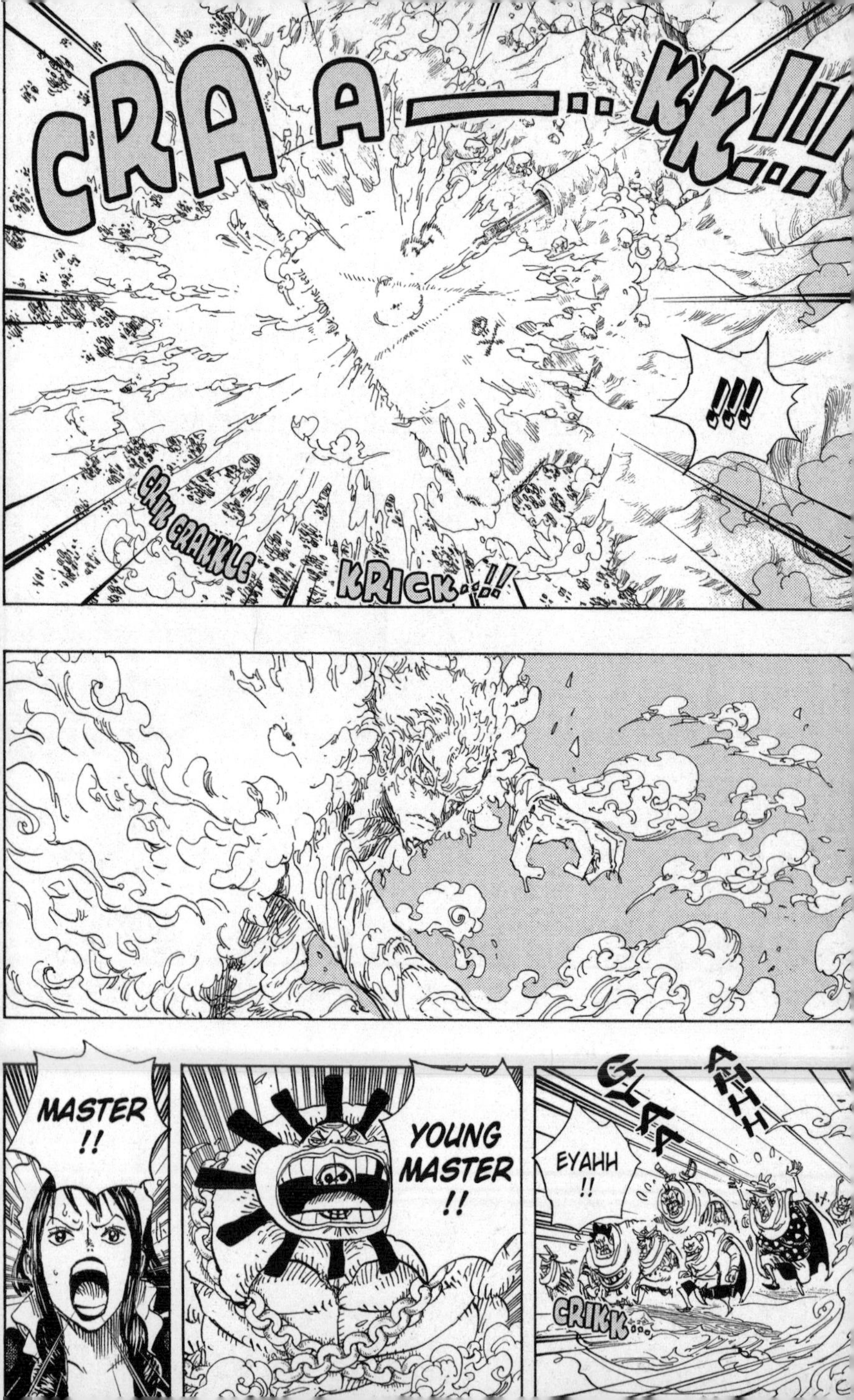
CRAA—...KK!!!...
!!!
CRIK CRAKKLE
KRICK...!!
GYAAAHHH
EYAHH !!
CRIKK...
YOUNG MASTER !!
MASTER !!

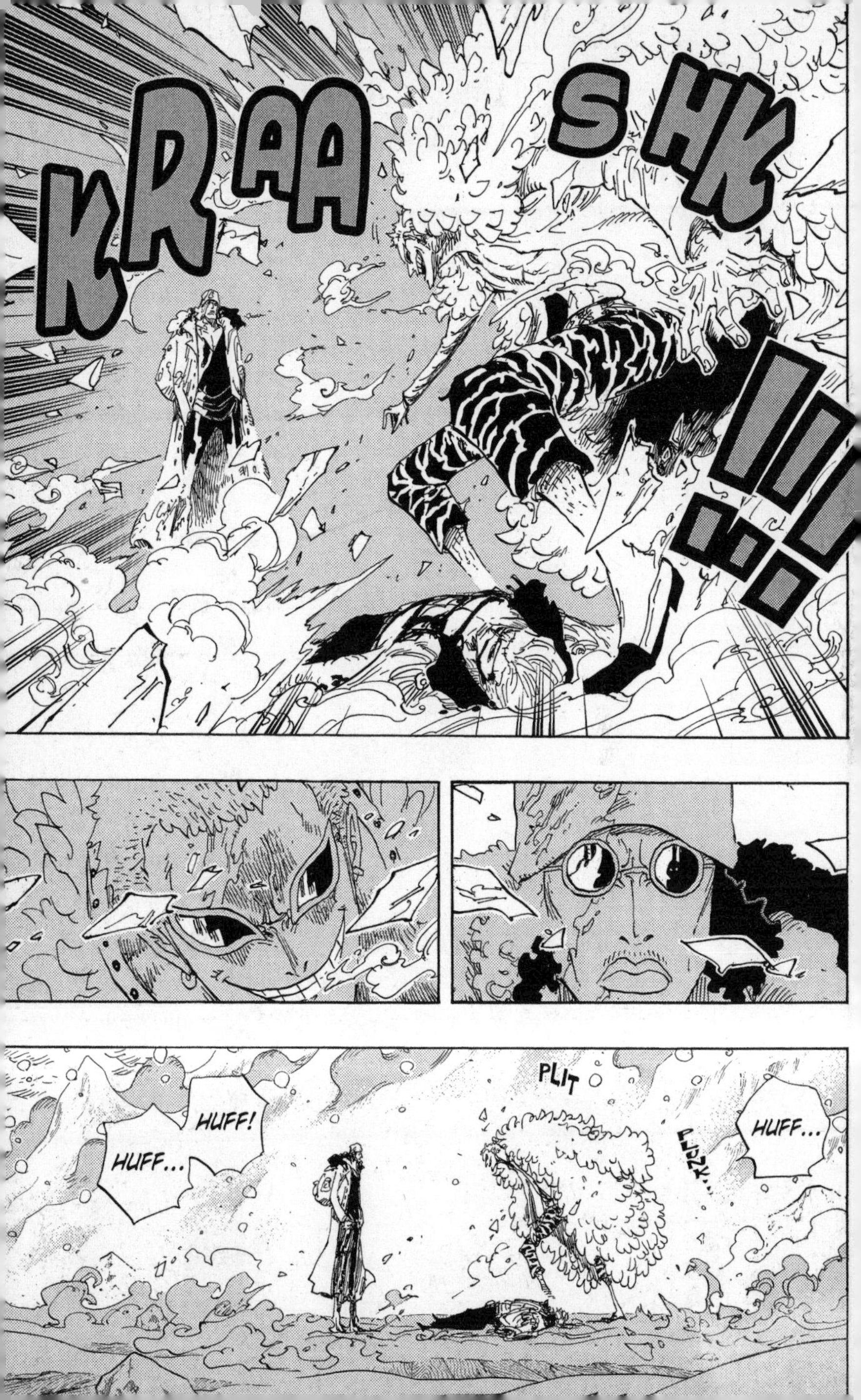
KRAA SHK!!
HUFF...
PLUNK...
PLIT
HUFF!
HUFF...

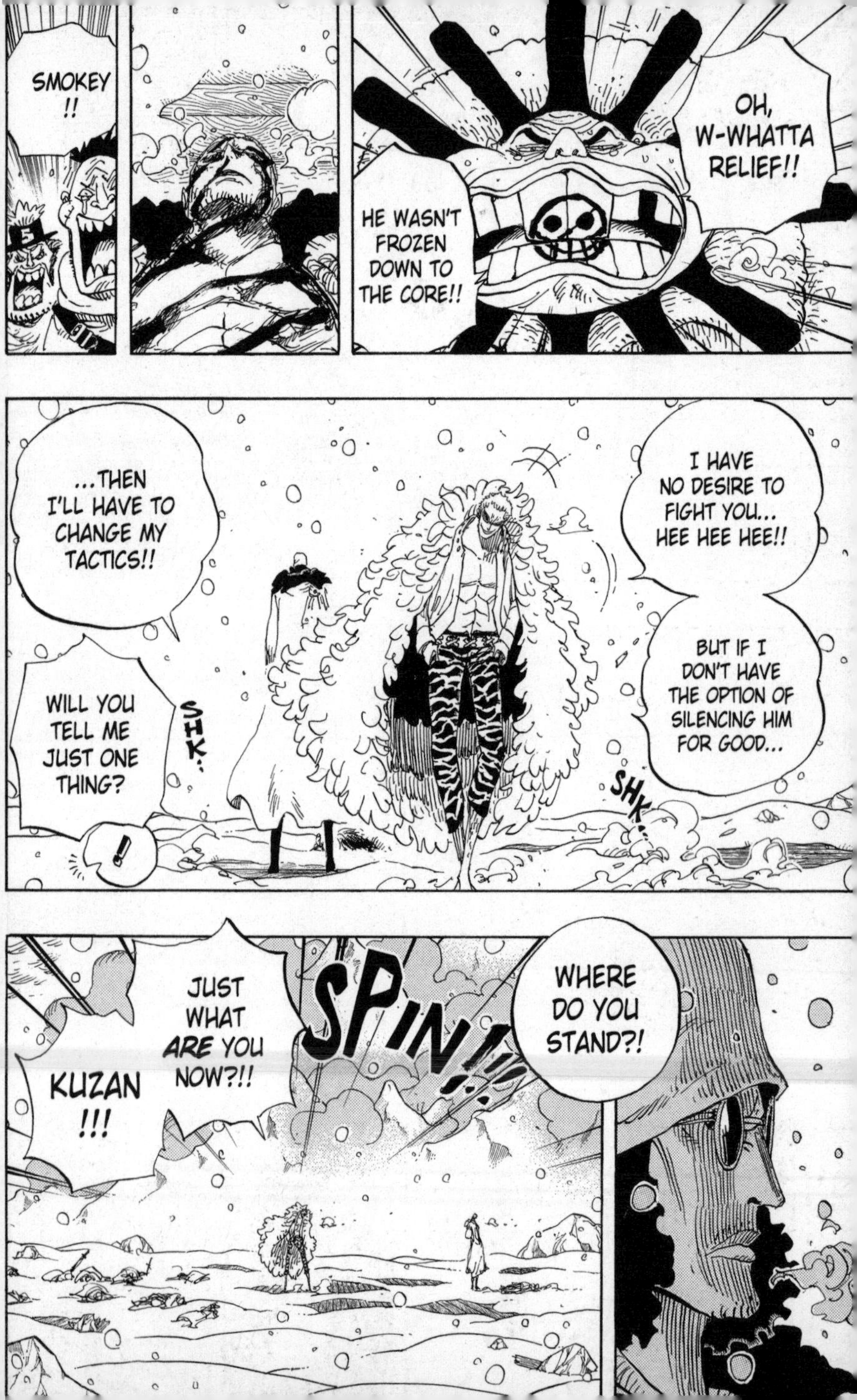
OH, W-WHATTA RELIEF!!
HE WASN'T FROZEN DOWN TO THE CORE!!
SMOKEY !!
I HAVE NO DESIRE TO FIGHT YOU... HEE HEE HEE!!
BUT IF I DON'T HAVE THE OPTION OF SILENCING HIM FOR GOOD...
SHK...
...THEN I'LL HAVE TO CHANGE MY TACTICS!!
SHK...
WILL YOU TELL ME JUST ONE THING?
!
WHERE DO YOU STAND?!
SPIN!!!
JUST WHAT ARE YOU NOW?!!
KUZAN !!!

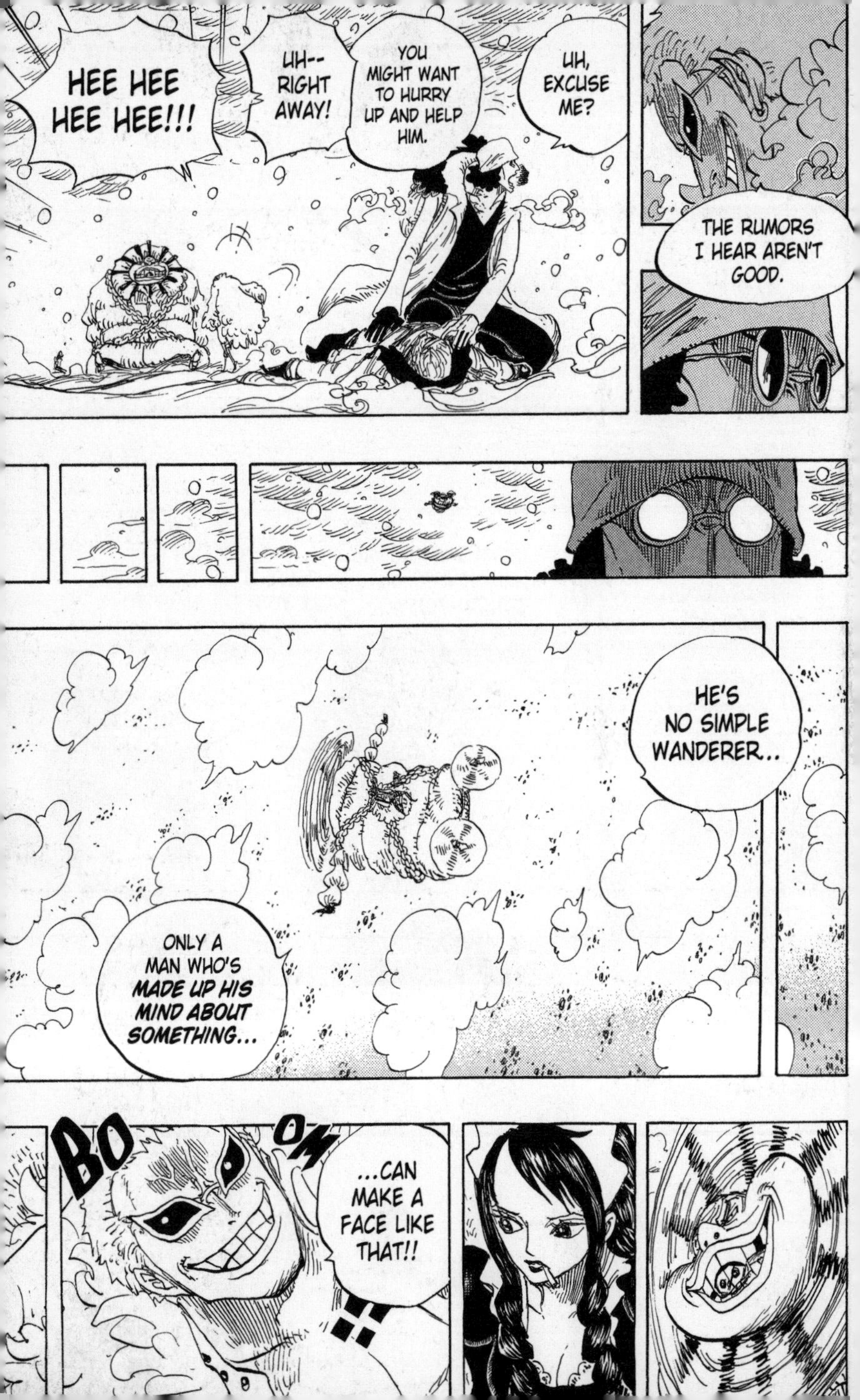
THE RUMORS I HEAR AREN'T GOOD.
UH, EXCUSE ME?
YOU MIGHT WANT TO HURRY UP AND HELP HIM.
UH-- RIGHT AWAY!
HEE HEE HEE HEE!!!
HE'S NO SIMPLE WANDERER...
ONLY A MAN WHO'S *MADE UP HIS MIND ABOUT SOMETHING*...
...CAN MAKE A FACE LIKE THAT!!
BOOM

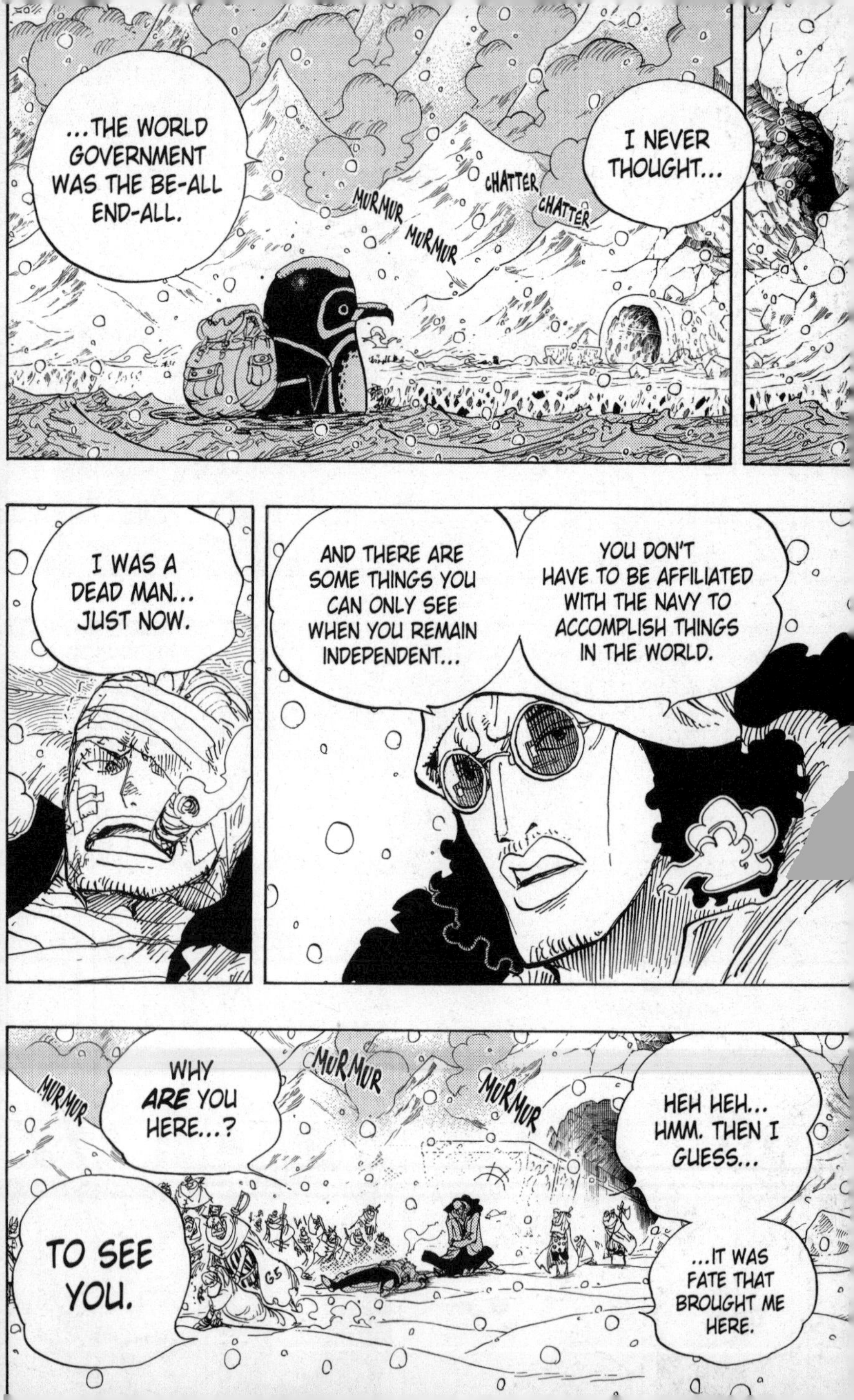
I NEVER THOUGHT...
CHATTER CHATTER
MURMUR MURMUR
...THE WORLD GOVERNMENT WAS THE BE-ALL END-ALL.
YOU DON'T HAVE TO BE AFFILIATED WITH THE NAVY TO ACCOMPLISH THINGS IN THE WORLD.
AND THERE ARE SOME THINGS YOU CAN ONLY SEE WHEN YOU REMAIN INDEPENDENT...
I WAS A DEAD MAN... JUST NOW.
HEH HEH... HMM. THEN I GUESS...
...IT WAS FATE THAT BROUGHT ME HERE.
MURMUR
MURMUR
WHY *ARE* YOU HERE...?
MURMUR
TO SEE YOU.

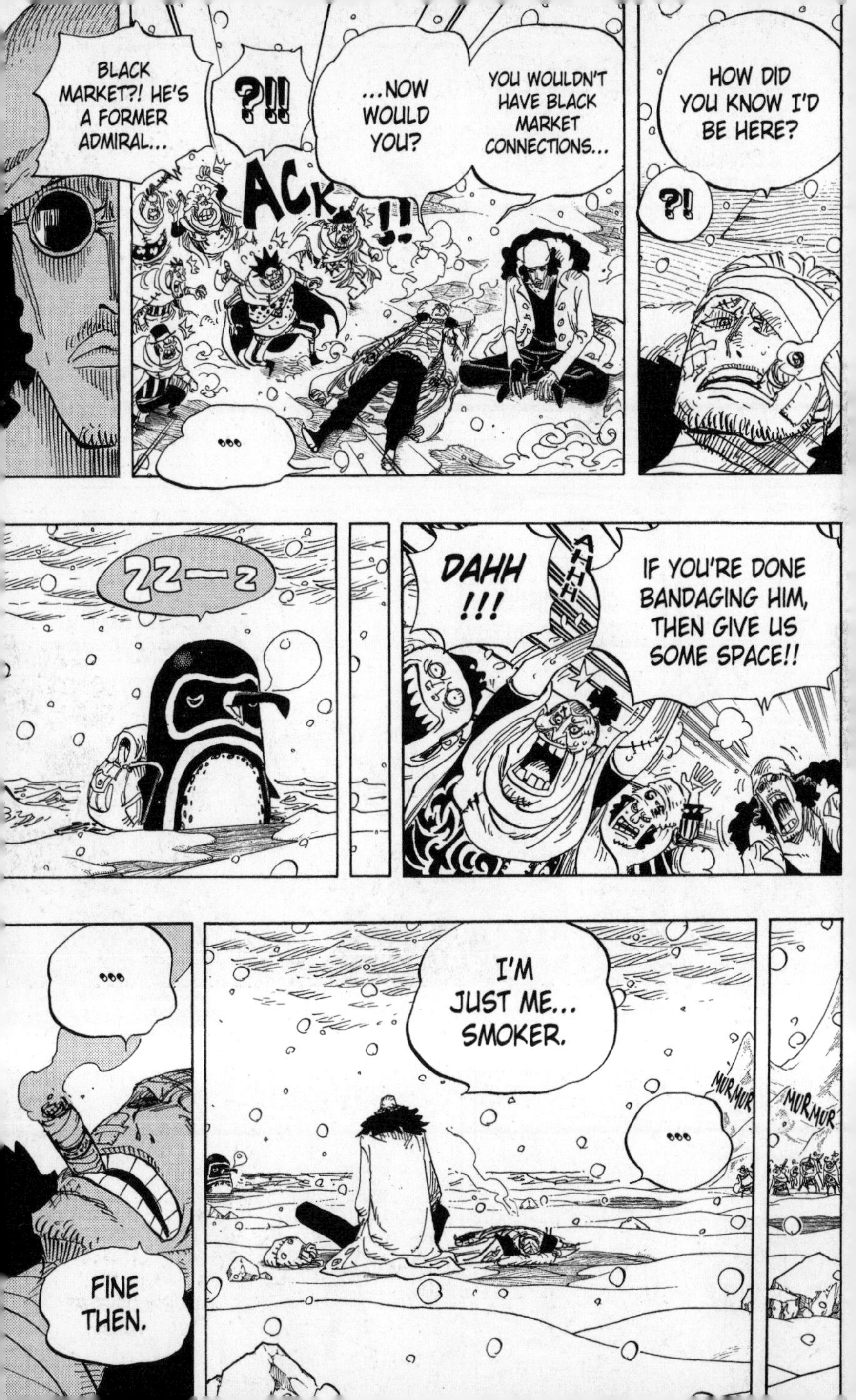
HOW DID YOU KNOW I'D BE HERE?
?!
YOU WOULDN'T HAVE BLACK MARKET CONNECTIONS...
...NOW WOULD YOU?
?!!
ACK!!
...
BLACK MARKET?! HE'S A FORMER ADMIRAL...
IF YOU'RE DONE BANDAGING HIM, THEN GIVE US SOME SPACE!!
AHHH
DAHH!!!
ZZ—Z
MURMUR
MURMUR
...
I'M JUST ME... SMOKER.
...
FINE THEN.

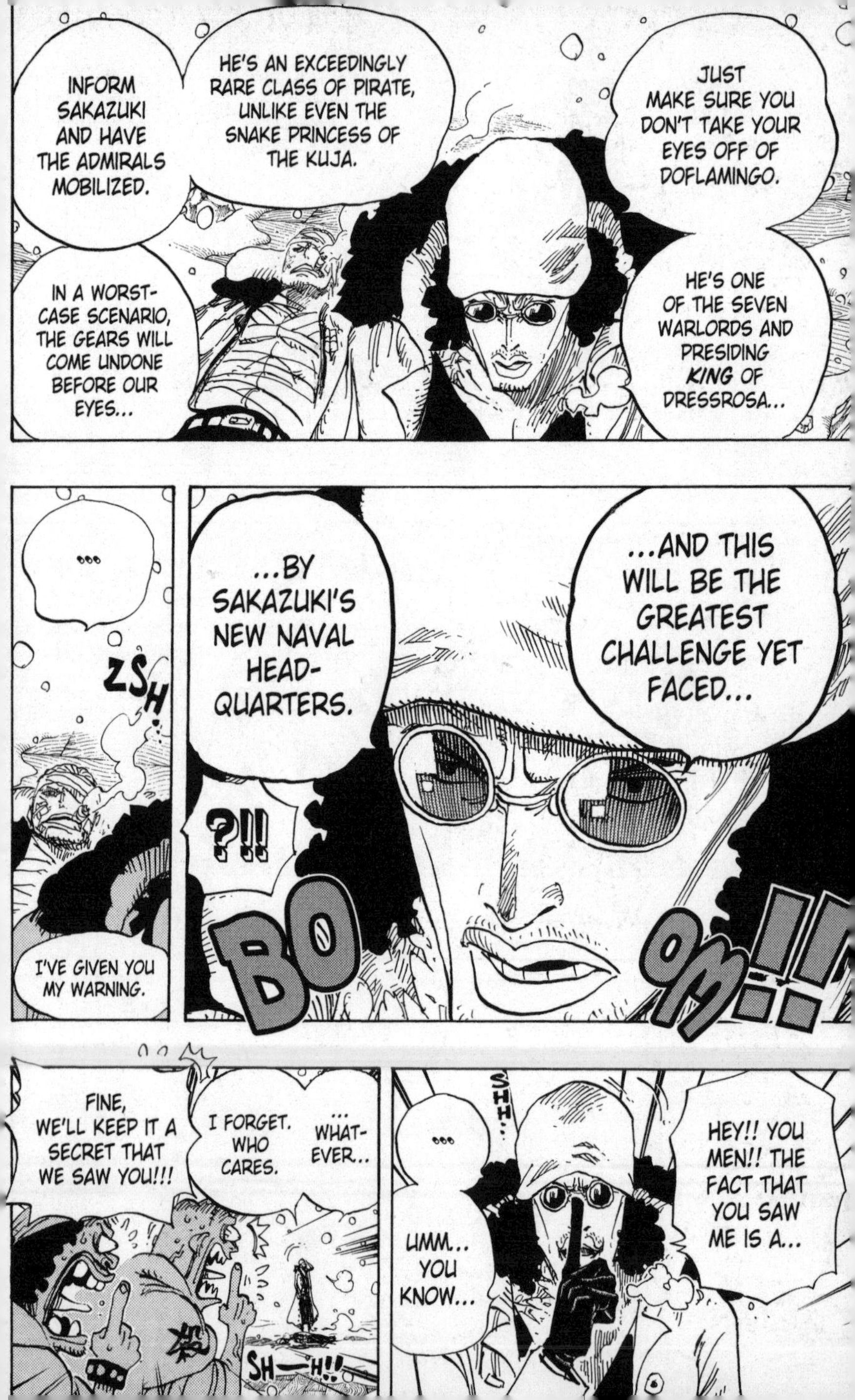
JUST MAKE SURE YOU DON'T TAKE YOUR EYES OFF OF DOFLAMINGO.
HE'S ONE OF THE SEVEN WARLORDS AND PRESIDING KING OF DRESSROSA...
HE'S AN EXCEEDINGLY RARE CLASS OF PIRATE, UNLIKE EVEN THE SNAKE PRINCESS OF THE KUJA.
INFORM SAKAZUKI AND HAVE THE ADMIRALS MOBILIZED.
IN A WORST-CASE SCENARIO, THE GEARS WILL COME UNDONE BEFORE OUR EYES...
...AND THIS WILL BE THE GREATEST CHALLENGE YET FACED...
...BY SAKAZUKI'S NEW NAVAL HEAD-QUARTERS.
?!!
BOOM!!
...
ZSH
I'VE GIVEN YOU MY WARNING.
SHH...
HEY!! YOU MEN!! THE FACT THAT YOU SAW ME IS A...
...
UMM... YOU KNOW...
... WHAT-EVER..
I FORGET. WHO CARES.
FINE, WE'LL KEEP IT A SECRET THAT WE SAW YOU!!!
SH—H!!

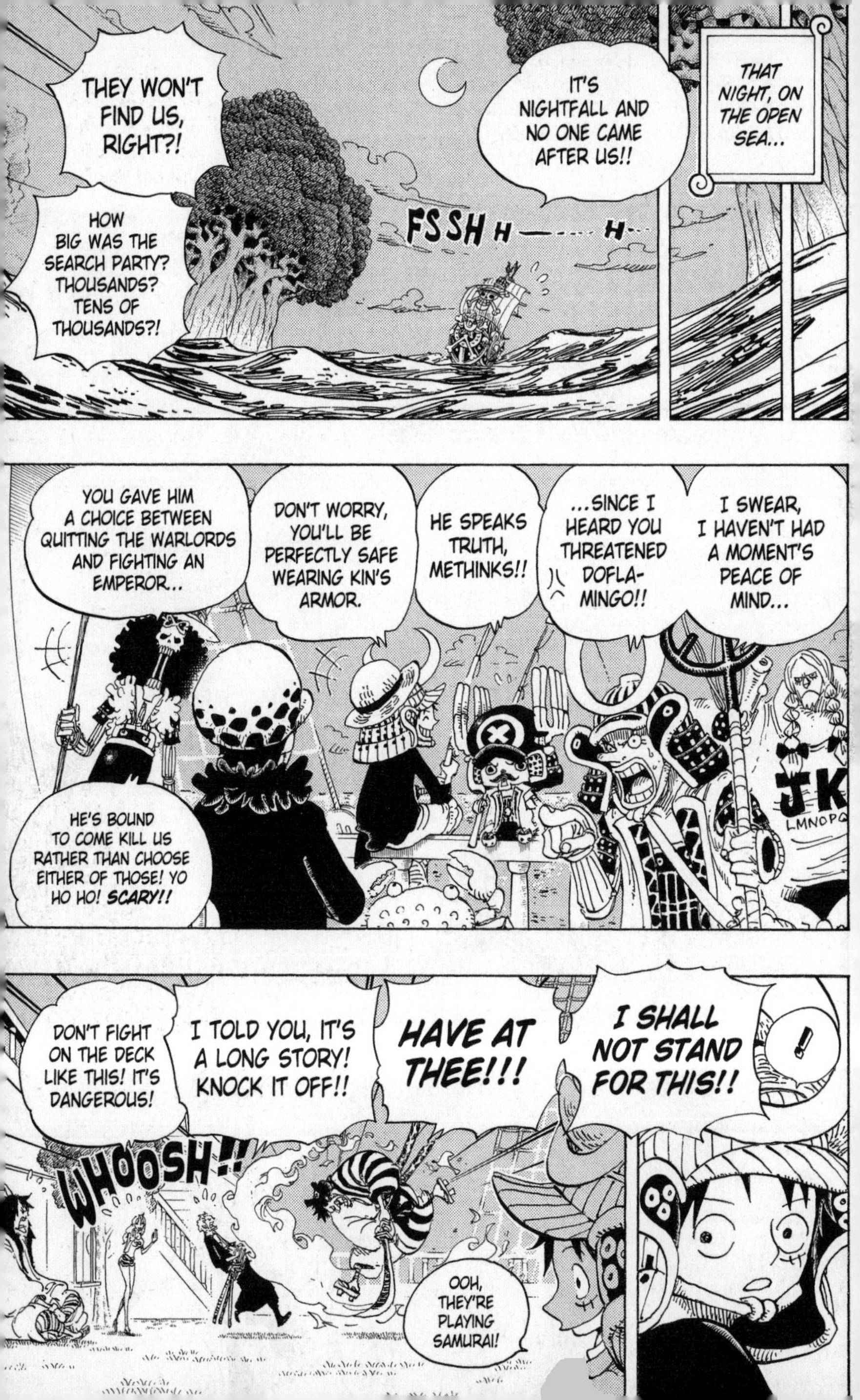

THAT NIGHT, ON THE OPEN SEA...
IT'S NIGHTFALL AND NO ONE CAME AFTER US!!
FSSHH—H
THEY WON'T FIND US, RIGHT?!
HOW BIG WAS THE SEARCH PARTY? THOUSANDS? TENS OF THOUSANDS?!
I SWEAR, I HAVEN'T HAD A MOMENT'S PEACE OF MIND...
...SINCE I HEARD YOU THREATENED DOFLAMINGO!!
HE SPEAKS TRUTH, METHINKS!!
DON'T WORRY, YOU'LL BE PERFECTLY SAFE WEARING KIN'S ARMOR.
YOU GAVE HIM A CHOICE BETWEEN QUITTING THE WARLORDS AND FIGHTING AN EMPEROR...
HE'S BOUND TO COME KILL US RATHER THAN CHOOSE EITHER OF THOSE! YO HO HO! SCARY!!
JK
LMNOPQ
!
I SHALL NOT STAND FOR THIS!!
HAVE AT THEE!!!
I TOLD YOU, IT'S A LONG STORY! KNOCK IT OFF!!
DON'T FIGHT ON THE DECK LIKE THIS! IT'S DANGEROUS!
WHOOSH!!
OOH, THEY'RE PLAYING SAMURAI!

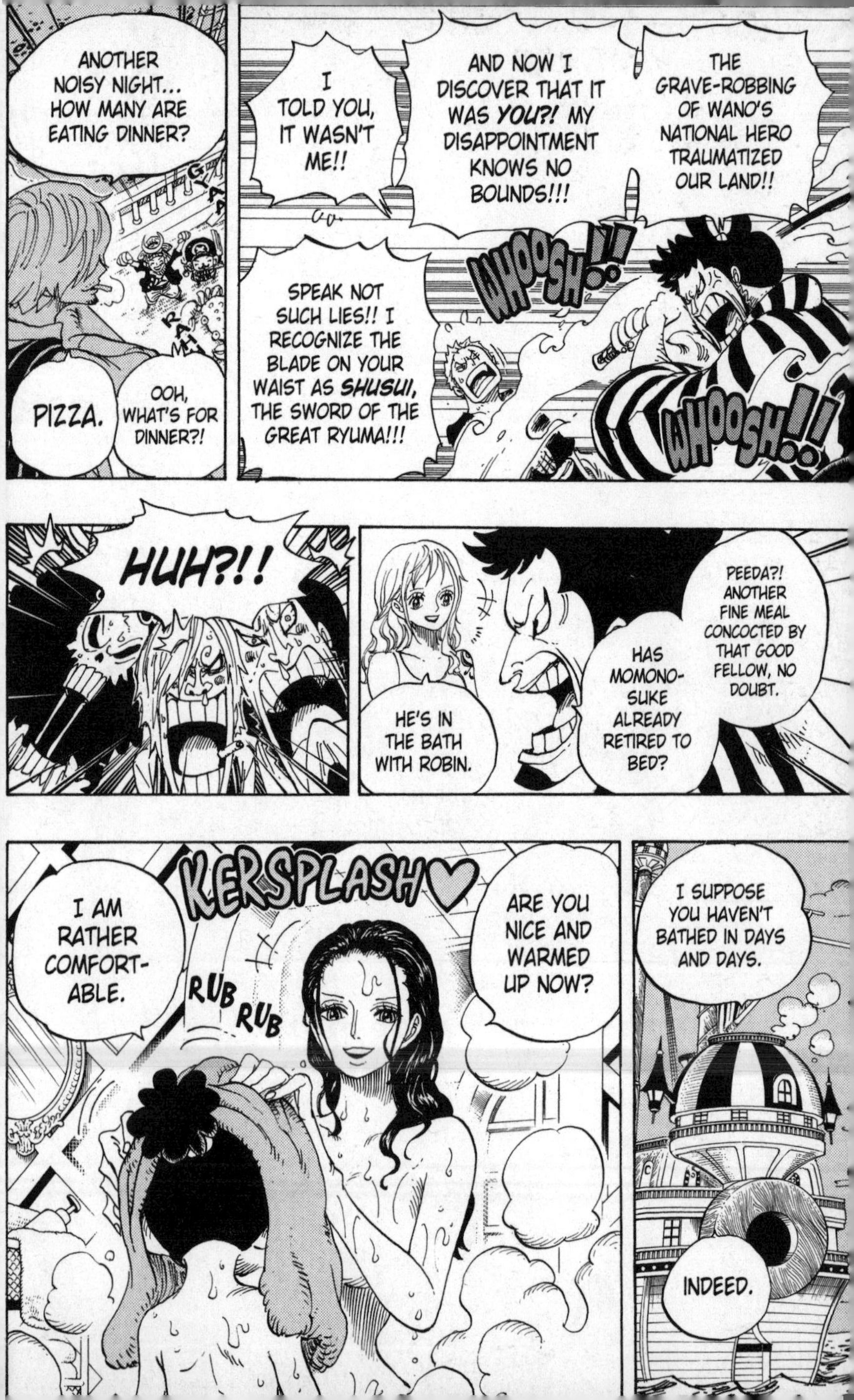
THE GRAVE-ROBBING OF WANO'S NATIONAL HERO TRAUMATIZED OUR LAND!!
AND NOW I DISCOVER THAT IT WAS YOU?! MY DISAPPOINTMENT KNOWS NO BOUNDS!!!
I TOLD YOU, IT WASN'T ME!!
WHOOSH!!
SPEAK NOT SUCH LIES!! I RECOGNIZE THE BLADE ON YOUR WAIST AS SHUSUI, THE SWORD OF THE GREAT RYUMA!!!
WHOOSH!!
ANOTHER NOISY NIGHT... HOW MANY ARE EATING DINNER?
OOH, WHAT'S FOR DINNER?!
PIZZA.
PEEDA?! ANOTHER FINE MEAL CONCOCTED BY THAT GOOD FELLOW, NO DOUBT.
HAS MOMONOSUKE ALREADY RETIRED TO BED?
HE'S IN THE BATH WITH ROBIN.
HUH?!!
I SUPPOSE YOU HAVEN'T BATHED IN DAYS AND DAYS.
INDEED.
ARE YOU NICE AND WARMED UP NOW?
KERSPLASH♥
I AM RATHER COMFORTABLE.
RUB RUB

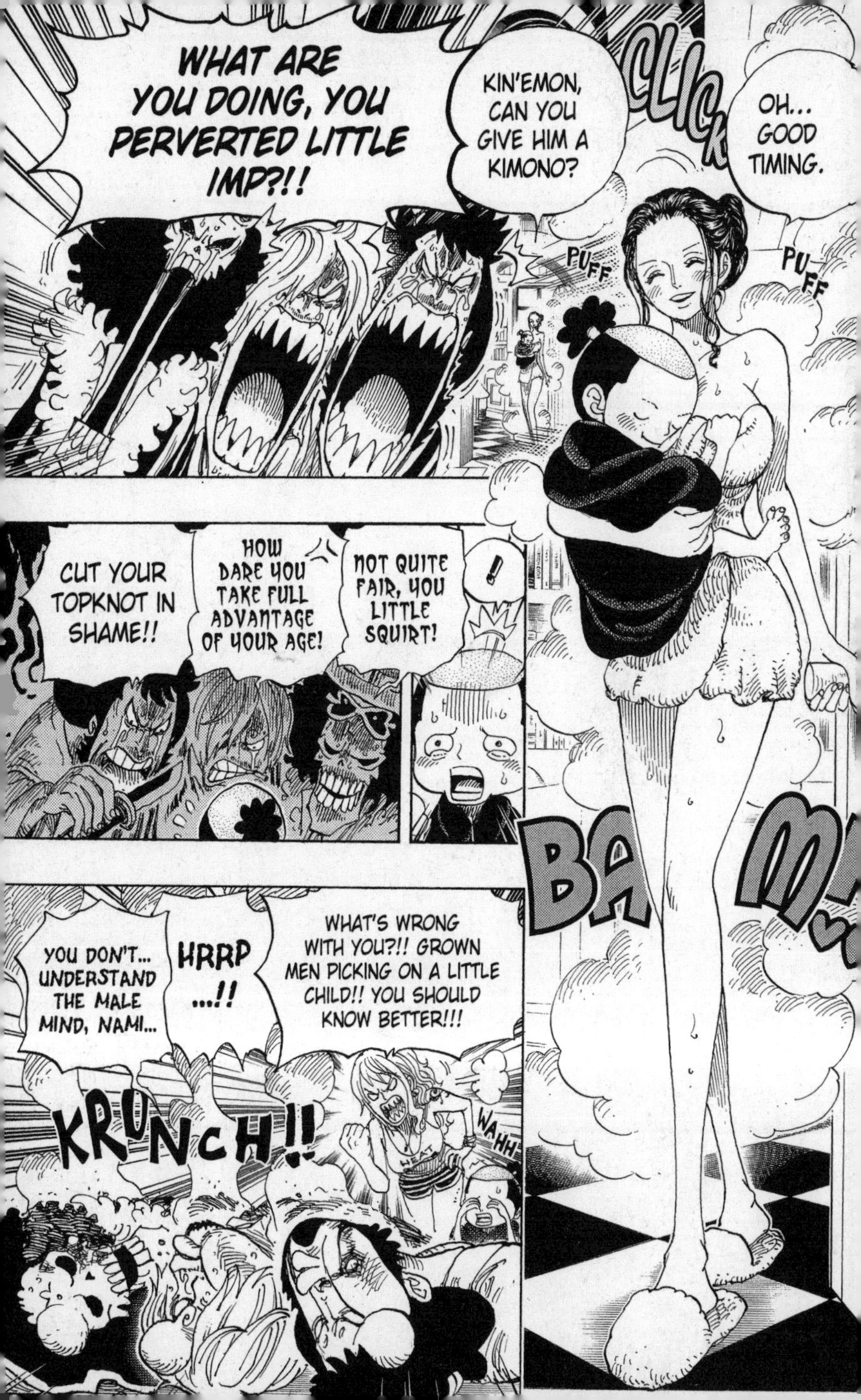
CLICK
OH... GOOD TIMING.
KIN'EMON, CAN YOU GIVE HIM A KIMONO?
PUFF
PUFF
BAMM
WHAT ARE YOU DOING, YOU PERVERTED LITTLE IMP?!!
!
NOT QUITE FAIR, YOU LITTLE SQUIRT!
HOW DARE YOU TAKE FULL ADVANTAGE OF YOUR AGE!
CUT YOUR TOPKNOT IN SHAME!!
WHAT'S WRONG WITH YOU?!! GROWN MEN PICKING ON A LITTLE CHILD!! YOU SHOULD KNOW BETTER!!!
WAHH
HEAT
HRRP ...!!
YOU DON'T... UNDERSTAND THE MALE MIND, NAMI...
KRUNCH!!

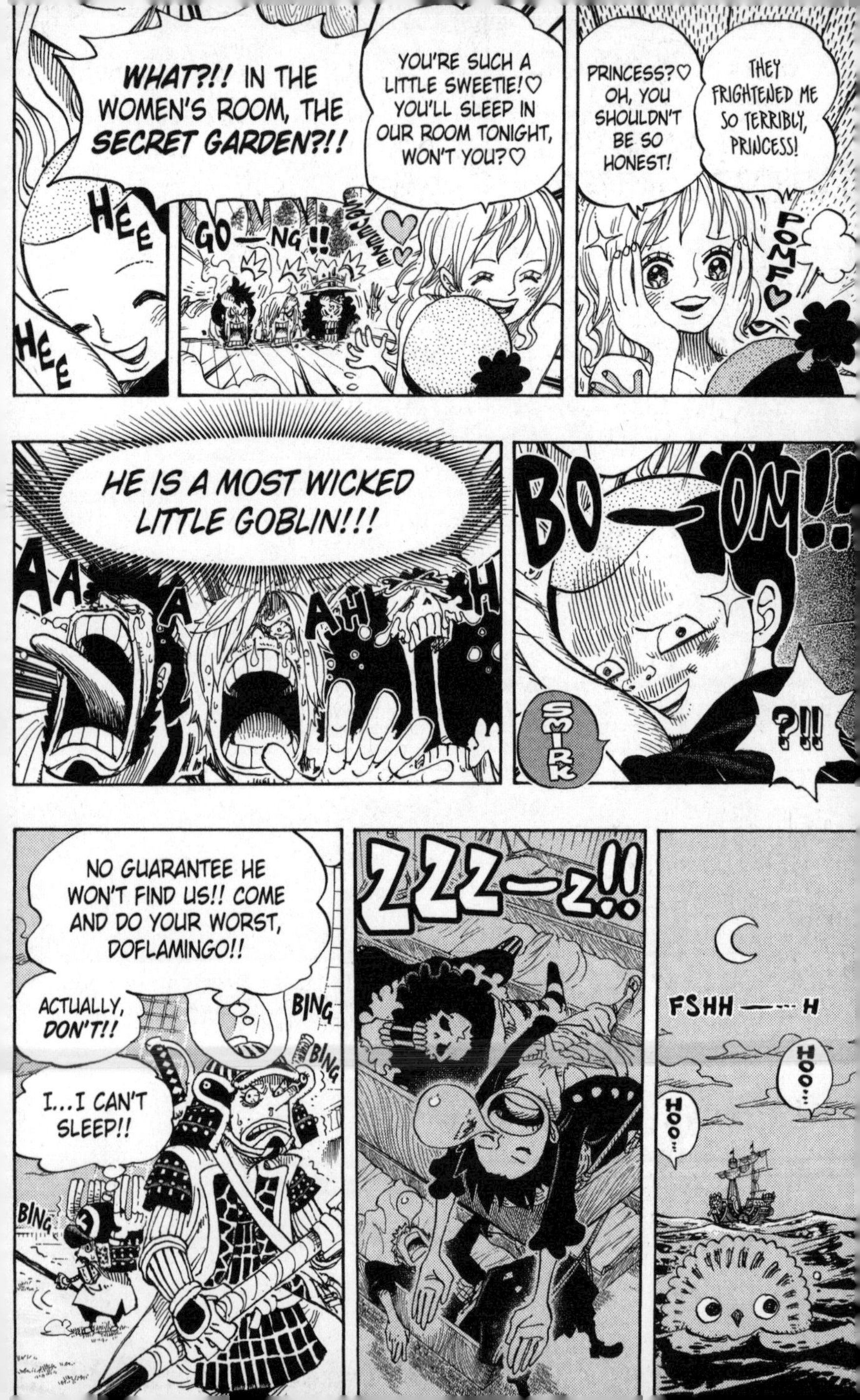
THEY FRIGHTENED ME SO TERRIBLY, PRINCESS!
PRINCESS?♡ OH, YOU SHOULDN'T BE SO HONEST!
POMF♡
YOU'RE SUCH A LITTLE SWEETIE!♡ YOU'LL SLEEP IN OUR ROOM TONIGHT, WON'T YOU?♡
GO—NG!!
WHAT?!! IN THE WOMEN'S ROOM, THE SECRET GARDEN?!!
HEE
HEE
BO—OM!!
SMIRK
?!!
HE IS A MOST WICKED LITTLE GOBLIN!!!
AAAAH
FSHH——H
HOO...
HOO...
ZZZ—Z!!
NO GUARANTEE HE WON'T FIND US!! COME AND DO YOUR WORST, DOFLAMINGO!!
ACTUALLY, DON'T!!
BING
BING
I...I CAN'T SLEEP!!
BING

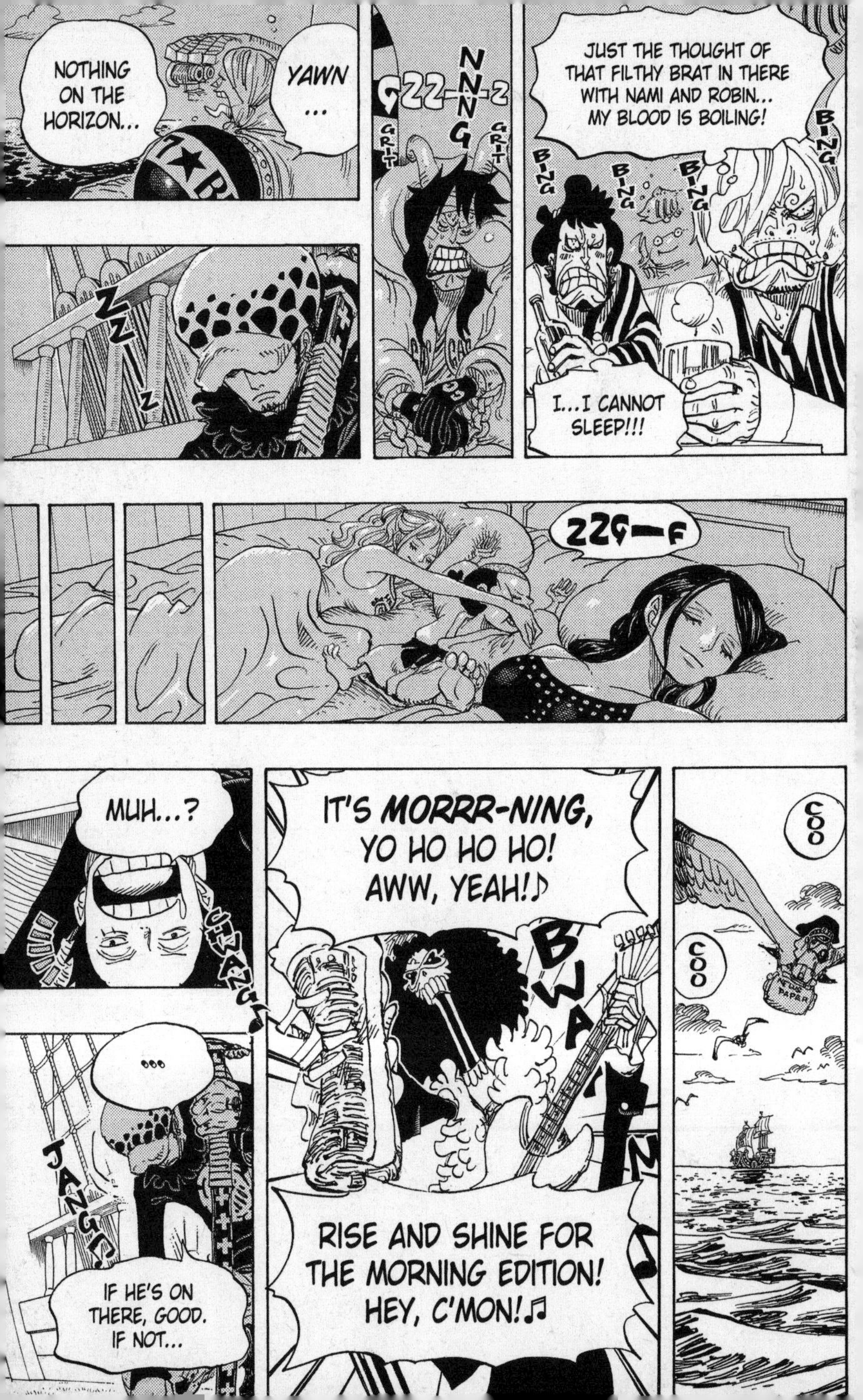

JUST THE THOUGHT OF THAT FILTHY BRAT IN THERE WITH NAMI AND ROBIN... MY BLOOD IS BOILING!
BING
BING
BING
BING
I...I CANNOT SLEEP!!!
GZZ-NNNG-Z
GRIT
GRIT
NOTHING ON THE HORIZON...
YAWN ...
ZZZ
Z
ZZG—F
COO
COO
IT'S MORRR-NING, YO HO HO HO! AWW, YEAH!♪
BWANN
RISE AND SHINE FOR THE MORNING EDITION! HEY, C'MON!♫
MUH...?
CHWANG♪
...
JANG♪
IF HE'S ON THERE, GOOD. IF NOT...

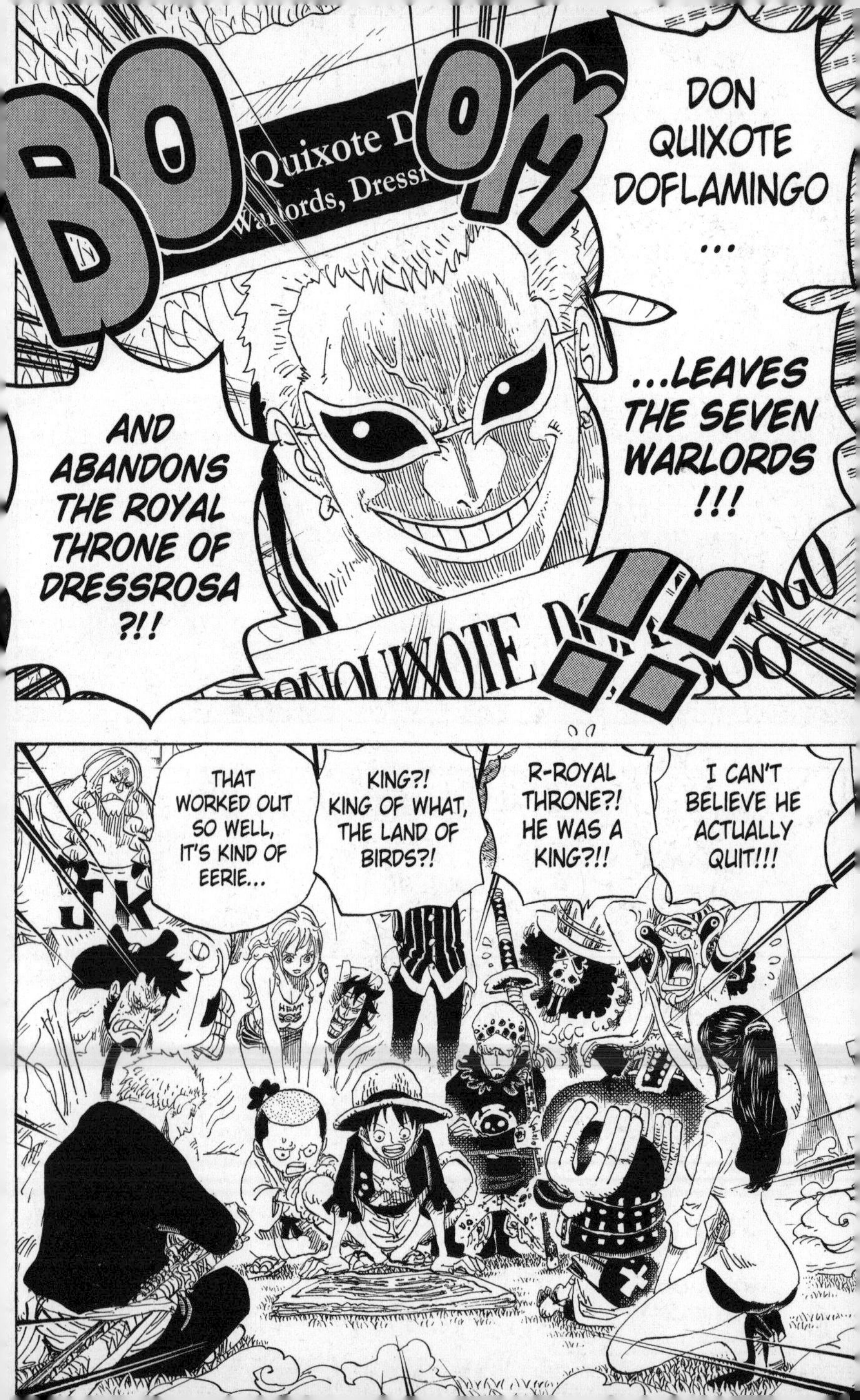
DON QUIXOTE DOFLAMINGO ...
BOOM
...LEAVES THE SEVEN WARLORDS !!!
AND ABANDONS THE ROYAL THRONE OF DRESSROSA ?!!
I CAN'T BELIEVE HE ACTUALLY QUIT!!!
R-ROYAL THRONE?! HE WAS A KING?!!
KING?! KING OF WHAT, THE LAND OF BIRDS?!
THAT WORKED OUT SO WELL, IT'S KIND OF EERIE...

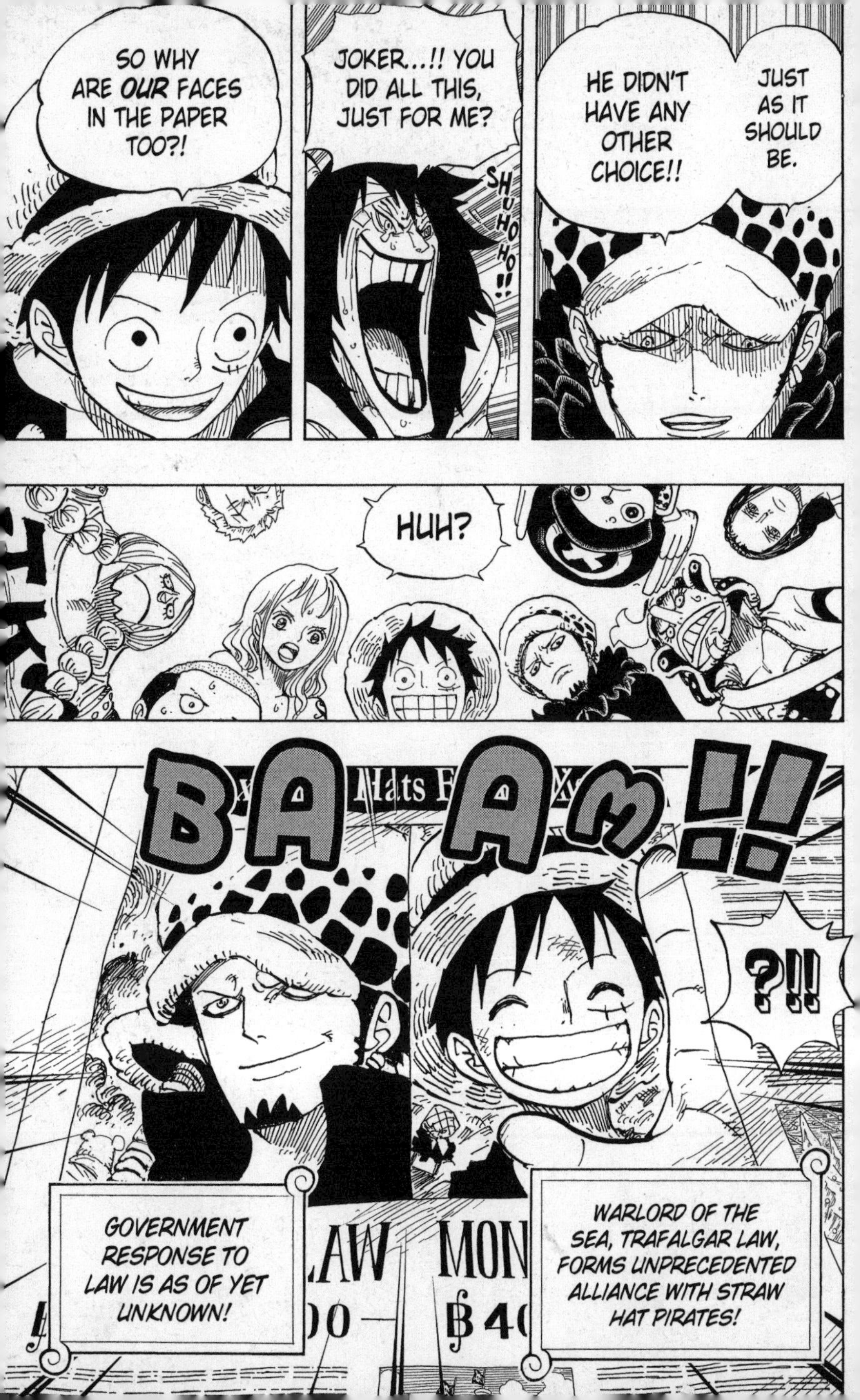
JUST AS IT SHOULD BE.
HE DIDN'T HAVE ANY OTHER CHOICE!!
JOKER...!! YOU DID ALL THIS, JUST FOR ME?
SHUHOHO!!
SO WHY ARE *OUR* FACES IN THE PAPER TOO?!
HUH?
BAAM!!
?!!
WARLORD OF THE SEA, TRAFALGAR LAW, FORMS UNPRECEDENTED ALLIANCE WITH STRAW HAT PIRATES!
GOVERNMENT RESPONSE TO LAW IS AS OF YET UNKNOWN!

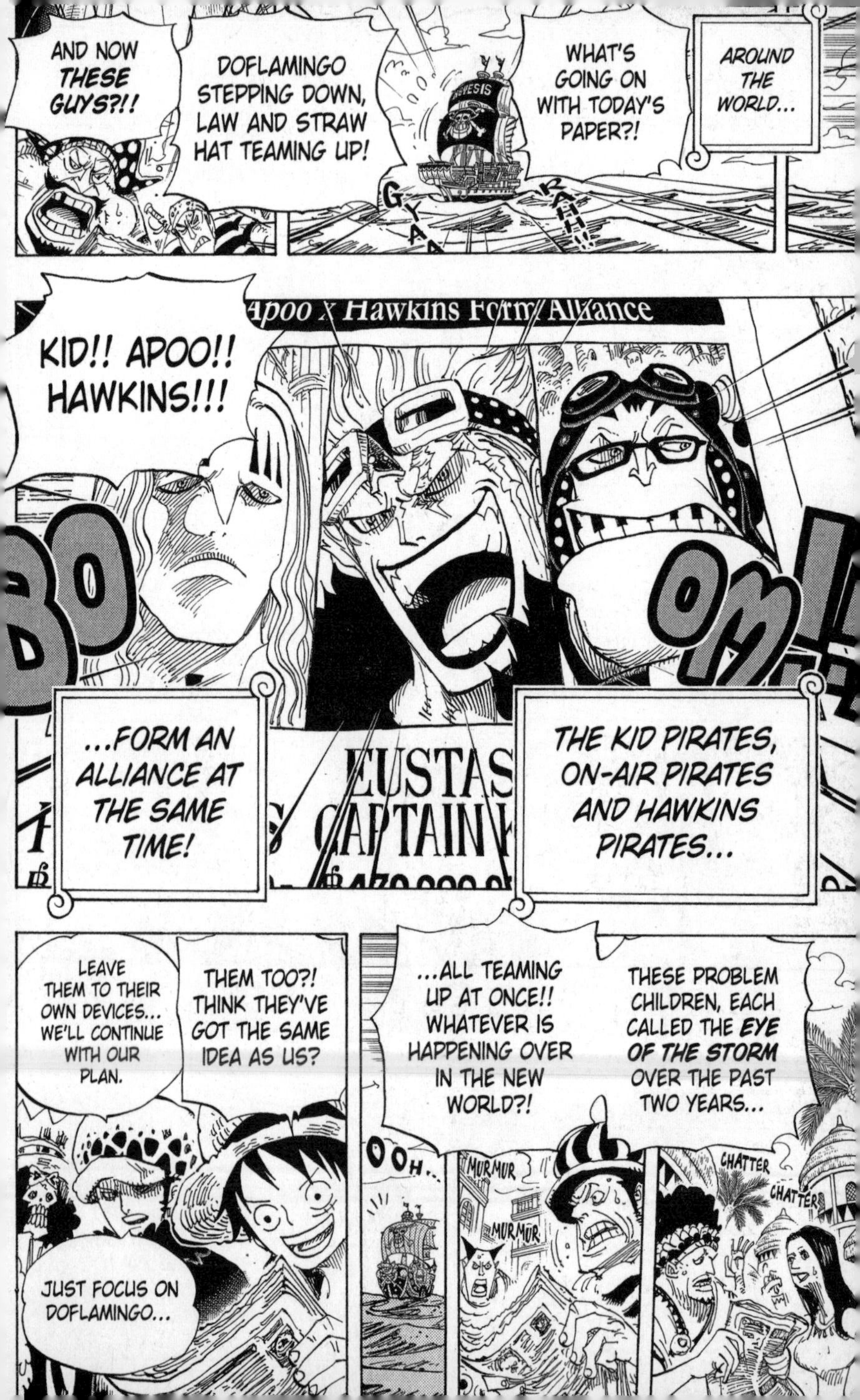
AROUND THE WORLD...
WHAT'S GOING ON WITH TODAY'S PAPER?!
GYAA
RAHH!!
DOFLAMINGO STEPPING DOWN, LAW AND STRAW HAT TEAMING UP!
AND NOW THESE GUYS?!!
Apoo x Hawkins Form Alliance
KID!! APOO!! HAWKINS!!!
BOOM!!
EUSTAS
CAPTAIN
THE KID PIRATES, ON-AIR PIRATES AND HAWKINS PIRATES...
...FORM AN ALLIANCE AT THE SAME TIME!
THESE PROBLEM CHILDREN, EACH CALLED THE EYE OF THE STORM OVER THE PAST TWO YEARS...
CHATTER
CHATTER
...ALL TEAMING UP AT ONCE!! WHATEVER IS HAPPENING OVER IN THE NEW WORLD?!
MURMUR
MURMUR
OOH...
THEM TOO?! THINK THEY'VE GOT THE SAME IDEA AS US?
LEAVE THEM TO THEIR OWN DEVICES... WE'LL CONTINUE WITH OUR PLAN.
JUST FOCUS ON DOFLAMINGO...

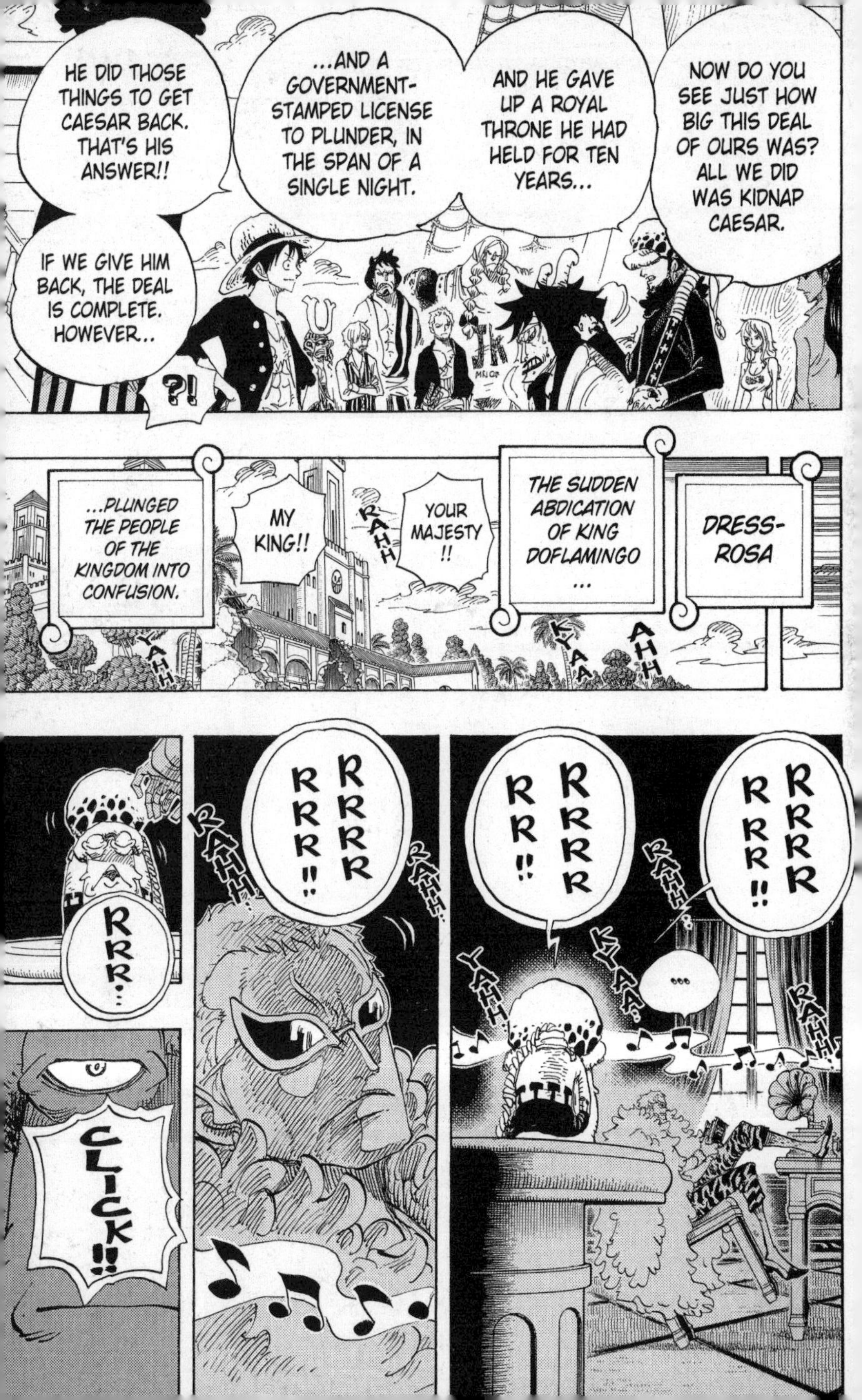
NOW DO YOU SEE JUST HOW BIG THIS DEAL OF OURS WAS? ALL WE DID WAS KIDNAP CAESAR.
AND HE GAVE UP A ROYAL THRONE HE HAD HELD FOR TEN YEARS...
...AND A GOVERNMENT-STAMPED LICENSE TO PLUNDER, IN THE SPAN OF A SINGLE NIGHT.
HE DID THOSE THINGS TO GET CAESAR BACK. THAT'S HIS ANSWER!!
IF WE GIVE HIM BACK, THE DEAL IS COMPLETE. HOWEVER...
?!
DRESS-ROSA
THE SUDDEN ABDICATION OF KING DOFLAMINGO...
AHH
KYAA
YOUR MAJESTY!!
RAHH
MY KING!!
...PLUNGED THE PEOPLE OF THE KINGDOM INTO CONFUSION.
YAHH
RRRR RRR!!
RAHH
KYAA
...
RAHH
YAHH
RRRR RRR!!
RRRR RRR!!
RAHH
RAHH
RRR..
CLICK!!

SBS Question Corner

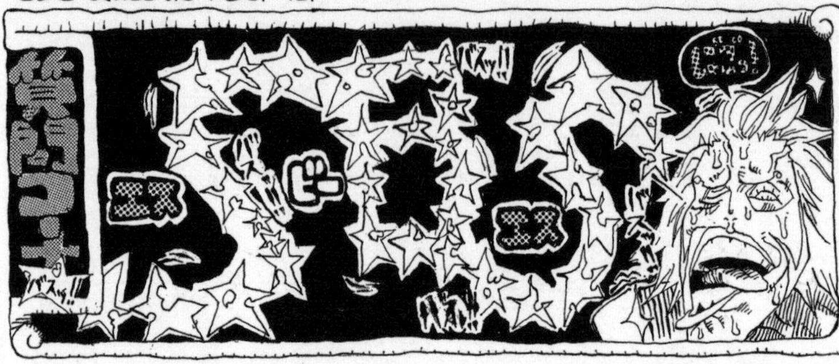

(Satomo, Yamanashi)

Q: What do you think of how young people are driving cars less and less?
--Maeda A.K.A. Kimotowa

A: Hmmmmm... Hmmmm. I don't care.

Q: Tell me the name of the penguin Mr. Kuzan was riding! Is he related to the Galapagos penguin?! Was he treading water under the surface the entire time he was waiting for Mr. Kuzan?! He's so cute, I can't help but want to know more! Tell me!!
--Kunugi

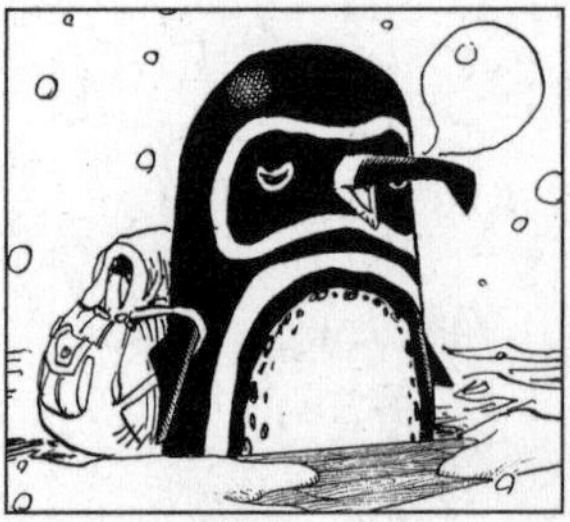

A: Yep, that's a big penguin. He's a member of the "super penguin" species, which is very adept at treading water. He fits well with Kuzan's Chilly-Chilly style, and has been accompanying him since he left the Navy. His name is Camel. Also, he's a hardboiled dude, so don't call him cute or you'll get burned.

Q: I have a question. Is the character of Borsalino based on Kunie Tanaka's role of "Borsalino 2" from the movie *Truck Yaro: Bakuso Ichiban-boshi?*
--AkuaNoichigo

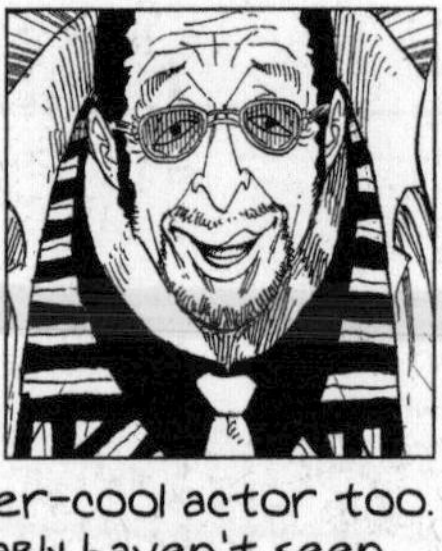

A: You saw that movie?! That's fantastic. It's quite an old film. I wonder if it's out on DVD and Blu-ray now. I have the entire Truck Yaro series on VHS tapes. You are correct, Borsalino comes from that role. There's an Alain Delon film called Borsalino as well, and I suspect that Kunie Tanaka's character was named in homage to that movie. Alain Delon's a super-cool actor too. His movies are older, so most people probably haven't seen them. I don't mind, though. I did this to satisfy myself.
That's all for this installment of the SBS! See you again soon!!

Chapter 700:
HIS MOMENTUM

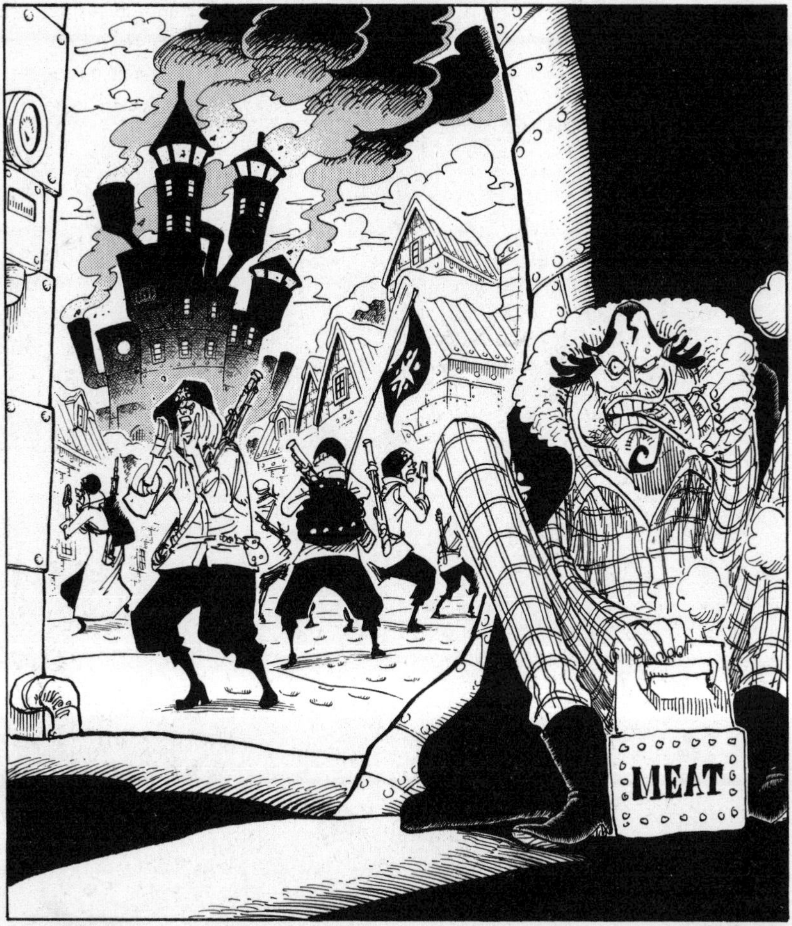
MEAT

CARIBOU'S NEW WORLD KEE HEE HEE, VOL. 21: "GOT CURIOUS AND RETURNED TO TOWN, WHERE I'M A WANTED MAN"

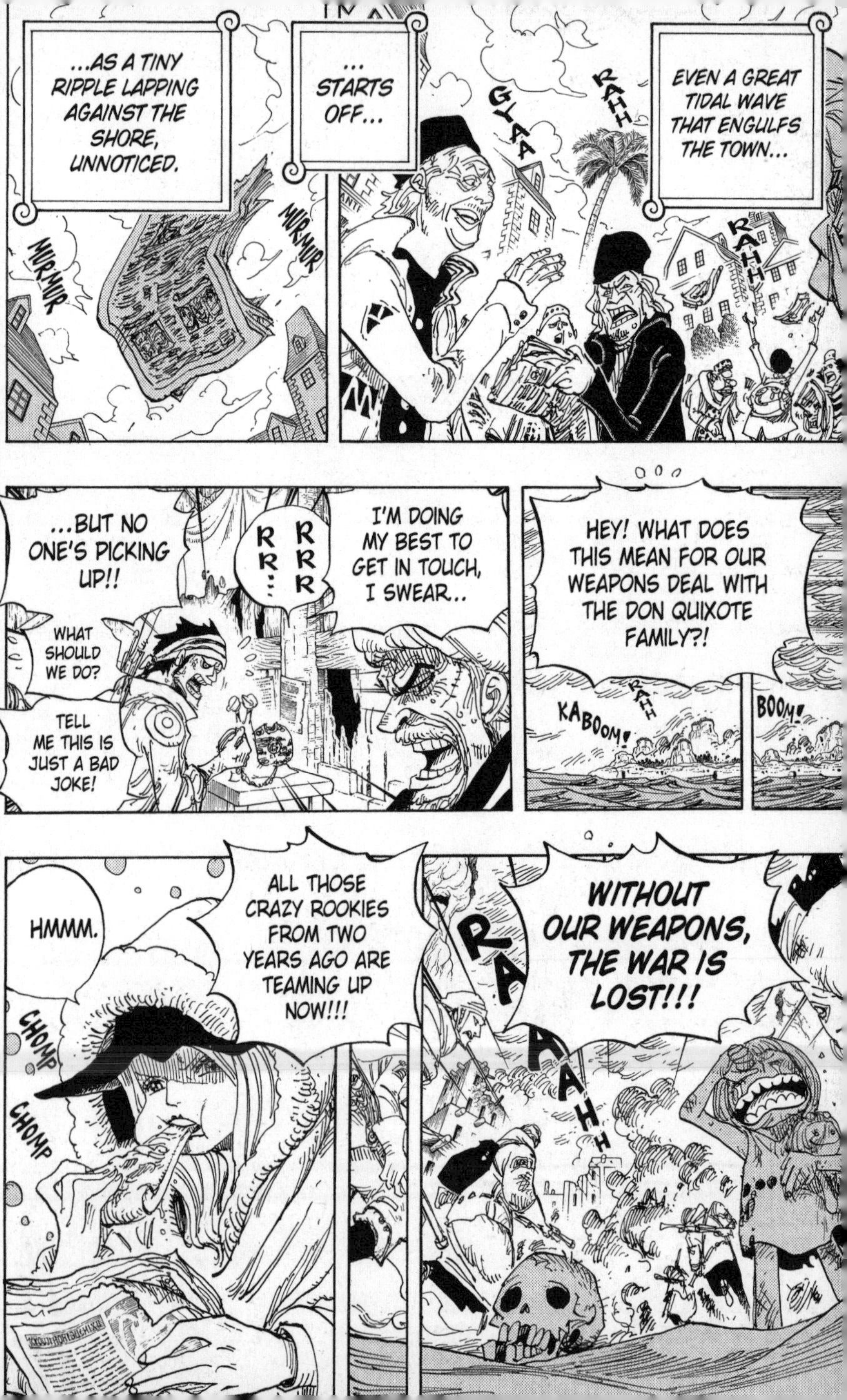
EVEN A GREAT TIDAL WAVE THAT ENGULFS THE TOWN...
RAHH
GYAA
RAHH
... STARTS OFF...
...AS A TINY RIPPLE LAPPING AGAINST THE SHORE, UNNOTICED.
MURMUR
MURMUR
HEY! WHAT DOES THIS MEAN FOR OUR WEAPONS DEAL WITH THE DON QUIXOTE FAMILY?!
KABOOM!
RAHH
BOOM!
I'M DOING MY BEST TO GET IN TOUCH, I SWEAR...
RRR
RR...
...BUT NO ONE'S PICKING UP!!
WHAT SHOULD WE DO?
TELL ME THIS IS JUST A BAD JOKE!
WITHOUT OUR WEAPONS, THE WAR IS LOST!!!
RAAAHH
ALL THOSE CRAZY ROOKIES FROM TWO YEARS AGO ARE TEAMING UP NOW!!!
HMMM.
CHOMP
CHOMP

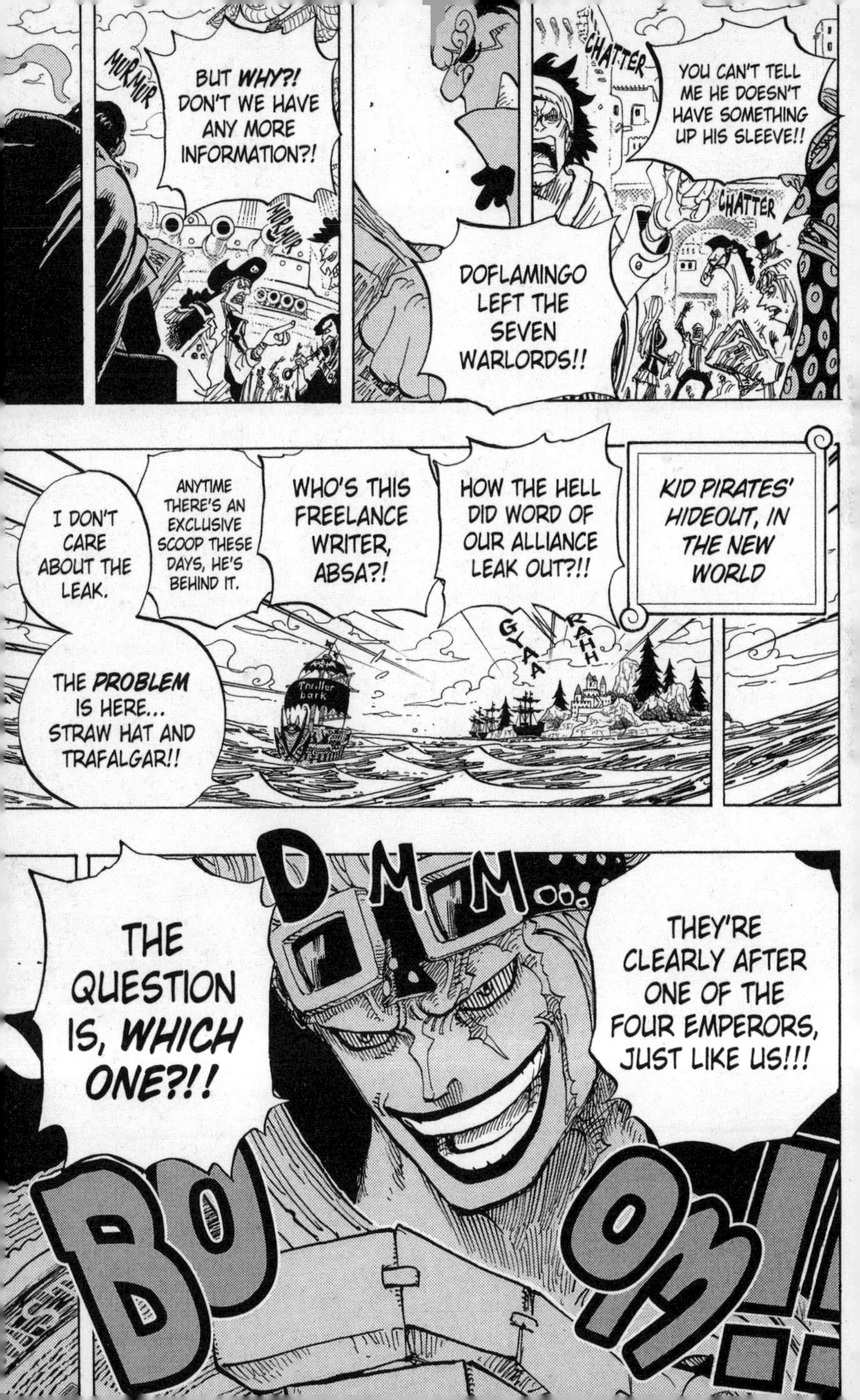
CHATTER
YOU CAN'T TELL ME HE DOESN'T HAVE SOMETHING UP HIS SLEEVE!!
CHATTER
DOFLAMINGO LEFT THE SEVEN WARLORDS!!
MURMUR
BUT WHY?! DON'T WE HAVE ANY MORE INFORMATION?!
MURMUR
KID PIRATES' HIDEOUT, IN THE NEW WORLD
HOW THE HELL DID WORD OF OUR ALLIANCE LEAK OUT?!!
WHO'S THIS FREELANCE WRITER, ABSA?!
ANYTIME THERE'S AN EXCLUSIVE SCOOP THESE DAYS, HE'S BEHIND IT.
I DON'T CARE ABOUT THE LEAK.
THE PROBLEM IS HERE... STRAW HAT AND TRAFALGAR!!
RAHH
GYAA
Thriller bark
THEY'RE CLEARLY AFTER ONE OF THE FOUR EMPERORS, JUST LIKE US!!!
THE QUESTION IS, WHICH ONE?!!
DMMM...
BOOM!!

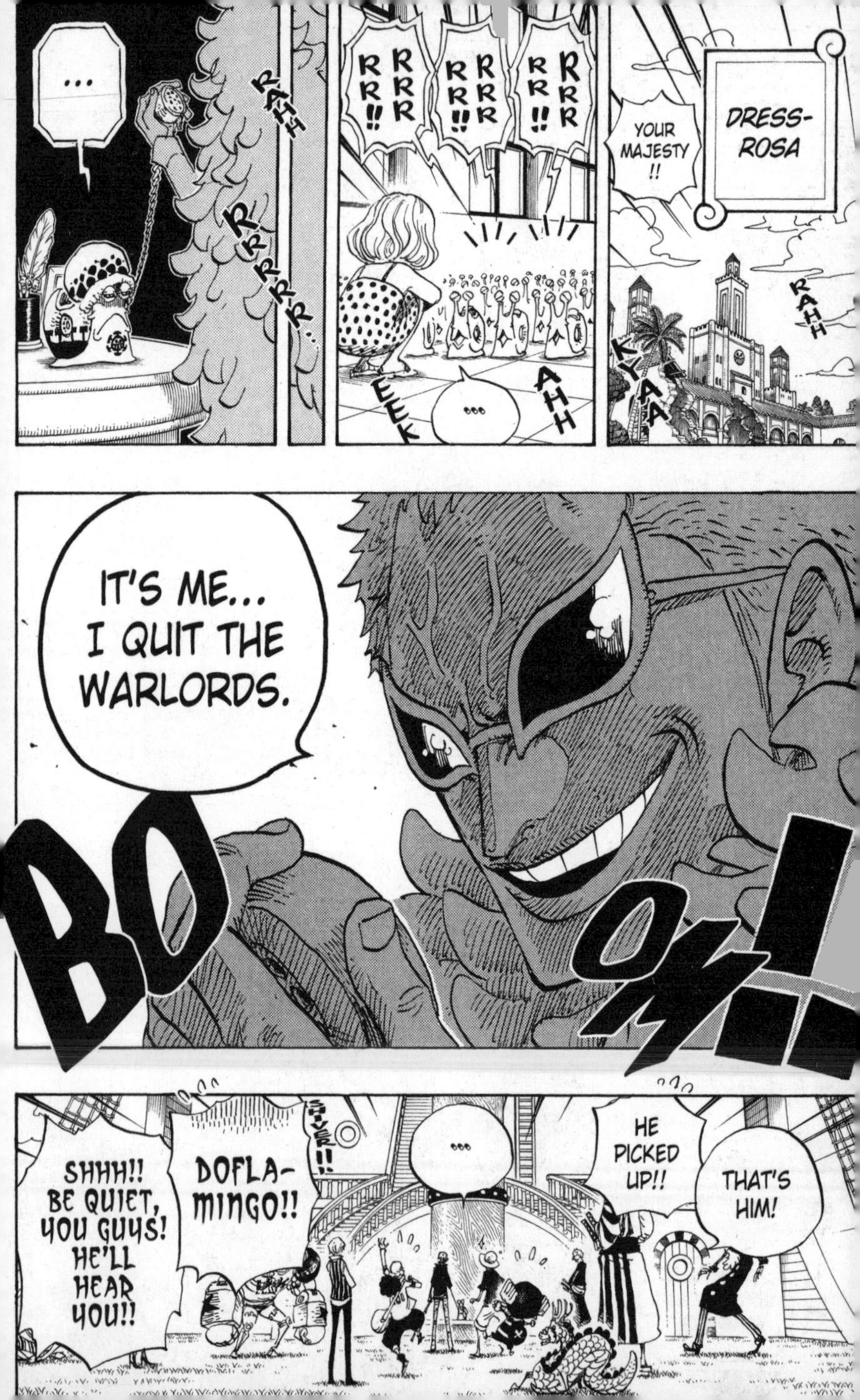
DRESS-ROSA
YOUR MAJESTY !!
RAHH
KYAAA
RRRRR!!
RRRRR!!
RRRRR!!
AHH
...
EEK
RAHH
RRRRRR...
...
IT'S ME... I QUIT THE WARLORDS.
BOOM!!
THAT'S HIM!
HE PICKED UP!!
...
SHIVER!!
DOFLA-MINGO!!
SHHH!! BE QUIET, YOU GUYS! HE'LL HEAR YOU!!

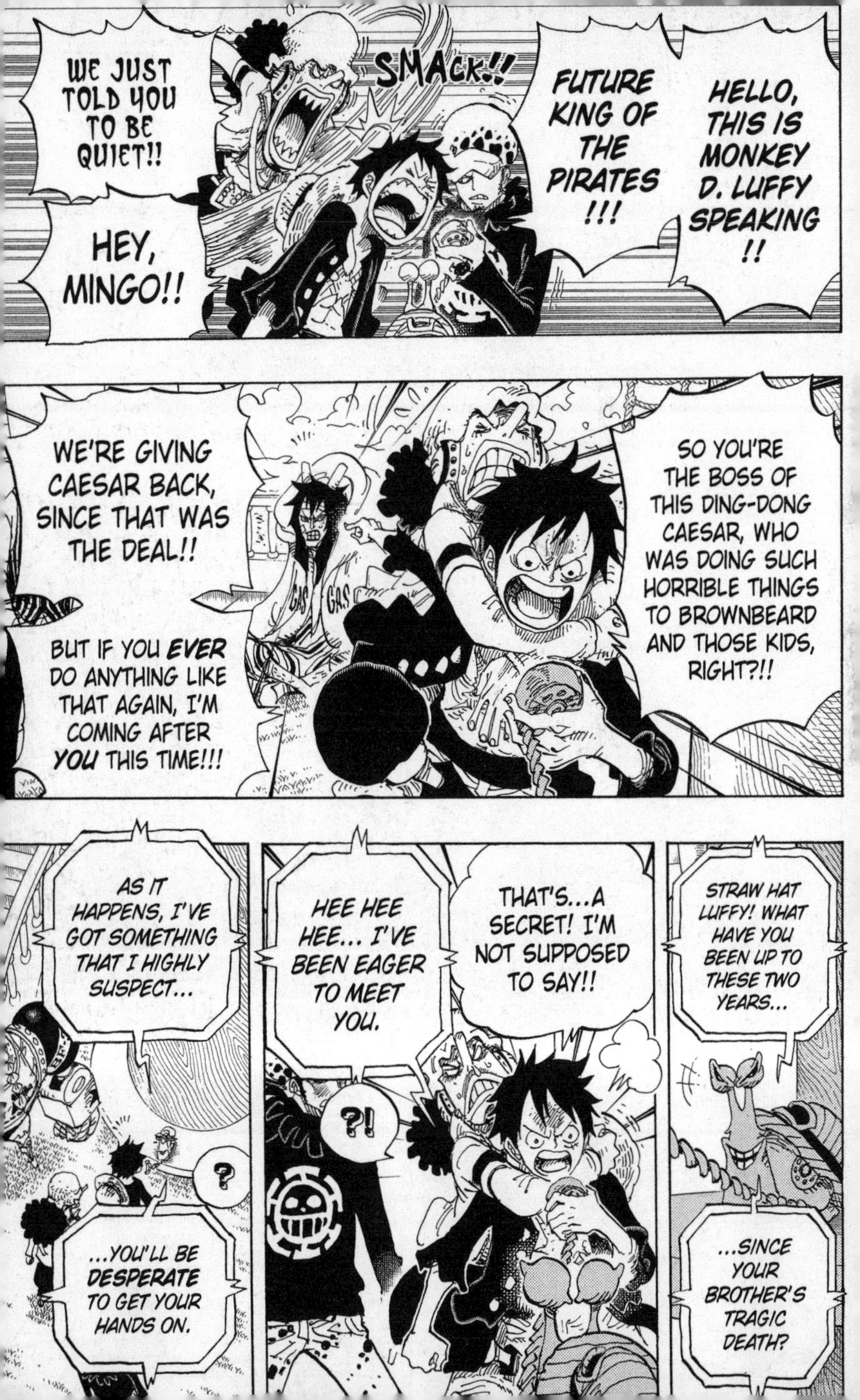
HELLO, THIS IS MONKEY D. LUFFY SPEAKING!!
FUTURE KING OF THE PIRATES!!!
SMACK!!
WE JUST TOLD YOU TO BE QUIET!!
HEY, MINGO!!
SO YOU'RE THE BOSS OF THIS DING-DONG CAESAR, WHO WAS DOING SUCH HORRIBLE THINGS TO BROWNBEARD AND THOSE KIDS, RIGHT?!!
WE'RE GIVING CAESAR BACK, SINCE THAT WAS THE DEAL!!
BUT IF YOU **EVER** DO ANYTHING LIKE THAT AGAIN, I'M COMING AFTER **YOU** THIS TIME!!!
STRAW HAT LUFFY! WHAT HAVE YOU BEEN UP TO THESE TWO YEARS...
...SINCE YOUR BROTHER'S TRAGIC DEATH?
THAT'S...A SECRET! I'M NOT SUPPOSED TO SAY!!
HEE HEE HEE... I'VE BEEN EAGER TO MEET YOU.
?!
AS IT HAPPENS, I'VE GOT SOMETHING THAT I HIGHLY SUSPECT...
?
...YOU'LL BE **DESPERATE** TO GET YOUR HANDS ON.

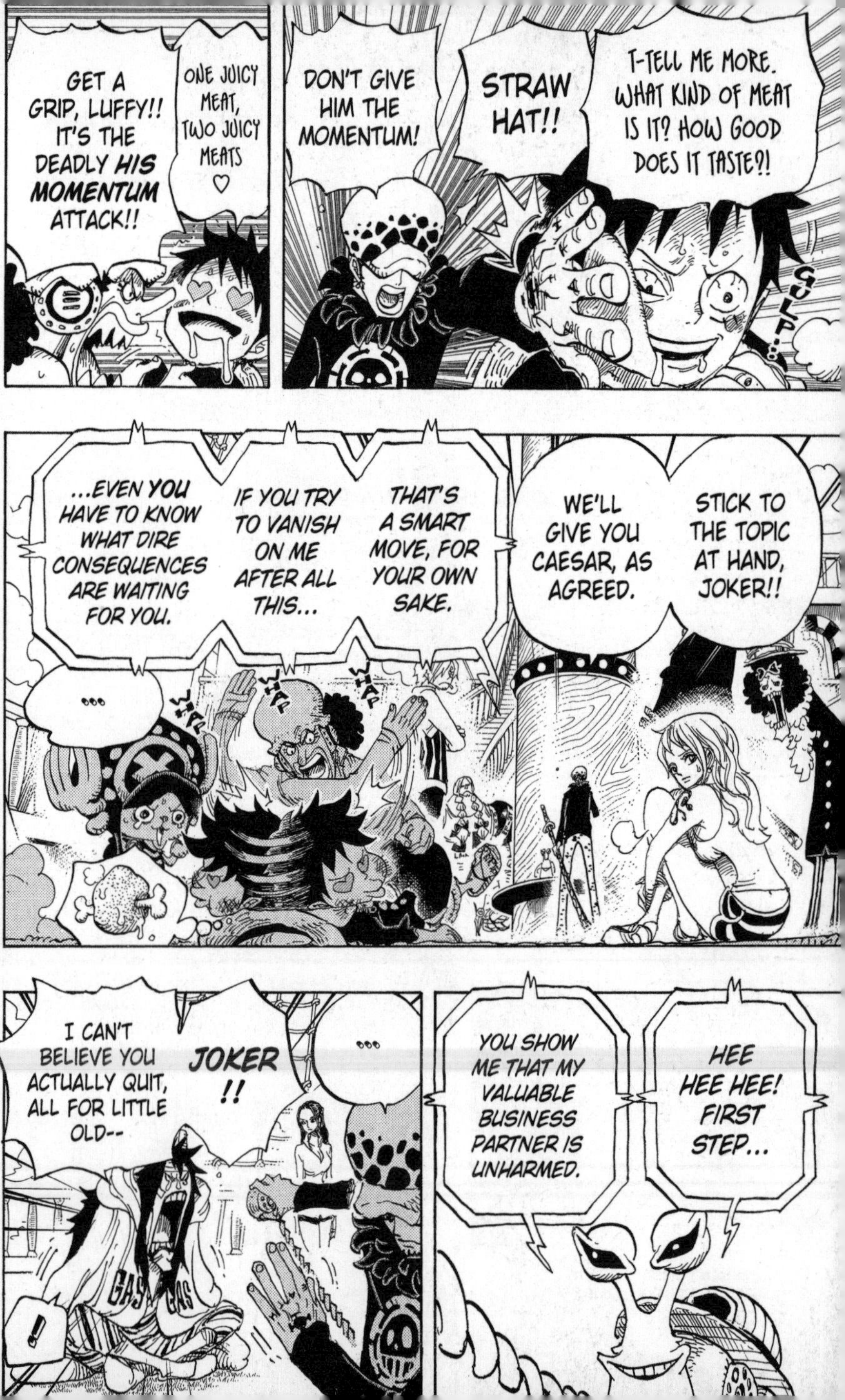
T-TELL ME MORE. WHAT KIND OF MEAT IS IT? HOW GOOD DOES IT TASTE?!
STRAW HAT!!
DON'T GIVE HIM THE MOMENTUM!
GULP...
ONE JUICY MEAT, TWO JUICY MEATS ♡
GET A GRIP, LUFFY!! IT'S THE DEADLY **HIS MOMENTUM** ATTACK!!
STICK TO THE TOPIC AT HAND, JOKER!!
WE'LL GIVE YOU CAESAR, AS AGREED.
THAT'S A SMART MOVE, FOR YOUR OWN SAKE.
IF YOU TRY TO VANISH ON ME AFTER ALL THIS...
...EVEN **YOU** HAVE TO KNOW WHAT DIRE CONSEQUENCES ARE WAITING FOR YOU.
WHAP
WHAP
WHAP
...
HEE HEE HEE! FIRST STEP...
YOU SHOW ME THAT MY VALUABLE BUSINESS PARTNER IS UNHARMED.
...
JOKER !!
I CAN'T BELIEVE YOU ACTUALLY QUIT, ALL FOR LITTLE OLD--
!
GAS
GAS

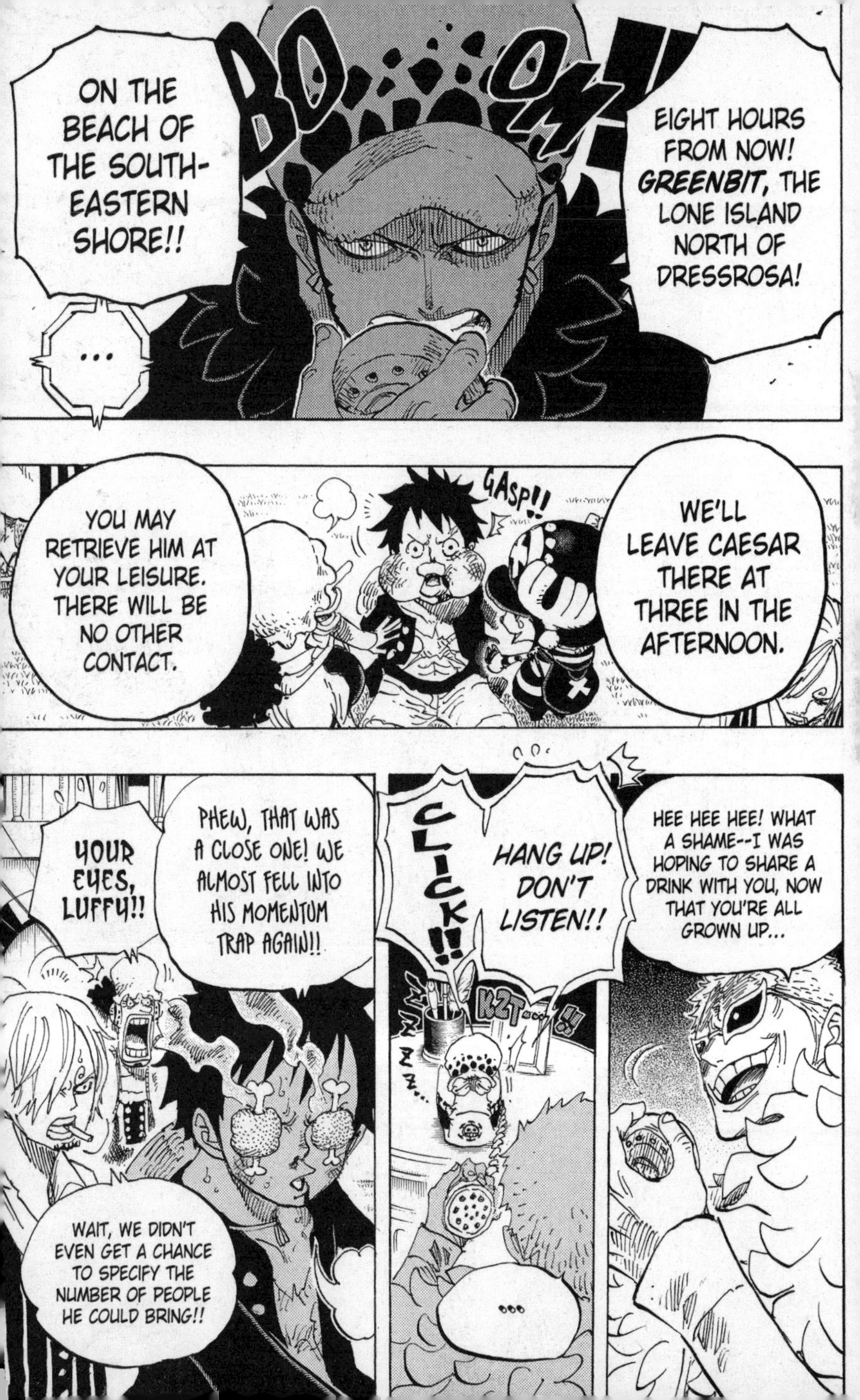

BO...OM!!
EIGHT HOURS FROM NOW! GREENBIT, THE LONE ISLAND NORTH OF DRESSROSA!
ON THE BEACH OF THE SOUTH-EASTERN SHORE!!
...
WE'LL LEAVE CAESAR THERE AT THREE IN THE AFTERNOON.
GASP!!
YOU MAY RETRIEVE HIM AT YOUR LEISURE. THERE WILL BE NO OTHER CONTACT.
HEE HEE HEE! WHAT A SHAME--I WAS HOPING TO SHARE A DRINK WITH YOU, NOW THAT YOU'RE ALL GROWN UP...
HANG UP! DON'T LISTEN!!
CLICK!!
KZT...!!
Z Z Z...
...
PHEW, THAT WAS A CLOSE ONE! WE ALMOST FELL INTO HIS MOMENTUM TRAP AGAIN!!
YOUR EYES, LUFFY!!
WAIT, WE DIDN'T EVEN GET A CHANCE TO SPECIFY THE NUMBER OF PEOPLE HE COULD BRING!!

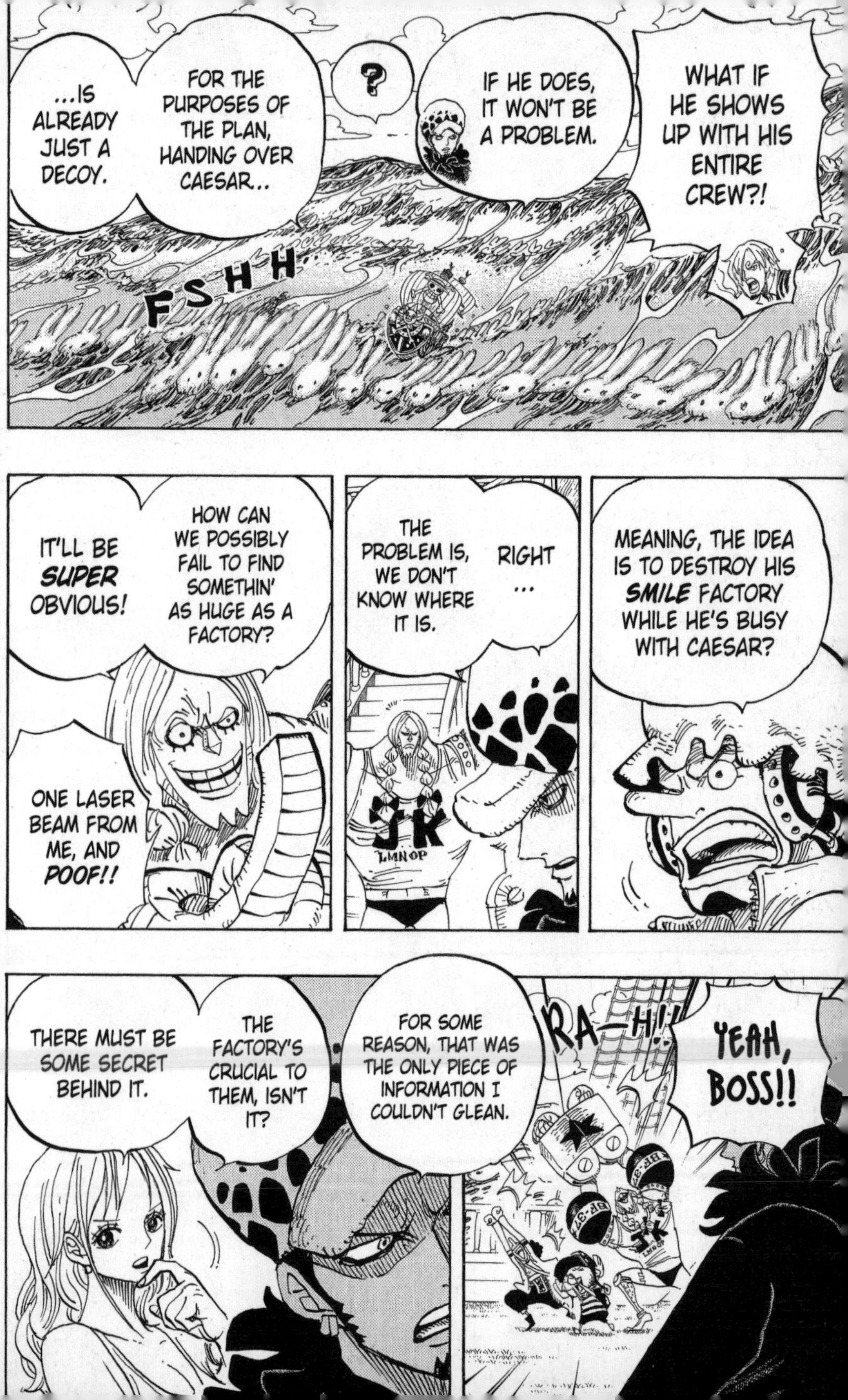
WHAT IF HE SHOWS UP WITH HIS ENTIRE CREW?!
IF HE DOES, IT WON'T BE A PROBLEM.
?
FOR THE PURPOSES OF THE PLAN, HANDING OVER CAESAR...
...IS ALREADY JUST A DECOY.
FSHH
MEANING, THE IDEA IS TO DESTROY HIS *SMILE* FACTORY WHILE HE'S BUSY WITH CAESAR?
RIGHT...
THE PROBLEM IS, WE DON'T KNOW WHERE IT IS.
HOW CAN WE POSSIBLY FAIL TO FIND SOMETHIN' AS HUGE AS A FACTORY?
IT'LL BE *SUPER* OBVIOUS!
ONE LASER BEAM FROM ME, AND *POOF!!*
YEAH, BOSS!!
RA-H!!
FOR SOME REASON, THAT WAS THE ONLY PIECE OF INFORMATION I COULDN'T GLEAN.
THE FACTORY'S CRUCIAL TO THEM, ISN'T IT?
THERE MUST BE SOME SECRET BEHIND IT.

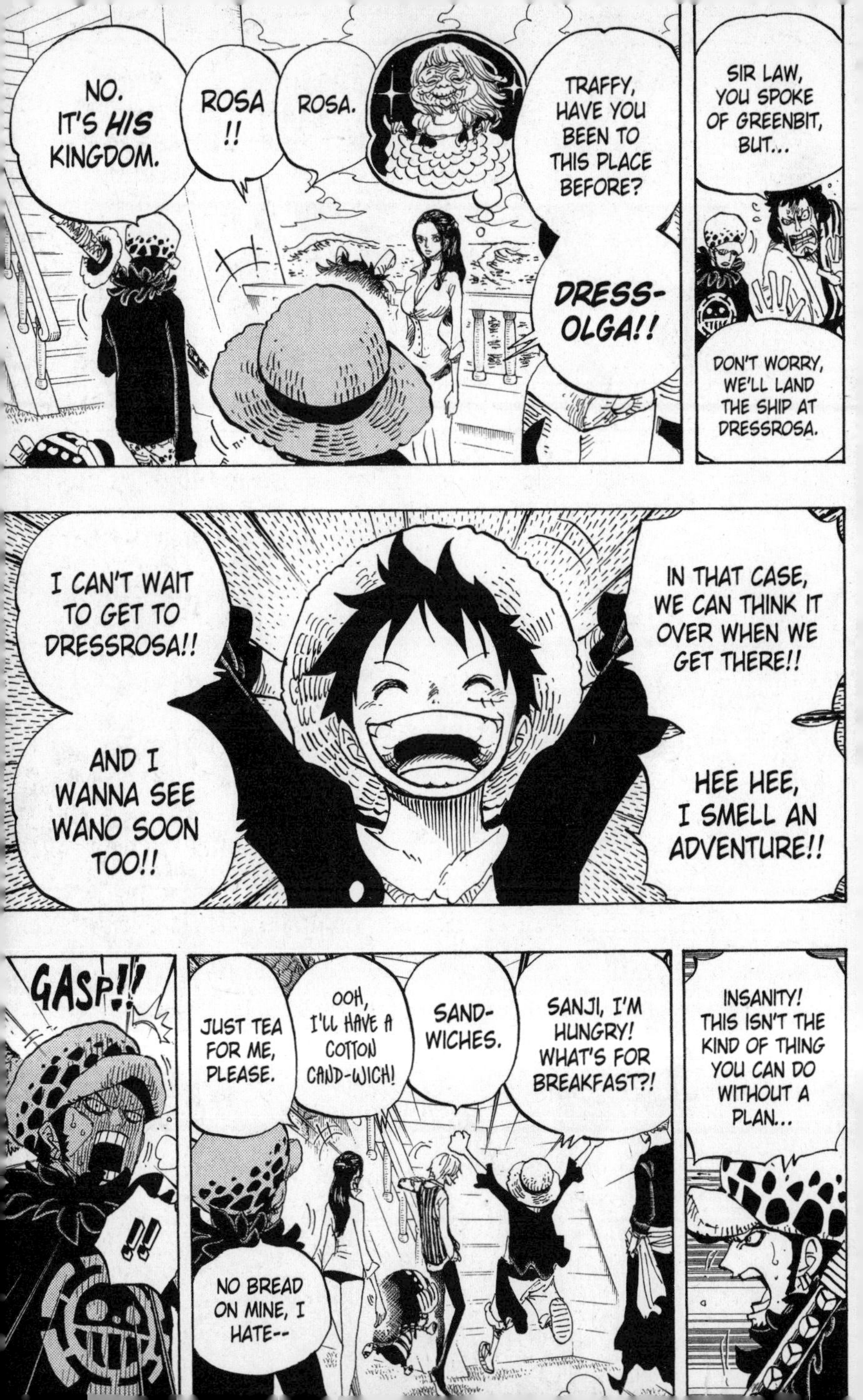
SIR LAW, YOU SPOKE OF GREENBIT, BUT...
DON'T WORRY, WE'LL LAND THE SHIP AT DRESSROSA.
TRAFFY, HAVE YOU BEEN TO THIS PLACE BEFORE?
DRESS-OLGA!!
ROSA.
ROSA !!
NO. IT'S *HIS* KINGDOM.
IN THAT CASE, WE CAN THINK IT OVER WHEN WE GET THERE!!
HEE HEE, I SMELL AN ADVENTURE!!
I CAN'T WAIT TO GET TO DRESSROSA!!
AND I WANNA SEE WANO SOON TOO!!
INSANITY! THIS ISN'T THE KIND OF THING YOU CAN DO WITHOUT A PLAN...
SANJI, I'M HUNGRY! WHAT'S FOR BREAKFAST?!
SAND-WICHES.
OOH, I'LL HAVE A COTTON CAND-WICH!
JUST TEA FOR ME, PLEASE.
NO BREAD ON MINE, I HATE--
GASP!!
!!

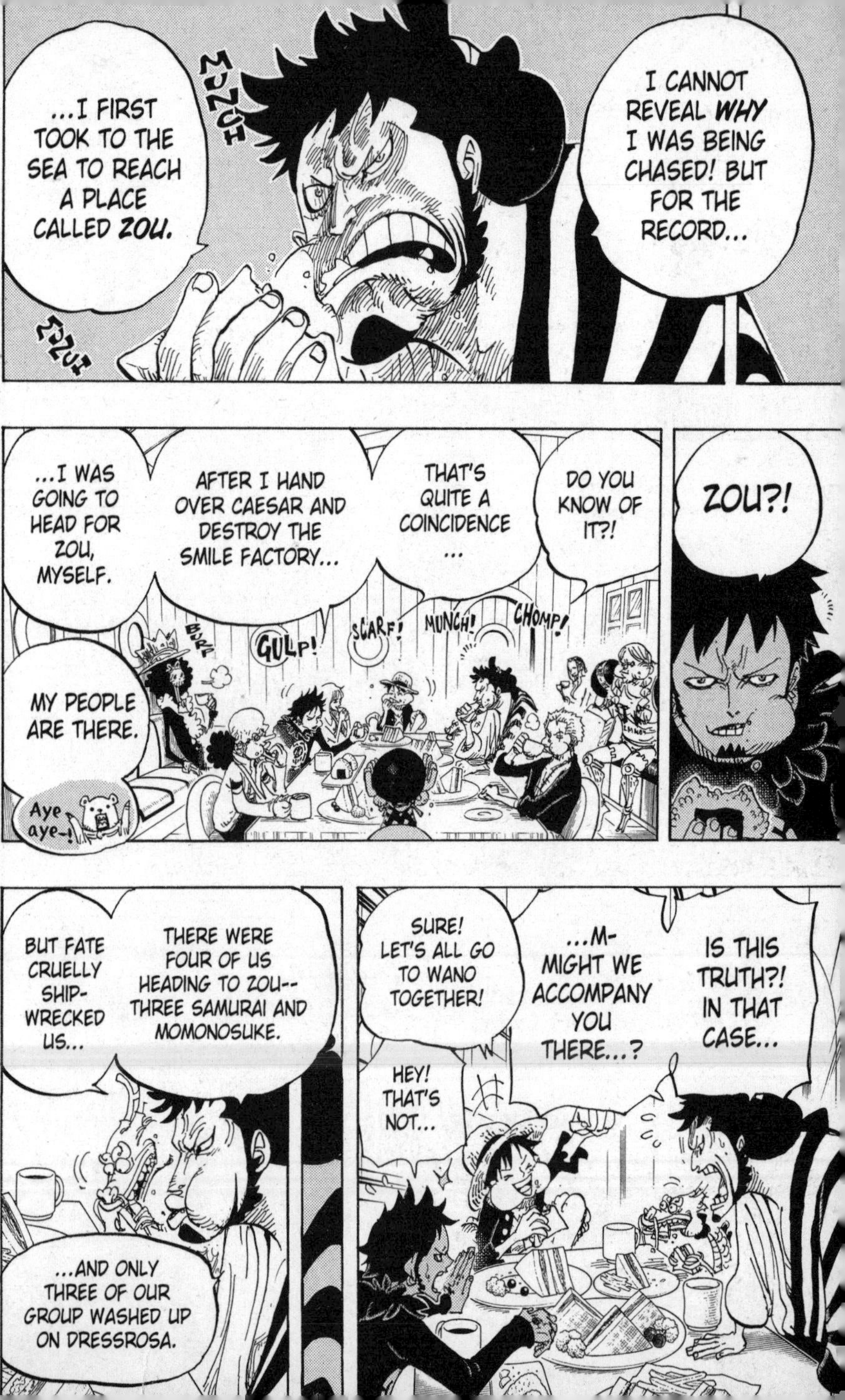
I CANNOT REVEAL WHY I WAS BEING CHASED! BUT FOR THE RECORD...
MUNCH
...I FIRST TOOK TO THE SEA TO REACH A PLACE CALLED ZOU.
MUNCH
ZOU?!
DO YOU KNOW OF IT?!
THAT'S QUITE A COINCIDENCE...
AFTER I HAND OVER CAESAR AND DESTROY THE SMILE FACTORY...
...I WAS GOING TO HEAD FOR ZOU, MYSELF.
CHOMP!
MUNCH!
SCARF!
GULP!
BURP
MY PEOPLE ARE THERE.
Aye aye-!
IS THIS TRUTH?! IN THAT CASE...
...M-MIGHT WE ACCOMPANY YOU THERE...?
SURE! LET'S ALL GO TO WANO TOGETHER!
HEY! THAT'S NOT...
THERE WERE FOUR OF US HEADING TO ZOU--THREE SAMURAI AND MOMONOSUKE.
BUT FATE CRUELLY SHIP-WRECKED US...
...AND ONLY THREE OF OUR GROUP WASHED UP ON DRESSROSA.

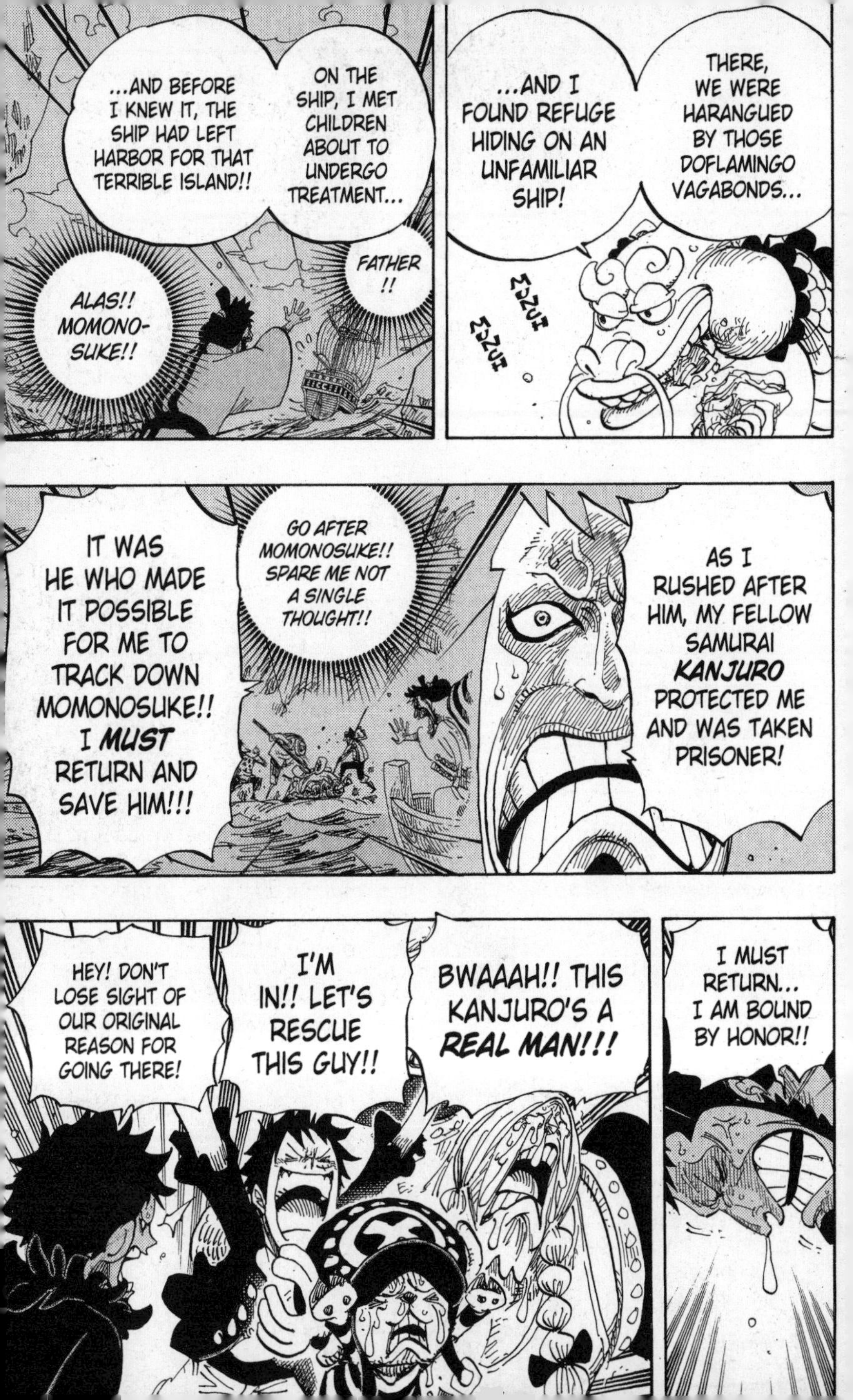
THERE, WE WERE HARANGUED BY THOSE DOFLAMINGO VAGABONDS...
...AND I FOUND REFUGE HIDING ON AN UNFAMILIAR SHIP!
ZUZUI
ZUZUI
ON THE SHIP, I MET CHILDREN ABOUT TO UNDERGO TREATMENT...
...AND BEFORE I KNEW IT, THE SHIP HAD LEFT HARBOR FOR THAT TERRIBLE ISLAND!!
FATHER !!
ALAS!! MOMONOSUKE!!
AS I RUSHED AFTER HIM, MY FELLOW SAMURAI KANJURO PROTECTED ME AND WAS TAKEN PRISONER!
GO AFTER MOMONOSUKE!! SPARE ME NOT A SINGLE THOUGHT!!
IT WAS HE WHO MADE IT POSSIBLE FOR ME TO TRACK DOWN MOMONOSUKE!! I MUST RETURN AND SAVE HIM!!!
I MUST RETURN... I AM BOUND BY HONOR!!
BWAAAH!! THIS KANJURO'S A REAL MAN!!!
I'M IN!! LET'S RESCUE THIS GUY!!
HEY! DON'T LOSE SIGHT OF OUR ORIGINAL REASON FOR GOING THERE!

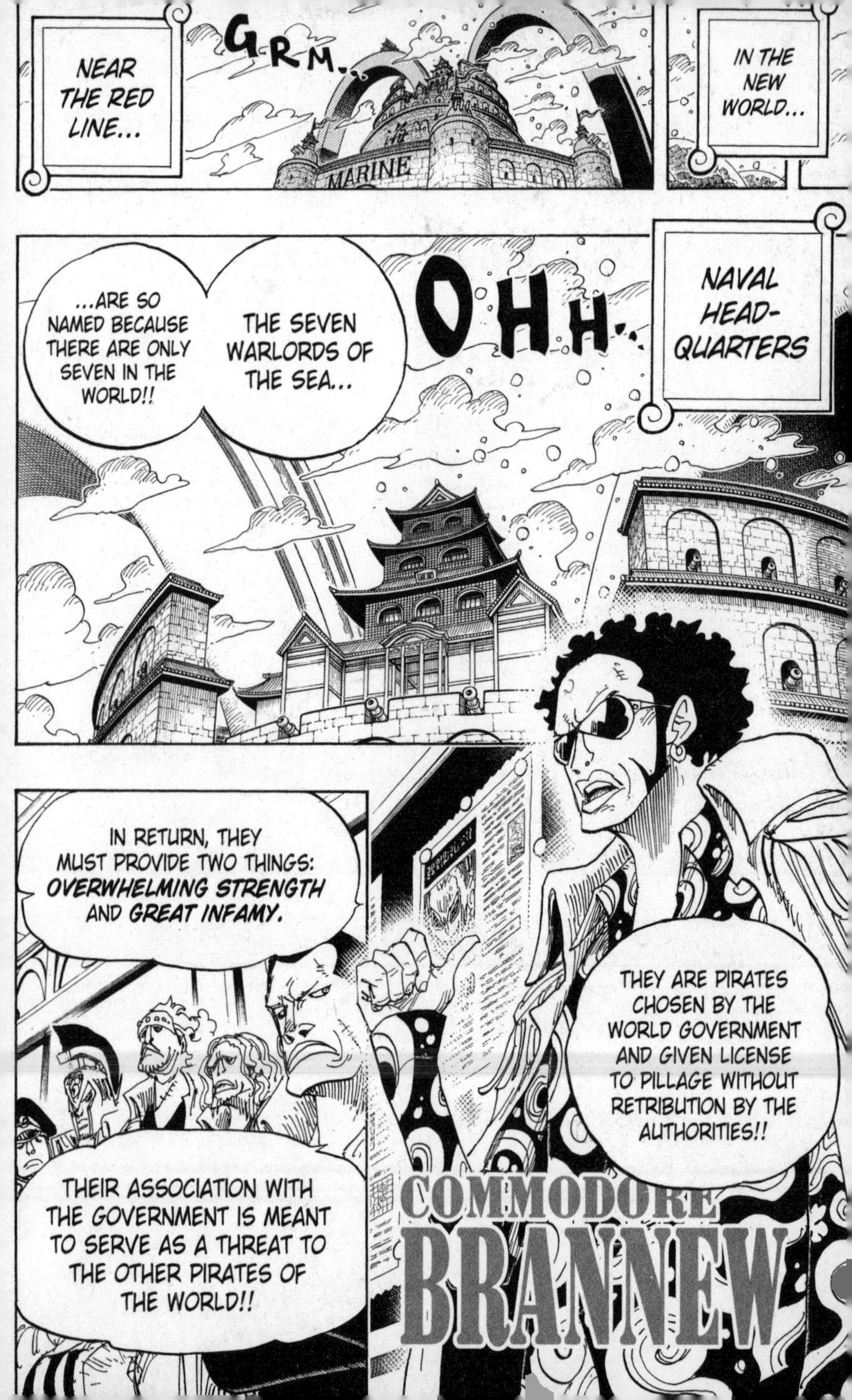
IN THE NEW WORLD...
NEAR THE RED LINE...
GRM...
MARINE
NAVAL HEAD-QUARTERS
OHH...
THE SEVEN WARLORDS OF THE SEA...
...ARE SO NAMED BECAUSE THERE ARE ONLY SEVEN IN THE WORLD!!
THEY ARE PIRATES CHOSEN BY THE WORLD GOVERNMENT AND GIVEN LICENSE TO PILLAGE WITHOUT RETRIBUTION BY THE AUTHORITIES!!
COMMODORE BRANNEW
IN RETURN, THEY MUST PROVIDE TWO THINGS: *OVERWHELMING STRENGTH* AND *GREAT INFAMY.*
THEIR ASSOCIATION WITH THE GOVERNMENT IS MEANT TO SERVE AS A THREAT TO THE OTHER PIRATES OF THE WORLD!!

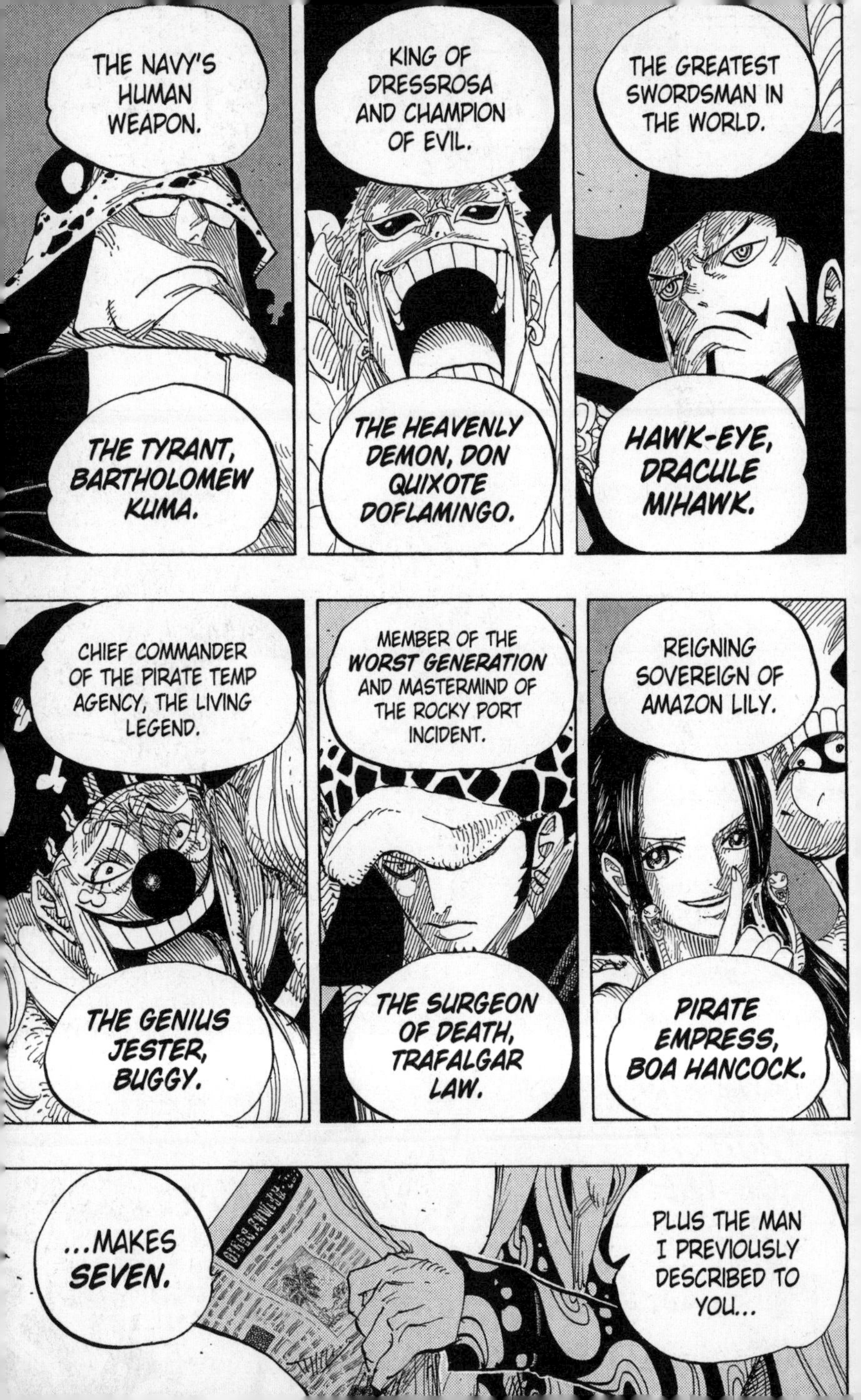
THE GREATEST SWORDSMAN IN THE WORLD.
HAWK-EYE, DRACULE MIHAWK.
KING OF DRESSROSA AND CHAMPION OF EVIL.
THE HEAVENLY DEMON, DON QUIXOTE DOFLAMINGO.
THE NAVY'S HUMAN WEAPON.
THE TYRANT, BARTHOLOMEW KUMA.
REIGNING SOVEREIGN OF AMAZON LILY.
PIRATE EMPRESS, BOA HANCOCK.
MEMBER OF THE WORST GENERATION AND MASTERMIND OF THE ROCKY PORT INCIDENT.
THE SURGEON OF DEATH, TRAFALGAR LAW.
CHIEF COMMANDER OF THE PIRATE TEMP AGENCY, THE LIVING LEGEND.
THE GENIUS JESTER, BUGGY.
PLUS THE MAN I PREVIOUSLY DESCRIBED TO YOU...
...MAKES SEVEN.

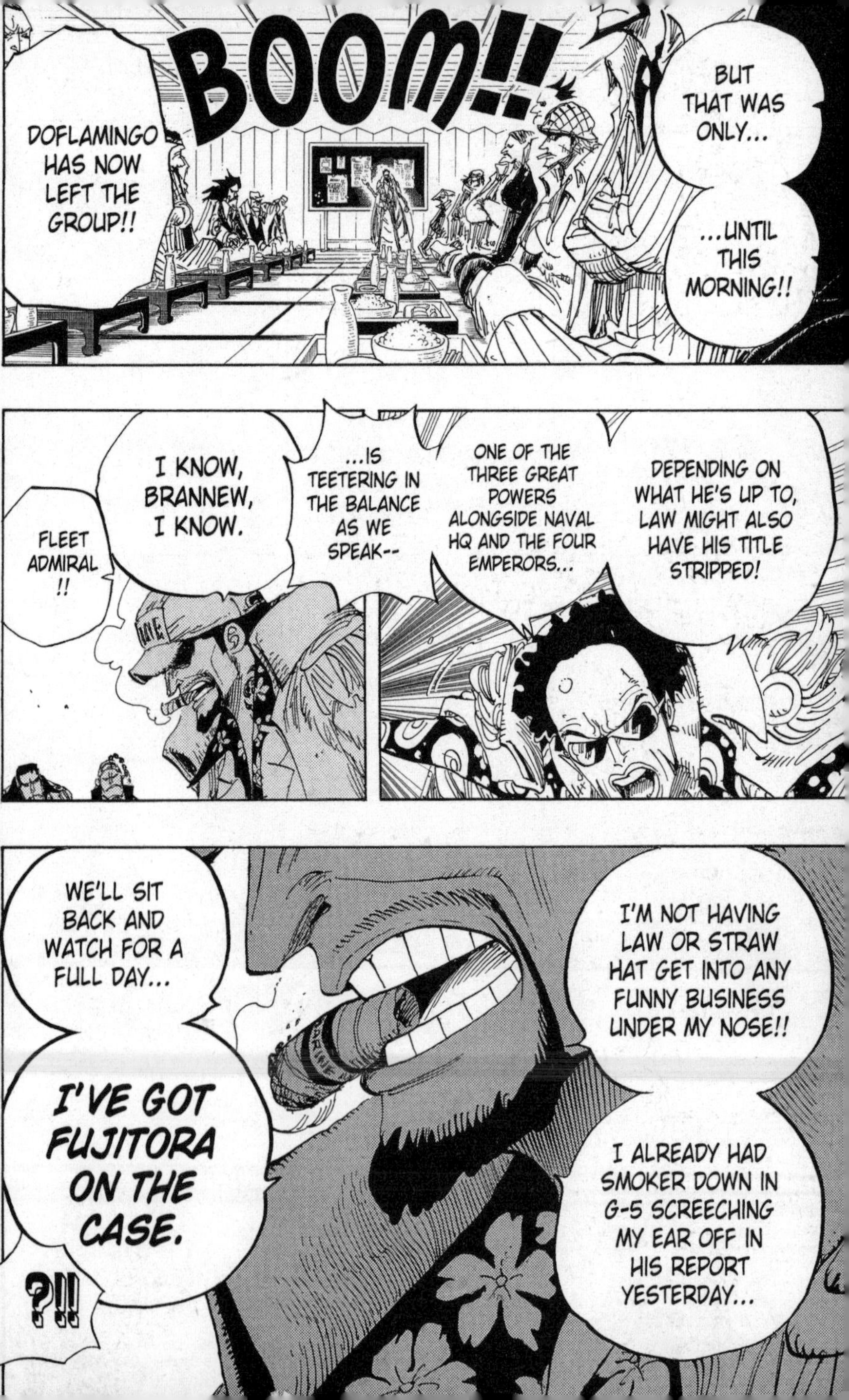
BUT THAT WAS ONLY...
...UNTIL THIS MORNING!!
BOOM!!
DOFLAMINGO HAS NOW LEFT THE GROUP!!
DEPENDING ON WHAT HE'S UP TO, LAW MIGHT ALSO HAVE HIS TITLE STRIPPED!
ONE OF THE THREE GREAT POWERS ALONGSIDE NAVAL HQ AND THE FOUR EMPERORS...
...IS TEETERING IN THE BALANCE AS WE SPEAK--
I KNOW, BRANNEW, I KNOW.
FLEET ADMIRAL !!
I'M NOT HAVING LAW OR STRAW HAT GET INTO ANY FUNNY BUSINESS UNDER MY NOSE!!
I ALREADY HAD SMOKER DOWN IN G-5 SCREECHING MY EAR OFF IN HIS REPORT YESTERDAY...
WE'LL SIT BACK AND WATCH FOR A FULL DAY...
I'VE GOT FUJITORA ON THE CASE.
?!!

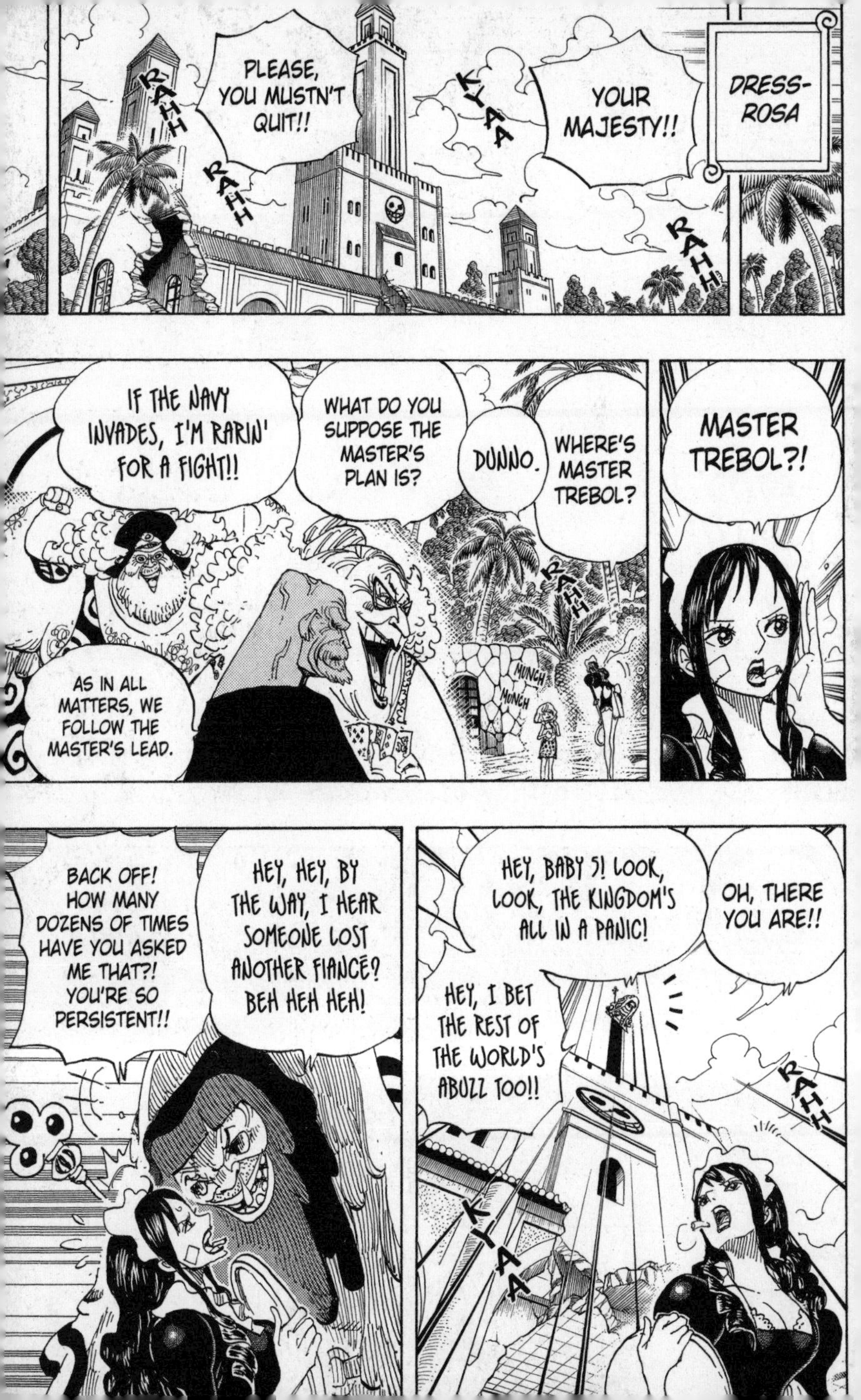
DRESS-ROSA
YOUR MAJESTY!!
KYAA
RAHH
PLEASE, YOU MUSTN'T QUIT!!
RAHH
RAHH
MASTER TREBOL?!
WHERE'S MASTER TREBOL?
DUNNO.
RAHH
WHAT DO YOU SUPPOSE THE MASTER'S PLAN IS?
IF THE NAVY INVADES, I'M RARIN' FOR A FIGHT!!
MUNCH
MUNCH
AS IN ALL MATTERS, WE FOLLOW THE MASTER'S LEAD.
OH, THERE YOU ARE!!
HEY, BABY 5! LOOK, LOOK, THE KINGDOM'S ALL IN A PANIC!
RAHH
HEY, I BET THE REST OF THE WORLD'S ABUZZ TOO!!
KYAA
HEY, HEY, BY THE WAY, I HEAR SOMEONE LOST ANOTHER FIANCE? BEH HEH HEH!
BACK OFF! HOW MANY DOZENS OF TIMES HAVE YOU ASKED ME THAT?! YOU'RE SO PERSISTENT!!

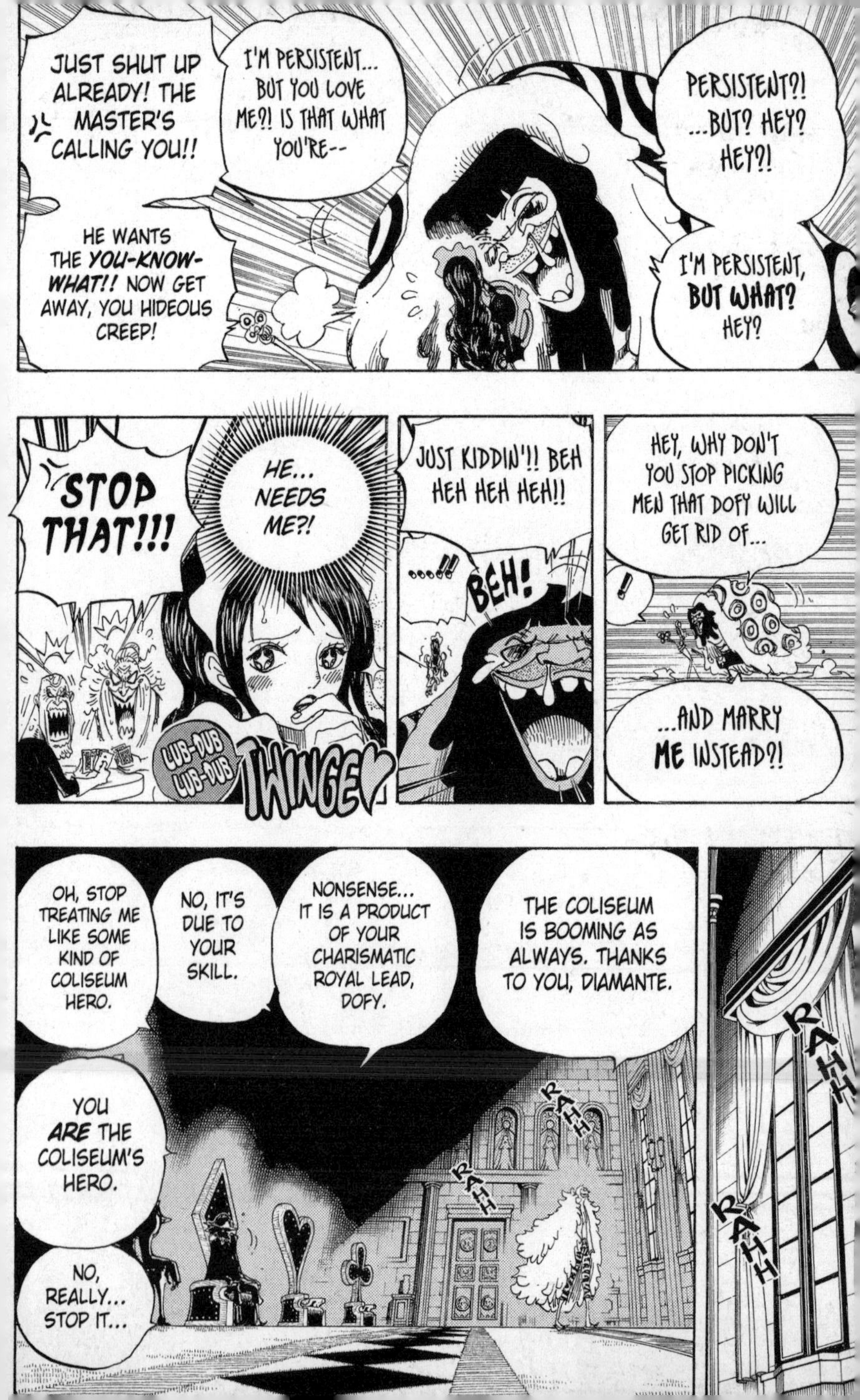
PERSISTENT?! ...BUT? HEY? HEY?!
I'M PERSISTENT, **BUT WHAT?** HEY?
I'M PERSISTENT... BUT YOU LOVE ME?! IS THAT WHAT YOU'RE--
JUST SHUT UP ALREADY! THE MASTER'S CALLING YOU!!
HE WANTS THE ***YOU-KNOW-WHAT!!*** NOW GET AWAY, YOU HIDEOUS CREEP!
HEY, WHY DON'T YOU STOP PICKING MEN THAT DOFY WILL GET RID OF...
!
...AND MARRY **ME** INSTEAD?!
JUST KIDDIN'!! BEH HEH HEH HEH!!
BEH!
....!!
HE... NEEDS ME?!
STOP THAT!!!
LUB-DUB LUB-DUB
TWINGE
RAHH
RAHH
THE COLISEUM IS BOOMING AS ALWAYS. THANKS TO YOU, DIAMANTE.
NONSENSE... IT IS A PRODUCT OF YOUR CHARISMATIC ROYAL LEAD, DOFY.
NO, IT'S DUE TO YOUR SKILL.
OH, STOP TREATING ME LIKE SOME KIND OF COLISEUM HERO.
RAHH
RAHH
YOU ***ARE*** THE COLISEUM'S HERO.
NO, REALLY... STOP IT...

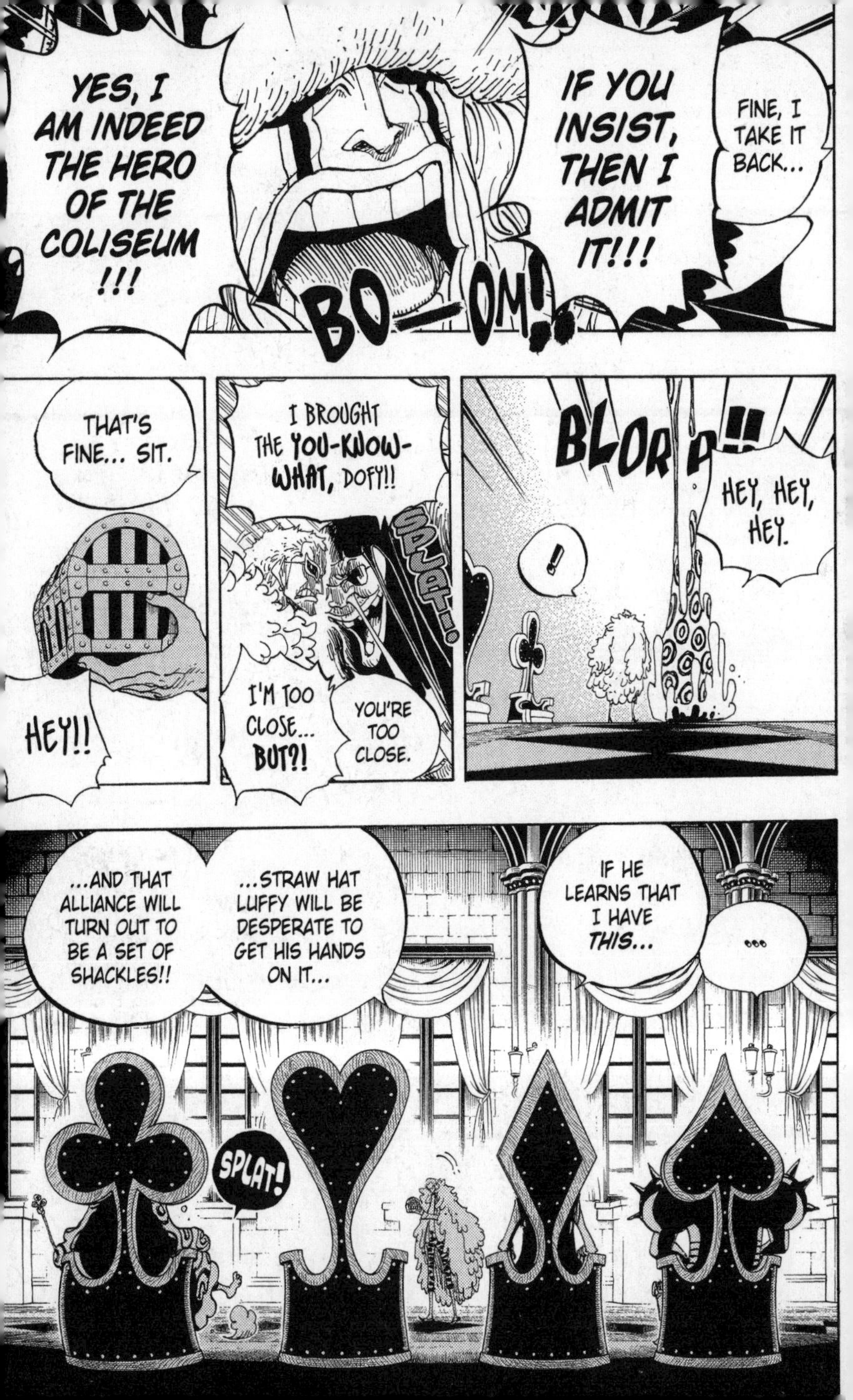
FINE, I TAKE IT BACK...
IF YOU INSIST, THEN I ADMIT IT!!!
YES, I AM INDEED THE HERO OF THE COLISEUM !!!
BO—OM!!
BLORP!!
HEY, HEY, HEY.
!
I BROUGHT THE YOU-KNOW-WHAT, DOFY!!
SPLAT!
YOU'RE TOO CLOSE.
I'M TOO CLOSE... BUT?!
THAT'S FINE... SIT.
HEY!!
...
IF HE LEARNS THAT I HAVE THIS...
...STRAW HAT LUFFY WILL BE DESPERATE TO GET HIS HANDS ON IT...
...AND THAT ALLIANCE WILL TURN OUT TO BE A SET OF SHACKLES!!
SPLAT!

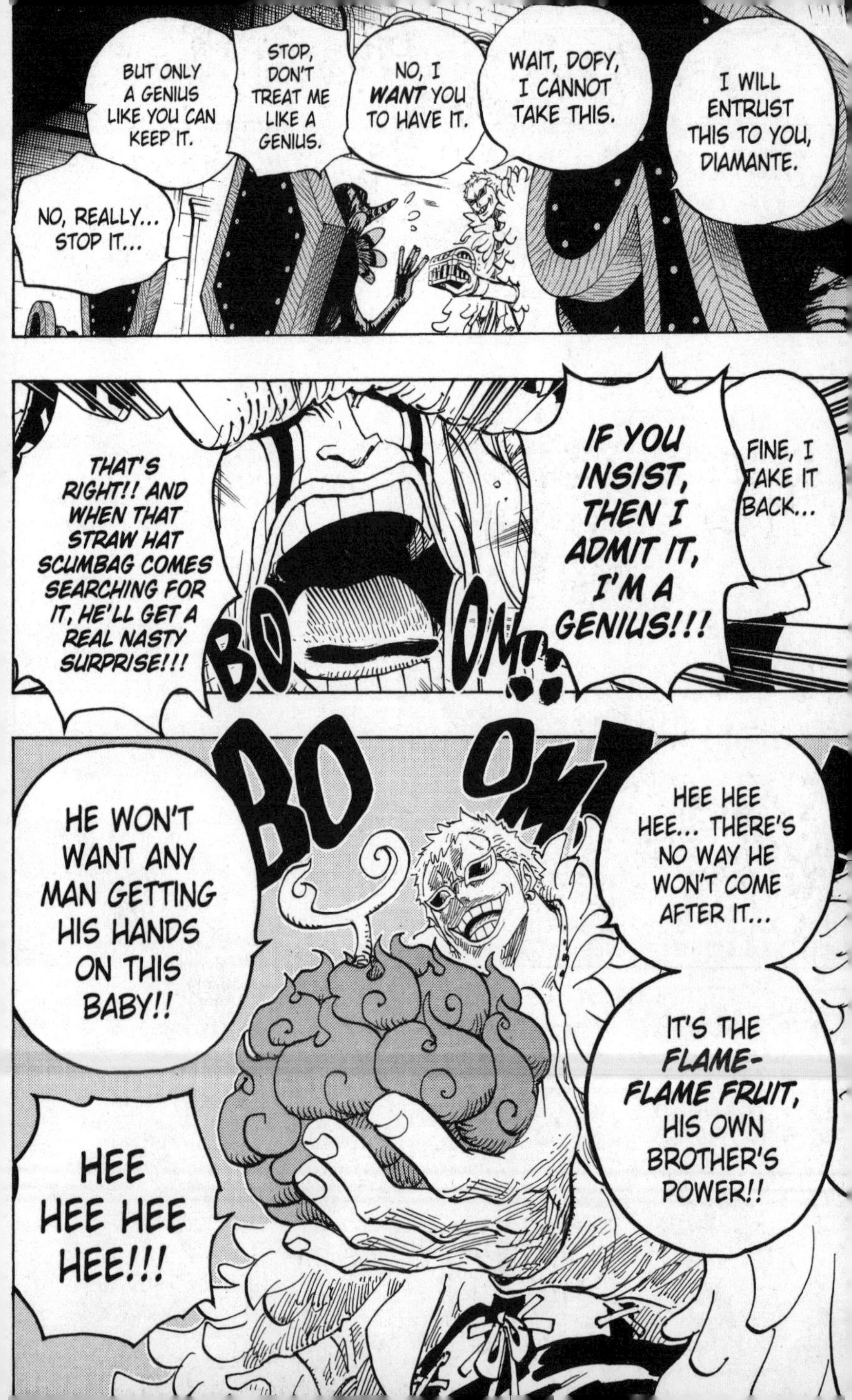
I WILL ENTRUST THIS TO YOU, DIAMANTE.
WAIT, DOFY, I CANNOT TAKE THIS.
NO, I *WANT* YOU TO HAVE IT.
STOP, DON'T TREAT ME LIKE A GENIUS.
BUT ONLY A GENIUS LIKE YOU CAN KEEP IT.
NO, REALLY... STOP IT...
FINE, I TAKE IT BACK...
IF YOU INSIST, THEN I ADMIT IT, I'M A GENIUS!!!
THAT'S RIGHT!! AND WHEN THAT STRAW HAT SCUMBAG COMES SEARCHING FOR IT, HE'LL GET A REAL NASTY SURPRISE!!!
BOOM!!
BOOM
HEE HEE HEE... THERE'S NO WAY HE WON'T COME AFTER IT...
IT'S THE *FLAME-FLAME FRUIT*, HIS OWN BROTHER'S POWER!!
HE WON'T WANT ANY MAN GETTING HIS HANDS ON THIS BABY!!
HEE HEE HEE HEE!!!

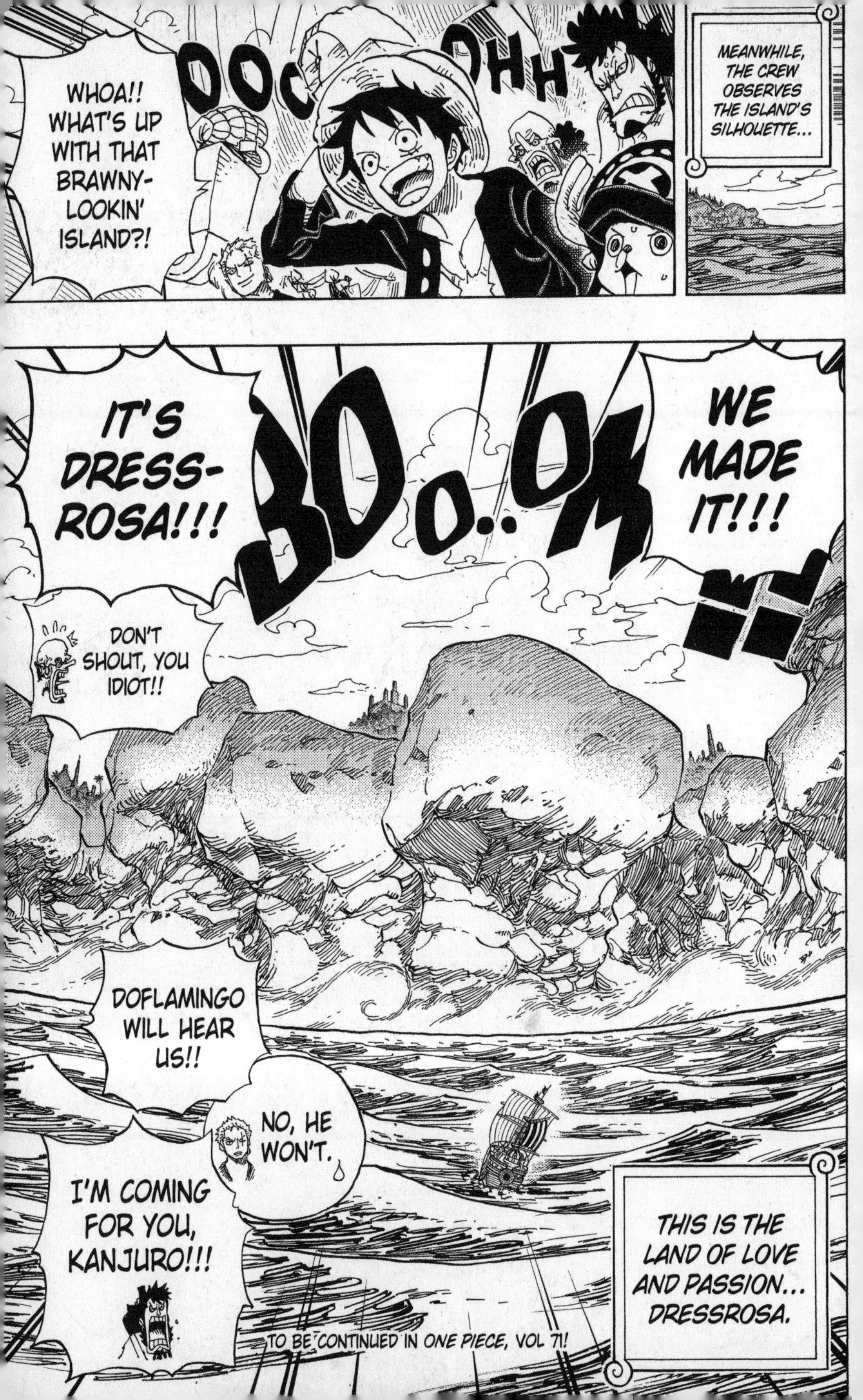
MEANWHILE, THE CREW OBSERVES THE ISLAND'S SILHOUETTE...
WHOA!! WHAT'S UP WITH THAT BRAWNY-LOOKIN' ISLAND?!
WE MADE IT!!!
BOo..OM
IT'S DRESS-ROSA!!!
DON'T SHOUT, YOU IDIOT!!
THIS IS THE LAND OF LOVE AND PASSION... DRESSROSA.
NO, HE WON'T.
DOFLAMINGO WILL HEAR US!!
I'M COMING FOR YOU, KANJURO!!!
TO BE CONTINUED IN ONE PIECE, VOL 71!

COMING NEXT VOLUME:

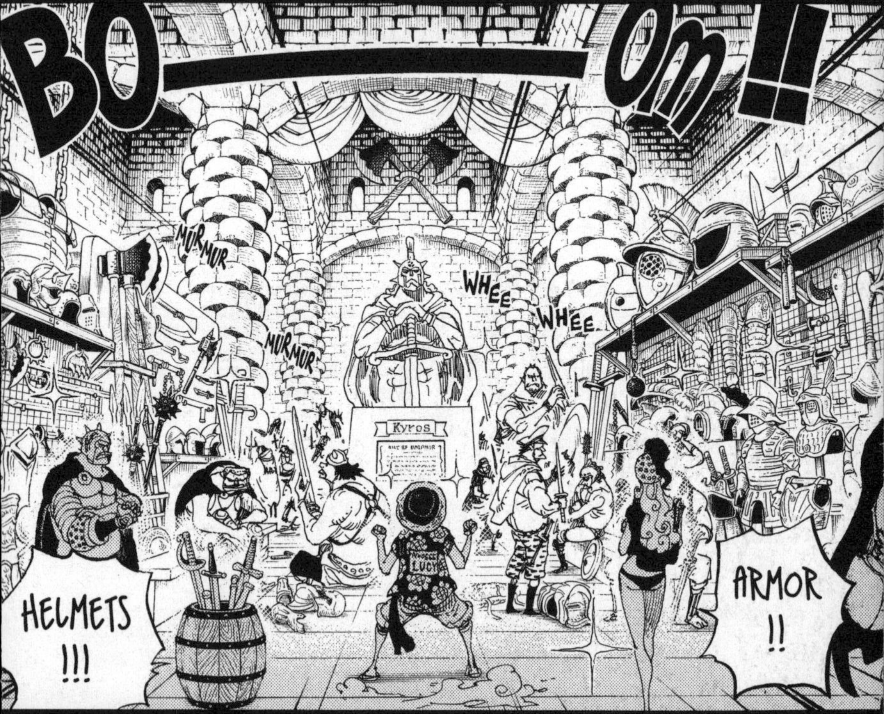
BO—om!!
MURMUR
MURMUR
WHEE
WHEE
Kyros
LUCY
HELMETS !!!
ARMOR !!

The Straw Hats arrive in the Kingdom of Dressrosa, Doflamingo's home turf. Dressrosa is one of the weirdest places Luffy has ever seen, and the land is hiding many dark secrets. And when Doflamingo opens a fighting tournament with the Flame-Flame Fruit as the prize, there's no way Luffy can stay away!

ON SALE JUNE 2014!

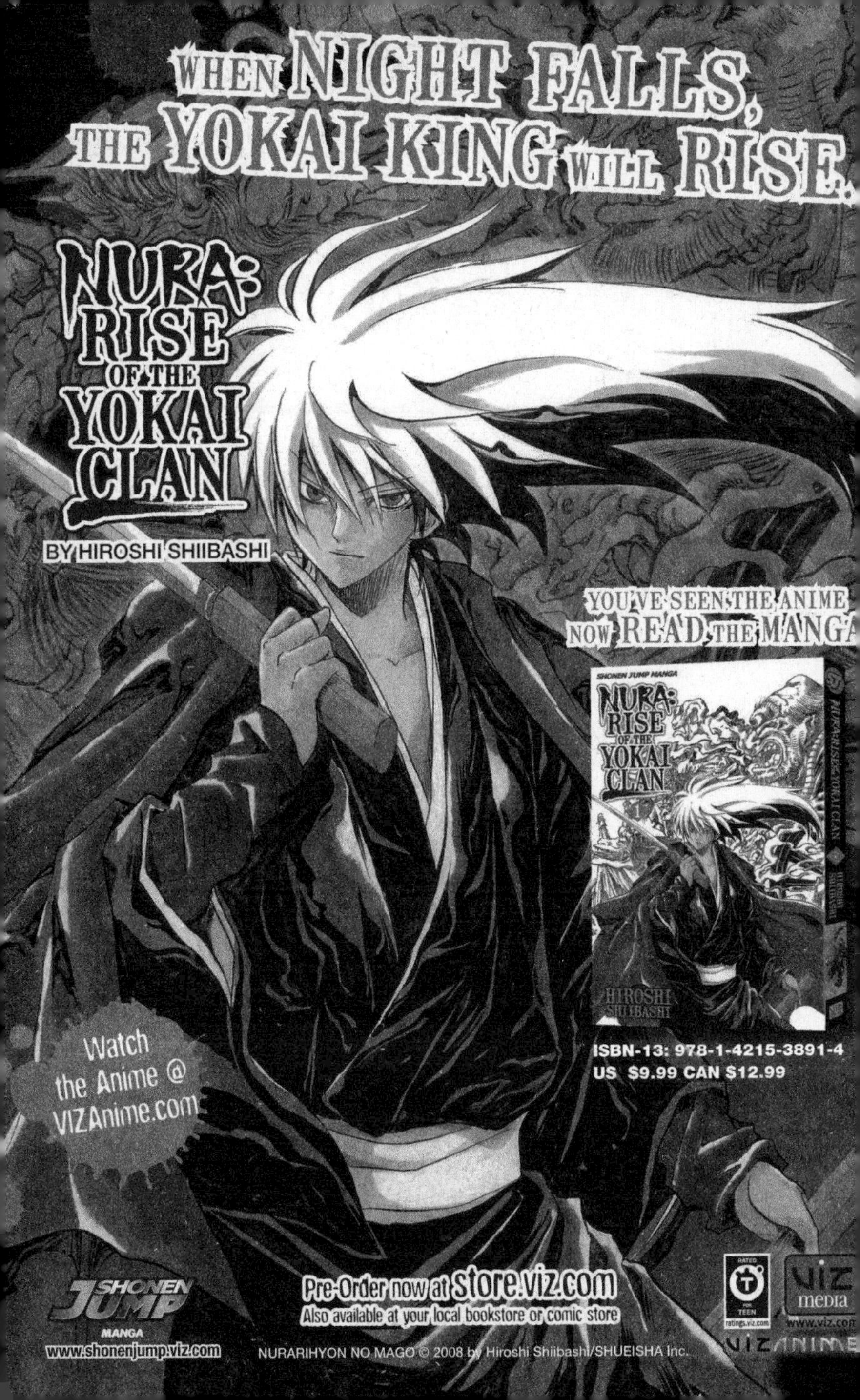

WHEN NIGHT FALLS, THE YOKAI KING WILL RISE.
NURA: RISE OF THE YOKAI CLAN
BY HIROSHI SHIIBASHI
YOU'VE SEEN THE ANIME NOW READ THE MANGA
SHONEN JUMP MANGA
NURA: RISE OF THE YOKAI CLAN
HIROSHI SHIIBASHI
ISBN-13: 978-1-4215-3891-4
US $9.99 CAN $12.99
Watch the Anime @ VIZAnime.com
SHONEN JUMP MANGA
www.shonenjump.viz.com
Pre-Order now at Store.viz.com
Also available at your local bookstore or comic store
RATED T FOR TEEN
ratings.viz.com
VIZ media
www.viz.com
VIZ ANIME
NURARIHYON NO MAGO © 2008 by Hiroshi Shiibashi/SHUEISHA Inc.

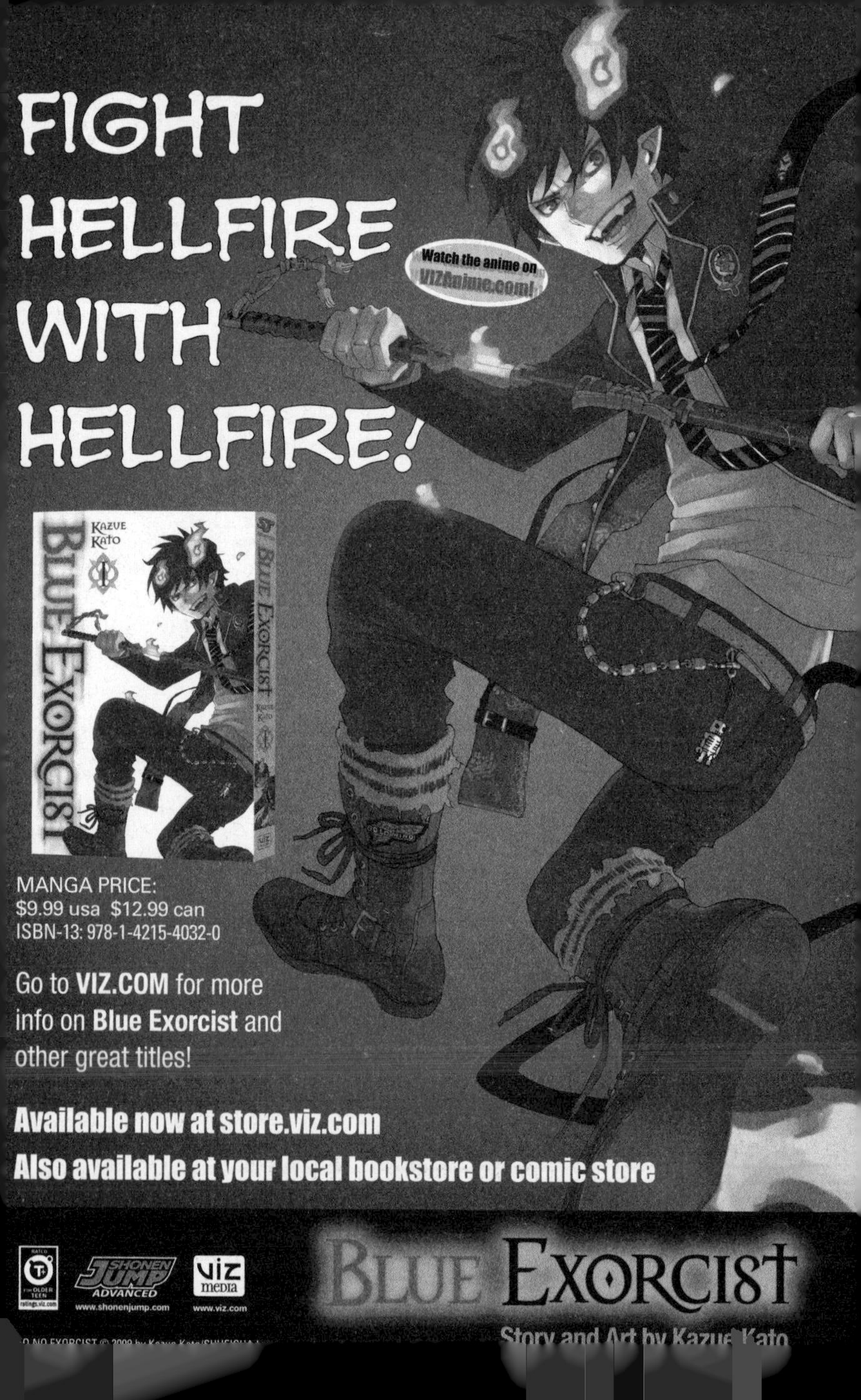

FIGHT HELLFIRE WITH HELLFIRE!
Watch the anime on VIZAnime.com!
KAZUE KATO
BLUE EXORCIST
1
MANGA PRICE:
$9.99 usa $12.99 can
ISBN-13: 978-1-4215-4032-0
Go to VIZ.COM for more info on Blue Exorcist and other great titles!
Available now at store.viz.com
Also available at your local bookstore or comic store
RATED T+ FOR OLDER TEEN
ratings.viz.com
SHONEN JUMP ADVANCED
www.shonenjump.com
viz media
www.viz.com
BLUE EXORCIST
Story and Art by Kazue Kato

You're Reading in the Wrong Direction!!

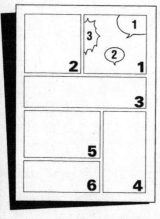

Whoops! Guess what? You're starting at the wrong end of the comic!

...It's true! In keeping with the original Japanese format, **One Piece** is meant to be read from right to left, starting in the upper-right corner.

Unlike English, which is read from left to right, Japanese is read from right to left, meaning that action, sound effects and word-balloon order are completely reversed...something which can make readers unfamiliar with Japanese feel pretty backwards themselves. For this reason, manga or Japanese comics published in the U.S. in English have sometimes been published "flopped"— that is, printed in exact reverse order, as though seen from the other side of a mirror.

By flopping pages, U.S. publishers can avoid confusing readers, but the compromise is not without its downside. For one thing, a character in a flopped manga series who once wore in the original Japanese version a T-shirt emblazoned with "M A Y" (as in "the merry month of") now wears one which reads "Y A M"! Additionally, many manga creators in Japan are themselves unhappy with the process, as some feel the mirror-imaging of their art skews their original intentions.

We are proud to bring you Eiichiro Oda's **One Piece** in the original unflopped format. For now, though, turn to the other side of the book and let the journey begin...!

—Editor